NEW HORIZONS OF
PARALLEL AND
DISTRIBUTED COMPUTING

NEW HORIZONS OF PARALLEL AND DISTRIBUTED COMPUTING

edited by

Minyi Guo
The University of Aizu, Japan

Laurence Tianruo Yang
St. Francis Xavier University, Canada

 Springer

Minyi Guo
The University of Aizu
Dept. of Computer Software
Aizu-Wakamatsu City, FUKUSHIMA
65-8580 JAPAN
minyi@u-aizu.ac.jp

Laurence T. Yang
Department of Computer Science
St. Francis Xavier University
Antigonish, NS, B2G 2W5, Canada
Email: lyang@stfx.ca

Library of Congress Cataloging-in-Publication Data

A C.I.P. Catalogue record for this book is available
from the Library of Congress.

New Horizons of Parallel and Distributed Computing
edited by Minyi Guo and Laurence Tianruo Yang

ISBN 978-1-4419-3747-6   e-ISBN 978-0-387-28967-0

Printed on acid-free paper.

Printed in the United States of America.

9 8 7 6 5 4 3 2 1

springeronline.com

Contents

Preface

In the past decades parallel and distributed computing played a key role that were stimulated by the availability of faster, more reliable, and cheaper super-computers and distributed systems. It will also become technologies in shaping future research and development activities in academia and industry. In the not too distant future, most of researchers in science and engineering fields will have to understand parallel and distributed computing. With hyperthreading in Intel processors, hypertransport links in next generation AMD processors, multicore silicon in today's high-end microprocessors, emerging cluster and grid computing, parallel/distributed computing has moved into the mainstream of computing. To fully exploit these advances, researchers must start to write parallel or distributed software and algorithms to cope with large and complex problems with very tight timing schedules.

This book is a collection of self-contained chapters written by pioneers and active researchers in parallel and distributed computing. It reports the recent important advances in the area of parallel and distributed computing and pro-vides an opportunity for practitioners and researchers to explore the connec-tion between various techniques in computer science and develop solutions to problems that arise in the rapidly emerging field of parallel and distributed computing.

This book is intended for researchers and graduate students in computer science and electrical engineering, as well as researchers and developers in industry. We believe all of these chapters will not only provide novel ideas, work in progress and state-of-the-art techniques in the field, but also stimulate the future research activities in the area of parallel and distributed computing with applications. This book can be used as a textbook and a reference for use by students, researchers, and developers.

The book is mainly divided into four parts. Chapters 1 to 3 (Part 1) cover programming models and supporting tools. Part 2, Chapters 4 to 8 describes high performance parallel and distributed algorithms including task scheduling algorithms, solving NP-complete problems based on DNA computing. Part 3, Chapters 9 to 15 covers the area of network, parallel computer architec-tures and distributed systems. Finally, Part 4, Chapters 16 to 21, covers paral-lel/distributed applications.

In the following sections, we will discuss the chapters of this book in more detail so that readers can better plan their perusal of the material. Extensive external citations are not given here but will be found in the individual chapters.

Part 1: programming models and support tools

In the first paper, Tsujita et al. develop a flexible MPI library, called Stampi, to enable MPI operations on a heterogeneous computing environment. Users can call the functions in Stampi without awareness of underlying commu-nication mechanism. In Chapter 2, Cao and Sun present a Graph-Oriented

Programming (GOP) model that provides flexible graph constructs and graph-oriented primitives to build a programming paradigm based on graph topology, and also provides a formal specification of software architecture for distributed programs. Saber and Mirenkov describe an outline of the approach to programming cellular automata systems in Chapter 3. They also discuss the concepts and features of a program generator in the system and how the parallel template programs support the automatic generation of executable codes from the multimedia specifications.

Part 2: algorithms

To achieve high performance on distributed memory machines with processing nodes, one has to attain both high single-processor performance and high parallel efficiency at the same time. In Chapter 4, Yamamoto et al. propose a general framework for designing 1-D FFT based on a 3-dimensional representation of the data that can satisfy both of these requirements. Two algorithms are shown to be optimal from the viewpoint of both parallel performance and usability. Experiments on Hitachi SR2201 show their algorithms can get 48% of the peak performance when computing the FFT of 2^{26} points using 64 nodes. Guo and Chang present an algorithm to solve an NP-complete problem, vertex-cover problem based on a molecular supercomputer model in Chapter 5. Their molecular computer model is called Adleman-Lipton model, which has a computational power for solving NP-complete problem using DNA computing. In Chapter 6, Hwang et al. propose a special design concept to construct a generalized group-oriented cryptosystem (GGOC). Any group can use their method to construct a GGOC which provides a secure environment for a sender to send confidential messages to it. Chapter 7 addresses the problem of scheduling tasks in the Non-Uniform Memory Access (NUMA) multiprocessor system with a bounded number of available processors. An algorithm is proposed to schedule tasks by considering the intertask communication overhead and the contentions among communication channels. The proposed algorithm also exploits the schedule-holes in schedules. In Chapter 8, Lin and Ng describe a static scheduling approach to integrate task mapping, scheduling and voltage selection to minimize energy consumption of real-time dependent tasks executing on a number of heterogeneous processors. Their approach is based on genetic algorithms. In Chapter 9, Vidyarthi et al. describe a cluster-based dynamic allocation scheme for distributed computing systems. A fuzzy function is used for both the task clustering and processor clustering. This paper shows how the dynamic allocation of stream of tasks, with minimum knowledge, is possible in a distributed computing system.

Part 3: networking, architectures, and distributed systems

In the first paper of this part, Chapter 10, Liang and Wang propose a scheme to improve existing on-demand routing protocols by creating a mesh and multiple alternate routes by overhearing the data packet transmission for ad hoc network. Their scheme establishes the mesh and alternate routes without transmitting any extra control message. Chapter 11 presents a cost-effective fault-tolerant routing strategy for optical-electronic grids. Loh and Hsu design a fully adaptive, both deadlock-free and livelock-free, fault-tolerant routing strategy for multi-hop grid networks. In Chapter 12, Kim et al. address information hiding using steganography technique. They improve generalized Lowbit Encoding method and apply this method with CDMA to level up information hiding. Chapter 13 addresses a proposal for the Synergy Distributed Shared Memory System and its integration with the virtual memory, group communication and process migration services of the Genesis Cluster Operating System. In order to retrieve fresh information, Sato et al. explain a distributed search engine that they developed, called Cooperative Search Engine (CSE) in Chapter 14. In CSE, a local search engine located in each Web server makes an index of local pages, and a meta search integrates these local search engines in order to realize a global search engine. In Chapter 15, Sreenivas and Bhalla provide exact conditions for an arbitrary checkpoint in distributed systems. Their method does not require expensive global computations and it is based on independent dependency tracking within clusters of nodes. The proposed computations can be performed by a node to identify existing global checkpoints. The nodes can also compute conditions to make a checkpoint, or conditions, such that a collection of checkpoints, can belong to a global snapshot.

Part 4: applications

In this part, Liu and Guo, in Chapter 16, describe a framework of an interactive data mining system based on PC cluster environments that they are developing. The system is an interactive and dynamic visual. In Chapter 17, the author analyzes the mobile Internet transition from the social process viewpoint first. A two-year tracing of mobile email transition observed on a commercial mobile web service shows the two-staged transition to cope with the bulk email problems. Then, the author, Yamakami, proposes an identity transition factor model to describe the social process of the forced email address changes in the mobile Internet. Chapter 18 presents two approaches for an efficient polygonal approximation on distributed systems and parallel computers. The authors describe how to use parallel and distributed algorithms to allow maximum efficiency on grid of computers and to minimize communications by distributing the geometric grid elements. In Chapter 19, Xie and Shen present a novel efficient geometric registration algorithm based on the shape of the closed-regions. Their registration algorithm takes advantage of shape information of the closed-regions bounded by contours in images. Chapter 20, presents MAPFS as a flexible and high-performance platform for data-intensive applications and, more specifically, for data grid applications whose major goal is to provide efficient access to data. In Chapter 21, Zhu et al. introduce and analyze an efficient Key Message (KM) approach to supporting parallel computing in cluster environments. Their goal is to reduce the communication overhead and thus the completion time of a parallel application. Experiments demonstrate that when the network background load increases or the computation to communication ratio decreases, the analysis results show a significant improvement on communication of a parallel application over the system which does not use the KM approach.

Acknowledgments

We would like to thank the all authors for their excellent contributions and patience in assisting us. We are also grateful for Susan Lagerstrom-Fife and Sharon Palleshi of Kluwer Academic Publishers for their patience and support to make this book possible. Finally, the fundamental work of all reviewers on these chapters is also very warmly acknowledged.

MINYI GUO AND LAURENCE TIANRUO YANG

I

PROGRAMMING MODELS AND SUPPORT TOOLS

Chapter 1

FLEXIBLE MESSAGE PASSING INTERFACE FOR A HETEROGENEOUS COMPUTING ENVIRONMENT

Yuichi Tsujita,* Toshiyuki Imamura,† Nobuhiro Yamagishi

Center for Promotion of Computational Science and Engineering,
Japan Atomic Energy Research Institute
693 HigashiUeno, Taitoku, Tokyo 1100015, Japan
tsujita@hiro.kindai.ac.jp, imamura@im.uec.ac.jp, yama@koma.jaeri.go.jp

Hiroshi Takemiya

Hitachi East Japan Solutions, Ltd.
21610 Honcho, Aobaku, Sendai, Miyagi 9800014, Japan

Abstract   A flexible MPI library, Stampi, has been developed to enable MPI operations on a heterogeneous computing environment. APIs are based on the MPI-1 and the MPI-2 standards. Users can call these functions without awareness of underlying communication mechanism. In message transfer, a vendor-supplied MPI library and TCP/IP socket are used selectively among MPI processes. Introducing its own router process mechanism hides a complex network configuration in inter-machine data transfer. In addition, the MPI-2 extensions, functionalities of dynamic process creation and MPI-I/O, are also implemented. MPI-I/O on the Stampi library realizes both local and remote I/O operations due to the request of user applications. We have evaluated performance of primitive MPI functions in Stampi and sufficient performance has been achieved and effectiveness of our flexible implementation has been confirmed.

Keywords: Stampi, MPI, router process, dynamic process creation, MPI-I/O processes

*Corresponding author, Present address: Department of Electric Engineering and Computer Science, Faculty of Engineering, Kinki University
1 Umenobe, Takaya, HigashiHiroshima, Hiroshima 7392116, Japan
† Present address: Department of Computer Science, The University of ElectroCommunications
151 Chofugaoka, Chofu, Tokyo 1828585, Japan

1.   Introduction

Recent applications in computational science handle huge amounts of memories, storages in addition to computation power. Nevertheless amounts of computational resources have recently grown hugely, a parallel computer has a limit on these resources due to physical constraints. As one of the solutions to overcome this limit, construction of a huge scale of computing environment by connecting computers via network has been focused because of its cheaper cost in construction and high bandwidth network connections.

As MPI (Message Passing Interface) [1, 2] has become the de facto standard in distributed parallel computation, almost all computer vendors have implemented their own MPI libraries. Although parallel computation coupled with several types of computers requires inter-machine communication, any vendor-supplied MPI library does not provide it generally. To realize such communication, we have developed an intermediate library named Stampi [3]. This library plays a role of the glue between a user program and underlying communication libraries, and it relays a messages between them and hides complexity and heterogeneity among computers. MPI communication inside a computer is realized using a vendor-supplied MPI library. On the other hand, TCP/IP socket connections are used among computers. Those two communication modes are selected flexibly by an intermediate communication library of Stampi.

In MPI communication, all processes are supposed to be accessible each other generally. But communications from/to computation nodes in private network or via firewall are difficult due to several underlying problems in such environment. Although MPI communications using administrative method such as network address translation (NAT) or virtual private network (VPN) can be considered, the authors selected to develop a flexible communication library which provides dynamic control capability to user program. A router process is invoked on an IP-reachable node, and it relays messages to the processes in the private or firewalled networks. The number of router processes is valuable and users can select it in order to gain higher throughput.

In some cases, users can not get fully computational resources of each computer. Dynamic resource usage is a key technology for effective use of computational resources. This method can be realized using dynamic process creation defined in the MPI-2 standard [2]. Stampi realizes this functionality in a heterogeneous distributed computing environment. Stampi also supports the dynamic process creation with a secure communication path.

Handling huge amounts of data is also significant in parallel computation. In such data-intensive computation, almost all applications tend to have access to noncontiguous data rather than contiguous data. Because UNIX I/O APIs are not effective to have access to noncontiguous data, MPI-I/O APIs have been proposed in the MPI-2 standard. As the MPI-I/O APIs give useful and flexible interfaces for both contiguous and noncontiguous accesses in parallel-I/O operations, MPI-I/O functions are realized in several kinds of vendor-supplied

MPI libraries. But none of them provide MPI-I/O operations among different hardware platforms yet.

To realize such mechanism, we have designed and developed an MPI-I/O library, Stampi-I/O [4], as a part of Stampi, using a flexible communication mechanism of Stampi. Users can call MPI-I/O functions in both local and remote I/O operations with the same API defined in the MPI-2 standard. Stampi-I/O has been designed to work on any computer where a vendor-supplied MPI library is available. Besides, if a vendor-supplied MPI-I/O library is available, high performance parallel I/O operations is realized using the library. Otherwise Stampi-I/O executes MPI-I/O operations using UNIX I/O functions.

In this paper, outline, architecture and preliminary results of Stampi, including Stampi-I/O, are described.

2. Stampi: A Flexible MPI Library for Heterogeneous Computing Environment

Stampi has been developed to provide a computing environment which hides heterogeneity among computers for flexible MPI operations. The features of Stampi are summarized as follows;

1 flexible communication mechanism among computers,

2 dynamic process creation and remote I/O operation mechanisms based on the MPI-2 standard,

3 flexible mechanism in both local and remote I/O operations, and

4 support of external32 data format among multiple platforms.

Users can execute functions including MPI-I/O functions across multiple platforms using Stampi without awareness of differences in communication mechanism and I/O system. Rest of this section describes the details of Stampi.

2.1 Flexible communication mechanism

Stampi has inter-operability between intra-machine and inter-machine data transfers with the same APIs defined in the and the standards. Architectural view of Stampi is illustrated in Figure 1.1. It is assumed that master user processes and slave user processes are running on parallel computers A and B, respectively. In intra-machine data transfer, Stampi uses a well-tuned vendor-supplied MPI library with the help of the vendor-supplied communication mechanism (VSCM). On the other hand, the common communication mechanism interface (CCMI) is used in inter-machine data transfer. In the CCMI layer, TCP/IP is applied to have inter-operability on any platform.

When user processes are in private or firewalled networks, a router process, which is invoked on an IP-reachable node, relays messages to/from those processes. If computers have multiple network interface cards (NICs), multiple

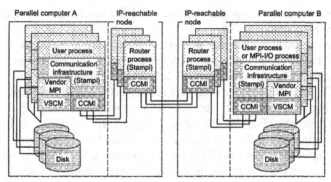

CCMI : Common Communication Mechanism Interface (TCP/IP)
VSCM : Vendor Supplied Communication Mechanism

Figure 1.1. Architectural view of Stampi. MPI communications and MPI-I/O operations are available across computers.

routers are invoked in order to gain higher throughput in inter-machine MPI communication. Users can select the number of in their programs by using key parameters in an info object.

Inter-operability among different kinds of MPI implementations is also an important issue in parallel computation on a heterogeneous computing environment. The Stampi library also has an inter-operable interface to other MPI implementations using an IMPI [5] interface. MPI operations between a Stampi program and a LAM/MPI [6] program has been realized using the IMPI interface.

2.2   Dynamic process creation and remote I/O operation mechanisms based on the MPI-2 standard

and MPI-I/O operations in the MPI-2 standard are important features in distributed parallel computation. These mechanisms have been implemented in Stampi for dynamic use of computational resources and flexible I/O operations. Using these methods, users can execute their programs in the manager-worker fashion. Some useful key parameters (user-ID, node name, partition name, batch queue name, etc.) are supported for the mechanisms. For MPI-I/O operations among computers, we introduced an MPI-I/O process which plays parallel-I/O operations on a remote machine. are invoked on a remote machine according to key parameters passed to the MPI_File_open function using the spawn mechanism of Stampi.

In execution of an MPI program, Stampi supports interactive and batch modes both. Here, we would like to explain how child MPI processes and MPI-I/O processes are created with a Stampi library on a batch system. Figure 1.2 depicts mechanism of the spawn operation and the remote I/O operation under

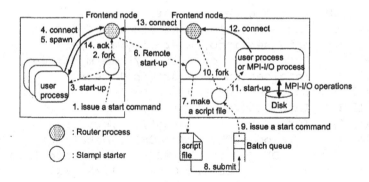

Figure 1.2. Spawn operation and remote I/O operation of Stampi under the batch mode.

the batch mode. Firstly user processes are initiated by a Stampi start-up command (starter) on a computer in the left side. When those user processes call MPI_Comm_spawn or MPI_File_open, a router process kicks off a starter process on a computer in the right side with the help of remote shell command (rsh, ssh, etc.) and it generates a script file which is submitted to a batch queue system according to a specified queue class in an info object. Secondly, the starter written in the script file kicks off user processes or MPI-I/O processes in the case of MPI_Comm_spawn or MPI_File_open, respectively. Besides, a router process is invoked on an IP-reachable node if it is required. Finally, a network connection between both computers is established.

In addition to the dynamic process creation, Stampi supports a static process creation based on the MPI-1 standard on a heterogeneous computing environment. In process creation on a remote machine, the dynamic process creation mechanism is used inside the Stampi library. Users can execute their programs across computers using Stampi.

2.3   Flexible mechanism in local and remote I/O operations

MPI-I/O functions are available not only inside a computer but also among computers using Stampi. When user processes call MPI_File_open, a Stampi library is called first. Then the Stampi library selects the most efficient I/O method possible between any two processes flexibly according to a target computer in the info object specified by users.

When MPI_INFO_NULL is specified in MPI_File_open, the I/O operation on a local file system is carried out. On the other hand, the remote I/O method is selected when key parameters such as target host name are set in the info object by MPI_Info_set and the info is used in MPI_File_open. The remote I/O operations are processed with TCP socket connections via a router process and an MPI-I/O process.

An example code of an MPI-I/O program is shown in Figure 1.3. In this

```
call MPI_Info_create(info,err)
call MPI_Info_set(info,'host','comp-b',err)
call MPI_Info_set(info,'user','myname',err)
call MPI_Info_set(info,'wdir','/home/mydir',err)
call MPI_Info_set(info,'nqsq','pb1',err)
call MPI_Info_set(info,'node','3',err)
call MPI_Info_set(info,'mpiio','vendor',err)
call MPI_Info_set(info,'io-np','2',err)
call MPI_File_open(MPI_COMM_WORLD,'datafile',
        MPI_MODE_WRONLY|MPI_MODE_CREATE,info,fh,err)
call MPI_File_set_view(fh,0,MPI_INT,MPI_INT,
        'external32',MPI_INFO_NULL,err)
call MPI_File_write(fh,buf,nints,MPI_INT,status,err)
call MPI_File_seek(fh,(MPI_Offset)0,MPI_SEEK_SET,err)
call MPI_File_sync(fh,err)
call MPI_File_read(fh,buf,nints,MPI_INT,status,err)
call MPI_File_close(fh,err)
```

Figure 1.3. An example code of an MPI-I/O program for remote I/O operations.

example code, several key parameters for remote I/O operations are specified by MPI_Info_set. The key parameters, *nqsq* and *node*, are used to specify parameters of the batch queue system. Users can also give *mpiio* to specify an MPI-I/O library to be used (a vendor-supplied MPI-I/O library or a UNIX I/O library). Multiple MPI-I/O processes can be created on a remote machine using a key parameter, *io-np*, to gain higher throughput when a vendor-supplied MPI-I/O library is available. The number of MPI-I/O processes is variable up to the number of user processes.

2.4   Support of external32 data format

To assure inter-operability in data handling among multiple platforms, external32 is supported as a common data format in Stampi. It is also available in MPI-I/O operations using Stampi-I/O. When external32 is designated in the data format, data conversion from native data format to external32 and vice versa is carried out automatically. Thus users need not pay attention to the difference on each hardware platform.

3.   Performance measurement of Stampi

Performance measurement of MPI functions in Stampi was carried out on two typical hardware configurations in computational science. One configuration is interconnected supercomputers, a Fujitsu VPP5000 and a Hitachi SR8000 in Japan Atomic Energy Research Institute, and another one is interconnected Linux machines, a Linux workstation and a Linux cluster with an

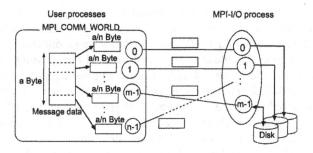

Figure 1.4. Schematic view of I/O operations with multiple user processes.

SCore PC cluster system [7]. On both cases, the systems are interconnected via Gigabit Ethernet based LAN.

In computational science, coupled simulation on interconnected supercomputers has been focused due to the lack of computational resources. As the SR8000 and the VPP5000 have different architecture in both hardware and software, performance can be improved in some kinds of coupled simulation codes using architectural merits of each supercomputer. Besides, MPI-I/O operations using a vendor-supplied MPI-I/O library is available on the VPP5000. Stampi has been implemented on many kinds of supercomputers including them to realize MPI communication on interconnected supercomputers. Besides MPI-I/O functions have been supported on supercomputers where a vendor-supplied MPI-I/O library is available. To show high availability and flexible architecture of Stampi, we evaluated performance of Stampi, typically performance of MPI-I/O operations, on the interconnected supercomputers.

Recently PC clusters have been focused for its cost-effective high performance and high availability. Stampi has been implemented on an SCore cluster system to realize coupled parallel computation among a PC cluster and other machines [8]. To show sufficient performance of Stampi on a PC cluster, peak performance of MPI communications were measured using Stampi.

In the following subsections, data size is denoted as the whole data size to be transfered. Data was distributed among user processes equally as shown in Figure 1.4. In performance measurement of round-trip communication, we calculated transfer rate as (message data size)/(RTT/2), where RTT is round trip time for ping-pong communication between user processes. In addition, we defined the latency as RTT/2 for 0 Byte message.

3.1 Performance measurement between a Hitachi SR8000 and a Fujitsu VPP5000

Firstly, we mention about performance measurement between the Hitachi SR8000 and the Fujitsu VPP5000. Hereafter, they are denoted as SR and VPP, respectively. The SR consists of 20 computation nodes, and they are all IP-reachable. Interconnection among those nodes is established with high performance cross-bar network with 1 GB/s bandwidth for single direction. While the VPP consists of one frontend node and 64 backend (computation) nodes and those nodes are interconnected with high performance cross-bar network with 1.6 GB/s bandwidth. Those backend nodes are in private network and they are all accessible only from the frontend node. High performance and flexible I/O operation is available with the FPFS (Flexible and high Performance File System) [9]. The FPFS has multiple disks for file striping and round-robin I/O operations. The FPFS and the backend nodes are interconnected with four Fibre Channel connections (theoretical peak bandwidth is 100 MB/s per link.).

In this test, peak performance of raw TCP socket connections and inter-machine MPI communications between the SR and the VPP was measured at first. Next, peak performance of collective blocking I/O operations was measured using MPI_File_write_at_all and MPI_File_read_at_all for both local and remote operations. In addition, performance of remote operations using multiple MPI-I/O processes was measured. In all MPI-I/O operations, I/O operations were carried out on the FPFS.

3.1.1 Performance results of round-trip raw TCP socket connections.

At first, we measured performance of round-trip point-to-point inter-machine data transfer using raw TCP socket connections. It is reported that appropriate TCP buffer size can improve performance of raw TCP socket connections in [10]. We tried to find appropriate TCP buffer size for inter-machine data transfer between the SR and the VPP. In addition, TCP_NODELAY option in setsockopt was specified to optimize the inter-machine data transfer.

We measured performance of inter-machine data transfer between the SR and a frontend node of the VPP and between the frontend node of the VPP and a backend node of the VPP. Table 1.1 shows the performance results. Transfer rate between the SR and the frontend node of the VPP was about 10 % of theoretical bandwidth. The most appropriate TCP buffer size was considered to be 512 KByte and latency in this case was 3 ms. In inter-machine data transfer between the frontend node and the backend node of the VPP was much higher than that between the SR and the frontend node of the VPP. In this case, the TCP buffer size is not a significant parameter for the communication performance.

3.1.2 Performance results of inter-machine data transfer using Stampi.

Next, we measured performance of point-to-point inter-machine data transfer with several TCP buffer sizes and TCP_NODELAY option using Stampi. To optimize inter-machine data transfer, these parameters can be specified from a Stampi start-up command. For example, next command;

```
% jmpirun -np 1 -sockbufsize 512 -tcpnodelay program
```

Table 1.1. Performance results of round-trip point-to-point inter-machine data transfer between a Hitachi SR8000 (SR) and a Fujitsu VPP5000 (VPP) using raw TCP socket connections. Unit of numbers in this table is MB/s.

TCP buffer size (Byte)	Latency	Data size (Byte)				
		512 K	1 M	16 M	64 M	128 M
SR → VPP(Frontend)						
128 K	3.08 ms	11.9	12.3	12.5	12.3	12.3
512 K	2.99 ms	11.9	12.2	12.7	12.7	12.7
1 M	3.09 ms	12.0	12.2	8.12	8.83	7.52
VPP(Frontend) ↔ VPP(Backend)						
128 K	0.13 ms	166.2	167.8	162.1	169.7	170.0
512 K	0.13 ms	159.3	159.9	169.8	164.6	168.4
1 M	0.12 ms	159.6	159.1	170.0	169.8	170.9

Table 1.2. Performance results of ping-pong inter-machine MPI communication using Stampi between a Hitachi SR8000 and a Fujitsu VPP5000 with several TCP buffer sizes. Unit of numbers in this table is MB/s.

TCP buffer size (Byte)	Latency	Data size (Byte)				
		512 K	1 M	16 M	64 M	256 M
128 K	7.87 ms	7.89	7.20	7.65	7.63	7.48
512 K	10.7 ms	10.2	9.89	11.1	9.75	9.67
1 M	11.2 ms	10.6	9.48	10.4	7.24	7.00

initiates a process (program) on a local machine with a TCP buffer size of 512 KByte and TCP_NODELAY option for an inter-machine data transfer. Once inter-communicator is established between executed user processes and spawned processes, MPI communication starts with the help of raw TCP socket connections via the inter-communicator.

In our test, ping-pong message transfer was operated between the SR and the VPP using MPI_Send and MPI_Recv. Table 1.2 shows performance results. From this table, we notice that appropriate TCP buffer size is 512 KByte. The appropriate TCP buffer size was 512 KByte in both raw TCP socket connections and inter-machine MPI communication. Therefore we consider that the most appropriate TCP buffer size in this case is 512 KByte for remote I/O operations using Stampi. In addition, we notice that latency of inter-machine MPI communication using Stampi is about 3 times larger than that of raw TCP socket connections. We consider that this additional latency was introduced by implementation of a Stampi library.

3.1.3   Performance results of local I/O operations.   Performance of local I/O operations with Stampi was measured using a vendor-

(a)   (b)

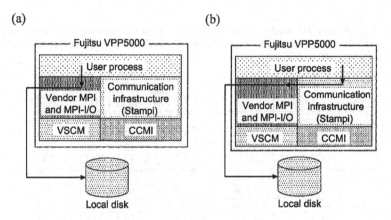

Figure 1.5. Functional diagram of (a) vendor-supplied execution method and (b) Stampi-supplied execution method.

supplied MPI-I/O library [11] on the VPP. In this test, vendor-supplied and Stampi-supplied execution methods were used. Functional diagram of these methods are depicted in Figs 1.5 (a) and (b), respectively. In the vendor-supplied execution method, a user process directly calls a vendor-supplied MPI-I/O library. On the other hand, a user process calls a Stampi library first. Next, the Stampi library calls the vendor-supplied MPI-I/O library. We examined whether overhead time for implementing the Stampi library was negligible or not compared with the execution time in the vendor-supplied execution method.

Performance results of local I/O operations using MPI_File_write_at_all and MPI_File_read_at_all are shown in Table 1.3. In this table, *Write* and *Read* correspond to MPI_File_write_at_all and MPI_File_read_at_all, respectively. Besides, *Vendor* and *Stampi* mean vendor-supplied and Stampi-supplied execution methods, respectively and *np* denotes the number of user processes. From this table, performance advantage for two and four user processes is obvious.

In the vendor-supplied MPI-I/O library of the VPP, disk cache mechanism is equipped on an I/O node of the VPP for performance improvement. In this mechanism, the number of cache blocks is 256 and the size of each block is 64 KByte. Thus, total size of the cache is 16 MByte. It is considered that performance degradation for the over 16 MByte was caused by inefficiency of the mechanism when the cache was almost full with data.

Furthermore, there was no significant degradation in the Stampi-supplied method compared with the vendor-supplied one. Thus, implementation of the Stampi library does not affect the performance of local I/O operations.

3.1.4   Performance results of remote I/O operations.   In remote I/O test, a user program was initiated on the SR and I/O operations

Table 1.3. Performance results of local I/O operations with MPI_File_write_at_all and MPI_File_read_at_all on a Fujitsu VPP5000. In this table, *Write* and *Read* correspond to MPI_File_write_at_all and MPI_File_read_at_all, respectively. Besides, *Vendor* and *Stampi* mean vendor-supplied and Stampi-supplied execution methods, respectively. Unit of numbers in this table is MB/s.

	np	512 K	1 M	4 M	8 M	16 M	64 M	256 M
		Data size (Byte)						
Write	1	308.1	312.6	312.9	1060.4	96.9	58.1	30.5
	2	2164.5	2272.7	2357.1	2371.8	141.5	109.8	68.0
(Vendor)	4	3906.3	4219.4	4640.4	4725.3	398.4	244.3	106.0
Write	1	300.3	305.3	305.2	1061.0	93.6	53.5	32.9
	2	2155.2	2267.6	2359.9	2373.9	136.8	106.2	66.0
(Stampi)	4	3876.0	4273.5	4640.4	7719.8	380.6	222.7	111.3
Read	1	115.0	110.0	106.1	1272.7	103.1	81.5	55.4
	2	2325.6	2439.0	2528.4	2534.9	109.7	109.4	109.6
(Vendor)	4	4237.3	4651.2	2515.7	5047.3	560.1	533.1	218.9
Read	1	114.7	109.8	106.1	1272.9	103.2	81.2	55.5
	2	2304.1	2427.2	2523.7	2535.7	109.7	108.8	108.9
(Stampi)	4	4166.7	4524.9	4956.6	5044.1	497.9	507.6	218.7

was carried out on the VPP. In this test, MPI-I/O processes using a vendor-supplied MPI-I/O library and a single router process were created on the VPP. Performance was measured in the user program on the SR. We specified the best TCP buffer size (512 KByte) and TCP_NODELAY option to gain higher throughput.

Transfer rate of remote I/O operations with MPI_File_write_at_all and MPI_File_read_at_all between the SR and the VPP was measured using Stampi. User processes were initiated on the SR and one or two MPI-I/O processes were created on the VPP. Table 1.4 shows performance results. In most cases, performance for two MPI-I/O processes was higher. Considering the I/O operations on the VPP, the I/O mechanism on the VPP in the two MPI-I/O processes case is similar to that of local I/O operations for two user processes. Therefore we consider that this improvement was realized due to the performance improvement mentioned in local I/O operations for two user processes (Table 1.3). As inter-machine data transfer time was dominant compared with local I/O operation time in remote I/O operations, the improvement realized by two MPI-I/O processes in remote I/O operations was not drastic compared with that in the local I/O operations.

In addition, we notice that performance of read operations was better than that of write operations although there was not significant difference in performance between local write and read operations. In the remote write and read operations between the SR to the VPP, almost all inter-machine data transfers were carried out from the SR to the VPP and vice versa. To find reasons, we measured performance of one-way trip inter-machine data transfer using raw

Table 1.4. Performance results of MPI_File_write_at_all and MPI_File_read_at_all in remote I/O operations from a Hitachi SR8000 (SR) to a Fujitsu VPP5000 (VPP). Unit of numbers in this table is MB/s. In this table, *np* and *io-np* denote the numbers of user processes and MPI-I/O processes, respectively.

	np	io-np	Data size (Byte)					
			512 K	1 M	8 M	16 M	64 M	256 M
MPI_File_write_at_all (SR → VPP)	2	1	7.67	10.2	8.63	8.72	8.23	5.82
	2	2	7.69	10.5	13.5	14.1	13.5	9.27
	4	1	6.38	9.48	5.38	7.71	5.78	5.11
	4	2	6.82	11.2	1.60	11.5	14.8	9.12
	8	1	1.28	1.39	0.30	1.63	1.20	2.86
	8	2	1.35	1.32	0.53	3.10	3.39	6.53
MPI_File_read_at_all (SR ← VPP)	2	1	7.27	10.3	8.26	13.0	9.77	8.21
	2	2	12.2	17.2	22.5	23.3	21.4	18.7
	4	1	3.94	7.40	17.1	18.5	17.9	17.1
	4	2	7.12	13.1	19.5	17.8	20.2	18.3
	8	1	1.89	3.66	14.1	16.8	17.5	19.8
	8	2	3.76	7.22	18.7	22.5	20.8	21.9

Table 1.5. Performance results of one-way trip inter-machine data transfer using raw TCP socket connections between a Hitachi SR8000 (SR) and a Fujitsu VPP5000 (VPP). Unit of numbers in this table is MB/s.

	Latency	Data size (Byte)				
		512 K	1 M	16 M	64 M	128 M
SR → VPP(Frontend)	1.41 ms	83.1	21.9	11.8	11.5	11.4
VPP(Frontend) → VPP(Backend)	0.038 ms	126.8	105.2	91.2	94.0	94.9
SR ← VPP(Frontend)	1.14 ms	23.7	22.0	17.1	16.0	15.7
VPP(Frontend) ← VPP(Backend)	0.547 ms	101.9	97.8	98.3	97.5	97.3

TCP sockets from the SR to the VPP and vice versa. Performance results are shown in Table 1.5. According to these results, we consider that performance of remote write operations is lower than that of remote read operations because inter-machine data transfer from the SR to the VPP is lower than that from the VPP to the SR.

There was performance degradation in remote I/O operations with multiple user processes on the SR compared with the single user process case as shown in Table 1.4. To find reasons, we measured performance of inter-machine data transfer of MPI_Send and MPI_Recv between the SR and the VPP using a Stampi communication library. In this test, slave processes on the VPP were

Table 1.6. Performance results of inter-machine data transfer with MPI_Send and MPI_Recv between a Hitachi SR8000 (SR) and a Fujitsu VPP5000 (VPP). In this table, *np(SR)* and *np(VPP)* denotes the numbers of processes on the SR8000 and the VPP5000, respectively. Unit of numbers in this table is MB/s.

	np(SR)	np(VPP)	Latency	Data size (Byte) 64 M	256 M
	1	1	4.35 ms	4.82	8.40
SR(MPI_Send) →	2	1	4.61 ms	2.93	6.65
VPP(MPI_Recv)	4	1	4.81 ms	1.77	4.71
	8	1	6.76 ms	0.954	2.97
	1	1	17.2 ms	19.7	19.1
SR(MPI_Recv) ←	2	1	17.3 ms	22.5	22.4
VPP(MPI_Send)	4	1	18.9 ms	15.8	17.6
	8	1	11.5 ms	15.9	19.5

created by master processes on the SR. Performance results are summarized in Table 1.6, where *np(SR)* and *np(VPP)* are the numbers of processes on the SR and the VPP, respectively. As shown in this table, performance of MPI_Send was lower than that of MPI_Recv on the SR. We consider that this result is caused partly by the performance difference in inter-machine data transfer by TCP raw socket connections shown in Table 1.5. We notice that performance of inter-machine data transfer is lower with increase of the number of processes on the SR. From these results, it is considered that the performance of remote I/O operations with multiple user processes was degraded due to the poor performance in one-way trip inter-machine data transfer from the SR to the VPP with multiple user processes.

3.2   Performance measurement between an SCore PC cluster and a Linux workstation

Performance of MPI communication was also measured on the interconnected Linux machines, a Linux PC cluster using the SCore PC cluster system (an SCore PC cluster) and a Linux workstation (dual 600 MHz Pentium III CPU node, Linux SMP kernel 2.4.17). The SCore PC cluster has one server node and eight computation nodes. Each node was a dual 1.26 GHz Pentium III CPU node. All the nodes except the server node have dual network connections, Gigabit Ethernet (1 Gbps, full duplex mode) and Myrinet2000 (2 Gbps) via a Gigabit Ethernet switch and a Myrinet2000 switch, respectively. Each computation node has a 64-bit PCI NIC (Intel PRO/1000). The server node was connected to the Gigabit Ethernet switch with 100 Mbps bandwidth and full duplex mode. The SCore PC cluster was connected to the Linux workstation with Gigabit Ethernet via two Gigabit Ethernet switches (NetGear GS524T).

Table 1.7. Latencies and transfer rates of raw TCP socket connections between a computation node in an SCore PC cluster and a Linux workstation via Gigabit Ethernet. Unit of numbers in this table is MB/s.

	Message data size (Byte)				
Latency	64 K	1 M	8 M	64 M	256 M
61 μs	30.1	37.2	37.3	36.9	36.8

Table 1.8. Latencies and transfer rates of inter-machine MPI communication between an SCore PC cluster and a Linux workstation. In this table, *dynamic* and *static* denotes dynamic and static process creation modes, respectively. *np(SCore)* and *np(Linux)* are the numbers of processes on the SCore PC cluster and the Linux workstation, respectively. Unit of numbers in this table is MB/s.

	np(SCore)	np(Linux)	Latency	Message data size (Byte)				
				64 K	1 M	8 M	64 M	256 M
dynamic	1	1	57.0 μs	19.5	33.9	34.6	34.9	35.0
static	1	1	106.5 μs	18.9	33.7	35.0	35.3	35.4

3.2.1 Performance results of inter-machine data transfer using raw TCP socket connections. Firstly, we measured performance of inter-machine data transfer using raw TCP socket connections between a computation node in the SCore PC cluster and the Linux workstation. Performance results are shown in Table 1.7. From this table, it is considered that up to 30 % of theoretical bandwidth of Gigabit Ethernet has been achieved. These values are compared with performance values of inter-machine MPI communications later to examine whether there is performance degradation in implementing Stampi or not.

3.2.2 Performance results of inter-machine MPI communication. Secondly, we measured performance of inter-machine MPI communication in the dynamic and the static process creation modes. In the dynamic mode, a single user process was initiated on the SCore PC cluster and an another user process was invoked on the Linux workstation by a spawn function. On the other hand, we initiated a single user process on a computation node in the SCore PC cluster and the Linux workstation each in the static mode. Performance results are shown in Table 1.8. From these results, we consider that the performance in both modes is quite comparable to that of the raw TCP socket connections.

4. Related Work

There are several MPI implementations which intend to support a heterogeneous computing environment such as MPICH [12], MPICH-G2 [13], PACX-

MPI [14] and so on. There are differences in design policy of MPI implementations such as extensibility for future computer architecture, flexible communication mechanism in heterogeneous computing environment, well-tuned communication method and support of Grid computing environment.

Inter-machine MPI communication is established by direct connections among all the computers in MPICH. On the other hand, MPICH-G2 and PACX-MPI uses router process mechanism for inter-machine MPI communication. The number of router processes is fixed in both cases. MPICH-G2 uses Globus [15] as an underlying communication library to support inter-machine MPI communication on a Grid computing environment. This library is used as a de facto standard MPI library in Grid computing. It realizes MPI communications across multiple computers which are distributed in a wide-area network. In this library, a vendor-supplied MPI library is used inside a computer, while TCP sockets are used via Globus communication libraries among computers. In Stampi, router process is dynamically created according to communication mechanism of computers or user's explicit configuration requests. In addition, the number of router processes is selectable in a user program. Stampi selects the most appropriate MPI library according to a destination of MPI communication. A vendor-supplied MPI library is used inside a computer, while TCP sockets are used in inter-machine MPI communication.

There is an MPI-I/O library named ROMIO [16] in MPICH. Interface to a lower level library is supplied by ADIO [17]. ADIO supports several kinds of file systems. On the other hand, Stampi was developed as a glue for MPI communication and MPI-I/O operations between different platforms. It provides users a computing environment which hides heterogeneity among computers for MPI operations. In MPI-I/O operations using Stampi, a vendor-supplied MPI-I/O library is used inside a computer, while remote I/O operation is carried out by inter-machine communication mechanism of Stampi and a newly developed MPI-I/O process. On an I/O server, a vendor-supplied MPI-I/O library is used as default.

Since MPICH is designed to be able to replace the communication drivers into well-tuned native one, it has several versions based on the hardware platforms. MPICH-GM [18] is one of the derivations of the MPICH library. It uses a GM [18] driver for a Myrinet PC cluster. It exploits lower latency and higher transfer rates of Myrinet networks. A cluster system, SCore [7], also supports Myrinet and Ethernet interconnections among PC nodes. A built-in MPI library, MPICH-SCore [19], uses a PM2 [20] driver in intra-machine MPI communication with higher throughput.

5.   Summary

We have reported outline, architecture and preliminary performance results of Stampi.

In Stampi, not only MPI-1 functions but also MPI-2 functions are supported to realize flexible MPI operations in a heterogeneous computing environment. We have implemented a router process to relay messages from/to user processes in private or firewalled networks. In addition, an MPI-I/O process has been introduced to realize MPI-I/O operations on a remote machine.

Through performance measurement test, we observed effectiveness of Stampi in both MPI communications and MPI-I/O operations. We observed that peak performance of MPI communication from a Hitachi SR8000 to a Fujitsu VPP5-000 is lower than that in the opposite direction. We also observed the similar degradation in raw TCP socket communications. Thus we consider that performance of MPI communication from the SR8000 to the VPP5000 was degraded by lower performance of raw TCP socket communications in the same direction.

MPI communications based on the MPI-2 standard has been also realized on an SCore cluster system. Users can select dynamic process creation mode based on the MPI-2 standard in addition to static process creation mode based on the MPI-1 standard. We achieved sufficient performance in MPI communications.

Currently, Stampi is supported on several platforms, for example, scalar parallel computers (Hitachi SR8000, IBM SP3, SGI Origin, SGI Onyx, etc.), vector parallel computers (Fujitsu VPP5000, NEC SX-5, etc.), workstation/PC clusters (Solaris, HP-UX, Linux, FreeBSD, SCore, etc.) and so on.

Acknowledgments

The authors would like to thank Prof. Genki Yagawa, University of Tokyo and director of Center for Promotion of Computational Science and Engineering (CCSE), Japan Atomic Energy Research Institute (JAERI), for his continuous encouragement. The authors would like to thank the staff at CCSE, JAERI, particularly Toshio Hirayama, Norihiro Nakajima, and Kenji Higuchi for their sincere support in this work.

References

[1] Message Passing Interface Forum. (1995). MPI: A Message-Passing Interface Standard.

[2] Message Passing Interface Forum. (1997). MPI-2: Extensions to the Message-Passing Interface Standard.

[3] T. Imamura, Y. Tsujita, H. Koide, and H. Takemiya. (2000). An Architecture of Stampi: MPI Library on a Cluster of Parallel Computers. LNCS 1908, Recent Advances in Parallel Virtual Machine and Message Passing Interface, Springer, pp. 200–207.

[4] Y. Tsujita, T. Imamura, H. Takemiya, and N. Yamagishi (2002). Stampi-I/O: Flexible Distributed Parallel-I/O Library for Heterogeneous Computing Environment. LNCS 2474, Recent Advances in Parallel Virtual Machine and Message Passing Interface, Springer, pp. 288–295.

[5] J. M. Squyres, A. Lumsdaine, W. L. George, J. G. Hagedorn, and J. E. Devaney (2000). The Interoperable Message Passing Interface (IMPI) Extensions to LAM/MPI. MPI Developer's Conference, Ithica, NY, USA.

[6] G. Burns, R. Daund, and J. Vaigl (1994). LAM: An open cluster environment for MPI. In *Proceedings of Supercomputing Symposium '94*, University of Toronto, pp. 379–386.

[7] PC Cluster Consortium. http://www.pccluster.org/.

[8] Y. Tsujita, T. Imamura, N. Yamagishi, and H. Takemiya (2003). MPI-2 Support in Heterogeneous Computing Environment Using an SCore Cluster System. LNCS 2745, Parallel and Distributed Processing and Applications, Springer, pp. 139–144.

[9] http://primepower.fujitsu.com/hpc/en/vpp5000e/.

[10] B. Tierney. (2001). TCP Tuning Guide for Distributed Application on Wide Area Networks. *Usenix; login*, February 2001.

[11] Fujitsu UXP/V MPI User's Manual V20.

[12] W. Gropp, E. Lusk, N. Doss, and A. Skjellum. (1996). A high-performance, portable implementation of the MPI message passing interface standard. *Parallel Computing*, 22(6), pp. 789–828.

[13] N. Karonis, B. Toonen, and I. Foster. (2003). MPICH-G2: A Grid-Enabled Implementation of the Message Passing Interface. *Journal of Parallel and Distributed Computing* 63(5), pp. 551–563.

[14] E. Gabiriel, M. Resch, T. Beisel, and R. Keller. (1998). Distributed Computing in a Heterogeneous Computing Environment. LNCS 1497, Recent Advances in Parallel Virtual Machine and Message Passing Interface, Springer, pp. 180-188.

[15] I. Foster and C. Kesselman (1998). The Globus project: A status report. In *Proceedings of the Heterogeneous Computing Workshop*, IEEE Computer Society Press, pp. 4–18.

[16] R. Thakur, W. Gropp, and E. Lusk. (1999). On Implementing MPI-IO Portably and with High Performance. In *Proceedings of the 6th Workshop on I/O in Parallel and Distributed Systems*, pp. 23–32.

[17] R. Thakur, W. Gropp, and E. Lusk. (1996). An Abstract-Device Interface for Implementing Portable Parallel-I/O Interfaces. In *Proceedings of the 6th Symposium on the Frontiers of Massively Parallel Computation*, pp. 180–187.

[18] Myricom, Inc. http://www.myri.com/.

[19] M. Matsuda, T. Kudoh, and Y. Ishikawa. (2003). Evaluation of MPI Implementations on Grid-connected Clusters using an Emulated WAN Environment. In *Proceedings of the 3rd IEEE/ACM International Symposium on Cluster Computing and the Grid (CCGrid 2003)*, pp. 10–17.

[20] T. Takahashi, S. Sumimoto, A. Hori, H. Harada, and Y. Ishikawa. (2000). PM2: High Performance Communication Middleware for Heterogeneous Network Environments. In *SC2000: High Performance Networking and Computing Conference*, IEEE.

Chapter 2

GOP: A GRAPH-ORIENTED PROGRAMMING MODEL FOR PARALLEL AND DISTRIBUTED SYSTEMS*

Jiannong Cao, Alvin T.S. Chan
Internet and Mobile Computing Lab, Department of Computing
The Hong Kong Polytechnic University, Hung Hom, Kowloon Hong Kong
csjcao@comp.polyu.edu.hk

Yudong Sun
School of Computing Science
University of Newcastle upon Tyne, Newcastle upon Tyne, NE1 7RU UK
yudong.sun@ncl.ac.uk

Abstract   The advances of parallel and distributed computing demand high-level programming models that support efficient software development and execution. Graphs can effectively represent the logical structures of distributed systems and applications so as to facilitate the programming of distributed applications and support efficient mapping of programs to hardware architecture. This chapter presents a Graph-Oriented Programming (GOP) model that provides flexible graph constructs and graph-oriented primitives to build a programming paradigm based on graph topology and also provides a formal specification of software architecture for distributed programs. The GOP model creates an abstract programming framework and supports dynamic reconfiguration of distributed computing system to implement adaptive computation and fault-tolerance. Various computing environments have been developed based on GOP for cluster computing, web service, and component-based computation.

Keywords: Graph-oriented programming, distributed computing, software architecture

*This work is partially supported by Hong Kong Polytechnic University under HK PolyU Research Grant H-ZJ80.

1.   Introduction

Parallel and distributed systems have been providing a pervasive computing platform, along with the significant advances in network and Internet technologies, for developing and executing various applications. The application areas span from large-scale scientific computing to web service and E-commerce. The programming methodologies for parallel and distributed computing are still an active research area. Due to the high diversity in application areas and system architectures, the modeling of parallel and distributed applications is not a plain deed.

At present, parallel and distributed programming mainly employs the computing paradigms such as message-passing, data-parallel, divide-and-conquer, and master-slave models. These paradigms have the limitations in representing the structuring characteristics of parallel and distributed applications and systems. Therefore, high-level programming model is required, which demand high flexibility to describe distinctive features of different application requirements on the model. The model should be able to describe the logical structure of different applications in identical way so that a uniform programming methodology can be created. It should be scalable to represent computations on clusters and on wide-area systems. It should be adaptive to the dynamic evolution of the computational pattern of an application and the architectural configuration of the underlying system.

A parallel and distributed application is composed of a collection of functional components called *tasks* that can be executed concurrently, possibly on different machines, with necessary interaction and cooperation. Graph is ideally suited to represent such a logical program structure. The nodes represent the tasks and the edges denote the interactions between the tasks. The graph structure is flexible to represent different computation and communication patterns. A graph can be scalable to the size of a program and an underlying system. A graph is pliable to make dynamic modification to reflect the evolution of the computational requirement of a program and the architectural evolution of underlying system. Different program code can be bound to the nodes to build a MPMD program. Attributes can be assigned to the nodes and edges to represent the features of a program and the performance of system resources. The graphs can be used in an abstract framework to define supportive services in parallel and distributed computing, such as task naming and grouping, communication and coordination, load balancing, and fault tolerance. The graph-oriented programming model can conform to object-oriented programming model and provide a powerful support to the development of graph constructs, primitives, and programs.

This chapter presents a *Graph-Oriented Programming model*, called *GOP*, for developing parallel and distributed programs. The GOP model provides a high-level abstraction by which a parallel / distributed program is depicted as a *logical graph*. In the graph, the nodes represent the computational tasks and the edges represent the communication and synchronization between the tasks. The operations performed by the tasks are defined as *local programs* that are bound to the nodes. Therefore, a distributed program can be specified. The GOP model can also specify a task-to-processor mapping to execute the program. GOP specifies the graph constructs for user to build a program. It provides a library of primitives to be called by local programs for varied operations based on the graph structure.

The GOP model has also provided a formal specification method for the software architecture of parallel and distributed software. It is a versatile model for various computing environments such as cluster computing, web-based applications, and component-based computation.

The rest of the chapter is organized as follows. Section 2 discusses the related work. Section 3 specifies the GOP model and its features. Section 4 introduces the computing frameworks based on the GOP model. Section 5 gives the conclusions and future work.

2. Related Work

Graph-based programming has been a prosperous approach of parallel computing for decade. Graphical programming languages, libraries, and environments have been developed as visual programming tools to ease parallel programming and assist the software development on parallel systems.

CODE [1, 15] is a graphical parallel programming language in which a user can create a parallel program by drawing a *dataflow* graph that shows the communication structure of the program. The graph consists of nodes to represent computations (or shared variables) and arcs to represent the data flow. HeNCE [3] is a graphical language for creating and running parallel programs over a heterogeneous collection of computers. Differing from CODE, the graph in HeNCE shows the *control flow* of a program [16]. PYRROS [26, 27] is a compile-time scheduling and code generation tool for parallel program on distributed-memory architecture. It provides a task graph language for creating the task graph for a program, editing the associated C code, specifying the weights of computation and communication operations, and the maximum number of available processors. VPE [17] is a visual parallel programming environment that provides a simple GUI for creating message-passing programs and supports automatic compilation, execution, and animation of the programs.

Some graphical programming tools provide pre-defined computational tasks or program structures for specific applications. VDCE [23, 24] is a software development environment that provides task libraries for building large-scale applications on the network of heterogeneous computers at geographically distributed sites. CAPSE environment [12] provides tools for performance prediction in the development of parallel programs based on the graphical creation and editing of the scalable workload characterizations of MIMD algorithms.

Some graphical programming environments aim to support code reuse. Tracs [2] is a graphical programming environment that promotes a modular approach for application development across heterogeneous machines on a local network. P-RIO [13] is a modular parallel programming environment that provides an object-based software construction methodology with modularity and code reuse.

Finally, there are visual programming environments that adopt object-oriented technology. Prograph [20, 22] is an object-oriented visual programming language and a development environment on Macintosh platforms. Visper [21] is a distributed object-oriented environment that supports visual programming development, object (process) groups, and agent-based system management.

The projects discussed above are graph-based programming languages and environments in which graph is simply used as a visual representation of a program structure. The code, especially the inter-node communication and synchronization, is programmed in the convention of procedural languages (e.g., C, FORTRAN) and message passing libraries (e.g., MPI, PVM, SOAP). A major shortcoming of these existing works is that the design model is not mapped to the implementation model, thus there is a big gap between the design and implementation support. Differently, our GOP model harnesses *graph-oriented* concept. Aa graph is not only used as the representation of program structure but also specifies the operations of the program based on the topology of a graph. For example, the communication primitives can be defined using the relative references of source and destination nodes in the graph, such as precedent and successor, parent and children, root and leaves, instead of using node IDs. The graph-oriented approach creates a flexible high-level programming model which allows a program adaptive to the parameters of the program and the underlying system such as problem size and number of processors. As an abstract representation of software, the GOP model also provides a framework for the specification of software architecture. It can also support dynamic reconfiguration to match the evolution of computational requirements and system resources. With an object-orientation extension, this can be achieved through reflection.

3.   GOP Model

GOP (Graph-Oriented Programming) is a graphical programming model for parallel and distributed programming. It specifies the graph constructs and primitives to develop different programs. With the graph-oriented concept, GOP provides a high-level abstraction of program structure that is appropriate to be defined and implemented in object-oriented method and other programming paradigms.

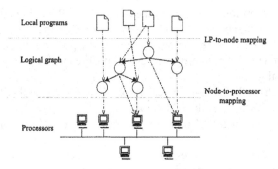

Figure 2.1. The GOP model

3.1   Graph Specification

In GOP, a program is defined as a *logical graph, G(N, E)*, where N is a set of *nodes* and E is a set of *edges*. The nodes represent the computational tasks of the program. Each edge links a pair of nodes, denoting the relationship between them. The relationship can be execution precedence, data dependency, and communication requirement. The graph represents the logical structure of the program. The edges can be *directed* to denote unidirectional data flow or control flow. Otherwise, an edge without direction allows bi-directional interaction between the nodes.

Associated with the nodes is a collection of local programs (LPs). Each node is bound with an LP that provides the program code to be executed by the node. The communication operations specified on the edges are implemented in the LPs by calling correspondent message-passing primitives. The nodes of a graph can be allocated to multiple processors and be executed concurrently. The GOP model can specify the node-to-processor mapping. In general, the GOP model consists of the following components.

(1) *Logical graph*: a logical graph (directed or undirected) defines the structure of a program in which the nodes represent the computational tasks and the edges specify the relationships between the nodes.

(2) *Local programs*: a collection of local programs (LPs) specifies the operations performed by the nodes.

(3) *LP-to-node mapping*: the mapping binds the LPs to the nodes.

(4) *Node-to-processor mapping* (optional): the mapping allocates the nodes to the processors to execution. When a program does not explicitly specify this mapping, the runtime system will use a default mapping strategy.

Figure 2.1 manifests the construction of the GOP model. In the GOP-based programming, a programmer first constructs a logical graph to describe the abstract structure of a program and writes associated logical programs. The LPs can be written in any languages supported by the implementation system. The LPs also invoke the pre-defined primitives to perform the communication and coordination operations specified by the edges. The LPs are bound to the nodes by a LP-to-node mapping. The node-to-processor mapping is an optional component that can be specified before submitting the program to execution. The constructs of a GOP-based program can be specified as following:

(1) Logical graph

Let LGraph be the class of logical graph. *Graph-name* is the identifier of a logical graph. *Node_no* is the ID of a node.

$<Logical\text{-}graph>$ ::= LGraph *Graph-name* '=' '{' '{'$<set\text{-}of\text{-}nodes>$'}', '{' $<list\text{-}of\text{-}edges>$'}' '}' .

$<set\text{-}of\text{-}nodes>$ ::= $<range\text{-}of\text{-}nodes>|<node\text{-}list>$.

$<range\text{-}of\text{-}nodes>$ ::= $<node\_no>..<node\_no>$.

$<node\text{-}list>$ ::= $<node\text{-}list>, <node\_no>|<node\_no>$.

$<list\text{-}of\text{-}edges>$ ::= $<list\text{-}of\text{-}edges>$, '{' *node_no, node_no* '}' |'{' *node_no, node_no* '}' | ϵ .

$<node\_no>$ ::= $\{ 0 | 1 | 2 | 3 | 4 | 5 | 6 | 7 | 8 | 9 \}$.

(2) Local programs

$<Local\text{-}program>$ ::= *code of a programming language and a library of primitives*.

(3) LP-to-node mapping

Let LMap be the class of LP-to-node mapping. *Lmap-name* is the identifier of an LP-to-node mapping. *LP_id* is the name of a local program. An LP-to-node mapping is defined as a set of {*node_no, LP_id*} pairs that binds the node *node_no* with the local program *LP_id*.

$<LP\text{-}to\text{-}node\text{-}mapping>$ ::= LMap *Lmap-name* '=' '{' $<node\text{-}lp\text{-}pair>$'}'.

$<node\text{-}lp\text{-}pair>$ ::= $<node\text{-}lp\text{-}pair>$, '{' $<node\_no>, <LP\_id>$'}' |'{' $<node\_no>, <LP\_id>$'}' | ϵ .

$<LP\_id>$ ::= $\{$ a-z | A-Z | _ | 0-9 $\}$.

(4) Node-to-processor mapping

Let PMap be the class of node-to-processor mapping. *Nmap-name* is the identifier of a node-to-processor mapping. *Processor_id* is the ID of a processor. A node-to-processor mapping is specified as a set of {*node_no, processor_id*} pairs by which *node_no* is mapped to *processor_id*. The node-to-processor mapping is an optional construct. If omitted, a default mapping will be used.

$<Node\text{-}to\text{-}processor\text{-}mapping>$ ::= PMap *Nmap-name* '=' '{' $<node\text{-}processor\text{-}pair>$'}' .

$<node\text{-}processor\text{-}pair>$ ::= $<node\text{-}processor\text{-}pair>$, '{' $<node\_no>, <processor\_id>$'}' |'{' $<node\_no>, <processor\_id>$'}' | ϵ .

$<processor\_id>$ ::= *system-dependent id* .

The GOP model is independent from any language and platform. It can be implemented on different hardware and software platforms such as clusters and distributed systems on top of PVM, MPI, and CORBA. The local programs can

Figure 2.2. Logical graph of a master-slave algorithm

be written in different languages (such as Java, C, and C++), depending on the implementation.

The GOP model builds a high-level framework for software architecture [10, 11] which supports the architectural definition of parallel and distributed software. The GOP modularizes a program as a graph. With regard to the non-intuitive structures of parallel and distributed programs, GOP enables programmer to visually describe the abstract structure and specify the semantic context of a program such as data dependency, task precedence, and synchronization among concurrent tasks. The GOP model establishes a foundation to the architectural design of parallel and distributed programs, which is helpful to improve the efficiency of software development. The model can enhance the understandability of the complex logical structures of parallel and distributed programs.

As the support for software architecture, the GOP model is convenient to define the abstract structure of a family of software system. Using GOP, for example, we can depict the generic structure of a master-slave algorithm. Figure 2.2 shows a logical graph of master-slave computation with one master and four slaves. Node 0 is the master that runs the local program *Master*. It is the coordinator of entire computation. Other nodes are slaves running the local program *Slave* to perform certain computation. They are under the control of the master.

With the GOP graph constructs, the master-slave program can be defined as:

(1) Logical graph: LGraph msgraph = {{0..4}, {{0,1}, {0,2}, {0,3}, {0,4}}};

(2) LP-to-node mapping: LMap lmsmap = {{0, "Master"}, {1, "Slave"}, {2, "Slave"}, {3, "Slave"}};

(3) Node-to-processor mapping: PMap pmsmap = {{0, "host0"}, {1, "host1"}, {2, "host2"}, {3, "host3"}}; where host0 to host3 are the names of the hosts to run the program.

The master-slave program can implement any computation specified by the local programs. For example, the programs can implement client-server computing such as file server and web server. The programs can also accomplish parallel computing where the master acts as the task allocator and the slaves run the tasks in parallel. Hence, the GOP model provides an abstract representation for a family of programs that have an identical structure.

3.2   Graph-oriented Operations

In the GOP model, a library of graph-oriented programming primitives can be defined based upon the semantics of graph. The LPs can call these primitives to implement various operations in the graph-oriented programming. Users can also define custom primitives in the similar graph-oriented semantics. The graph-oriented primitives can be basically classified into four categories:

- *Communication and synchronization*

  These primitives support communication operations for passing messages from one node to others, such as unicast, multicast, and broadcast. The LPs call the primitives to fulfill the communications associated with the edges and to synchronize the operations of the nodes.

- *Subgraph derivation*

  The primitives aim to derive subgraphs, such as the shortest path and spanning tree, of a graph. Many distributed algorithms include the construction of some form of subgraph deriving from an original graph to obtain optimal solution. The primitives are useful to these algorithms.

- *Query*

  The primitives examine the attributes of a graph such as the number of nodes, the current binding of an LP to a node and whether an edge exists between two nodes. The query provides a basis for the operations of system control and reconfiguration.

- *Graph update*

  The primitives support dynamic reconfiguration of a graph. For example, there are primitives to insert or delete nodes and edges in a graph. Also, the LP-to-node mapping and node-to-processor mapping can be dynamically altered at runtime. The dynamic reconfiguration of a program graph reflects the adaptation of distributed computing in response to varying computational requirements and available resources.

In the graph-oriented primitives, the references to nodes and edges are generally based on *relative naming*. The primitives do not explicitly indicate the nodes and edges involved. Instead, the relative positions of the nodes and edges are specified such as *precedents*, *successors* and *neighbors*. For example, in Figure 2.2, the "Precedents" of the master are all slave nodes and the "Successor" of all slaves is the master node. In a GOP-based program, new references can be derived by carrying out *set operations* on existing references. For example, the *neighbors* of a node are the union of its precedents and successors.

A collection of message passing primitives including *unicast, multicast* and *anycast* can be called in the LPs for inter-node communication. In Figure 2.2, the master can multicast a message to the slaves by the multicast primitive Msend() using the reference "Precedents":

    Msend(Precedents, message);

Each slave node can receive the message by the anycast primitive Arecv() that receives a message from any of the nodes specified by the reference "Successor", which refers to the master in this example:

    Arecv(Successor, message);

The interaction between the master and the slaves can be accomplished by a composite of communication primitives. For example, the master can send a message to query all slaves and wait for the responses using Msend() and Mrecv() primitives:

    Msend(Precedents, query_command);
    Mrecv(Successors, result_buffer);

On the other side, each slave receives the query and sends the result back to the master as:

    Arecv (Successor, command);
    if (command == query) {
        process the query;
        Asend (Successor, result);
    }

The class of logical graph *LGraph* specified in Section 3.1 provides a general specification of a graph structure. It can be used to describe any type of graphs. However, an algorithm is usually designed on a specific graph topology, e.g., tree, hypercube, or mesh. The algorithm needs to operate with specific semantics and constraints on a particular graph topology. To support the topology-specific operations, the GOP model allows programmers to derive new graph type, such as a tree or a star, from the basic *LGraph* along with new primitives based on topology-specific semantics and operations. For a tree, for example, there is one root and each node has one ancestor and one or more descendants. The primitives for tree-specific operations can be defined with the references as *parent, children, siblings, root,* and *leaves*.

An example of graph derivation is a new graph type created for the master-slave computation shown in Figure 2.2. The new type of graph is called *Star* that is derived from the class of *LGraph*:

    <Star-graph>::= Star *Star-name* '=' '{' *<Logical-graph>*, '{' *<center-node>*'}', '{' *<set-of-leaves* >'}' '}' .

    <center-node>::= *<node_no* >.   // master node

    <set-of-leaves>::= *<node-list* >.   // all slave nodes

where *<Logical-graph>*, *<node_no* >, and *<node-list>* are specified in Section 3.1. This new type of graph constrains the topology as a star that consists of one center node and a number of leaf nodes. Every leaf is connected to the center node.

With the type of star, the primitives can be redefined to directly implement intuitive, star-specific operations. To perform the query operations as above, the master at the center can make use of the star-specific primitives where the reference to the slaves is omitted because it is implied in the primitives:

SendToLeaves(query_command);
RecvFromLeaves(result_buffer);

The slave nodes receive the query command and send the result back to the master using the primitives as:

RecvFromCenter(command);
SendToCenter(result);

3.3   Dynamic Reconfiguration

As a framework for software architecture, the GOP model also manifests the dimensions in which the software can evolve. Distributed applications demand the capability of dynamic reconfiguration to adapt to the evolving computational requirements and execution environment. GOP facilitates the dynamic reconfiguration of a software system with the support of graph-oriented operations.

Traditionally, the configuration of a parallel / distributed software contains: (a) a set of software components; (b) the interconnections between the components that specify the interactions between the components; (c) the mapping of the components to target hosts [5]. The configuration is closely related to the concept of software architecture. Dynamically reconfigurable software system is sometimes called a system with *dynamic architecture* [18].

Dynamic reconfiguration is needed in many circumstances of distributed computing. In distributed applications, the workload is often dynamically generated in individual components. The applications require dynamic transformation in its structure to handle the change of workload distribution. New nodes can be added to a graph to share the increasing workload. A node can also be removed from a graph when the node fails to work.

The characteristics of the GOP model determine the feasibility for dynamic reconfiguration. In GOP, local programs (LPs) are separated from a graph topology. The LPs may not share any information except the structure of a logical graph. The LPs need no direct reference to each other for interaction. The LPs bound to individual nodes communicate with one another through relative naming. This feature allows the modification to a graph meanwhile keeping the compatibility of the LPs on the altered graph. The GOP model specifies the query primitives to examine the structure of a graph by which the proper reconfiguration can be determined. Furthermore, the scope of valid reconfiguration can be constrained within a specific graph topology as the valid primitives of graph update are specified based on the graph topology. The

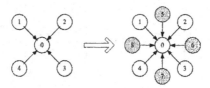

Figure 2.3. Add new leaves to the graph

reconfiguration of a graph can be defined at a high level in terms of logical graph, making it easier to understand and manage.

With an object-oriented extension, the GOP model can support dynamic reconfiguration through inheritence and reflection. As an example, consider the dynamic reconfiguration of the master-slave graph shown in Figure 2.2. The master can dynamically add new slaves to or remove existing slaves from the graph according to the runtime workload. Figure 2.3 shows that four slaves are added to the graph. A new slave can be added to the graph using the primitives of graph update as following:

Node newLeaf = new Node(node_no); // create new leaf

Edge newEdge = new Edge(newLeaf, center_node); // create new edge

AddNode(graph-name, newLeaf);   // add new leaf to graph

AddEdge(graph-name, newEdge);   // add new edge to graph

The dynamic reconfiguration in Figure 2.3 preserves the star topology. Nevertheless, dynamic reconfiguration can also create a new graph topology that is different from the original one. The GOP model implements such a dynamic reconfiguration by deriving a new graph type that extends the original one. The primitives of the new graph type can be invoked to transform the original graph to the new topology. Let us use the graph derivation to reconfigure the graph on the right side of Figure 2.3. Assume that the master is finally overloaded as more and more slave nodes are added to the system, a new master node will be added into the graph. To achieve this goal, a new type of graph called *StarMC* is defined which extends the star topology to permit the coexistence of more than on center. Figure 2.4 shows such a reconfiguration that adds an additional master to the original star. In the multi-center star, each slave is linked to each of the masters. This reconfiguration can be implemented by the following primitives:

Node newCenter = new Node(node_no); // create a new center

AddNode (graph-name, newCenter);   // add new center to graph

for(each leaf in the graph) {

Edge newEdge = new Edge(leaf, newCenter); // create a new edge between each leaf and the new center.

AddEdge = (graph-name, newEdge); // add the edge to the graph

}

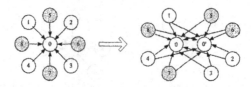

Figure 2.4. Add a new center to a star

The behavior of the master-slave program with multiple centers should be adjusted accordingly. In *StarMC*, some primitives should be redefined. For example, the communication primitive SendToCenter( ) should be redefined for the leaves to send a message to one of the centers to balance the workload between the masters. The primitive of adding a new leaf should be redefined to link the new leaf to each of the centers. On the other hand, the original local programs are still usable on the new topology because the graph-oriented operations will be automatically adjusted based on the adaptive implementation of the primitives in the *StarMC*.

4.   Applications of GOP

We have developed different programming environments to implement the GOP model for cluster computing, web-based computation, and component-based computation.

4.1   ClusterGOP

ClusterGOP [8] is a software environment to implement the GOP model for cluster computing. It provides a visual user interface and a framework for developing parallel and distributed programs on cluster systems. The user interface is a visual programming environment. When building an application, a programmer starts to draw a logical graph in the graph design editor. Then, the programmer uses the text editor to write the LP code and binds to the nodes of the logical graph. After that, the whole application is ready for compilation and execution. To run the program, the graph nodes will be mapped to the processors in the cluster according to the user-specified node-to-processor mapping or a default mapping strategy.

The ClusterGOP environment provides a library of primitives for communication, synchronization, query, and graph update. The LPs can call these primitives. The communication and synchronization primitives closely conform to the MPI (Message Passing Interface) standard [14] and are implemented with the MPI functions.

When compiling the application, the ClusterGOP environment converts the logical graph into XML (Extensible Markup Language) format [25]. Then, ClusterGOP transfers the necessary data (including the XML graph, LPs, and ClusterGOP library) to target machines and compiles the application. After that, ClusterGOP starts to execute the application. Each target machine contains two runtimes to run the programs. One is the ClusterGOP runtime, which is a background process to support the query, update and consistency of a graph structure. When updating a graph, the runtime will block other machines from updating the graph and synchronize the graph update made on different machines. The other is the MPI runtime, which implements the ClusterGOP communication and synchronization primitives. ClusterGOP uses the MPI library as the low-level implementation of inter-process communication.

4.2   WebGOP

WebGOP [6] is a framework for constructing web-based distributed applications. WebGOP uses object-oriented method to support software architecture. It specifies the architecture of a distributed computing system with the graph objects that are separated from the programming of functional components. The object-oriented method also benefits the reusability of the functional components and the software architecture. With the graph objects and the built-in graph-update facilities, dynamic reconfiguration of an application can be implemented.

The WebGOP framework defines the graph constructs as the foundation to build the GOP-based web applications. The framework consists of a Web-GOP runtime, a monitoring and management module, and a security protection module. The core of the WebGOP runtime is the distributed representation and management of a graph on which a set of graph-oriented message passing primitives and a set of basic graph update primitives are provided as the APIs for programming web applications. The WebGOP runtime translates the graph nodes and nodes groups into web addresses. Several graph derivation operations such as the shortest path, minimum spanning tree are built in the runtime.

The monitoring and management model is responsible for helping user to manage, debug and monitor the applications. The module also acts as the front-end user interface for application loading, deployment, activation, and dynamic reconfiguration.

Reliable and flexible security protection is essential to the web applications. As an open system running over different administrative domains, WebGOP should control user access to the resources by discerning the permissions. The security protection module is provided for this purpose based on cryptic communication and digital signature identification.

A prototype of WebGOP is developed in a heterogeneous network environment consisting of a Sun Ultra Enterprise server 10000, several Sun Solaris workstations and Microsoft Windows 2000 workstations. The prototype is implemented with Java and Apache SOAP (Simple Object Access Protocol) [4]. Since SOAP has become *de facto* standard protocol for web services, WebGOP uses it to realize the compatibility in the web environment. The prototype provides a communication middleware to support the interactions between the components of distributed web applications and a graph-oriented framework for architectural modeling and programming. Sample applications have been developed on the WebGOP framework to evaluate the performance of the prototype. For example, a master-slave system is constructed for web service and the dynamic reconfigurations shown in Figure 2.3 and Figure 2.4 are implemented.

4.3   ComponentGOP

ComponentGOP [7] provides a new approach to support the creation and reconfiguration of distributed component-based software (CBS). Distributed software can be viewed as a collection of building blocks (called *components*) that interact with each other through message passing. ComponentGOP implements the GOP model in component-based computing based on a generic middleware such as CORBA [9]. ComponentGOP creates a graph-oriented framework for modeling and constructing component-based software. The architectural design of CBS can be simplified to a higher level with graph abstraction and pre-defined graph patterns. It also acts as the communication middleware for distributed components.

The ComponentGOP framework consists of a configuration manager module, a consistency maintenance module, and a runtime module. The ComponentGOP runtime includes the APIs that provides a set of graph-oriented primitives for programming component-based software and the ComponentGOP LIB for compiling and executing the applications. The kernel of the runtime is the distributed representation and management of graphs. Based on the kernel, a set of graph-oriented primitives are created for message passing, graph update, and query. The configuration manager module acts as the front-end user interface for component loading, deployment, activation, and dynamic reconfiguration management. When a graph needs dynamic reconfiguration, software consistency should be maintained among distributed components. The consistency maintenance module is used for this purpose.

A prototype of ComponentGOP has been implemented on top of CORBA using Java and VisiBroker (a CORBA compliant platform) in a heterogeneous network environment with Sun Solaris workstations and Windows 2000 workstations. In the prototype, the ComponentGOP LIB is divided into two sublibs: GOPORB_LIB and GOP_LIB. The GOPORB_LIB mainly implements the communication-related primitives that are mapped to the CORBA method invocations. The implementation of GOPORB_LIB is based on CORBA DII (Dynamic Invocation Interface), DSI (Dynamic Skeleton Interface) and CORBA compiled client stubs and server skeletons. The GOP_LIB implements other primitives such as graph update and query. ComponentGOP encapsulates the complicated CORBA programming details in abstract, graph-oriented components so that the component-based programming can be simplified.

5.   Conclusions

In this chapter, we have presented the GOP model for graph-oriented programming. The GOP model provides a new framework for constructing the logical structure of a distributed program in terms of graph. The operations of the program are specified on the graph structure. The model presents a high-level abstraction of program logic to support the formal specification of software architecture. Distributed programs built on the GOP model are suited to undertake dynamic reconfiguration at runtime in response to the evolution of computational requirements and underlying systems. New computing frameworks and middleware can be developed based on GOP to implement graph-oriented programming in different parallel and distributed environments. We have implemented the graph-oriented computing environments for cluster computing, web-based computation, and component-based computation.

We will design a formal specification of the graph-oriented model. We believe that the graph grammar based formalism is a suitable approach for the formal specification. For the prototype implementation, we will enrich the graph-oriented programming tools including graph editor, task scheduler, and program visualization. We are investigating the integration of the GOP-based environments such as ClusterGOP, WebGOP, and ComponentGOP under a unified interface that can be used for application programming in different systems.

References

[1] D. Banerjee and J. Browne, "Complete Parallelization of Computations: Integration of Data Partitioning and Functional Parallelism for Dynamic Data Structures", *Proc. 10th IEEE Int'l Parallel Processing Symp.* (IPPS'96), Honolulu, Hawaii, April 15-19, 1996, pp.354-361.

[2] A. Bartoli, P. Corsini, G. Dini and C. Prete, "Graphical Design of Distributed Applications Through Reusable Components", *IEEE Concurrency*, Vol. 3, No. 1, Spring 1995, pp.37-50.

[3] A. Beguelin, J. Dongarra, A. Geist, R. Manchek and K. Moore, "HeNCE: A Heterogeneous Network Computing Environment", *Scientific Programming*, Vol. 3, No. 1, 1994, pp.49-60.

[4] D. Box, D Ehnebuske, G. Kakivaya, A. Layman, N. Mendelsohn, H. Nielsen, S. Thatte and D. Winer, "Simple Object Access Protocol (SOAP) 1.1", W3C Note, May 8, 2000, available at http://www.w3.org/TR/SOAP/

[5] J. Cao, A. Chan, C. Lee and K. Yu, "A Dynamic Reconfiguration Manager for Graph-Oriented Distributed Programs", *Proc. 1997 Int'l Conf. on Parallel and Distributed Systems (ICPADS'97)*, Seoul, Korea, Dec 1997, pp.216-221.

[6] J. Cao, X. Ma, A. Chan and J. Lu, "WEBGOP: A Framework for Architecting and Programming Dynamic Distributed Web Applications", *Proc. 2002 Int'l Conf. on Parallel Processing (ICPP'02)*, Vancouver, Canada, August 2002, pp.266-275.

[7] J. Cao, M. Cao and A. Chan, "Architecture Level Support for Dynamic Reconfiguration and Fault Tolerance in Component-Based Distributed Software", *Proc. 2002 Int'l Conf. on Parallel and Distributed Systems (ICPADS'02)*, Dec. 2002, Taiwan, pp.251-256.

[8] F. Chan, J. Cao and Y. Sun, "High-level Abstractions for Message-passing Parallel Programming", *Parallel Computing*, Vol.29, No.11-12, 2003, pp.1589-1621.

[9]   CORBA, http://www.corba.org/

[10] D. Garlan and M. Shaw, "An Introduction to Software Architecture", in *Advances in Software Engineering and Knowledge Engineering*, Vol. II, World Scientific Publishing, 1993.

[11] D. Garlan and D. Perry, "Software Architecture: Practice, Potential, and Pitfalls", *Proc. 16th Int'l Conf. on Software Engineering*, Sorrento, Italy, May 16-21, 1994, pp.363-364.

[12] B. Gruber, G. Haring, J. Volkert and D. Kranzlmüler, "Parallel Programming with CAPSE - A Case Study", *Proc. 4th EUROMICRO Workshop on Parallel and Distributed Processing (PDP'96)*, Braga, Portugal, Jan. 1996, pp.130-137.

[13] O. Loques and J. Leite, "P-RIO: A Modular Parallel-Programming Environment", *IEEE Concurrency*, Vol. 6, No. 1, Jan-Mar 1998, pp.47-57.

[14] The Message Passing Interface (MPI) Standard, http://www-unix.mcs.anl.gov/mpi/

[15] P. Newton and J. Browne, "The CODE 2.0 Graphical Parallel Programming Language", *Proc. ACM Int'l Conf. on Supercomputing (Supercomputing'92)*, Washington D.C., July 1992, pp.167-177.

[16] P. Newton, "Visual Programming and Parallel Computing", *Workshop on Environments and Tools for Parallel Scientific Computing*, Walland, TN, May 26-27, 1994.

[17] P. Newton and J. Dongarra, "Overview of VPE: A Visual Environment for Message-Passing", *Proc. 4th Heterogeneous Computing Workshop*, Santa Barbara, CA, April 25, 1995.

[18] P. Oreizy and R.Taylor, "On the Role of Software Architecture in Runtime System Reconfiguration", *IEE Proceedings-Software Engineering*, Vol. 145, No. 5, October 1998, pp.137-145.

[19] PVM, http://www.csm.ornl.gov/pvm/

[20] T. Smedley and P. Cox, "Visual Languages for the Design and Development of Structured Objects", *Journal of Visual Languages and Computing*, Vol. 8, No. 1, 1997, pp.57-84.

[21] N. Stankovic and K. Zhang, "A Distributed Parallel Programming Framework", *IEEE Transactions on Software Engineering*, Vol. 28, No. 5, May, 2002, pp.478-493.

[22] S. Steinman and K. Carver, *Visual Programming with Prograph CPX*, Manning Publications, 1995.

[23] H. Topcuoglu, S. Hariri, W. Furmanski, J. Valente, I. Ra, D. Kim, Y. Kim, X. Bing and B. Ye, "The Software Architecture of a Virtual Distributed Computing Environment", *Proc. 6th Int'l Symp. on High Performance Distributed Computing (HPDC'97)*, Portland, OR, Aug. 5-8, 1997, pp.40-49.

[24] H. Topcuoglu, S. Hariri, D. Kim, Y. Kim, X. Bing, B. Ye, I. Ra and J. Valente, "The Design and Evaluation of a Virtual Distributed Computing Environment", *Cluster Computing*, Vol. 1, No. 1, 1998, pp.81-93.

[25] XML, http://www.xml.org/

[26] T. Yang and A. Gerasoulis, "PYRROS: Static Task Scheduling and Code Generation for Message Passing Multiprocessors", *Proc. ACM Int'l Conf. on Supercomputing (Supercomputing'92)*, Washington D.C., July 1992, pp.428-437.

[27] T. Yang and A. Gerasoulis, "A Parallel Programming Tool for Scheduling on Distributed Memory Multiprocessors", *Proc. the Scalable High Performance Computing Conference*, Williamsburg, Virginia, April 26-29, 1992, pp.350-357.

Chapter 3

PROGRAMMING CELLULAR AUTOMATA-LIKE SYSTEMS IN A MULTIMEDIA PARALLEL ENVIRONMENT

Mahmoud A. Saber and Nikolay Mirenkov

Graduate Department of Information Systems

The University of Aizu, Japan

8032101@u-aizu.ac.jp,nikmir@u-aizu.ac.jp

Abstract   The cellular automata (CA) models and corresponding algorithms have a rich theoretical basis. They have also been used in a great variety of applications. A number of programming languages and systems have been developed to support the implementation of the CA models. However, these languages focus on computational and performance issues, and do not pay enough attention to programming productivity, usability, understandability, and other aspects of software engineering. In this chapter,we provide an outline of our approach to programming cellular automata systems. We also provide a brief explanation of a user interface subsystem and discuss concepts and features of a program generator subsystem in this environment. We pay special attention to the parallel template programs supporting the automatic generation of executable codes from the multimedia specifications.

Keywords: Cellular automata, self-explanatory components, algorithmic film format,template programs, multimedia interface

1.   Introduction

In this chapter, We present a environment oriented to programming cellular automata systems where global behavior arises from the collective effect of many locally interacting, simple components. CA systems are distinguished from parallel computing systems based on the scale of number of processors involved in each of them. Most parallel computers contain no more than a few dozen processors. In the parallel computing systems, the term massively parallel usually describes those few machines that consists of several thousand, or, at most tens of thousands of processors. Cellular automata systems involve parallelism on a much larger scale, with a number of cells often measured by the exponential notion 10^x. In addition, CAs are extreme manifestation of true concurrency, because they does not explicitly specify neither the order (in time) nor the place (in space) of performing computational steps. They are started in the cellular space then and there, when and where the respective readiness conditions are met.Cellular automata systems have long needed a way to understand their essential features and global behaviors during all phases of the life cycle. We designed and implemented a new multimedia environment that can be used to specify, present, and execute computational algorithms from the field of cellular automata (CA) systems.

The Active Knowledge Studio (AKS) group at the University of Aizu is studying, design-ing, and developing multimedia programming environments for various domains; see, for example, [1]- [5]. These special purpose environments are developed within the framework of a global environment and based on common design and implementation approaches. However, because of the orientation to different domains, each environment possesses its own features represented through specific multimedia objects and interface panels. The multimedia programming environment is based on self-explanatory components approach [6]. Self-explanatory components constitute a framework for visual representation and specification of objects/processes, based on the idea of multiple views and algorithmic multimedia skeletons. A series of multimedia frames represents a set of algorithm features in an algorithmic "film" format . In this format, computational algorithms become components that are accessed and manipulated through a number of views related to its dynamic, static, and hierarchical features [7]. algorithmic "Film" is used as a new type of abstraction to represent computational algorithms by combining mathematical and physical concepts [6]. Mathematical concepts are used to convey the arithmetic/logic aspects of algorithmic activities. Physical concepts are used mainly to convey the spatial and temporal aspects of computation. A film is a series of multimedia frames (stills.) One frame represents a view (aspect) of an algorithm; many frames represent many algorithmic aspects. Frame views are arranged into six special groups. The first three groups visualize 1) computational steps and data structures, 2) variables attached to the structures and formulas used in space-time points of algorithm activity, and 3) input/output operations. The fourth group consists of frames of an integrated view where important features from previous groups are presented altogether. Groups 5 and 6 are auxiliary views related to the film title, authorship, registration date, and links to other algorithms, additional explanations, statistics of the usage, etc. Films as pieces of "active" knowledge are acquired in a film database. The film frames are watchable and editable in a nonlinear order according to the user's demands. Therefore, the conventional animation (movie) is a mere partial case of our film concept. We also consider our films as self-explanatory components, because multiple views are an excel-lent basis for bridging the gap between "syntax and semantics" and understanding the component meaning.

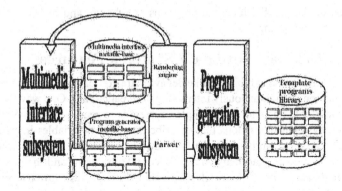

Figure 3.1. The architecture of the multimedia parallel programming environment

An overall architecture of the multimedia environment comprises a multi-media interface subsystem, a program generation subsystem, a rendering engine, a parser, a template programs library, and metafiles bases (see Figure 3.1). We will explain main parts of the environment's architecture in Sections 3-5. The work presented here is situated in the context of several research areas like pixel rewriters, pixel-level computation, and fine grain parallel computation. Some of them include software visualization techniques. Pixel rewriters are used to explore the variety of interesting computations on, and manipulation of, shape directly in the pixels [8]. These are close to Furnas's BITPICT system [9], a pixel rewriting system proposed as a possible model for "purely graphical" reasoning. A work of the same area is Yamamoto's VISULAN system [10]. It is an extension of Furnas's pixel rewrite programming language. Pixel-level computations are used extensively in the early stages of processing and parsing images in the area of computer vision. Filters highlight edges by enhancing brightness gradients in the pixel array [11]. In morphological analysis [12], noisy edges are healed by first dilation. Image processing is central to photo manipulation applications of Photoshop type, using pixel operations like blurring, sharpening, and color substitution. WinALT [13],[14] is a simulating system of fine grain algorithms and structures that have a recognizable and intuitively clear interface which eases the learning of the system. Graphics is used to represent the intermediate and resulting data visually. However, these systems usually focus on computational and performance issues, and provide a rather "conventional" view of the algorithm description. They pay not enough attention to the human abilities, and reserve the graphics and colors to represent the intermediate and final results only, while the algorithm structures and steps of computation are described in a pure textual form. The rest of this chapter is organized as follows. In Section 2, we reconsider the modeling of CA systems and in Section 3, the multimedia interface subsystem is briefly explained. In Sections 4 the program generator subsystem is described. In Section 5, the features of the parallel template programs are shown, and in Section 6, the conclusion is presented.

2.   Cellular Automata Systems Features

Most entities that exhibit life-like behavior are complex systems made up of many elements simultaneously interacting with each other. One way to understand the global behavior of a complex system is to model that behavior with a simple system of equations that describe how global variables interact. By contrast, the characteristic approach followed in artificial life is to construct lower-level models that them-selves are complex systems and then to iterate the models and observe the resulting global behavior. Such lower-level models are sometimes called agent- or individual-based models, because the whole system's behavior is represented only indirectly and arises merely out of the interactions of a collection of directly represented parts (agents or individuals). As complex system changes over time, each element changes according to its state and the state of those neighbors with which it interacts. Complex systems typically lack any central control, though they may have boundary conditions. The elements of a complex system are often simple compared to the whole system, and the rules by which the elements interact are also often simple. The behavior of a complex system is simply the aggregate of the changes over time of all of the system's elements. In rare cases the behavior of a complex system may actually be derived from the rules governing the elements' behavior, but typically, a complex system's behavior cannot be discerned short of empirically observing the emergent behavior of its constituent parts. The elements of a complex system may be connected in a regular way, e.g. on an Euclidean lattice, or in an irregular way, e.g. on a random network. Interactions between elements may also be without a fixed pattern, as in molecular dynamics of a chemical soup or interaction of autonomous agents. When adaptation is part of a complex system's dynamics, it is sometimes described as a complex adaptive system. For long time it has been very difficult to study the behavior of complex systems because the formal models describing them were so hard that the main computational modality, represented by the integration of differential equations, was intractable even using powerful parallel computers. The development of computer science in the latest years considerably enlarged its application boundaries because of the continuous rise of computing power. At the same time research in parallel computing showed evidence of the significant potential of parallel computing models, such as cellular automata and neural networks, in representing a valid alternative to differential calculus in the description of complex phenomena [15]. This occurs especially when differential equations cannot efficiently be solved because of their complexity or when is very difficult to model the problem being solved in terms of differential equations. Cellular automata (CA) are very effective in modeling complex systems because they can capture the essential features of systems in which the global behaviour arises from the collective effect of large numbers of locally interacting simple components. CAs are decentralized spatially extended systems consisting of large numbers of simple identical components with local connectivity. Such systems have the potential to perform complex computations with a high degree of efficiency and robustness, as well as to model the behavior of complex systems in nature. For these reasons, CAs and related architectures have been studied extensively in the natural sciences, mathematics, and in computer science. They have been used as models of physical and biological systems, such as fluid flow, galaxy formation, earthquakes, and biological pattern formation. They have been considered as mathematical objects about which formal properties can be proved. They have been used as parallel computing devices, both for the high-speed simulation of scientific models and for computational tasks such as image processing. In addition, CAs have been used as abstract models for studying emergent cooperative or collective behavior in CA systems [16]-[18]. Many programming languages and systems were developed to implement cellular automata (CA) based algorithms (see, for example [19]-[21].) After a study of the interesting features of the CA model, we had the motivation to create a new multimedia representation of the CA model that can be manipulated with user-oriented visual interface, and translated to efficient parallel programs, as we are going to explain in the following sections.

3.   Multimedia Interface Subsystem

In the case of a conventional language, a source program is input as a text with some support of a text editor. In our case of the film language, a source program can be input as collection of icons, colored shapes, in addition to text whenever it is more expressive than other media. Figure 3.2 depicts the contents of the multimedia interface subsystem. A special module to perform searching and opening operations for films, scenes, and frames is considered as a multimedia navigator that helps the users to get their needs from the filmbase in a user-friendly few steps. The users can create there own films from scratch based on their own experience or with the help of an interactive wizard. After these operations, the user can watch a film or its parts and perform editing and composing manipulation. Editing mode allows the specification of cellular models. The power of a specification method is mainly related to its flexibility, generality, and capability to customize visualizations [22]. While watching a film is close to algorithm animation field, an algorithm animation visualizes the behavior of an algorithm by producing an abstraction of both data and the operations of the algorithm (for a comprehensive view of the field, see [23].) These manipulations are divided into six groups depending on algorithmic film features (as we have mentioned in the Introduction, these features are directly represented by six groups of film frames). As a result, the editing/watching/composing module is created as six sub-modules. Each sub-module is a multimedia interface to edit, watch, and compose frames of a cor-

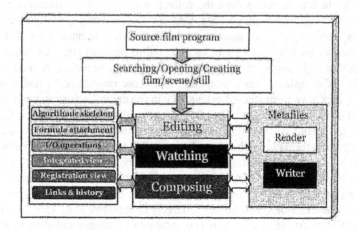

Figure 3.2.   The multimedia interface subsystem

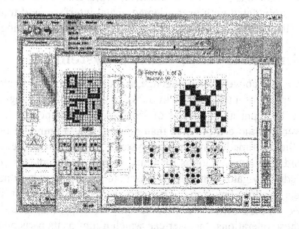

Figure 3.3.   Panels of Multimedia interface subsystem

responding group. A metafile reader/writer module is responsible for storing the specifications of the manipulated films in the metafile bases, and fetching them to the interface modules whenever they are re-quested. The multimedia interface subsystem is developed in JAVA. Figure 3.3 shows some of the panels (editing, watching, and, formula attaching panels) developed and used for the CA domain. See [24]-[25], for more details about the design and implementation of this subsystem. In the film format, a CA is specified by a series of frames (computational steps) and repetitive constructs on sub-series of these frames. Each step is defined by a set of substitution rules and a partial order to apply on the rules. In its turn, each substitution rule is specified as a parallel

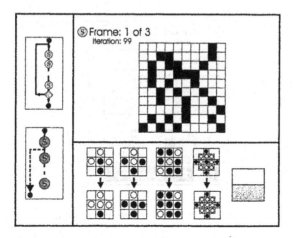

Figure 3.4. A Frame example

operation of "find & replace" type applied on all CA cells. Each frame shows a view (some features) of an algorithmic step. The frames can be watched in either static or dynamic (animated) views. To represent contents of frames and orders of their execution, a special icon language has been developed. A frame contains a sample grid, and pairs of micro-icons that represent substitution rules applied on the grid, control micro-icons that represent an iteration scheme applied on a set of frames, and micro-icons for introducing some irregularity and priority conditions applied on the rules and iteration schemes.

In Figure 3.4, a frame example divided into three sections is shown. On the upper-left section, a sample image where substitution rules can be applied. On the bottom section, five pairs of micro-icons are placed down, they are to describe rules, and three micro-icons are put up-right; they are -from left to right - to define a type of the frame iteration, scheme irregularity, and rule priorities. The shown iteration scheme is applied for one scene that consists of three frames (1:3). All rules have the same priority. To specify a CA model, a set of the illustrated visual elements should be selected, and edited by few mouse clicks, then watched in the multimedia user interfaces, after that the user can obtain the corresponding executable code as we are going to describe in the following section.

4. Generating Executable Code

After watching the film specification from different points of view, and performing new editing/composing operations, a metafile writer module generates a program generator metafile. The writer module is considered as a multimedia scanner that analyzes film sections (scene by scene, frame by frame, etc.), then

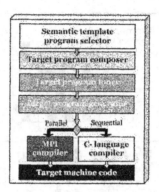

Figure 3.5.   The program generator subsystem

writes their description in a metafile used in later stages of the program generation. The program generator metafiles have a common outline that consists of a header and body parts. The header part stores global information about the film; it consists of the following records: A system (source) grid of cells, The size of the grid, Variables declared on the grid, Frame transformations, Types of iterations, irregularity of iterations, grid boundaries, and cell neighborhood.

The body part includes priority conditions to be applied to frame substitutions, types of substitutions, and data of the pairs of cellular patterns to be found and replaced. Next, a parsing unit (system parser) performs the analysis of the program generator metafile, that is a global type checking. This parsing unit recognizes the syntactic structures of algorithmic skeletons. After that, an executable code generation takes place. The program generator (PG) (depicted in Figure 3.5) consists of semantic template program selector (STPS), target program composer (TPC), target program tuner (TPT), target program generator (TPGs), and conventional compilers. The final product of PG subsystem is a target machine (sequential/parallel) executable code.

PG has a read-only access to the template program library which will be discussed later in this section. STPS defines hand-coded template programs to be called for representing corresponding computational schemes. STPS selects templates based on a type of the grid (1D, 2D, 3D, etc.), a size of the grid (small, medium, big, huge), the number of expected operations on each cell of the grid, in addition to, types of boundaries (close/open), neighborhood, iterations, and overlapping solving schemes. TPC adjusts the selected template programs to be parts of one program. In other words, it creates a program of template programs by adjusting them from a whole program view. TPT uses the declarations of variables, formulas, etc. related to the above mentioned syntactic structures to tune the composed program on an "indivisual" basis. The tuner output is used by a program generator to create either a sequential or parallel C-program which is compiled by a conventional compiler to obtain a target machine code. During the program generation phase, the template programs library (TPL) is accessed frequently, so, it is important to mention a few features related to TPL. Like any library of programs, the contents must be high-tech pieces of code written by expert developpers in order to be used by users of various levels of skills and experiences. TPL consists of three major modules: searchable index, a sequential template programs pool, and a parallel template programs pool. The searchable index is an interface between the entire library and outsiders. It facilitate the process of finding the most suitable templates in a short time. TPL uses adaptive searching techniques that accumulate its experience over time to improve the searching process. Sequential template programs pool is a collection of light-load computational codes to be used on a single processor architecture. Meanwhile, parallel template programs pool is a collection of heavy-load computational codes which are used on a parallel architecture. In the following section, we will talk in details about parallel template programs.

5.   Creating Parallel Programs

In this section, we provide some details of parallel template programs (PTP): back-ground, classification of parallel template programs, and a look inside a parallel template program.

5.1   Target Machines and Parallel Model

At the University of Aizu, we use MPICH [26] implementation of Message Passing Interface (MPI) [27], on a network of Fujitsu GP400 S machines with " Sun UltraSPARC-Iii" processors. A parallel program can be executed over a variable number of machines reaches 96 machines connected by 100 Mbps network. MPI parallel computational model (Figure 3.6) posits a set of processes that have only local memory but are able to communicate with other processes by sending and receiving messages. It is a defining feature of the message-passing model that data transfer from the local memory of one process to the local memory of another requires operations to be performed by both processes. Message-passing model has become widely used for many reasons like universality, expressivity, ease of debugging, and providing high performance computation. Two levels of parallelism are supported: (1) coarse grain and (2) fine grain parallelism. The coarse grain parallelism is especially valid for the strategies of parallelism like master-worker and macro-pipelines, where the communication activity is relatively small in comparison with the computation performed. In the fine grain parallelism, there is a relatively large amount of communication in comparison with the computation done.

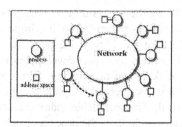

Figure 3.6.   The message passing model

5.2   Classification of Parallel Template Programs

It is too difficult to create a single parallel program that enjoy every feature of the parallel computational model because of the complex nature of parallelism. We classify PTP into several categories that are expandable over time to satisfy user needs and cover the recent technologies and programming techniques. PTPs are selected based on this classification to generate executable codes. PTP are classified accord-ing to:

- Granularity of tasks (coarse grain/fine grain)

- Parallelism model (data/functional)

- Task assignment (static/semi static/dynamic)

5.3   Inside Parallel Template Program

A generic parallel template program (Figure 3.7) consists of non-changeable and changeable parts. The non-changeable part is prepared as a ready-made program to implement a computational scheme written in C&MPI. It is usually a set of nested loops with formal parameters, variables, and bodies of formal operations. The changeable part including the formal parameters, variables, bodies of formal operations, and positions to be filled out by real parameters, variables, and operation bodies, which are specified by user's operations performed through the multimedia inter-faces. For CA models, the PTPs have common functions to process the cellular grid; the first basic function is the pattern discovery, which is responsible for finding all in-stances of the specified patterns in the grid. Two approaches to search the cellular grid are implemented. The first approach directly searches the whole grid for each pattern in turn. This means if there are N patterns related to different substitutions, the grid is searched N times. The second approach is to compose N patterns into a single larger pattern, and to search the grid for that pattern. Selecting the proper searching approach is based on the nature of the CA system. The second function is the overlapping detection. Its main task is to analyze the discovered instances of patterns; if an overlapping occurs among them, this function selects one of the over-lapped patterns to be replaced and discard all

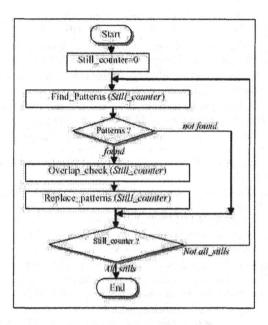

Figure 3.7. A generic template program chart

others. This decision is taken based on a priority condition specified by the user in earlier stages. The third function is pattern replacement. Its task is to apply the substitution rules to the processed grid after solving all overlaps by the previous function.

6. Conclusion

In this chapter, we overviewed the modeling of cellular automata systems, briefly explained multimedia interface, described the program generation, and showed the features of the parallel template programs. We demonstrated how in designing our multimedia environment, we abstract the knowledge as much as possible from the underlying computational infrastructure. We also presented our approach to provide higher level environments that allow the users to effectively manage their knowledge, experience, and abilities, as well as, their computational resources and domain environments. As a future work, we are working on empirical study to measure the self-explanatory factors of our multimedia environment. The feedback will be used in improving our work. In addition, we will run experiments to measure the improvement of performance of our parallel template programs.

References

[1] R. Yoshioka, N. Mirenkov: Visual Computing within Environment of Self-explanatory components, *Soft Computing*, Vol. 7, No. 1, Springer-Verlag, p.20-32 (2002)

[2] T. Ebihara, N. Mirenkov: Self-explanatory Ssoftware Components for Computation on Pyramids, *J. Three Dimensional Images*, 14, 4, p.158-163 (2000)

[3] T. Hirotomi, N. Mirenkov: Multimedia Representation of Computation on Trees, *J. Three Dimensional Images*, 13, p.146-151 (1999)

[4] A. Vazhenin, N. Mirenkov, D. Vazhenin: Multimedia Representation of Matrix Computations and Data, *Information Sciences*, 141, Elsevier Science, p.97-122 (2002)

[5] N. Mirenkov, Oleg Monakov, R. Yoshioka: Self-explanatory Components: Visualization of Graph Algorithms, , *In the Proceedings of Visual Computing (VC'02)*, published in *The Proceedings of the Eighth International Conference on Distributed Multimedia Systems (DMS2002)*, p.562-567 (2002)

[6] N.Mirenkov, A. Vazhenin, R. Yoshioka, T. Ebihara, T. Hirotomi, T. Mirenkova: Self-explanatory Components: A New Programming Paradigm, *International Journal of Software and Knowledge Engineering*, Vol. 11, No. 1, World Scientific, p.5-36 (2001)

[7] R. Yoshioka, N. Mirenkov: A Multimedia System to Render and Edit Self-explanatory Components, *Journal of Internet Technology*, Vol.3, No.1 (2002)

[8] Furnas, George W. and Qu, Yan: Shape Manipulation Using Pixel Rewrites. *In the Proceedings of Visual Computing (VC'02)*, published in *The Proceedings of the Eighth International Conference on Distributed Multimedia Systems (DMS2002)*, p.630-639 (2002)

[9] Furnas, G.W.: New Graphical Reasoning Models for Understanding Graphical Interfaces. *Proc. of CHI '91 Conf. on Hum. Factors in Comp. Sys.* 1991, p.71-78 (1991)

[10] Yamamoto, Kakuya: Visulan: A Visual Programming Language for Self-Changing Bitmap. *Proc. of International Conference on Visual Information Systems*, Victoria Univ. of Tech. cooperation with IEEE (Melbourne, Australia), p.88-96 (1996)

[11] Russ, John C.: *The Image Processing Handbook 3rd Ed*, Boca Raton, FL: CRC Press (1998)

[12] Serra, Jean: Image Analysis and Mathematical Morphology, *New York: Academic Press* (1982)

[13] D.Beletkov, M. Ostapkevich, S. Piskunov, I. Zhileev: WinALT, a Software Tool for Fine-grain Algorithms and Structures Synthesis and Simulation, *lecture notes in computer science.* 1662, p.491-496 (1999)

[14] M.B. Ostapkevich, S.V. Shashkov: Basic Constructions of Models in WinALT, *Bulletin of the Novosibirsk computer center*, issue 14 (2001)

[15] T. Toffoli: Cellular Automata as an Alternative to (Rather than an Approximation of) Differential Equations in Modelling Physics", *Physica* 10D, pp. 117-127 (1984)

[16] M. Resnick: Turtles, Termites, and Traffic Jams, *MIT Press*, Cambridge, Mass. (1994)

[17] B. Chopard and M. Droz: Cellular Automata Modelling of Physical Systems, *Cambridge Univ. press*, Cambridge, England (1998)

[18] D. Talia and P.Sloot, eds., *Future Generation Computer Systems*, Dec.1999.

[19] M. Sipper, The Emergence of Cellular Computing, IEEE Computer society, *COMPUTER magazine*, Vol. 32, No. 7, July (1999), p. 18-26

[20] G. Spezzano and D. Talia, CARPET: a Programming Language for Parallel Cellular Processing. In *proc. 2nd European school on parallel programming tools (ESPPE'96)*, p. 71-74, Alpe d'Huez,April (1996)

[21] Di Napoli, C., Giordano, M., Mango Furnari, M., Mele, F., and Napolitano, R.: CANL: a Language for Cellular Automata Network Modeling. In R. Vllmar, W. Erhard, and V.

jossifov, editors, Parcella '96, number 96 in *Mathematical research*, p.101-111, Berlin. Akademie Verlag, (1996)

[22] C. Demetrescu, I. Finocchi, and Stasko J.: Specifying Algorithm Visualizations, *Lecture notes in computer science*; 2269, Springer, p.16-29 (2002)

[23] Kerren A., and Stasko J.: Introduction to Algorithm Animation, chapter 1, *Lecture notes in computer science*; 2269, Springer, p.1-15 (2002)

[24] M. Saber, N. Mirenkov: Filmification of Methods: Cellular Programming Approach, *Journal of Three Dimensional Images*, Vol.15, No. 1, 3D Forum, p.110-115 (2001)

[25] M. Saber, N. Mirenkov: Visual Cellular Programming Based on Self-Explanatory Components Technology, In *the Proceedings of the Second International Workshop on Intelligent Multimedia Computing and Networking (IMMCN'2002)*, published in *The proceedings of the Sixth Joint Conference on Information Sciences (JCIS'2002)*, p.931-935

[26] MPICH-A Portable Implementation of MPI http://www.unix.mcs.anl.gov/mpi/mpich/index.html

[27] William Gropp, Ewing Lusk, and Anthony Skjellum: Using MPI: Portable Parallel Programming with the Message Passing Interface, 2nd edition, *MIT Press*, Cambridge, MA (1999)

II

ALGORITHMS

Chapter 4

VECTOR-PARALLEL ALGORITHMS FOR 1-DIMENSIONAL FAST FOURIER TRANSFORM

Yusaku Yamamoto*
Dept. of Computational Science and Engineering, Nagoya University
yamamoto@na.cse.nagoyau.ac.jp

Hiroki Kawamura
Hitachi Software Engineering Corp.
kawamu_h@itg.hitachi.co.jp

Mitsuyoshi Igai
Hitachi ULSI Systems Corp.
igai@hitachiul.co.jp

Abstract

We review 1-dimensional FFT algorithms for distributed-memory machines with vector processing nodes. To attain high performance on this type of machine, one has to achieve both high single-processor performance and high parallel efficiency at the same time. We explain a general framework for designing 1-D FFT based on a 3-dimensional representation of the data that can satisfy both of these requirements. Among many algorithms derived from this framework, two variants are shown to be optimal from the viewpoint of both parallel performance and usability. We also introduce several ideas that further improve performance and flexibility of user interface. Numerical experiments on the Hitachi SR2201, a distributed-memory parallel machine with pseudo-vector processing nodes, show that our program can attain 48% of the peak performance when computing the FFT of 2^{26} points using 64 nodes.

Keywords: fast Fourier transform, distributed-memory, vector processor, parallel algorithm, Stockham's algorithm, cyclic distribution, block cyclic distribution, SR2201

*This work was done while the author was at the Central Research Laboratory, Hitachi Ltd.

1. Introduction

The Fourier transform is one of the most fundamental tools in science and engineering and has applications in such diverse areas as signal processing, time series analysis and solution of partial differential equations. While a straightforward computation of the Fourier transform of N points requires $O(N^2)$ work, Cooley and Tukey proposed a novel algorithm called the *fast Fourier transform* (FFT) that requires only $O(N \log N)$ work in 1965 [6]. Since then, many variants of the FFT have been proposed so far, including autosort FFT [12][15], FFT for general N [1], FFT for real data [9][15] and so on.

The FFT has a large degree of parallelism in each stage of the computation, and accordingly, its implementations on parallel machines have been well studied. See, for example, [5] [13] for implementations on shared-memory parallel machines and [2] [7] [9] [10] [13] [14] [16] for implementations on distributed-memory parallel machines.

In this article, we review 1-dimensional FFT algorithms for distributed-memory machines with (pseudo-)vector processing nodes. This type of machines have become increasingly popular recently in high-end applications such as weather forecasting and electronic structure calculation. Representative machines that fall into this category include NEC SX-7, Fujitsu VPP5000 and Hitachi SR2201 and SR8000.

To attain high performance on this type of machine, one has to achieve both high single-processor performance and high parallel efficiency at the same time. The former is realized by maximizing the length of the innermost loops, while the latter is realized when the volume and frequency of inter-processor communication is minimized. We explain a general framework for 1-dimensional FFT based on a 3-dimensional representation of the data [2][14] that satisfies both of these requirements. In designing an FFT routine using this framework, one can consider several possible variants which differ in the way the data is distributed among the processing nodes at each stage of computation. We examine these variants and point out that two of them are optimal from the viewpoint of both parallel performance and usability. They need only one global transposition and input/output data using cyclic distribution. One of them called the *variant zzx* coincides with the algorithm proposed by Takahashi [14].

Next, we introduce several ideas to further improve the performance and flexibility of user interface. Specifically, we describe methods for enhancing single-processor performance by increasing the length of the innermost loops and enhancing parallel efficiency by overlapping interprocessor communication with computation. We also propose an extension that enables the routine to input/output data using general block cyclic distributions. The block sizes for input/output data can be specified independently by the user and this flexibility is realized without increase in the amount of interprocessor communication.

The rest of this paper is organized as follows: In section 2 we describe the general framework for 1-D FFT based on the 3-dimensional representation and find out the best variants among those derived from this framework. Ideas for further improving their performance and flexibility of user interface are introduced in section 3. Section 4 shows the performance of our program on the Hitachi SR2201. Conclusions are given in the final section.

2. A general framework for 1-D FFT on vector-parallel machines

In this section, we will explain a general framework for designing a 1-dimensional FFT routine on vector-parallel machines following [2] [3] [14]. It is intended to achieve both high single-processor performance and high parallel efficiency at the same time and is based on a 3-dimensional representation of the data. To derive the framework, we start with the case of 1-D FFT algorithms for vector machines.

2.1 A 1-D FFT algorithm for vector machines based on a 2-dimensional representation of data

The discrete Fourier transform of a 1-dimensional complex sequence $\{f_0, f_1, \ldots, f_{N-1}\}$ is defined as follows:

$$c_k = \sum_{j=0}^{N-1} f_j \omega_N^{jk} \qquad (k = 0, 1, \ldots, N-1), \qquad (4.1)$$

where $\omega_N = \exp(-2\pi i / N)$ and $i = \sqrt{-1}$.

When N can be factored as $N = N_x N_y$, the indices j and k can be expressed in a two-dimensional form:

$$j = j_x N_y + j_y \quad (j_x = 0, \ldots, N_x - 1, \quad j_y = 0, \ldots, N_y - 1), \quad (4.2)$$
$$k = k_x + k_y N_x \quad (k_x = 0, \ldots, N_x - 1, \quad k_y = 0, \ldots, N_y - 1). \quad (4.3)$$

Accordingly, $\{f_j\}$ and $\{c_k\}$ can be regarded as two-dimensional arrays:

$$f_{j_x, j_y} = f_{j_x N_y + j_y}, \qquad (4.4)$$
$$c_{k_x, k_y} = c_{k_x + k_y N_x}. \qquad (4.5)$$

Using these notations, we can rewrite eq. (4.1) as follows:

$$
\begin{aligned}
c_{k_x, k_y} &= \sum_{j_y=0}^{N_y-1} \sum_{j_x=0}^{N_x-1} f_{j_x, j_y} \omega_N^{(j_x N_y + j_y)(k_x + k_y N_x)} \\
&= \sum_{j_y=0}^{N_y-1} \left(\left(\sum_{j_x=0}^{N_x-1} f_{j_x, j_y} \omega_{N_x}^{j_x k_x} \right) \omega_N^{j_y k_x} \right) \omega_{N_y}^{j_y k_y}. \qquad (4.6)
\end{aligned}
$$

This shows that the Fourier transform of $\{f_j\}$ can be computed by the following algorithm proposed by Bailey [3]:

[Algorithm 1]

1 Compute $c'_{k_x,j_y} = \sum_{j_x=0}^{N_x-1} f_{j_x,j_y} \omega_{N_x}^{j_x k_x}$ by repeating N_x-point FFT N_y times.

2 Multiply c'_{k_x,j_y} by $\omega_N^{j_y k_x}$.

3 Compute $c_{k_x,k_y} = \sum_{j_y=0}^{N_y-1} c'_{k_x,j_y} \omega_{N_y}^{j_y k_y}$ by repeating N_y-point FFT N_x times.

The factor $\omega_N^{j_y k_x}$ appearing in step 2 is called *twiddle factor* and the step 2 is called *twiddle factor multiplication*. This algorithm requires about the same amount of computational effort as the FFT of N data points. It is especially suited to vector machines if N_y and N_x are chosen so that both of them are $O(\sqrt{N})$ and the loops over j_y and k_x are used as the innermost loops in steps 1 and 3, respectively. Then the innermost loops will have a fixed length of $O(\sqrt{N})$. Moreover, the factor ω is a constant within these loops and can be loaded outside the loops.

2.2   The five-step FFT based on a 3-dimensional representation of data

In the algorithm explained in the previous subsection, we decompose the 1-D FFT into multiple FFTs of smaller size and use the multiplicity for vectorization. In the case of distributed-memory vector-parallel machines, we need another dimension to use for parallelization. To this end, we factor N as $N = N_x N_y N_z$ and introduce a three-dimensional representation for the indices j and k:

$$j = j_x N_y N_z + j_y N_z + j_z \tag{4.7}$$
$$(j_x = 0, \ldots, N_x - 1, \quad j_y = 0, \ldots, N_y - 1, \quad j_z = 0, \ldots, N_z - 1),$$
$$k = k_x + k_y N_x + k_z N_x N_y \tag{4.8}$$
$$(k_x = 0, \ldots, N_x - 1, \quad k_y = 0, \ldots, N_y - 1, \quad k_z = 0, \ldots, N_z - 1).$$

By regarding the input and output sequences as three-dimensional arrays f_{j_x,j_y,j_z} and c_{k_x,k_y,k_z}, we can rewrite eq. (4.1) as follows:

$$c_{k_x,k_y,k_z} = \tag{4.9}$$
$$\sum_{j_z=0}^{N_z-1} \left(\left(\sum_{j_y=0}^{N_y-1} \left(\left(\sum_{j_x=0}^{N_x-1} f_{j_x,j_y,j_z} \omega_{N_x}^{j_x k_x} \right) \omega_{N_x N_y}^{j_y k_x} \right) \omega_{N_y}^{j_y k_y} \right) \omega_N^{j_z(k_x+k_y N_x)} \right) \omega_{N_z}^{j_z k_z}.$$

This suggests the following five-step FFT [14]:

[Algorithm 2: Five-step FFT]

1 Compute $c'_{k_x,j_y,j_z} = \sum_{j_x=0}^{N_x-1} f_{j_x,j_y,j_z} \omega_{N_x}^{j_x k_x}$ by repeating N_x-point FFT $N_y N_z$ times.

2 Twiddle factor multiplication (I): multiply c'_{k_x,j_y,j_z} by $\omega_{N_x N_y}^{j_y k_x}$.

3 Compute $c''_{k_x,k_y,j_z} = \sum_{j_y=0}^{N_y-1} c'_{k_x,j_y,j_z} \omega_{N_y}^{j_y k_y}$ by repeating N_y-point FFT $N_x N_z$ times.

4 Twiddle factor multiplication (II): multiply c''_{k_x,k_y,j_z} by $\omega_N^{j_z(k_x+k_y N_x)}$.

5 Compute $c_{k_x,k_y,k_z} = \sum_{j_z=0}^{N_z-1} c''_{k_x,k_y,j_z} \omega_{N_z}^{j_z k_z}$ by repeating N_z-point FFT $N_x N_y$ times.

Because the operation in step 1 consists of $N_y N_z$ independent FFTs, we can, for example, use the index j_y for vectorization and the index j_z for parallelization. Steps 3 and 5 can be executed in a similar way.

2.3 A general framework for vector-parallel FFT based on the five-step algorithm

There are many possible ways to exploit the parallelism in Algorithm 2 for vectorization and parallelization. For example, in step 1, we can use the y-direction for vectorization and the z direction for parallelization, or vice versa. Similarly, we have two possible choices in each of steps 3 and 5. In total, there are $2^3 = 8$ possible variants. In this subsection, we clarify which variant is optimal from the viewpoint of both parallel performance and usability.

Let zxy denote the variant which uses z, x and y-directions for parallelization in steps 1, 3 and 5, respectively. In this variant, the 3-dimensional arrays are scattered along the z-direction among the nodes in step 1, while they are scattered in the x and y-direction in step 3 and 5, respectively. Accordingly, redistribution of the array is necessary after step 1 and step 3. This operation is called *global transposition*. Among the eight possible variants, yxy, yzx, yzy and zxy need two global transpositions. In contrast, variants yxx, zxx, zzx and zzy need only one global transposition and their communication overhead is half of the former ones. We can therefore expect that the latter group will achieve higher parallel performance and consider only them from now on. We illustrate the vectorization and parallelization in the zxx variant in Figure 4.1.

Now assume that the number of points (N_x, N_y and N_z) in the direction along which the array is scattered is divisible by P, the number of processing nodes, and that we adopt cyclic distribution for scattering the data in each direction. From eqs. (4.7) and (4.8), we know that the indices j and k change contiguously when indices j_z and k_x change contiguously, respectively. As a result, the input data is distributed in a cyclic manner in j when the array

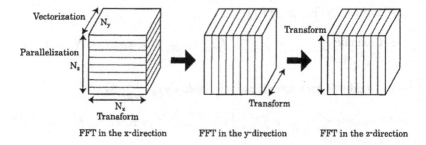

Figure 4.1. Vectorization and parallelization in the zxx variant.

is scattered in the z-direction, while it is distributed in a block cyclic manner with block size N_z when the array is scattered in the y-direction. Similarly, the output data is distributed in a cyclic manner in k when the array is scattered in the x-direction, while it is distributed in a block cyclic manner with block size N_x when the array is scattered in the y-direction. These observations are summarized in Table 4.1 for the four variants. Here, C and BC denote cyclic and block cyclic distribution, respectively.

From the table, we can see that the variants yxx and zzy use different data distributions for the input and output data, while zxx and zzx use the same (cyclic) distribution. From user's point of view, it seems more natural that the FFT routine uses the same data distribution for input and output data. Thus we can conclude that the variants zxx and zzx are the best ones judging both from parallel performance and usability among the eight variants that can be considered within our general framework. Of these two, the variant zzx has been proposed by Takahashi [14] as an algorithm suited to vector-parallel machines.

2.4   The detailed algorithm of the variant zxx

In this subsection, we describe a detailed algorithm of the 1-D parallel FFT based on the variant zxx. To this end, we first introduce some notations. Let $X_p^{(i)}$ denote the partial array allocated to node p at step i. We also define the

Table 4.1. Comparison of the four variants.

Step	Direction of transform	Direction of parallelization/vectorization			
		variant yxx	variant zxx	variant zzx	variant zzy
Input	–	BC	C	C	C
1	x	y/z	z/y	z/y	z/y
3	y	x/z	x/z	z/x	z/x
5	z	x/y	x/y	x/y	y/x
Output	–	C	C	C	BC

indices and their ranges as follows:

$$j_x = 0, \ldots, N_x - 1, \quad j_y = 0, \ldots, N_y - 1, \quad j_z = 0, \ldots, N_z - 1, \quad (4.10)$$
$$k_x = 0, \ldots, N_x - 1, \quad k_y = 0, \ldots, N_y - 1, \quad k_z = 0, \ldots, N_z - 1, \quad (4.11)$$
$$p = 0, \ldots, P - 1, \quad q = 0, \ldots, P - 1, \quad (4.12)$$
$$j_z' = 0, \ldots, N_z/P - 1, \quad (4.13)$$
$$k_x' = 0, \ldots, N_x/P - 1. \quad (4.14)$$

Here, j_z' and k_x' are local indices corresponding to j_z and k_x, respectively, and are related to the latter in the following way:

$$j_z = j_z' P + p, \quad (4.15)$$
$$k_x = k_x' P + p, \quad (4.16)$$

where p is the node number.

Using these notations, the algorithm can be described as follows:

[Algorithm 3: Detailed algorithm of the variant zxx]

1 Data input: $X_p^{(1)}(j_y, j_z', j_x) = f_{j_x N_y N_z + j_y N_z + j_z' P + p}.$

2 FFT in the x-direction:
$$X_p^{(2)}(j_y, j_z', k_x) = \sum_{j_x=0}^{N_x-1} X_p^{(1)}(j_y, j_z', j_x) \omega_{N_x}^{j_x k_x}.$$

3 Twiddle factor multiplication (I):
$$X_p^{(3)}(j_y, j_z', k_x) = X_p^{(2)}(j_y, j_z', k_x) \omega_{N_x N_y}^{j_y k_x}.$$

4 Data packing for global transposition:
$$X_p^{(4)}(j_y, j_z', k_x', q) = X_p^{(3)}(j_y, j_z', k_x' P + q).$$

5 Global transposition: $X_p^{(5)}(j_y, j_z', k_x', q) = X_q^{(4)}(j_y, j_z', k_x', p).$

6 Data unpacking:
$$X_p^{(6)}(j_z' P + q, k_x', j_y) = X_p^{(5)}(j_y, j_z', k_x', q).$$

7 FFT in the y-direction:
$$X_p^{(7)}(j_z, k_x', k_y) = \sum_{j_y=0}^{N_y-1} X_p^{(6)}(j_z, k_x', j_y) \omega_{N_y}^{j_y k_y}.$$

8 Twiddle factor multiplication (II):
$$X_p^{(8)}(k_x', k_y, j_z) = X_p^{(7)}(j_z, k_x', k_y) \omega_N^{j_z(k_x' P + p + k_y N_x)}.$$

9 FFT in the z-direction:
$$X_p^{(9)}(k_x', k_y, k_z) = \sum_{j_z=0}^{N_z-1} X_p^{(8)}(k_x', k_y, j_z) \omega_{N_z}^{j_z k_z}.$$

10 Data output: $c_{k_x' P + p + k_y N_x + k_z N_x N_y} = X_p^{(9)}(k_x', k_y, k_z).$

In this algorithm, the most computationally intensive parts are the FFTs in steps 2, 7 and 9. The indexing scheme for array $X_p^{(i)}$ is designed so that the index with respect to which the Fourier transform is performed comes last and the loop merging techniques to be described in subsection 3.2 can be applied easily.

The computational steps of this algorithm are illustrated in Figure 4.2 for the case of $N = 512$ and $P = 4$. Here we used the global 3-dimensional array rather than the partial 3-dimensional arrays for illustration to facilitate understanding. The numbers in the first and third 3-dimensional arrays correspond to the indices of input sequence f_j and output sequence c_k, respectively. The shaded area represents elements which are allocated to node 0, and the area enclosed by a thick line represents a set of elements used to perform a single FFT in the x, y or z-direction. It is apparent from the figure that (i) the FFTs in each direction can be computed within each node, (ii) there is only one global transposition, and (iii) the input and output data are scattered with a cyclic distribution, as required.

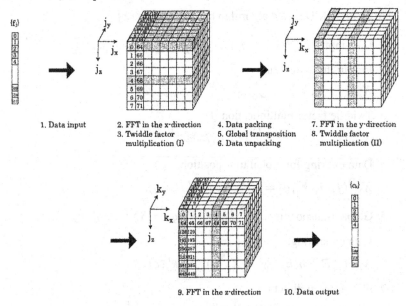

1. Data input   2. FFT in the x-direction   4. Data packing   7. FFT in the y-direction
                3. Twiddle factor   5. Global transposition   8. Twiddle factor
                   multiplication (I)   6. Data unpacking   multiplication (II)

9. FFT in the z-direction   10. Data output

Figure 4.2.   Computational steps of our FFT routine.

3.   Further improvements

In this section, we introduce several ideas that can further improve the performance and usability of the 1-dimensional vector-parallel FFT described in subsection 2.4. However, all the ideas apply to algorithms based on other variants as well.

3.1   Optimization of N_x, N_y and N_z

In the derivation given in subsection 2.3, N_x, N_y and N_z for the variant zxx were assumed to be arbitrary as long as N_x and N_z are divisible by P. We can use this freedom to increase the vector length. From Table 4.1 it can be seen that y, z and y-directions are used for vectorization in the FFTs in the x, y and z-directions, respectively. So we can maximize the single-processor performance by maximizing N_y and N_z subject to the above constraints.

3.2   Increasing the loop length by loop merging

To further extend the vector length, we can use loop merging techniques [14]. First, if $N_z/P > 1$, each processing node computes FFT for multiple values of j'_z in step 2 of Algorithm 3. So the loop over j'_z can be merged with the loop over j_y, extending the loop length to $N_y N_z/P$.

Second, we can use Stockham's algorithm [12][15] suited for vector processors in performing the FFT in each step. Let $n = 2^p$ and assume that we want to compute the FFT of an n-point sequence $Y_0(0,0), Y_0(1,0)$, $\ldots, Y_0(n-1,0)$. This can be done with the following algorithm.

[Algorithm 4: Stockham FFT]
> **do** $L = 0, p - 1$
> $\quad \alpha_L = 2^L$
> $\quad \beta_L = 2^{p-L-1}$
> $\quad$ **do** $m = 0, \alpha_L - 1$
> $\quad\quad$ **do** $l = 0, \beta_L - 1$
> $\quad\quad\quad Y_{L+1}(l, m) = Y_L(l, m) + Y_L(l + \beta_L, m) \omega_n^{m\beta_L}$
> $\quad\quad\quad Y_{L+1}(l, m + \alpha_L) = Y_L(l, m) - Y_L(l + \beta_L, m) \omega_n^{m\beta_L}$
> $\quad\quad$ **end do**
> $\quad$ **end do**
> **end do**

The result is stored in $Y_p(0,0), Y_p(0,1), \ldots, Y_p(0, n-1)$.

Notice that the ω in the innermost loop does not depend on l. This means that if we use this algorithm to compute the N_x-point FFT in step 2 of Algorithm 3, we can merge the loop over l with the loop over j_y. Combined with the loop merging mentioned above, the innermost loop length is finally extended to $N_y N_z \beta_L / P$.

Because the loop of length β_L appears α_L times in Stockham's algorithm, the average length of the innermost loops in step 2 is

$$\frac{N_y N_z}{P} \times \frac{\sum_{L=0}^{\log_2 N_x - 1} \alpha_L \beta_L}{\sum_{L=0}^{\log_2 N_x - 1} \alpha_L} = \frac{N_y N_z}{P} \times \frac{\frac{N_x}{2} \log_2 N_x}{N_x - 1}$$

$$\sim N_y N_z \log_2 N_x / 2P. \qquad (4.17)$$

Hence the loop length can be increased by a factor of $N_z \log_2 N_x / 2P$. Similarly, the innermost loop length in steps 7 and 9 can be extended to $N_x N_z \log_2 N_y / 2P$ and $N_x N_y \log_2 N_z / 2P$, respectively.

3.3   Overlapping the communication with computation

As we have shown in subsection 2.3, the variants yxx, zxx, zzx and zzy can attain higher parallel efficiency than other variants because they need only one global transposition. However, even one global transposition incurs considerable overhead because the amount of data each processing node has to transfer is $O(N/P)$ and is comparable to the computational work per node of $O(N \log N/P)$. This is expected to cause a severe problem for future-generation vector-parallel computers, for the speed of interprocessor data transfer evolves much more slowly than the processor speed.

To mitigate the problem, we can construct a modified algorithm in which the data transfer is overlapped with computation. In this algorithm, the data is divided into two parts depending on whether its j_y index is even or odd and one of them is transferred while the other is computed. The outline of the algorithm can be stated as follows:

[Algorithm 5: Overlapping the communication with computation]

1 Compute the FFT in the x-direction using only those elements with even j_y. Multiply the results with twiddle factors. $\omega_{N_x N_y}^{j_y k_x}$ for even j_y.

2 Compute the FFT in the x-direction using only those elements with odd j_y. Multiply the results with twiddle factors. At the same time, perform global transposition operation for those elements with even j_y.

3 Compute the first $\log_2 N_y - 1$ stages of the FFT in the y-direction using 5only those elements with even j_y. At the same time, perform global transposition operation for those elements with odd j_y.

4 Compute the first $\log_2 N_y - 1$ stages of the FFT in the y-direction 5using only those elements with odd j_y.

5 Compute the last stage of the FFT in the y-direction using all the data. Multiply 5the results with twiddle factors.

6 Compute the FFT in the $z$direction using all the data.

This algorithm exploits the fact that in the first $\log_2 N_y - 1$ steps of the y-FFT, 5computations involving elements with even j_y and those with odd j_y can be done separately [15]. As a result, the overhead due to global transposition can be hidden if the computing times in steps 2 and 3 are longer than the communication time in these steps.

3.4   Use of user-specified input/output block sizes

In the variant zxx and zzx, both the input and output data are scattered among the processing nodes 5 in a cyclic manner. However, some users may need more flexibility of data distribution. For example, block cyclic distribution is frequently used when solving linear simultaneous equations or eigenvalue problems on distributed-memory machines [4]. So if the user wants to connect the FFT routine with these routines, it is more convenient that the FFT routine can input/output data using block cyclic data distribution with user-specified block sizes. Note that the block sizes suitable for input and output data may not be the same, so it is more desirable if they can be specified independently.

To construct an FFT routine that meets these requirements, we can use the five-step FFT as a basis. Let the block sizes for input and output data be L_1 and L_2, respectively, and assume that N_z and N_x are divisible by $L_1 * P$ and $L_2 * P$, respectively. Now we scatter the three-dimensional array along the z-direction in steps 1 and 2 of Algorithm 2 using block cyclic distribution of block size L_1, and along the x-direction in steps 3-5 using block cyclic distribution of block size L_2. Then, from eq. (4.7), we know that the whole input sequence of length N is scattered with a block cyclic distribution of block size L_1. Likewise, the whole output sequence is scattered with a block cyclic distribution of block size L_2. This method requires only one global transposition like the variant zxx and leaves the room for vectorization using indices j_y, j_z and j_y in steps 1, 3 and 5, respectively.

One shortcoming of this approach is that N_y, which is the length of the innermost loops in steps 1 and 5, tends to become small because N_x and N_z need to be large enough to be multiples of $L_1 * P$ and $L_2 * P$, respectively. We can mitigate this problem by using loop merging techniques described in subsection 3.2. The readers are referred to [16] for more detailed description and performance evaluation of this approach.

4.   Experimental results

We implemented Algorithm 3 on the Hitachi SR2201 [8] and evaluated its performance. The SR2201 is a distributed-memory parallel machine with pseudo-vector processing nodes. Each node consists of a RISC processor with a pseudo-vector mechanism [11], which preloads the data from pipelined main memory to on-chip special register bank at a rate of 1 word per cycle. One node has peak performance of 300MFLOPS and 256MB of main memory. The nodes are connected via a multi-dimensional crossbar network, which enables all-to-all communication among P nodes to be done in $P - 1$ steps without contention [17].

Our FFT routine is written in FORTRAN and inter-processor communication is done using remote DMA, which enables data stored in the main memory of one node to be transferred directly to the main memory of another node without buffering. The FFT in the x, y and z direction in steps 2, 7 and 9 is performed using Stockham's radix 4 FFT [15], a variant of Algorithm 4 which saves both computational work and memory access by computing Y_{L+2} directly from Y_L.

To measure the performance of our FFT routine, we varied the problem size per node, N/P, from 2^{14} to 2^{20}. As for the number of nodes P, we measured the performance in two cases, namely, $P = 1$ and $P = 64$. We adopted optimization of N_x, N_y and N_z introduced in subsection 3.1, but did not incorporate the loop merging technique and overlapping of communication and computation. We didn't adopt the modifications to make the input/output block sizes user-specifiable, either. Readers interested in the last point are referred to the performance results given in [16]. The ω's used in the FFT and twiddle factor multiplication are pre-computed, so the time for computing them is not included in the execution time to be reported below.

Table 4.2 and Figure 4.3 shows the execution time and the performance of our routine. From these results, we can see that (i) the maximum performance on a single node is 176MFLOPS, which is more than 58% of the peak performance and (ii) parallel performance on 64 nodes is 9.18GFLOPS, which is about 48% of the peak performance.

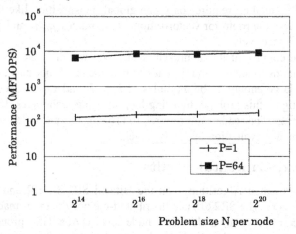

Figure 4.3. Performance results for $P = 1$ and $P = 64$.

From these results, we can conclude that the FFT algorithm described in this article can attain high performance on a (pseudo-)vector-parallel machine.

Table 4.2. Performance results for $P = 1$ and $P = 64$.

P	$N/P = 2^{14}$	$N/P = 2^{16}$	$N/P = 2^{18}$	$N/P = 2^{20}$
1	130.86MF	157.07MF	158.82MF	176.11MF
	43.33%	52.35%	52.94%	58.7%
64	6477.44MF	8477.41MF	8146.88MF	9175.07MF
	33.73%	44.15%	42.43%	47.78%

5. Conclusion

In this article, we reviewed 1-dimensional FFT algorithms for distributed-memory machines with vector processing nodes. We explained a general framework for designing 1-D FFT based on a 3-dimensional representation of the data that can achieve both high single-processor performance and high parallel efficiency at the same time. Among the many algorithms derived from this framework, we showed that two variants are optimal from the viewpoint of both parallel performance and usability. We also introduced several ideas that further improve performance and flexibility of user interface.

We implemented the algorithm on the Hitachi SR2201, a distributed-memory parallel machine with pseudo-vector processing nodes, and obtained the performance of 9175 MFLOPS, or 48% of the peak performance, when transforming 2^{26} point data on 64 nodes. It should be easy to adapt our method to other similar vector-parallel machines.

Acknowledgments

We would like to thank Dr. Mamoru Sugie at the Central Research Laboratory, Hitachi Ltd. for many valuable comments on the first version of this paper. We are also grateful to Mr. Nobuhiro Ioki and Mr. Shin-ichi Tanaka at the Software Development Division of Hitachi Ltd. for providing the environments for our computer experiments.

References

[1] R. C. Agarwal and J. W. Cooley: Vectorized Mixed Radix Discrete Fourier Transform Algorithms, *Proc. of IEEE*, Vol. 75, No. 9, pp. 1283-1292 (1987).

[2] R. C. Agarwal, F. G. Gustavson and M. Zubair: A High Prformance Parallel Algorithm for 1-D FFT, *Proc. of Supercomputing '94*, pp. 34-40 (1994).

[3] D. H. Bailey: FFTs in External or Hierarchical Memory, *The Journal of Supercomputing*, Vol. 4, pp. 23-35 (1990).

[4] L. Blackford, J. Choi, A. Cleary, E. D'Azevedo, J. Demmel, I. Dhillon, J. Dongarra, S. Hammarling, G. Henry, A. Petitet, K. Stanley, D. Walker and R. Whaley: ScaLAPACK User's Guide, SIAM, Philadelphia, PA, 1997.

[5] D. A. Carlson: Ultrahigh-Performance FFTs for the Cray-2 and Cray Y-MP Supercomputers, *Journal of Supercomputing*, Vol. 6, pp. 107-116 (1992).

[6] J. W. Cooley and J. W. Tukey: An Algorithm for the Machine Calculation of Complex Fourier Series, *Mathematics of Computation*, Vol. 19, pp. 297-301 (1965).

[7] A. Dubey, M. Zubair and C. E. Grosch: A General Purpose Subroutine for Fast Fourier Transform on a Distributed Memory Parallel Machine, *Parallel Computing*, Vol. 20, pp. 1697-1710 (1994).

[8] H. Fujii, Y. Yasuda, H. Akashi, Y. Inagami, M. Koga, O. Ishihara, M. Kashiyama, H. Wada and T. Sumimoto: Architecture and Performance of the Hitachi SR2201 Massively Parallel Processor System, *Proc. of IPPS '97*, pp. 233-241, 1997.

[9] M. Hegland: Real and Complex Fast Fourier Transforms on the Fujitsu VPP500, *Parallel Computing*, Vol. 22, pp. 539-553 (1996).

[10] S. L. Johnson and R. L. Krawitz: Cooley-Tukey FFT on the Connection Machine, *Parallel Computing*, Vol. 18, pp. 1201-1221 (1992).

[11] K. Nakazawa, H. Nakamura, H. Imori and S. Kawabe: Pseudo Vector Processor Based on Register-Windowed Superscalar Pipeline, *Proc. of Supercomputing '92*, pp. 642-651 (1992).

[12] P. N. Swarztrauber: FFT Algorithms for Vector Computers, *Parallel Computing*, Vol. 1, pp. 45-63 (1984).

[13] P. N. Swarztrauber: Multiprocessor FFTs, *Parallel Computing*, Vol. 5, pp. 197-210 (1987).

[14] D. Takahashi: Parallel FFT Algorithms for the Distributed-Memory Parallel Computer Hitachi SR8000, *Proc. of JSPP2000*, pp. 91-98, 2000 (in Japanese).

[15] C. Van Loan: Computational Frameworks for the Fast Fourier Transform, SIAM Press, Philadelphia, PA (1992).

[16] Y. Yamamoto, M. Igai and K. Naono: A Vector-Parallel FFT with a User-Specifiable Data Distribution Scheme, in M. Guo and L. T. Yang, eds., *Parallel and Distributed Processing and Applications*, Lecture Notes in Computer Science 2745, Springer-Verlag, pp. 362-374, 2003.

[17] Y. Yasuda, H. Fujii, H. Akashi, Y. Inagami, T. Tanaka, J. Nakagoshi, H. Wada and T. Sumimoto: Deadlock-Free Fault-Tolerant Routing in the Multi-Dimensional Crossbar Network and its Implementation for the Hitachi SR2201, *Proc. of IPPS '97*, pp. 346-352, 1997.

Chapter 5

TOWARDS SOLVING NP-COMPLETE PROBLEMS BY USING A MOLECULAR SUPERCOMPUTER MODEL

Minyi Guo

Department of Computer Software

The University of Aizu, Aizu-wakamatsu, Fukushima 965-8580, Japan

minyi@u-aizu.ac.jp

Weng-Long Chang

Department of Information Management

Southern Taiwan University of Technology, Tainan County, Taiwan

changwl@csie.ncku.edu.tw

Abstract   Cook's Theorem [5, 6] is that if one algorithm for an NP-complete problem will be developed, then other problems will be solved by means of reduction to that problem. Cook's Theorem has been demonstrated to be right in a general *digital electronic* computer. In this chapter, we propose a DNA algorithm for solving the *vertex-cover problem*. It is demonstrated that if the size of a reduced NP-complete problem is equal to or less than that of the vertex-cover problem, then the proposed algorithm can be directly used for solving the reduced NP-complete problem and Cook's Theorem is correct on DNA-based computing. Otherwise, Cook's Theorem is incorrect on DNA-based computing and a new DNA algorithm should be developed from the characteristic of NP-complete problems.

Keywords: Molecular Computing, DNA-based Parallel Computing, Cook's Theorem, NP-complete Problem.

Introduction

Nowadays, producing roughly 10^{18} DNA strands that fit in a test tube is possible through advances in molecular biology [1]. Those 10^{18} DNA strands can be employed for representing 10^{18} bit information. Basic biological operations can be applied to simultaneously operate 10^{18} bit information. This is to say that there are 10^{18} data processors to be executed in parallel. Hence, it is very clear that biological computing can provide very huge parallelism for dealing with the problem in real world.

Adleman wrote the first paper in which it was demonstrated that DNA (*DeoxyriboNucleic Acid*) strands could be applied for figuring out solutions to an instance of the NP-complete Hamiltonian path problem (HPP) [2]. Lipton wrote the second paper in which it was shown that the Adleman techniques could also be used to solving the NP-complete satisfiability (SAT) problem (the first NP-complete problem) [3]. Adleman and his co-authors proposed *sticker* for enhancing the Adleman-Lipton model [9].

In this chapter, we use *sticker* to constructing solution space of DNA library sequences for the *vertex-cover problem*. Simultaneously, we also apply DNA operations in the Adleman-Lipton model to develop a DNA algorithm. The main result of the proposed DNA algorithm shows that the vertex-cover problem is resolved with biological operations in the Adleman-Lipton model from solution space of sticker. Furthermore, if the size of a reduced NP-complete problem is equal to or less than that of the vertex-cover problem, then the proposed algorithm can be directly used for solving the reduced NP-complete problem.

1.   DNA Supercomputer Model

A DNA (*DeoxyriboNucleic Acid*) is a *molecule* that plays the main role in DNA based computing [10]. In the biochemical world of large and small *molecules, polymers*, and *monomers*, DNA is a polymer, which is strung together from monomers called *deoxyriboNucleotides*. The monomers used for the construction of DNA are deoxyribonucleotides, which each deoxyribonucleotide contains three components: a *sugar*, a *phosphate* group, and a *nitrogenous* base. This sugar has five carbon atoms - for the sake of reference there is a fixed numbering of them. Because the base also has carbons, to avoid confusion the carbons of the sugar are numbered from 1' to 5' (rather than from 1 to 5). The phosphate group is attached to the 5' carbon, and the base is attached to the 1' carbon. Within the sugar structure there is a hydroxyl group attached to the 3' carbon.

Distinct nucleotides are detected only with their bases, which come in two sorts: purines and pyrimidines [1, 10]. Purines include *adenine* and *guanine*, abbreviated A and G. Pyrimidines contain *cytosine* and *thymine*, abbreviated C and T. Because nucleotides are only distinguished from their bases, they are simply represented as $A, G, C,$ or T nucleotides, depending upon the sort of base that they have. The structure of a nucleotide is illustrated (in a very simplified way) in Figure 5.1. In Figure 5.1, **B** is one of the four possible bases $(A, G, C,$ or $T)$, **P** is the phosphate group, and the rest (the "stick") is the sugar base (with its carbons enumerated 1' through 5').

P——●—●—●—●—●——B

5' 4' 3' 2' 1'

Figure 5.1. A schematic representation of a nucleotide.

In the Adleman-Lipton model [2, 3], *splints* were used to correspond to the edges of a particular graph the paths of which represented all possible binary numbers. As it stands, their construction indiscriminately builds all splints that lead to a complete graph. This is to say that hybridization has higher probabilities of errors. Hence, Adleman et al. [9] proposed the sticker-based model, which was an abstract model of molecular computing based on DNAs with a random access memory and a new form of encoding the information, to enhance the Adleman-Lipton model.

The DNA operations in the Adleman-Lipton model are described below [2, 3, 7, 8]. These operations will be used for figuring out solutions of the vertex-cover problem.

The Adleman-Lipton model:

A (test) tube is a set of molecules of DNA (i.e. a multi-set of finite strings over the alphabet $\{A, C, G, T\}$). Given a tube, one can perform the following operations:

1 *Extract.* Given a tube P and a short single strand of DNA, S, produce two tubes $+(P, S)$ and $-(P, S)$, where $+(P, S)$ is all of the molecules of DNA in P which contain the strand S as a sub-strand and $-(P, S)$ is all of the molecules of DNA in P which do not contain the short strand S.

2 *Merge.* Given tubes P_1 and P_2, yield $\cup(P_1, P_2)$, where $\cup(P_1, P_2) = P_1 \cup P_2$. This operation is to pour two tubes into one, with no change of the individual strands

3 *Detect.* Given a tube P, say 'yes' if P includes at least one DNA molecule, and say 'no' if it contains none.

4 *Discard.* Given a tube P, the operation will discard the tube P.

5 *Read.* Given a tube P, the operation is used to describe a single molecule, which is contained in the tube P. Even if P contains many different molecules each encoding a different set of bases, the operation can give an explicit description of exactly one of them.

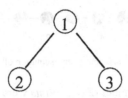

Figure 5.2.   the graph G of our problem.

2.   Using Sticker for Solving the Vertex-Cover Problem in the Adleman-Lipton Model

2.1   Definition of the Vertex-Cover Problem

Assume that G is a graph and $G = (V, E)$, where $V = \{v_1, \ldots, v_n\}$ is a set of vertices in G and $E = \{(v_a, v_b) \mid v_a$ and v_b are vertices in V, respectively$\}$ is a set of edges in G, and $|V| = n$ is the number of vertex in V and $|E| = m$ is the number of edge in E.

Mathematically, a *vertex cover* of a graph G is a subset $V^1 \subseteq V$ of vertices such that for each edge (v_a, v_b) in E, at lease one of v_a and v_b belongs to V^1 [5, 6]. The vertex-cover problem is to find a minimum-size vertex cover from G. The problem has been shown to be a NP-complete problem [6].

The graph in Figure 5.2. denotes such a problem. In Figure 5.2 , the graph G contains three vertices and two edges. The minimum-size vertex cover for G is $\{v_1\}$. Hence, the size of the vertex-cover problem in Figure 5.2 is one. It is indicated from [6] that finding a minimum-size vertex cover is a NP-complete problem, so it can be formulated as a search problem.

2.2   Using Sticker for Constructing Solution Space of DNA Sequence for the Vertex Cover Problem

The first step in the Adleman-Lipton model is to yield solution space of DNA sequences for those problems solved. Next, basic biological operations are used to remove illegal solution and find legal solution from solution space. Thus, the first step of solving the vertex-cover problem is to generate a test tube, which includes all of the possible vertex covers. Assume that an n-digit binary number corresponds to each possible vertex cover to any n-vertex graph, G. Also suppose that V^1 is a vertex cover for G. If the i-th bit in an n-digit binary number is set to 1, then it represents that the corresponding vertex is in V^1. If the i-th bit in an n-digit binary number is set to 0, then it represents that the corresponding vertex is out of V^1.

By this way, all of the possible vertex covers in G are transformed into an ensemble of all n-digit binary numbers. Hence, with the way above, Table 5.1 denotes the solution space for the graph in Figure 5.2. The binary number 000

3-digit binary number	The corresponding vertex cover
000	$\emptyset$
001	$\{v_1\}$
010	$\{v_2\}$
011	$\{v_2, v_1\}$
100	$\{v_3\}$
101	$\{v_3, v_1\}$
110	$\{v_3, v_2\}$
111	$\{v_3, v_2, v_1\}$

Table 5.1.   The solution space for the graph in Figure 5.2.

in Table 5.1 represents that the corresponding vertex cover is empty. The binary numbers 001, 010 and 011 in Table 5.1 represent that those corresponding vertex covers are $\{v_1\}$, $\{v_2\}$ and $\{v_2, v_1\}$, respectively. The binary numbers 100, 101 and 110 in Table 5.1 represent that those corresponding vertex covers, subsequently, are $\{v_3\}$, $\{v_3, v_1\}$ and $\{v_3, v_2\}$. The binary number 111 in Table 5.1 represents that the corresponding vertex cover is $\{v_3, v_2, v_1\}$. Though there are eight 3-digit binary numbers for representing eight possible vertex covers in Table 5.1, not every 3-digit binary number corresponds to a *legal* vertex cover. Hence, in next subsection, basic biological operations are used to develop an algorithm for removing illegal vertex covers and finding legal vertex covers.

To implement this way, assume that an unsigned integer X is represented by a binary number x_n, $x_{n-1}, \ldots, x_1$, where the value of x_i is 1 or 0 for $1 \leq i \leq n$. The integer X contains 2^n kinds of possible values. Each possible value represents a vertex cover for any n-vertex graph, G. Hence, it is very obvious that an unsigned integer X forms 2^n possible vertex cover. A bit x_i in an unsigned integer X represents the i-th vertex in G. If the i-th vertex is in a vertex cover, then the value of x_i is set to 1. If the i-th vertex is out of a vertex cover, then the value of x^i is set to 0.

To represent all possible vertex covers for the vertex-cover problem, *sticker* [9, 15] is used to construct solution space for that problem solved. For every bit, x_i, two distinct 15 base value sequences are designed. One represents the value 1 and another represents the value 0 for x_i. For the sake of convenience of presentation, assume that $x_i{}^1$ denotes the value of x_i to be 1 and $x_i{}^0$ defines the value of x_i to be 0. Each of the 2^n possible vertex covers is represented by a library sequence of $15*n$ bases consisting of the concatenation of one value sequence for each bit. DNA molecules with library sequences are termed library strands and a combinatorial pool containing library strands is termed a library. The probes used for separating the library strands have sequences complementary to the value sequences.

The Adleman program [15] is modified for generating those DNA sequences to satisfy the constraints above. For example, for representing the three vertices in the graph in Figure 5.2, the generated DNA sequences are:
$x_1{}^0 = AAAACTCACCCTCCT$, $x_2{}^0 = TCTAATATAATTACT$,

$x_3{}^0 = ATTCTAACTCTACCT$, $x_1{}^1 = TTTCAATAACACCTC$,
$x_2{}^1 = ATTCACTTCTTTAAT$ and $x_3{}^1 = AACATACCCCTAATC$.
Therefore, for every possible vertex cover to the graph in Figure 5.2, the corresponding library strand is synthesized by employing a mix-and-split combinatorial synthesis technique [16]. Similarly, for any n-vertex graph, all of the library strands for representing every possible vertex cover could be also synthesized with the same technique.

2.3   The DNA Algorithm for Solving the Vertex Cover Problem

The following DNA algorithm is proposed to solve the vertex cover problem.

Algorithm 1 *Solving the vertex cover problem.*

(1) *Input* (T_0), *where the tube* T_0 *includes solution space of DNA sequences to encode all of the possible vertex covers for any* n-*vertex graph* G, *with those techniques mentioned in the previous subsection.*

(2) *For* $k = 1$ *to* m, *where* m *is the number of edges in* G.
Assume that $e_k = (v_i, v_j)$, *is one edge in* G *and* v_i *and* v_j *are vertices in* G. *Also suppose that bits* x_i *and* x_j, *respectively, represent* v_i *and* v_j.
(a) $\theta^1 = +(T_0, x_i{}^1)$ *and* $\theta = -(T_0, x_i{}^1)$.
(b) $\theta^2 = +(\theta, x_j{}^1)$ *and* $\theta^3 = -(\theta, x_j{}^1)$.
(c) $T_0 = \cup(\theta^1, \theta^2)$.
EndFor

(3) *For* $i = 0$ *to* $n - 1$
For $j = i$ *down to* 0
(a) $T_{j+1}{}^{ON} = +(T_j, x_{i+1}{}^1)$ *and* $T_j = -(T_j, x_{i+1}{}^1)$.
(b) $T_{j+1} = \cup(T_{j+1}, T_{j+1}{}^{ON})$.
EndFor
EndFor

(4) *For* $k = 1$ *to* n
(a) If (detect $(T_k) = $ *'yes') then*
(b)Read (T_k) *and terminate the algorithm.*
EndIf

EndFor

Theorem 1 *From those steps in Algorithm 1, the vertex cover problem for any n-vertex graph G can be solved.*

Proof. In Step 1, a test tube of DNA strands, that encode all 2^n possible input bit sequences $x_n, \ldots, x_1$ is generated. It is very clear that the test tube includes all 2^n possible vertex covers for any n-vertex graph G.

From the definition of vertex cover [5, 6], Step 2(a) applies "extraction" operation from the tube T_0 to form two test tubes: θ^1 and θ. θ^1 contains all of the strands that have $x_i = 1$, while θ consists of all of the strands that have $x_i = 0$. It is very clear from the definition of vertex cover that the tube θ represents those sets which do not include the vertex v_i. Next, Step 2(b) also uses "extraction" operation from the tube θ to form two new test tubes: θ^2 and θ^3. θ^2 contains all of the strands that have $x_i = 0$ and $x_j = 1$, while θ^3 consists of all of the strands that have $x_i = 0$ and $x_j = 0$. The tubes θ^1 and θ^2 contain the strands, which satisfy the definition of vertex cover. Therefore, Step 2(c) applies "merge" operation to pour the tubes θ^1 and θ^2 into the tube T_0. After Steps 2(a) to 2(c) are repeated to execute m times, the tube T_0 includes the strands, which represent those legal vertex covers. When each time of the outer loop in Step 3 are executed, the number of execution for the inner loop is $(i + 1)$ times. The first time of the outer loop is executed, the inner loop is only executed one time. Therefore, Step 3(a) and 3(b) will also be executed one time. Step 3a uses "extraction" operation to form two test tubes: T_1^{ON} and T_0. T_1^{ON} contains all of the strands that have $x_1 = 1$. T_0 consists of all of the strands that have $x_1 = 0$. That is to say, the first tube encodes every vertex cover including the first vertex and the second tube represents every vertex cover not including the first vertex. Hence, Step 3(b) applies "merge" operation to pour the tube T_1^{ON} into the tube T_1. After repeat to execute Steps 3(a) and 3(b), it finally produces n new tubes. The tube T_k for $n \geq k \geq 1$ encodes those vertex covers that contain k vertices.

Because the vertex-cover problem is to find a minimum-size vertex-cover, the tube T_1 is detected with "detection" operation in Step 4(a). If it returns "yes", then T_1 contains those vertex covers which size is minimum. Therefore, Step 4(b) uses "read" operation to describe the sequence of a molecular in T_1 and the algorithm is terminated. Otherwise, repeat to execute Step 4(a) until a minimum-size vertex cover is found in the tube detected. $\square$.

2.4 The Complexity of the Proposed DNA Algorithm

The following theorems describe time complexity of Algorithm 1, volume complexity of solution space in Algorithm 1, the number of the tube used in Algorithm 1 and the longest library strand in solution space in Algorithm 1.

Theorem 2 *The vertex-cover problem for any undirected n-vertex graph G with m edges can be solved with $O(n^2)$ biological operations in the Adleman-Lipton model, where n is the number of vertices in G and m is at most equal to $(n * (n - 1)/2)$.*

Proof. Algorithm 1 can be applied for solving the vertex-cover problem for any undirected n-vertex graph G. Algorithm 1 includes three main steps. Step 2 is mainly used to determine legal vertex covers and to remove illegal vertex covers from all of the 2^n possible library strands. From Algorithm 1, it is very obvious that Steps 2(a) and 2(b) take $2 * m$ "extraction" operations and Step 2(c) takes m "merge" operations. Step 3 is mainly applied to figure out the number of element in every legal vertex cover. It is indicated from Algorithm 1 that Step 3(a) takes $(n * (n - 1)/2)$ "extraction" operations and Step 3(b) takes $(n*(n-1)/2)$ "merge" operations. Step 4 is used to find a minimum-size vertex cover from legal vertex cover. It is pointed out from Algorithm 1 that Step 4(a) at most takes n "detection" operations and Step 4(b) takes one "read" operation. Hence, from the statements mentioned above, it is at once inferred that the time complexity of Algorithm 1 is $O(n^2)$ biological operations in the Adleman-Lipton model. $\square$.

Theorem 3 *The vertex-cover problem for any undirected n-vertices graph G with m edges can be solved with sticker to construct $O(2^n)$ strands in the Adleman-Lipton model, where n is the number of vertices in G.*

Proof. Refer to Theorem 2. $\square$.

Theorem 4 *The vertex-cover problem for any undirected n-vertices graph G with m edges can be solved with $O(n)$ tubes in the Adleman-Lipton model, where n is the number of vertices in G.*

Proof. Refer to Theorem 2. $\square$.

Theorem 5 *The vertex-cover problem for any undirected n-vertices graph G with m edges can be solved with the longest library strand, $O(15 * n)$, in the Adleman-Lipton model, where n is the number of vertices in G.*

Proof. Refer to Theorem 2. $\square$.

2.5 Range of Application to Cook's Theorem in DNA Computing

Cook's Theorem [5, 6] is that if one algorithm for one NP-complete problem will be developed, then other problems will be solved by means of reduction to that problem. Cook's Theorem has been demonstrated to be right in a general digital electronic computer. Assume that a collection C is $\{c_1, c_2, \cdots, c_m\}$ of clauses on a finite set U of variables, $\{u_1, u_2, \cdots, u_n\}$, such that —$c_x$— is equal to 3 for $1 \leq x \leq m$. The 3-satisfiability problem (3-SAT) is to find whether there is a truth assignment for U that satisfies all of the clauses in C. The simple structure for the 3-SAT problem makes it one of the most widely used problems for other NP-completeness results [5]. The following theorems are used to describe the range of application for Cook's Theorem in molecular computing

Theorem 6 *Assume that any other NP-complete problems can be reduced to the vertex-cover problem with a polynomial time algorithm in a general electronic computer. If the size of a reduced NP-complete problem is not equal to or less than that of the vertex-cover problem, then Cook's Theorem is uncorrected in molecular computing.*

Proof. We transform the 3-SAT problem to the vertex-cover problem with a polynomial time algorithm [5]. Suppose that U is $\{u_1, u_2, \cdots, u_n\}$ and C is $\{c_1, c_2, \cdots, c_m\}$. U and C are any instance for the 3-SAT problem. We construct a graph $G = (V, E)$ and a positive integer $K \leq |V|$ such that G has a vertex cover of size K or less if and only if C is satisfiable. $\square$

For each variable u_i in U, there is a truth-setting component $T_i = (V_i, E_i)$, with $V_i = \{u_i, u_i^1\}$ and $E_i = \{\{u_i, u_i^1\}\}$, that is, two vertices joined by a single edge. Note that any vertex cover will have to contain at least one of u_i and u_i^1 in order to cover the single edge in E_i. For each clause c_j in C, there is a satisfaction testing component $S_j = (V_j^1, E_j^1)$, consisting of three vertices and three edges joining them to form a triangle:

$$V_j^1 = \{a_j[j], a_2[j], a_3[j]\}$$

$$E_j^1 = \{\{a_1[j], a_2[j]\}, \{\{a_1[j], a_3[j]\}, \{\{a_2[j], a_3[j]\}\}.$$

Note that any vertex cover will have to contain at least two vertices from V_j^1 in order to cover the edges in E_j^1.

The only part of the construction that depends on which literals occur in which clauses is the collection of communication edges. These are best viewed from the vantage point of the satisfaction testing components. For each clause c_j in C, assume that the three literals in c_j is denoted as x_j, y_j, and z_j. Then the communication edges emanating from S_j are given by:

$$E_j^2 = \{\{a_1[j], x_j\}, \{a_2[j], y_j\}, \{a_3[j], z_j\}\}.$$

The construction of our instance to the vertex-cover problem is completed by setting $K = n + 2 * m$ and $G = (V, E)$, where

$$V = (\bigcup_{i=1}^{n} V_i) \cup (\bigcup_{j=1}^{m} V_j^1)$$

and

$$E = (\bigcup_{i=1}^{n} E_i) \cup (\bigcup_{j=1}^{m} E_j^1) \cup (\bigcup_{j=1}^{m} V_E^2).$$

Therefore, the number of vertex and the number of edge in G are, respectively, $(2 * n + 3 * m)$ and $(n + 6 * m)$. Algorithm 1 is used to determine the vertex-cover problem for G with $2^{2*n+3*m}$ DNA strands. Because the limit of DNA strands is 10^{21}, n is equal to or less than 15 and m is also equal to or less than 15. That is to say that Algorithm 1 at most solves the 3-SAT problem with 15 variables and 15 clauses. However, a general digital electronic computer can be applied to directly resolve the 3-SAT problem with 15 variables and 15 clauses. Hence, it is at once inferred that if the size of a reduced NP-complete problem is not equal to or less than that of the vertex-cover problem, then Cook's Theorem is uncorrected in molecular computing.

From Theorem 3– 6, if the size of a reduced NP-complete problem is equal to or less than that of the vertex-cover problem, then Algorithm 1 can be directly used for solving the reduced NP-complete problem. Otherwise, a new DNA algorithm should be developed according to the characteristic of NP-complete problems.

3. Experimental Results of Simulated DNA Computing

We finished the modification of the Adleman program [15] in a PC with one Pentium(R) 4 and 128 MB main memory. Our operating system is Window 98 and the compiler is C++ Builder 6.0. This modified program is applied to generate DNA sequences for solving the vertex-cover problem. We added some subroutines to the Adleman program for simulating biological operations in the Adleman-Lipton model in Section 2. We also added the subroutines to the Adleman program to simulate Algorithm 1.

The Adleman program is used for constructing each 15-base DNA sequence for each bit of the library. For each bit, the program is applied for generating two 15-base random sequences (for 1 and 0) and checking to see if the library strands satisfy the seven constraints in subsection 2.2 with the new DNA sequences added. If the constraints are satisfied, the new DNA sequences are greedily accepted. If the constraints are not satisfied then mutations are introduced one by one into the new block until either: (A) the constraints are satisfied and the new DNA sequences are then accepted or (B) a threshold for the number of mutations is exceeded and the program has failed and so it exits, printing the sequence found so far. If n-bits that satisfy the constraints are found then the program has succeeded and it outputs these sequences.

Consider the graph in Figure 5.2. The graph includes three vertices: v_1, v_2 and v_3. DNA sequences generated by the Adleman program modified were shown in Table 5.2. This program, respectively, took one mutation, one mutation and ten mutations to make new DNA sequences for v_1, v_2 and v_3. With the nearest neighbor parameters, the Adleman program was used to calculate the enthalpy, entropy, and free energy for the binding of each probe to its corresponding region on a library strand. The energy was shown in Table 5.3. Only G really matters to the energy of each bit. For example, the delta G for the probe binding a '1' in the first bit is thus estimated to be 24.3 kcal/mol and the delta G for the probe binding a '0' is estimated to be 27.5 kcal/mol.

Vertex	5' → 3' DNA Sequence
hline $x_3{}^0$	ATTCTAACTCTACCT
$x_2{}^0$	TCTAATATAATTACT
$x_1{}^0$	AAAACTCACCCTCCT
$x_3{}^1$	AACATACCCCTAATC
$x_2{}^1$	ATTCACTTCTTTAAT
$x_1{}^1$	TTTCAATAACACCTC

Table 5.2. Sequences chosen to represent the vertices in the graph in Figure 5.2.

Vertex	Enthalpy energy (H)	Entropy energy (S)	Free energy (G)
$x_3{}^0$	105.2	277.1	22.4
$x_2{}^0$	104.8	283.7	19.9
$x_1{}^0$	113.7	288.7	27.5
$x_3{}^1$	112.6	291.2	25.6
$x_2{}^1$	107.8	283.5	23
$x_1{}^1$	105.6	271.6	24.3

Table 5.3. The energy for the binding of each probe to its corresponding region on a library strand.

The program simulated a mix-and-split combinatorial synthesis technique [16] to synthesize the library strand to every possible vertex cover. Those library strands are shown in Table 5.4, and represent eight possible vertex covers: $\emptyset, \{v_1\}, \{v_2\}, \{v_2, v_1\}, \{v_3\}, \{v_3, v_1\}, \{v_3, v_2\}$ and $\{v_3, v_2, v_1\}$, respectively. The program is also applied to figure out the average and standard deviation for the enthalpy, entropy and free energy over all probe/library strand interactions. The energy is shown in Table 5.5. The standard deviation for delta G is small because this is partially enforced by the constraint that there are 4, 5, or 6 Gs (the seventh constraint in subsection 3.2) in the probe sequences.

The Adleman program is employed for computing the distribution of the types of potential mishybridizations. The distribution of the types of potential mishybridizations is the absolute frequency of a probe-strand match of length k from 0 to the bit length 15 (for DNA sequences) where probes are not supposed to match the strands. The distribution is, subsequently, 106, 152, 183, 215, 216, 225, 137, 94, 46, 13, 4, 1, 0, 0, 0 and 0. It is pointed out from the last four zeros that there are 0 occurrences where a probe matches a strand at 12, 13, 14, or 15 places. This shows that the third constraint in subsection 3.2 has been satisfied. Clearly, the number of matches peaks at 5 (225). That is to say that there are 225 occurrences where a probe matches a strand at 5 places.

4.   Conclusions

Cook's Theorem is that if one algorithm for one NP-complete problem will be developed, then other problems will be solved by means of reduction to that problem. Cook's Theorem has been demonstrated to be right in a general

5'-ATTCTAACTCTACCTTCTAATATAATTACTAAAACTCACCCTCCT-3'
3'-TAAGATTGAGATGGAAGATTATATTAATGATTTTGAGTGGGAGGA-5'
5'-ATTCTAACTCTACCTTCTAATATAATTACTTTTCAATAACACCTC-3'
3'-TAAGATTGAGATGGAAGATTATATTAATGAAAAGTTATTGTGGAG-5'
5'-ATTCTAACTCTACCTATTCACTTCTTTAATAAAACTCACCCTCCT-3'
3'-TAAGATTGAGATGGATAAGTGAAGAAATTATTTTGAGTGGGAGGA-5'
5'-ATTCTAACTCTACCTATTCACTTCTTTAATTTTCAATAACACCTC-3'
3'-TAAGATTGAGATGGATAAGTGAAGAAATTAAAAGTTATTGTGGAG-5'
5'-AACATACCCCTAATCTCTAATATAATTACTAAAACTCACCCTCCT-3'
3'-TTGTATGGGGATTAGAGATTATATTAATGATTTTGAGTGGGAGGA-5'
5'-AACATACCCCTAATCTCTAATATAATTACTTTTCAATAACACCTC-3'
3'-TTGTATGGGGATTAGAGATTATATTAATGAAAAGTTATTGTGGAG-5'
5'-AACATACCCCTAATCATTCACTTCTTTAATAAAACTCACCCTCCT-3'
3'-TTGTATGGGGATTAGTAAGTGAAGAAATTATTTTGAGTGGGAGGA-5'
5'-AACATACCCCTAATCATTCACTTCTTTAATTTTCAATAACACCTC-3'
3'-TTGTATGGGGATTAGTAAGTGAAGAAATTAAAAGTTATTGTGGAG-5'

Table 5.4. DNA sequences chosen represent all possible vertex covers.

	Enthalpy energy (H)	Entropy energy (S)	Free energy (G)
Average	108.283	282.633	23.7833
Standard deviation	3.58365	6.63867	2.41481

Table 5.5. The energy over all probe/library strand interactions.

digit electronic computer. From Theorem 4–6, if the size of a reduced NP-complete problem is equal to or less than that of the vertex-cover problem, then Cook's Theorem is right in molecular computing. Otherwise, Cook's Theorem is uncorrected in molecular computing and a new DNA algorithm should be developed from the characteristic of NP-complete problems.

Chang and Guo [12, 14] applied splints to constructing solution space of DNA sequence for solving the vertex-cover problem in the Adleman-Lipton. This causes that hybridization has higher probabilities for errors. Adleman and his co-authors [9] proposed *sticker* to decrease probabilities of errors to hybridization in the Adleman-Lipton. The main result of the proposed algorithms shows that the vertex cover problem is solved with biological operations in the Adleman-Lipton model from solution space of sticker. Furthermore, this work represents clear evidence for the ability of DNA based computing to solve NP-complete problems.

Currently, there are still lots of NP-complete problems not to be solved because it is very difficulty to basic biological operations for supporting mathematical operations. We are not sure whether molecular computing can be applied for dealing with every NP-complete problem. Therefore, in the future, our main work is to solve other NP-complete problem unsolved with the Adleman-Lipton model and the sticker model, or develop a new model.

References

[1] R. R. Sinden. *DNA Structure and Function*. Academic Press, 1994.

[2] L. Adleman. *Molecular computation of solutions to combinatorial problems*. Science, 266:1021-1024, Nov. 11, 1994.

[3] R. J. Lipton. *DNA solution of hard computational problems*. Science, 268:542:545, 1995.

[4] A. Narayanan, and S. Zorbala. DNA algorithms for computing shortest paths. *In Genetic Programming 1998: Proceedings of the Third Annual Conference*, J. R. Koza et al. (Eds), 1998, pp. 718–724.

[5] T. H. Cormen, C. E. Leiserson, and R. L. Rivest. *Introduction to algorithms*.

[6] M. R. Garey, and D. S. Johnson. *Computer and intractability. Freeman*, San Fransico, CA, 1979.

[7] D. Boneh, C. Dunworth, R. J. Lipton and J. Sgall. On the computational Power of DNA. *In Discrete Applied Mathematics, Special Issue on Computational Molecular Biology*, Vol. 71 (1996), pp. 79-94.

[8] L. M. Adleman. On constructing a molecular computer. *DNA Based Computers*, Eds. R. Lipton and E. Baum, DIMACS: series in Discrete Mathematics and Theoretical Computer Science, American Mathematical Society. 1-21 (1996)

[9] S. Roweis, E. Winfree, R. Burgoyne, N. V. Chelyapov, M. F. Goodman, Paul W.K. Rothemund and L. M. Adleman. Sticker Based Model for DNA Computation. *2nd annual workshop on DNA Computing*, Princeton University. Eds. L. Landweber and E. Baum, DIMACS: series in Discrete Mathematics and Theoretical Computer Science, American Mathematical Society. 1-29 (1999).

[10] G. Paun, G. Rozenberg and A. Salomaa. *DNA Computing: New Computing Paradigms*. Springer-Verlag, New York, 1998. ISBN: 3-540-64196-3.

[11] W.-L. Chang and M. Guo. Towards Solution of the Set-splitting Problem on Gel-based DNA Computing. *Future Generation Computer Systems*, accepted, to appear, 2004.

[12] W.-L. Chang and M. Guo. Solving the Clique Problem and the Vertex Cover Problem in Adleman-Liptons Model. *IASTED International Conference, Networks, Parallel and Distributed Processing, and Applications*, Japan, 2002, pp. 431-436.

[13] W.-L. Chang, M. Guo. Solving the Set-cover Problem and the Probram of Exact Cover by 3-sets in the Adleman-Lipton Model. *BioSystems*, Vol. 72, No. 3, pp.263–275, 2003.

[14] W.-L. Chang and M. Guo. Solving the 3-Dimensional Matching Problem and the Set Packing Problem in Adleman-Lipton's Mode. *IASTED International Conference, Networks, Parallel and Distributed Processing, and Applications*, Japan, 2002, pp. 455-460.

[15] Ravinderjit S. Braich, Clifford Johnson, Paul W.K. Rothemund, Darryl Hwang, Nickolas Chelyapov and Leonard M. Adleman.Solution of a satisfiability problem on a gel-based DNA computer. *Proceedings of the 6th International Conference on DNA Computation* in the Springer-Verlag Lecture Notes in Computer Science series.

[16] A. R. Cukras, Dirk Faulhammer, Richard J. Lipton, and Laura F. Landweber. Chess games: A model for RNA-based computation. In *Proceedings of the 4th DIMACS Meeting on DNA Based Computers*, held at the University of Pennsylvania, June 16-19, 1998, pp. 27-37.

[17] T. H. LaBean, E. Winfree and J.H. Reif. Experimental Progress in Computation by Self-Assembly of DNA Tilings. *Theoretical Computer Science*, Volume 54, pp. 123-140, (2000).

Chapter 6

A DESIGN CONCEPT OF GENERALIZED GROUP-ORIENTED CRYPTOSYSTEM WITHOUT TRUSTED PARTIES

Ren-Junn Hwang

Department of Computer Science and Information Engineering,
Tamkang University, Tamsui, Taipei, Taiwan 251, R. O. C.
junhwang@ms35.hinet.net

Chin-Chen Chang

Institute of Computer Science and Information Engineering,
National Chung Cheng University, Chiayi, Taiwan 621, R. O. C.
ccc@cs.ccu.edu.tw

Sheng-Hua Shiau

Department of Computer Science and Information Engineering,
Tamkang University, Tamsui, Taipei, Taiwan 251, R. O. C.
aaron@mail.mine.tku.edu.tw

Abstract   A special design concept to construct a generalized group-oriented cryptosystem (GGOC) is proposed in this chapter. Any group can use our design concept to construct a GGOC which provides a secure environment for a sender to send confidential messages to it. The constructed GGOC does not need the assistance of any trusted party. We also propose a practical and efficient generalized secret sharing scheme based on simple operations. We apply our design concept to construct a GGOC based on this generalized secret sharing scheme, RSA and DES. As a result, our new GGOC is simple and easy to implement in hardware. We also show that our proposed GGOC is practical and is more efficient than Chang and Lee's GGOC.

Keywords: Information security, Generalized Group-Oriented Cryptosystem, Generalized Secret Sharing Scheme

1.   Introduction

Due to the rapid prevalence of computer networks and communications, we usually prefer processing and transmitting data in computer network environments than communicating by means of traditional paperwork. In these network environments, cryptosystems are the major technique to protect confidential data from being destroyed, disclosed, or altered by unauthorized users. The conventional cryptosystems, e.g., symmetric cryptosystems and asymmetric cryptosystems, are usually only used to send confidential messages to an individual; namely, they cannot be adapted when confidential messages are intended for a group instead of an individual [7]. However, in our real world, messages are frequently addressed to a group of people, such as a board of directors. "How to transmit confidential messages to a group ?" is a very important issue. The messages, which are intended for a group, are usually divided into three types by their implicit properties [10].

(1) *important messages* : these messages are so important that only some specific subsets of the recipient group are authorized to decrypt them in order to keep the message secure.

(2) *urgent messages* : these messages are so urgent that each legal member of the recipient group is authorized to decrypt them in order to make the communication convenient and fast.

(3) *particular messages* : these messages are transmitted to an individual, so only the specific individual is authorized to decrypt them for the sake of privacy and secrecy.

The cryposystem which satisfies the preceding issues is named Group Oriented Cryptosystem(GOC)[7].

Desmedt first proposed a scheme [7] to solve the GOC problem, but, unfortunately, his scheme was impractical. However, since then, there have been many researchers [7, 8, 9, 10, 17] proposing new (k, n) threshold cryptosystems trying to solve GOC-related problems. In their (k, n) threshold cryptosystems, any k legal members of the recipient group can cooperate to decipher the encrypted message. They still cannot satisfy the need of having some specified subset of legal recipients cooperate to decipher the encrypted message. This (k, n)-threshold policy is too simple in many applications because it assumes that each member of the recipient group is equally trusted and equally authorized with regard to a same encrypted message. Benaloh and Leichter [1] showed that a (k, n) threshold scheme could only handle a small fraction of the ideal secret sharing policy which we might follow. Laih and Harn [14], however, proposed a generalized threshold cryptosystem and claimed that it could be implemented on any secret sharing policy, but Langford [12] soon pointed out that Laih and Harn's scheme is not secure for some access structures.

Chang and Lee [5] proposed a Generalized Group-Oriented Cryptosystem (GGOC) without a trusted party. The difference between GGOC and GOC is that GGOC can handle any secret sharing policy. As a matter of fact, Chang and Lee's GGOC can not only be implemented on any secret sharing policy but also work without the assistance of a trusted party. In most cryptographic applications, a trusted party does not exist in a group [11]. This situation becomes more common in commercial or international applications. Thus the GGOC without a trusted party is very attractive. However, in some cases, an undesired side effect is that the number of primes required by their scheme grows exponentially in accordance with the number of memberships [15]. In other words, Chang and Lee's scheme is neither practical nor efficient when there are many members in the recipient group. In this chapter, we propose a design concept of GGOC and the GGOC constructed by our design concept does not need the assistance of any trusted party. Each group can employ our design concept to construct a secure GGOC based on a secure generalized secret sharing scheme [1], and an asymmetric cryptoscheme, and a symmetric cryptoscheme. We shall also propose an efficient generalized secret sharing scheme and use our design concept to construct a secure GGOC based on it, RSA [18], and DES [16]. The newly proposed GGOC is practical and more efficient than Chang and Lee's GGOC.

This chapter is organized into five sections. Section 2 introduces our generalized secrete sharing scheme. The discussions and security analysis of our generalized secret sharing scheme is described in the subsection 2.2. Section 3 provides our GGOC design concept and we also apply our design concept to construct a GGOC based RSA, DES and our generalized secret sharing scheme. We discuss the security, computational and communication costs in Section 4. Finally, we make some conclusions in Section 5.

2. A New Generalized Secret Sharing Scheme

Without loss of generality, we assume that a secret K is shared by a set of n participants $U = \{U_1, U_2, \ldots, U_n\}$. The generalized secret sharing scheme is a method which divides the secret K into n shadows $K_1, K_2, \ldots, K_n$ according to the secret sharing policy. The trusted party distributes every shadow K_i to a relative participant U_i through a secure channel. Let Γ be a set of subsets of participants U, where the subsets in Γ are those subsets of U that should be able to reconstruct the secret K. Γ is named an access structure, and each element in Γ is called a qualified subset of the secret sharing policy. By the definition of the access structure Γ, these shadows have to satisfy the following conditions:

(1) If a qualified subset of participants pool their shadows, then they can reconstruct the secret K.

(2) If an unqualified subset of participants pool their shadows, then they can reconstruct nothing about the secret K.

In the following subsection, we show our generalized secret sharing scheme and analyze its security and computational cost.

2.1   Basic Scheme

The new generalized secret sharing scheme uses a publicly accessible board where the trusted party can give away true information for all the participants to access. This board is named a bulletin board. If memory and communication are inexpensive, the trusted party can transmit the true public information to the participants instead of storing it centrally. Thus, a public bulletin board is necessary for all existing secret sharing schemes to publish the access structure and the number of participants.

With this public bulletin board mechanism, our scheme can be divided into two parts: the distribution part and the reconstruction part. In the following, we shall give a general description of our scheme according to this division, where n is the number of shadows, and the access structure is Γ.

Part 1: Distribution

In this part, the trusted party generates and distributes the shadows to the participants as the following steps. Step D-1 uses a concept of super-increasing set. It is defined as follows:

Definition

Give an integer set $\{a_1, a_2, \ldots, a_n\}$. This set is named a super-increasing set if it satisfies the condition

$$\sum_{i=1}^{j-1} a_i < a_j \text{, for } 1 \le j \le n.$$

D-1. Randomly generate two distinct super-increase sets $\{a'_1, a'_2, \ldots, a'_n\}$ and $\{b'_1, b'_2, \ldots, b'_n\}$. Permute these two sets and let the new sets be $\{a_1, a_2, \ldots, a_n\}$ and $\{b_1, b_2, \ldots, b_n\}$ so that neither $< a_1, a_2, \ldots, a_n >$ nor $< b_1, b_2, \ldots, b_n >$ is an increasing or decreasing sequence.

D-2. Distribute the integer pair (a_i, b_i) to the participant U_i as her/his shadow through a secure channel.

D-3. For each access instance V in Γ, compute D_V so that

$$D_V = K - \left(\sum_{\forall U_i \in V} a_i \oplus \sum_{\forall U_i \in V} b_i \right), \tag{6.1}$$

where '$\oplus$' represents a bitwise exclusive-OR operation.

D-4. Publish D_V on the bulletin board.

Part 2: Reconstruction

In this part, any qualified subset V of participants can cooperate to reconstruct the secret K as follows:

R-1. Pool their shadows (a_i, b_i)'s together.

R-2. Get the public parameter D_V from the bulletin board.

R-3. Reconstruct

$$K = D_V + \left(\sum_{\forall U_i \in V} a_i \oplus \sum_{\forall U_i \in V} b_i \right). \tag{6.2}$$

In Equations (6.1) and (6.2), we should alter some data types. First, the results of $\sum_{\forall U_i \in V} a_i$ and $\sum_{\forall U_i \in V} b_i$ are two integers, their types should be changed to the binary form with the same bit length before performing the exclusive-OR operation. Second, the binary result of $\left(\sum_{\forall U_i \in V} a_i \oplus \sum_{\forall U_i \in V} b_i \right)$ should be changed to the integer type. Finally, we perform the subtraction and addition operations to get K and D_V respectively.

2.2   Discussions and Security Analysis

It is obvious that the computational cost of our generalized secret sharing scheme depends on Steps D-1, D-3 and R-3. Step D-1 takes $2 \times n$ arithmetic additions to generate two distinct super-increase sets. Both Equation (6.1) of Step D-3 and Equation (6.2) of Step R-3 use only simple operations: arithmetic additions and bitwise exclusive-OR operations. As a result, our GGOC scheme is easy to implement in hardware. Incontestably, our scheme is practical and efficient.

The proposed scheme requires a public bulletin to publish information, e. g. access structure Γ and the parameter D_V for each qualified subset V. All participants can access the information, and yet the integrity and authenticity of such information are still assured. Cachin [3] pointed out that such a public bulletin is necessary for all the existing secret sharing schemes nowadays, and yet it contains at least the access structure and the number of participants. However, the access structure is a set of all qualified subsets, our generalized secret sharing scheme only adds a parameter D_V to each qualified subset V. It does not increase many burdens to the public bulletin. If there are many qualified subsets in the access structure, the public bulletin will be very large. It seems to be inefficient in this case, but all the generalized secret sharing schemes have this common drawback. Moreover, if the access structure includes all the k out of n participants subsets as the qualified subsets, we suggest that the user uses the (k, n) threshold schemes which will be more efficient than she/he uses any generalized secret sharing scheme.

In many generalized secret sharing schemes, e. g. Benaloh and Leichter [1], and Blundo et al.[2], each participant holds many integers as her/his shadows to share a secret with other participants, that the number of shadows held by each participant is dependent on the access structure. Each participant has to remember that each shadow she/he held is used in which qualified subset. In our scheme, each participant only holds two integers as her/his shadow and she/he can use these two integers to cooperate with other participants to recover the shared secret based on any qualified subset.

The security analysis of the generalized secret sharing scheme shall focus on whether an unqualified subset Q of participants can reconstruct the secret K. Theorem 1 proves that the participants of the unqualified subset Q can not reconstruct the shared secret by themselves.

Theorem 1.

The participants of the unqualified subset can not reconstruct the shared secret by using their shadows directly.

Proof:

By Equation (6.2), if the unqualified subset Q wants to reconstruct the shared secret K, they must know the correct parameter D_Q. Since the subset Q is unqualified, the dealer does not generate D_Q in the distribution part. Nobody knows this value D_Q. Clearly, the participants of the unqualified subset Q can reconstruct the shared secret K by using their shadows.   Q.E.D.

The unqualified subset Q may try to use the public information to reconstruct the shared secret. However, Theorem 5 proves that they also can not reconstruct the shared secret K by using the public information. Before describing Theorem 5, Theorem 2, Lemma 3 and Theorem 4 show some results which are used to prove Theorem 5.

Theorem 2.

Let us randomly select some distinct integers from a given super-increasing set $\{a_1, a_2, \ldots, a_n\}$ to form two integer sets $\{a_{i_1}, a_{i_2}, \ldots, a_{i_s}\}$ and $\{a_{j_1}, a_{j_2}, \ldots, a_{j_t}\}$, where $1 \leq s \leq n$ and $1 \leq t \leq n$. If $\{a_{i_1}, a_{i_2}, \ldots, a_{i_s}\} \neq \{a_{j_1}, a_{j_2}, \ldots, a_{j_t}\}$, then $\sum_{k=1}^{s} a_{i_k} \neq \sum_{k=1}^{t} a_{j_k}$.

Lemma 3.

Give $(a_1 + a_2) \oplus (b_1 + b_2) = c$. Let d be the maximal bit length of $(a_1 + a_2)$ and $(b_1 + b_2)$, then $(k \times 2^d + a_1 + a_2) \oplus (k \times 2^d + b_1 + b_2)$ equals c for any arbitrary positive integer k.

Proof:

By the format of binary bits, the first d bits of $(k \times 2^d + a_1 + a_2)$ are equal to the first d bits of $(k \times 2^d + b_1 + b_2)$ for any arbitrary positive integer k. The exclusive-OR of these d bits are '0' bits. Thus we conclude that $(k \times 2^d + a_1 + a_2) \oplus (k \times 2^d + b_1 + b_2) = c$ for any arbitrary positive integer k. $\qquad$ Q.E.D.

Theorem 4.

Let V, Q' and Q'' be subsets of participants with $V \cap Q = \phi$ and $V \cup Q' \in \Gamma$, $V \cup Q'' \in \Gamma$ for $Q', Q'' \subset Q$, and $Q' \neq Q''$. Given two pairs, $(\sum_{\forall U_i \in Q'} a_i, \sum_{\forall U_i \in Q'} b_i)$ and $(\sum_{\forall U_i \in Q''} a_i, \sum_{\forall U_i \in Q''} b_i)$, then the number of possible pairs $(\sum_{\forall U_i \in V} a_i, \sum_{\forall U_i \in V} b_i)$'s which satisfy Equation (6.3) is infinite.

$$
D_{V \cup Q'} - D_{V \cup Q''} = \left(\sum_{\forall U_i \in V} a_i, \sum_{\forall U_i \in Q'} a_i \right) \oplus \left(\sum_{\forall U_i \in V} b_i, \sum_{\forall U_i \in Q'} b_i \right)
$$
$$
- \left(\sum_{\forall U_i \in V} a_i, \sum_{\forall U_i \in Q''} a_i \right) \oplus \left(\sum_{\forall U_i \in V} b_i, \sum_{\forall U_i \in Q''} b_i \right). \quad (6.3)
$$

Proof:

Let $(\sum_{\forall U_i \in Q'} a_i, \sum_{\forall U_i \in Q'} b_i) = (G'_1, G'_2)$, $(\sum_{\forall U_i \in Q''} a_i, \sum_{\forall U_i \in Q''} b_i) = (G''_1, G''_2)$, and $(\sum_{\forall U_i \in V} a_i, \sum_{\forall U_i \in V} b_i) = (X_1, X_2)$. Then Equation (6.3) can be rewritten as

$$
D = ((X_1 + G'_1) \oplus (X_2 + G'_2)) - ((X_1 + G''_1) \oplus (X_2 + G''_2)). \quad (6.4)
$$

And we also know the values of G'_1, G'_2, G''_1, G''_2, and D. Let's assume that the pair (h_1, h_2) is one solution of (X_1, X_2) for Equation (6.4). Let d be the maximal bit length among $(h_1 + G'_1)$, $(h_2 + G'_2)$, $(h_1 + G''_1)$, and $(h_2 + G''_2)$. By Lemma 3, we know that the pairs $(k \times 2^d + h_1, k \times 2^d + h_2)$'s for all positive integer k's are solutions of (X_1, X_2) for Equation (6.4), too. In other words, the number of pairs (X_1, X_2)'s for Equation (6.4) is infinite. So, we conclude that the number of possible pairs $(\sum_{\forall U_i \in V} a_i, \sum_{\forall U_i \in V} b_i)$'s which satisfy Equation (6.3) is infinite. $\qquad$ Q.E.D.

Theorem 5.

The participants of the unqualified subset Q can not reconstruct the shared secret K by using the public information.

Proof:

By Equation (6.1), the difference between the secret K and the public parameter D_V is equal to $(\sum_{\forall U_i \in V} a_i \oplus \sum_{\forall U_i \in V} b_i)$, which is based on the mixing operations from different algebraic groups. These two kinds of operations, the bitwise exclusive-OR and the summation, are incompatible. We prove that $(\sum_{\forall U_i \in V} a_i \neq \sum_{\forall U_i \in W} a_i)$ and $(\sum_{\forall U_i \in V} b_i \neq \sum_{\forall U_i \in W} b_i)$ for all $V \neq W$ in Theorem 2. So the unqualified subset cannot reconstruct secret K

by exploiting one equation alone. However, the unqualified subset Q can link several equations through K or through $(\sum_{\forall U_i \in V} a_i \oplus \sum_{\forall U_i \in V} b_i)$. Linking two equations via K, they can get relations of the form

$$D_V - D_W = (\sum_{\forall U_i \in V} a_i \oplus \sum_{\forall U_i \in V} b_i) - (\sum_{\forall U_i \in W} a_i \oplus \sum_{\forall U_i \in W} b_i),$$

where V and W are any qualified subsets. Because the operation pair (bitwise exclusive-OR, summation) does not satisfy the distribution law and the association law, the members of Q cannot derive the value on the right-hand side of the equation above. Except for a single special case that $\sum_{\forall U_i \in V} a_i \oplus \sum_{\forall U_i \in V} b_i = \sum_{\forall U_i \in W} a_i \oplus \sum_{\forall U_i \in W} b_i$, which can be recognized on the bulletin by $D_V = D_W$, those linkings are of no use at all.

At the same time, the unqualified subset Q can link two equations via $\sum_{\forall U_i \in V} a_i \oplus \sum_{\forall U_i \in V} b_i$; they can obtain another relation

$$D_{V \cup Q'} - D_{V \cup Q''} = (\sum_{\forall U_i \in V} a_i, \sum_{\forall U_i \in Q'} a_i) \oplus (\sum_{\forall U_i \in V} b_i, \sum_{\forall U_i \in Q'} b_i)$$
$$- (\sum_{\forall U_i \in V} a_i, \sum_{\forall U_i \in Q''} a_i) \oplus (\sum_{\forall U_i \in V} b_i, \sum_{\forall U_i \in Q''} b_i). \quad (6.5)$$

where $V \cap Q = \phi$ and $V \cup Q' \in \Gamma$, $V \cup Q'' \in \Gamma$ for $Q', Q'' \subset Q$, and $Q' \neq Q''$. By Theorem 4, the members of the unqualified subset Q can compute infinite possible values for the unknown pair $(\sum_{\forall U_i \in V} a_i, \sum_{\forall U_i \in V} b_i)$ which satisfies Equation (6.5). However, the probability for the members of the unqualified subset Q to get the right pair $(\sum_{\forall U_i \in V} a_i, \sum_{\forall U_i \in V} b_i)$ which satisfies Equation (6.5) is very small. Thus the participants of the unqualified subset Q can hardly compute anything by using the public information.　　　　　　　Q.E.D. By Theorems 1 and 5, it is clearly that the participants in any unqualified subset can not recover the shared secret.

Theorem 6.

Suppose $\{a_1, a_2, \ldots, a_n\}$ is a super-increase set. Let $|a_1| = d$ and $|a_i| - \sum_{j=1}^{i-1} |a_j| = e > 0$, for $i = 2, 3, \ldots, n$, where $|x|$ denotes the bit length of x. Then $|a_h| = 2^{h-2}(d + e)$, for $h = 2, 3, \ldots, n$.

Proof:

1) Basis step: Since $|a_1| = d$, $|a_2| = d + e = 2^{2-2}(d + e)$ is clearly valid.
2) Inductive step: Assume that $|a_k| = 2^{k-2}(d + e)$ for some $k > 1$.

$$\text{Then } |a_{k+1}| \; = \; \sum_{j=1}^{k-1} |a_j| + e$$

$$= \; d + (d+e) + 2(d+e) + \ldots + 2^{k-2}(d+e) + e$$

$$= \; (d+e) + (d+e)(1 + 2 + \ldots + 2^{k-2}) = 2^{k-1}(d+e)$$

Hence, by the principle of finite induction, we conclude that $|a_h| = 2^{h-2}(d+e)$, for $h = 2, 3, \ldots, n$. $\hfill Q.E.D.$

It is not easily to exactly derive the relation between the bit length of each integer in the super-increase set and the number of elements in this set. Theorem 6 shows one case of the super-increase set. Let a_n be the largest integer of this set. The bit length of a_n is $2^{n-2}(d+e)$ in the case as Theorem 6. It will be large when n is large. The proposed scheme may be not practical in this case. However, many cryptographic techniques shall use a long binary bit string as the secret key or password against the brute-force attack. We suggest use the magnetic card to keep these shadows when they are large. In the GGOC of Section 3, the sender shall encrypt the shadows and send them with the ciphertext to the recipient group. The participants of the recipient group do not need to keep their shadows. Although the shadows are large, they do not affect the practicability of the application of Section 3.

In the case of Theorem 6, the difference of $|a_i|$ and $\sum_{j=1}^{i-1} |a_j|$ is a fixed value e, but Step D-1 should permute these integers before distributing them to the participants. It does not affect the security of the proposed scheme. Additionally, the attacker does not know d and e. It is hard for the attacker to derive these n integers from the large interval $(1, 2^{2^{n-2}(d+e)})$. Although d and e are small, the proposed scheme is still secure. In other word, the smallest integer of the su-per-increase set can be small.

Like many secret sharing schemes, we assume all of the participants pool their true shadows in Step R-1. In order to enhance the security, our scheme can be combined with other cheater detection schemes [4, 19] to check the validity of the shadows in Step R-1.

3.   The Design Concept of GGOC

In this section, we shall propose a design concept of constructing GGOC. The inspiration comes from Chang and Lee's GGOC [5]. The design concept to be proposed is built on three schemes: the generalized secret sharing scheme, the asymmetric cryptoscheme, and the symmetric cryptoscheme. Each group can put any set of a generalized secret sharing scheme, an asymmetric cryptoscheme, and a symmetric cryptoscheme under our design concept to construct a GGOC. The GGOC thus constructed does not need the assistance of a trusted party. The GGOC constructed by our design concept uses the selected generalized secret sharing scheme to make sure that only the qualified subset can read the sent message. The selected asymmetric cryptoscheme is used as a channel to send some secret information and the symmetric cryptoscheme is used to encrypt the sent message. In order to illustrate our idea clearly, we make an example of constructing a GGOC based on RSA [18], DES [16], and our generalized secret sharing scheme.

Two roles, the sender and the recipient group, appear in a GGOC issue. The recipient group selects and publishes one asymmetric cryptoscheme, one symmetric cryptoscheme, and one generalized secret sharing scheme in the initialization phase. Each member of the recipient group generates her/his public key and secret key based on the selected asymmetric cryptoscheme and then publishes her/his public key on the public bulletin. As a generalized secret sharing scheme is all about, we also use an access structure Γ to show which recipients can cooperate to decrypt the encrypted message in the GGOC. In our design concept, if the access structure is decided by the recipient group, then they have to publish their access structure on the public bulletin in the initialization phase. Otherwise, if the access structure of each message is dynamic and dependent on the sent message, then the access structure is decided by the sender. The sender shall send, or publish, the access structure Γ with its corresponding message.

Let's first define some notations used in the example of constructing GGOC as follows:

(1) $E_k(M)$: the encryption function of DES, where k is the encryption key and M is the plaintext.

(2) $D_k(C)$: the decryption function of DES, where k is the decryption key and C is the ciphertext.

(3) $PE_{p_k}(M)$: the encryption function of RSA, where p_k is the public key and M is the plaintext.

(4) $PD_{s_k}(C)$: the decryption function of RSA, where s_k is the secret key and C is the ciphertext.

In the initialization phase, each member U_i of the recipient group selects her/his secret key s_{k_i} and public key p_{k_i} based on RSA. She/he also publishes her/his public key in the bulletin.

In the following paragraph, we show how to use the GGOC based on our design concept to send a message M to a recipient group in three cases according to their implicit properties. We illustrate our idea by using RSA as the asymmetric cryptoscheme, DES as the symmetric cryptoscheme and our generalized secret sharing scheme proposed in Section 2 as the selected generalized secret sharing scheme. Practically, the interested reader can construct a new GGOC by replacing each scheme with another cognate scheme.

Case 1: M is an *important message*.

The message is so important that only some specific subsets of the recipient group are authorized to decrypt it. The sender encrypts and sends this message as follows:

(1) Select a private key K based on DES and compute $C = E_K(M)$.

(2) Construct the access structure Γ to specify the qualified subsets V's of the recipient group which are authorized to read this message. Alternatively, if Γ is specified by the recipient group, she/he gets Γ from the bulletin.

(3) Randomly generate two distinct super-increase sets $\{a'_1, a'_2, \ldots, a'_n\}$ and $\{b'_1, b'_2, \ldots, b'_n\}$. Permute these two sets and let the new sets be $\{a_1, a_2, \ldots, a_n\}$ and $\{b_1, b_2, \ldots, b_n\}$ so that neither $< a_1, a_2, \ldots, a_n >$ nor $< b_1, b_2, \ldots, b_n >$ is an increasing or decreasing sequence.

(4) Compute a pair (A_i, B_i) for each member U_i of the recipient group so that $A_i = PE_{pk_i}(a_i)$ and $B_i = PE_{pk_i}(b_i)$.

(5) Send the pair (A_i, B_i) to U_i, or, alternatively, the sender can use the Chinese Remainder Theorem to integrate all (A_i, B_i)'s into an integer pair and then transmit this integer pair to the recipient group or publish it on the bulletin instead of transmitting the cipher (A_i, B_i) to the member U_i individually.

(6) For each access instance V in the access structure Γ, compute and put a parameter D_V on the bulletin board so that

$$D_V = K - \left(\sum_{\forall U_i \in V} a_i \oplus \sum_{\forall U_i \in V} b_i \right).$$

(7) Send the ciphertext C to the recipient group.

Any qualified subset V of the recipient group can cooperate to decrypt the ciphertext C as follows:

(1) Generate the shadow (a_i, b_i) of each participant U_i in V by

$$a_i = PD_{s_{k_i}}(A_i) \text{ and } b_{n-i+1} = PD_{s_{k_i}}(B_i).$$

(2) Pool all the shadows (a_i, b_i)'s together.

(3) Get the public parameter D_V from the bulletin board.

(4) Reconstruct $K = D_V + \left(\sum_{\forall U_i \in V} a_i \oplus \sum_{\forall U_i \in V} b_i \right)$.

(5) Read the message M by $M = D_K(C)$.

Case 2: M is an *urgent message.*

The message M is so urgent that any legal member of the recipient group is authorized to decrypt it. The sender encrypts and transmits the message M as follows:

(1) Select a private key K based on DES.

(2) Compute $C = E_K(M)$.

(3) Compute S_i for each member U_i of the recipient group so that $S_i = PE_{pk_i}(K)$.

(4) Send S_i to U_i. Or, alternatively, use the Chinese Remainder Theorem to integrate all of these ciphers S_i's into one integer and then transmit this integer to the recipient group or publish it on the bulletin instead of transmitting the cipher S_i to the member U_i individually.

(5) Transmit the cipher C to the recipient group.

Each member of the recipient group can decrypt the ciphertext C as follows:

(1) Generate the private key K by $K = PD_{sk_i}(S_i)$.

(2) Read the message M by $M = D_K(C)$.

Case 3: M is an *particular message.*

The sender wants to send a particular message M to a particular member U_i of the recipient group, she/he encrypts and transmits the message M as follows:

(1) Retrieve the member U_i's public key pk_i from the public bulletin.

(2) Encrypt the message M by $C = PE_{pk_i}(M)$.

(3) Send the ciphertext to the recipient group.

The particular member U_i can read the message M by $M = PD_{sk_i}(C)$.

4.   Discussions

In many generalized secret sharing schemes, it is assumed that there is a trusted party who is responsible for generating and distributing a shadow to each participant according to the access structure and the shared secret. As for our design concept, by Step (2) of the Case 1, the sender shall make her-/himself responsible for generating and distributing shadows. That is why the GGOC based on our design concept does not need the assistance of the trusted party.

The security and the computational cost of the GGOC based on our design concept is dependent on the security and the computational cost of the

Table 6.1.   The comparison between our GGOC and Chang and Lee's GGOC.

types of messages		Schemes	our scheme	Chang and Lee's scheme
particular message	computational operations	sender	RSA	RSA
		recipient	RSA	RSA
	communication cost		$|N|$ bits	$|N|$ bits
urgent message	computational operations	sender	RSA+DES	RSA+DES
		recipient	RSA+DES	RSA+DES
	communication cost		$|N| \times n + |C|$ bits	$|N| \times n + |C|$ bits
important message	computational operations	sender	RSA+DES + addition + bitwise exclusive-OR	RSA+DES + multiplication + modular exponentiation
		recipient	RSA+DES + addition + bitwise exclusive-OR	RSA+DES + addition + multiplication + modular exponentiation
	communication cost		$2 \times n \times |N| + |C| + |I| \times |D|$ bits	$2 \times n \times |N| + |C| + |I| \times |D|$ bits

selected asymmetric cryptoscheme, symmetric cryptoscheme and generalized secret sharing scheme. Both of the asymmetric cryptoscheme and the symmetric cryptoscheme have efficient and secure commercial products such as RSA and DES. The analyses of the security and the computational cost of the newly constructed GGOC focus on the selected generalized secret sharing scheme. We have shown that our generalized secret sharing scheme is secure and efficient in Section 2. So the constructed GGOC in Section 3 is naturally secure and efficient.

Without loss of generality, we assume there are n members in the recipient group and the size of the confidential message is less than the block size of the RSA and DES. We also assume that the cipher of RSA is $|N|$ bits and the cipher of DES is $|C|$ bits. The communication cost of the newly GGOC is shown in Table 6.1. Moreover, Table 6.1 also shows the comparison of computational operations and communication cost between our GGOC and Chang and Lee's GGOC. It is clear that our GGOC is more efficient than Chang and Lee's GGOC. In Table 6.1, $|\Gamma|$ denotes the number of qualified subsets in access structure and $|D|$ denotes the average size of the public parameter D of Equation (6.1).

5.   Conclusions

This chapter propose a design concept to construct a GGOC. The GGOC provides a secure environment for a sender to send confidential messages to a group. We also propose a secure and efficient generalized secret sharing scheme. This generalized secret sharing scheme is based on simple operations. Furthermore, we use our design concept to construct a GGOC based on our generalized secret sharing scheme, RSA, and DES. The newly constructed GGOC has following properties:

1. It is more efficient than Chang and Lee's GGOC.

2. It only uses simple operations: additions and bitwise exclusive-OR operations.

3. It is easy to implement in hardware.

4. It does not need the assistance of a trusted party.

5. It permits the sender to specify qualified subsets of recipients.

6. It permits the sender to renew the encryption/decryption keys so as send to the confidential message in each transmission.

References

[1] Benaloh, J. and Leichter, J. "Generalized Secret Sharing and Monotone Functions," *Advances in Cryptology: Crypto'88*, New York: Springer-Verlag, 1989, pp. 27-35.

[2] Blundo, C., Santis, A. D., Crescenzo, G. D., Gaggia, A. G., and Vaccaro, U. "Multi-Secret Sharing Schemes," *Advances in Cryptology: Crypto'94*, New York: Springer-Verlag, 1995, pp. 150-163.

[3] Cachin, C. "On-line Secret Sharing," *Cryptography and Coding*, Springer-Verlag, Berlin, 1994, pp. 190-198.

[4] Chang, C. C. and Hwang, R. J. "An Efficient Cheater Identification Method for Threshold Schemes," *IEE Proceedings- Computers and Digital Techniques*, vol. 144, No. 1, 1997, pp.23-27.

[5] Chang, C. C. and Lee, H. C. "A New Generalized Group-Oriented Cryptoscheme Without Trusted Centers," *IEEE Journal on Selected Areas in Communications*, Vol. 11, No. 5, 1993, pp. 725-729.

[6] Denning, D. E. *Cryptography and Data Security*, Addison Wesely, Mass., 1982.

[7] Desmedt, Y. "Society and Group Oriented Cryptography: A New Concept," *Advances in Cryptology: Crypto'87*, New York: Springer-Verlag, 1988, pp. 120-127.

[8] Desmedt, Y. and Frankel, Y. "Threshold Cryptosystems," *Advances in Cryptology: Crypto'89*, New York: Springer-Verlag, 1989, pp. 307-315.

[9] Frankel, Y. "A Practical Protocol for Large Group Oriented Networks," *Advances in Cryp-tology: Eurpocrypt'89*, New York: Springer-Verlag, 1990, pp. 56-61.

[10] Hwang, T. "Cryptosystem for Group Oriented Cryptography," *Advances in Cryptology:Eurocrypt'90*, New York: Springer-Verlag, 1990, pp. 317-324.

[11] Ingemarsson, I. and Simmons, G. L. "A Protocol to Set up Shared Secret Schemes without the Assistance of a Mutually Trusted Party," *Advances in Cryptology:Eurocrypt'90*, New York: Springer-Verlag, 1990, pp. 266-282.

[12] Langford, S. K. "Weaknesses in Some Threshold Cryptosystems," *Advances in Cryptology: Crypto'96*, New York: Springer-Verlag, 1996, pp. 74-82.

[13] Lai, X. *On the Design and Security of Block Ciphers*, ETH Series in Information Processing, Konstanz: Hartung-Gorre Verlag, 1992.

[14] Laih, C. and Harn, L. "Generalized Threshold Cryptosystems," *Advances in Cryptology:Asiacrypt'91*, New York: Springer-Verlag, 1993, pp. 159-166.

[15] Lin, H. Y. and Harn, L. "A Cheater Resistant Generalized Secret Sharing Scheme," *Advances in Cryptology:Asiacrypt'91*, New York: Springer-Verlag, 1993, pp. 149-158.

[16] NBS FIPs PUB 46, "Data Encryption Standard," *National Bureau of Standards*, U. S. Department of Commerce, Jan. 1977.

[17] Pedersen, T. "A Threshold Cryptosystem without a Trusted Party," *Advances in Cryptology:Eurocrypt'91*, New York: Springer-Verlag, 1992, pp. 522-526.

[18] Rivest, R. L., Shamir, A. and Adleman, L. "A Method for Obtaining Digital Signatures and Public Key Cryptosystems," *Communications of ACM*, Vol. 21, No. 2, 1978, pp. 120-126.

[19] Wu, T. C. and Wu, T. S. "Cheating Detection and Cheater Identification in Secret Sharing Schemes," *IEE Proceedings- Computers and Digital Techniques*, Vol. 142, No. 5, 1995, pp.367-369.

Chapter 7

SCHEDULING PARALLEL TASKS ONTO NUMA MULTIPROCESSORS WITH INTER-PROCESSOR COMMUNICATION OVERHEAD

Guan-Joe Lai

National Taichung Teachers College, Taichung, Taiwan, R.O.C.

gjlai@mail.ntctc.edu.tw

Abstract   This chapter addresses the problem of scheduling tasks in the Non-Uniform Memory Access (NUMA) multiprocessor system with a bounded number of available processors. An algorithm is proposed here to schedule tasks by considering the intertask communication overhead and the contentions among communication channels. Communication contentions arise from the communication medium having insufficient capacity to serve all transmissions, causing significant contention delays. The proposed algorithm also exploits the schedule-holes in schedules; therefore, it could produce better schedules than that produced by existing algorithms. In this chapter, a sharper bound in the multiprocessor scheduling problem with the consideration of the communication delay is also shown. The proposed algorithm ensures performance within a factor of two times of the optimum scheduled lengths for general directed acyclic task graphs. Experimental results demonstrate the superiority of the proposed algorithm over that presented in literature.

Keywords: scheduling, NUMA, multiprocessor, communication, directed acyclic graph.

Introduction

Scalable shared-memory multiprocessors are emerging as attractive platforms for parallel applications. Examples of such architectures include the Data General nuSMP [1], HP/Convex Exemplar [3], Sequent STiNG [15], and SGI Origin 2000 [10]. What makes these machines attractive is the shared address space. In such a paradigm, programmers could write parallel programs easier, but still require substantial tuning effort to reduce the impact of long-latency memory accesses. The difficulty lies in the fact that both data

and programs must be partitioned and then distributed to processors for efficient parallel execution, resulting in communication overhead [9, 14]. The latency and bandwidth limitations induced by the interconnection network could
seriously degrade the gain obtained by parallelization. Additionally, access
contentions by several processors for the shared communication media (e.g.,
switches, memory modules, etc.) could further exacerbate the communication
time. Therefore, to exploit the potential of parallel processing, the scheduling
algorithms must be developed. Such algorithms allocate tasks to processors,
and determine the execution order to attain the minimum completion time.
This problem is usually considered as the multiprocessor scheduling problem.
However, it is recognized that certain relaxed or simplified cases of scheduling problems still fall into the class of NP-hard problems [9]. Consequently,
previous efforts have focused on finding heuristics for obtaining satisfactory
solutions in a reasonable time complexity.

Several researchers have studied the scheduling problem. For instance,
MCP [12] algorithm and Hwang's ETF algorithm [9] schedule tasks under the
assumption that the number of processors is limited. Kwok and Ahmad proposed two algorithms, DCP [18] and FASTEST [8], under the condition that
the number of processors is unlimited; Yang and Gerasoulis also presented
DSC [16] in the same assumption. Dynamic Level Scheduling (DLS) [4] and
MH [6] algorithms were introduced for arbitrary processor network architecture. In addition, MJD [11] and CPFD [7] algorithms were task-duplication-
based algorithms.

However, none of the above works considers the impact of the communication contention. They schedule tasks to attain the minimal completion time
for programs based on the macro-dataflow [17] model. In such a model, a
task node starts the execution after receiving all the necessary input operands
from its input edges, and then exports the computed results simultaneously
through its output edges. The assumption that there is no contention among
communication channels in this model is not reasonable [13]. Consequently,
the scheduled tasks cannot be adequately executed in real multiprocessor systems. Selvakumar and Siva [14] presented an algorithm for scheduling tasks
by considering the intertask communications and the contentions in communication channels. However, the disadvantages of their approach are that a) the
time complexity is apparently of a high order, and b) additional space is needed
for keeping free time slot lists.

An algorithm referred to as the Task Scheduling with Communication Contentions (TSCC) algorithm is presented here. The TSCC algorithm exploits the
schedule-holes [14] in schedules. It schedules tasks by considering the non-
negligible intertask communication and takes account of the communication
contentions created by data exchange. Communication contentions arise from
the communication medium having insufficient capacity to serve all transmissions, causing significant contention delays. In this chapter, a sharper bound
in the multiprocessor scheduling problem with the consideration of the com-

munication overhead is also shown. It is meaningful not only theoretically but also practically to give a better lower bound for evaluating the accuracy of the resultant heuristic solution more precisely. It could prune a larger number of meaningless branches that will never lead to an optimal solution under the branch-and-bound paradigm and even in the solution-based heuristic methods. For the comparative demonstration of the proposed algorithm's effectiveness, we apply two conventional algorithms. The experimental results reveal the superiority of our algorithm over that compared.

The rest of this chapter is organized as follows. Section 2 introduces the preliminaries and related works. Section 3 presents the proposed algorithm, and section 4 shows the lower performance bound. Experimental results are provided in section 5. Concluding remarks are finally made.

1. Preliminaries and Related Works

Previous works [8, 16, 18] assumed that there is an infinite number of processors such that the potential for exploiting the maximum parallelism within parallel programs could be investigated. However, it is impossible that the number of processors is infinite in real multiprocessor systems. The problem of exploiting schedule-hole [14] arises when the processor number is limited. Therefore, these algorithms could not be applied to the scheduling problem on a bounded number of processors.

This section opens with the description of the program model called the Shared Communication Resource (SCR) model [5], which enlarges the macro-dataflow program description to allow the employment of scheduling heuristics in NUMA systems. The SCR model is formally described as follows.

A program is represented as a directed acyclic graph (DAG) based on the SCR model. The DAG is defined by a quintuple $G=(N_t, N_s, E, C, T)$, where N_t is the set of tasks, N_s is the set of SCR nodes, C is the set of communication volumes, T is the set of computation costs, and E is the set of communication edges which define a partial order or precedence constraints on $N_t \cup N_s$. There is no communication edge between n_i and n_j, when $n_i, n_j \in N_t$ or $n_i, n_j \in N_s$. The value of $c_{ij} \in C$ is the communication volume occurring along the edge $e_{ij} \in E$, either $n_i \in N_t, n_j \in N_s$ or $n_i \in N_s, n_j \in N_t$. The value $\tau_i \in T$ is the computation time for node $n_i \in N_t$, and $\tau_i=0$ for all $n_i \in N_s$. When there is data dependence between tasks n_i and n_j, where $n_i, n_j \in N_t$, there exists a node $n_s \in N_s$ such that $e_{is}, e_{sj} \in E$.

In SCR model, a task is an indivisible unit of computation; once the task execution begins, it must continue to completion without interruption. Only one task at a time can access data from one SCR node. Two independent tasks must therefore access data from the same SCR node in sequence, making resource contention issue. Task execution is triggered by satisfying precedence constraints and by removing resource contentions. Precedence constraints occur when the execution of one task must be postponed until the arrival of all necessary data. The two kinds of resource contentions are that (a) a task executing contention, in which a task's execution must be deferred until all the tasks scheduled before it within the same processor complete their execution, and (b) a communication contention, in which data are received sequentially from the same communication channel, i.e., a task cannot receive data from all its predecessors simultaneously. Synchronization is just represented by a communication edge with zero data size. This is because that the synchronization overhead could not be obtained at the compile-time. However, we will study this problem in the future work. Experimental results [5] show that the adoption of the SCR model could achieve more realistic outcomes for the clustering/scheduling problem in NUMA systems.

Suppose next that a NUMA system is homogeneous, and that the communication is half-duplex. Each processor has a co-processor to deal with communications, which allows computations and communications that are independent of each other to be overlapped. Formally, let $P=\{p_i|\ i=1, \ldots, |P|\}$, $|P|$ ¡ ∞, be the set of homogeneous processors. Let $P(n_i)$ be the processor allocated by n_i, and $\eta(p_i, p_j)$ denote the latency required to transfer a message unit from p_i to p_j, where $p_i, p_j \in$ P.

Given a DAG and a system as described above, this problem is to obtain a non-preemptive schedule with the minimal completion time. To simplify the analysis, we neglect the additional overhead of transforming a serial algorithm into a parallel form, and assume that no additional processing cost is required to execute programs in multiprocessor systems. To avoid high complexity, only the non-backtracking approach is considered here. Aiming to simplify it, only two kinds of communication latencies are considered. Let $M=\{L_l, L_r\}$ be the set of latencies, where $L_l=\eta(p_i, p_i)$, $p_i \in$P, is the intraprocessor latency; and $L_r=\eta(p_i, p_j)$, where $p_i, p_j \in$P, and i$\neq$j, is the interprocessor latency.

Formally, let $N = N_t \cup N_s$, and $pred(n_i)$ be the set of immediate predecessors of n_i. After satisfying the precedence constraints and removing the communication contentions, the earliest starting time of node n_j, $est(n_j)$, is the earliest time when node n_j can start the execution. $\forall n_i \in pred(n_j)$, the earliest completion time of node n_i is defined as follows:

$$ect(n_i) = est(n_i) + \tau_i. \tag{7.1}$$

Let $succ(n_i)$ be the set of immediate successors of n_i and $lmt(P(n_i))$ be the last message time of the processor, which n_i is allocated. Consequently, the earliest starting transmission time of edge e_{ij} is defined as follows:

$$estt(e_{ij}) = max(ect(n_i), lmt(P(n_i))). \tag{7.2}$$

For node n_j, we claim that a chain of communication edges can be found as $X_j : e_{1j} \rightarrow e_{2j} \rightarrow \ldots \rightarrow e_{qj}$, such that $estt(e_{1j}) \leq estt (e_{2j}) \leq \ldots \leq estt(e_{qj})$, where $n_1, n_2, \ldots, n_q \in pred(n_j)$. Let $icti(e_{kj}, e_{ij})$ denote the idle communication time interval between two communication edges, e_{kj} and e_{ij}, in the chain X_j, $1 \leq k < i \leq q$; mathematically,

$$icti(e_{kj}, e_{ij}) = \begin{cases} 0, & \text{if } \Gamma < 0; \\ \Gamma, & \text{otherwise,} \end{cases} \qquad (7.3)$$

where $\Gamma = estt(e_{ij}) - estt(e_{kj}) - c_{kj} \times \eta(P(n_k), P(n_j))$. The idle communication time before the communication edge e_{ij} is defined to be $\Omega(e_{ij}) = min(icti(e_{kj}, e_{ij}))$, $1 \leq k < i$. Thus, $\forall n_i \in pred(n_j)$,

$$est(n_j) = max \begin{cases} min(estt(e_{ij})) + \sum(c_{ij} \times \eta(P(n_i), P(n_j)) + \Omega(e_{ij})), \\ max(estt(e_{ij}) + c_{ij} \times \eta(P(n_i), P(n_j))). \end{cases}$$
$$(7.4)$$

Let $st(e_{ij})$ denote the starting time for e_{ij} after scheduling; mathematically, $\forall n_k \in pred(n_j)$,

$$st(e_{ij}) = max \begin{cases} min(estt(e_{kj})) + \sum(c_{kj} \times \eta(P(n_k), P(n_j)) + \Omega(e_{kj})), \\ max(estt(e_{kj}) + c_{kj} \times \eta(P(n_k), P(n_j))), \end{cases}$$
$$(7.5)$$

where $1 \leq k < i \leq q$ in the chain X_j.

The least completion time of node n_i, $lct(n_i)$, is the longest execution time from this node to the sink node. Formally, $\forall n_i \in N$,

$$lct(n_i) = max(c_{ij} \times L_l + \tau_j + lct(n_j)), \qquad (7.6)$$

where $\forall n_j \in succ(n_i)$.

Initially, $\forall n_i \in N$ and $pred(n_i) = \emptyset$, let $est(n_i) = 0$.

2. TSCC Algorithm

The TSCC algorithm exploits the schedule-holes in schedules by considering the communication overhead and the contentions among communication channels. Selvakumar and Siva [14] stated "Scheduling-holes in a processor (communication channel) are the time intervals during which the processor (channel) is not scheduled provided these time intervals occur prior to the finish time of the task (communication) last scheduled to the processor (communication channel)." The schedule-holes are primarily due to that a task is scheduled after some tasks with higher priorities; however, it could be scheduled before these tasks with higher priorities and does not affect the earliest starting times of these tasks.

Figure 7.1 provides an example of exploiting schedule-holes to improve the quality of schedules. For instance, assume that there is a partial DAG, as shown in Figure 7.1(a). Figure 7.1(b) shows the schedule obtained by applying a list scheduling algorithm according to a scheduling priority. In this figure, after scheduling n_1 and n_2, the set of ready tasks is $\{n_3, n_4, n_5\}$, where the priority of scheduling n_3 is larger than that of n_4, and the priority of scheduling n_4 is larger than that of n_5. The applied algorithm schedules first n_3 and then n_4. However, n_5 could be scheduled before n_4 without affecting the earliest starting time of n_4, as shown in Figure 7.1(c). In such a situation, the schedule holes could be exploited, and the completion time could be shortened.

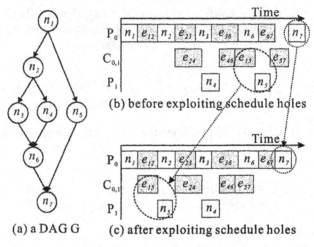

(a) a DAG G   (c) after exploiting schedule holes

Figure 7.1. An illustrative example of exploiting schedule holes.

Existing algorithms do not consider the conditions of exploiting schedule-holes. Therefore, the properties of exploiting schedule-holes are defined to ensure that the completion time of a DAG will be strictly curtailed after applying TSCC.

Property C1.   The task n_a could be scheduled to $P(n_a)$ before n_b, if the scheduling operation at step i-1, which schedules n_a to processor $P(n_a)$ to minimize $est(n_a)$, does not affect the strict reduction of $est(n_b)$ at some future step j, i < j, where the following conditions are satisfied:

1. $est(n_a) < est(n_b)$,

2. $\tau_a + lct(n_a) - est(n_a) < \tau_b + lct(n_b) - est(n_b)$, and

3. $P(n_a) = P(n_b)$.

To improve the performance of the TSCC algorithm, a further property for the completion time reduction warranty is defined to ensure that the completion time is strictly curtailed. For instance, assume that there is a partial DAG, as shown in Figure 7.2, where n_c and n_d have been allocated to some processors, n_a is ready and n_b still does not satisfy some precedence constraints or some resource contentions. Suppose that $P(n_c) \neq P(n_d)$ and that the dominant sequence passes through n_b and n_d. Scheduling n_a to $P(n_d)$ should not affect the strict reduction of $est(n_b)$ at some future step; otherwise, such a scheduling may lengthen the parallel completion time.

Property C2. The operation, which schedules n_a to minimize $est(n_a)$ at step i-1, should not affect the strict reduction of $est(n_b)$ at some future step j, i < j, where n_b is along the dominant sequence [16] which is the longest path of the scheduled DAG.

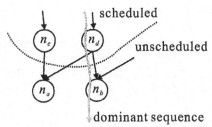

Figure 7.2. An illustrative example of the Property C2.

To improve the performance of the TSCC algorithm, the properties C1 and C2 for the completion time reduction warranty should also be considered. The reason for adopting the scheduling priority, $max(\tau_i + lct(n_i) - est(n_i))$, to select candidates is described as follows. When two nodes are ready and their least completion times are equal, the node that could be issued earlier should be scheduled first. When the two ready nodes have the same earliest starting time, the one which has the larger least completion time should also be scheduled first. If we mix these situations, the priority function will be $max(\tau_i + lct(n_i) - est(n_i))$.

The TSCC algorithm initially finds the *lct* for each node bottom-up, and then pre-schedules DAGs by a list scheduling algorithm that schedules tasks according to the priority, $max(\tau_i + lct(n_i) - est(n_i))$. Nodes without predecessors are selected first. A candidate with $max(\tau_i + lct(n_i) - est(n_i))$ is allocated to a schedule by considering the properties C1 and C2; the chosen candidate node is then examined. The algorithm repeats this procedure until all nodes have been examined.

The time complexity of pre-scheduling is $O(|N|(|N| + |E|))$ and the time complexity for calculating *lct* is $O(|N| + |E|)$, where $|N| = |N_t| + |N_s|$. The while loop is executed $O(|N|)$ times. The time complexity of finding the node, n_i, with $max(\tau_i + lct(n_i) - est(n_i))$ is $O(|N|)$. Checking the properties C1 and C2 is executed $O(|N||P|(|N|+|E|))$ times. The time complexity of TSCC algorithm then is $O(|P||N|^2(|N| + |E|))$. Consequently, in practical applications, the complexity of the TSCC algorithm is reasonable, because in [14] the corresponding complexity is $O(|N|^3|P||E|\log^2|P|)$.

TSCC algorithm
Input: a NUMA system M, and a DAG G.
Output: a schedule with the minimal parallel completion time.
{

    Initialization.
    Finding $lct(n_i)$, $\forall n_i \in N_t \cup N_s$.
    Pre-scheduling.
    unexam← $N_t \cup N_s$, *ready* ← $\emptyset$.
    While *unexam*≠ $\emptyset$
    {

        ready ← *ready* $\cup n_i$, $\forall n_i \in$ *unexam* and *pred* $(n_i) \cap$ *unexam* = $\emptyset$.
        Finding n_i with $max(\tau_i + lct(n_i) - est(n_i))$, $\forall n_i \in$ *ready*.
        $n_s \leftarrow n_i$ /*n_s is the selected candidate node*/
        If there is $n_k \in$ *ready*, $n_k \neq n_s$, which satisfies properties C1 and
C2

        $\{n_s \leftarrow n_k\}$.
        Scheduling n_s to its corresponding processor.
        unexam ← *unexam* - n_s, and *ready* ← *ready* - n_s.

    }

}

3.   Performance Bounds

This section introduces a sharper bound for the scheduling problem. It is meaningful not only theoretically in evaluating the accuracy of the resultant heuristic solution more precisely, but also practically in giving a better lower bound in the multiprocessor scheduling problem.

In the multiprocess scheduling problem, there are at least two kinds of the resource contention: one, in which execution of a task must be deferred until the completion of all the tasks scheduled before it in the same processor; and the other, that entails receiving data from immediate predecessors sequentially, i.e., a task that cannot receive data from all its predecessors simultaneously. The Lemma 1 and 2 describe the two kinds of the resource contention as follows.

Lemma 1.   For a communication e_{ij} in a schedule, only one of the following three cases should be considered. Case 1: Only one task and one communication have resource contention relationships with e_{ij}. Case 2: Only one task has a resource contention relationship with e_{ij}. Case 3: Only one communication has a resource contention relationship with e_{ij}.

Proof.   We prove Lemma 1 by contradiction. Three possibilities are available for a communication edge e_{ij} in a schedule:

1) Assume there is neither a computation task nor a communication that has a resource contention relationship with e_{ij}. This assumption would imply that we can advance the starting time of the communication edge, e_{ij}, or that we can advance the earliest starting time of computation task n_j. However, this contradicts Equation 7.4 for n_j, or Equation 7.5 for e_{ij}.

2) Assume that more than one computation task has resource contention relationships with e_{ij}. Two sub-possibilities are (a) these tasks are all allocated to the same processor. Since the tasks must be executed in order, only one can have a resource contention relationship with e_{ij}; or (b) the tasks are allocated to more than one processor. It is impossible for more than one processor to receive the communication data along e_{ij}.

3) Assume that more than one communication has resource contention relationships with e_{ij}. The proof is similar to that of the possibility 2).

Thus, the Lemma 1 is proven. §

Lemma 2. For a task n_i in a schedule, only one of the following three cases should be considered. Case 1: Only one task and one communication have resource contention relationships with n_i. Case 2: Only one task has a resource contention relationship with n_i. Case 3: Only one communication has a resource contention relationship with n_i.

Proof. Since the proof is similar to that of Lemma 1, we omit it. §

Theorem 1 *For any DAG $G = (N_t, N_s, E, C, T)$ to be scheduled to a NUMA system, the schedule length, ω, obtained by TSCC always satisfies*

$$\omega \leq \left(2 - \frac{1}{|P|}\right)\omega_{opt} + \sum_{i=1}^{x-1}\left(c_{i,i+1} \times \left(\eta_{max} - \left(\frac{|P|-1}{|P|}\right)\eta_{min}\right)\right), \quad (7.7)$$

where ω_{opt} is the length of the optimal schedule, $\eta_{max} = max(\eta(p_i, p_j))$ and $\eta_{min} = min(\eta(p_i, p_j))$, $\forall$ any pair $p_i, p_j \in P$.

Proof. The set of all points of time in $(0, \omega)$ could be partitioned into two sets A and B. A is defined as the set of all points of times for which all processors are executing some tasks, and B is defined as the set of all points of time for which at least one processor is idle. If B is empty, all processors complete their last assignment at ω and no idle interval can be found within $(0, \omega)$. The TSCC schedule is indeed optimal and, thus, the theorem holds obviously. Therefore, we assume that B is non-empty. Moreover, we also assume that B is the disjoint union of q open intervals as below: B=(I_{l1}, I_{r1}) $\cup (I_{l2}, I_{r2}) \cup \ldots \cup (I_{lq}, I_{rq})$, where $I_{l1} < I_{r1} < I_{l2} < I_{r2} < \ldots < I_{lq} < I_{rq}$.

Without loss of generality, we claim that a chain of tasks can be found, i.e., $X_q : n_1 \rightarrow n_2 \rightarrow \ldots \rightarrow n_x$, such that

$$\sum_{i=1}^{q} (I_{r,i} - I_{l,i}) \leq \sum_{k=1}^{x} \tau_k + \sum_{k=1}^{x-1} (c_{k,k+1} \times \eta(P(n_k), P(n_{k+1}))). \qquad (7.8)$$

Let n_x denote the task that finishes in the TSCC schedule at time ω. Let $st(n_x)$ denote the stating time scheduled by TSCC for n_x. Three possibilities regarding the starting time of n_x are

(a) $st(n_x) \leq I_{l1}$.

(b) $st(n_x) \in B$, i.e., $\exists$ an integer h, $h \leq q$, s.t. $I_{lh} < st(n_x) < I_{rh}$.

(c) $st(n_x) \in A$ but $st(n_x) > I_{l1}$, i.e., $\exists$ an integer h, $h \leq q - 1$, s.t. $I_{rh} \leq st(n_x) \leq I_{l,h+1}$ or $I_{r,q} \leq st(n_x)$.

If the first possibility occurs, the task n_x by itself constitutes a chain that satisfies our claim.

The second possibility is next considered. Suppose that h is the index satisfying (b). Then, n_x covers some part of B from its right end to somewhere in-between I_{lh} and I_{rh}. An attempt is made to add the second task, n_{x-1}, to the chain. According to the Lemma 1 and 2, there is some task n_g or some e_{gx} that has a resource contention relationship with n_x. Therefore, let $n_{x-1} = n_g$, and add n_{x-1} to the chain, X_q. The cycle can be repeated until the starting time of the last added task satisfies (a) or (c).

The third possibility is considered as follows. Suppose that h is the index satisfying (c). According to the Lemma 1 and 2, there is some task n_g or some e_{gx} that has a resource contention relationship with n_x. Therefore, let $n_{x-1} = n_g$, and add n_{x-1} to the chain, X_q. The cycle can be repeated until the starting time of the last added task satisfies (a) or (b).

The whole process is repeated by considering the above-mentioned three possibilities until $st(n_1) \leq I_{l1}$ is satisfied. Finally, a chain satisfying our claim (see Eq.7.8) is constructed. Consequently,

$$\sum_{\varepsilon \in \Phi} \tau_\varepsilon \leq (|P| - 1) \sum_{k=1}^{x} \tau_k + |P| \sum_{k=1}^{x-1} (c_{k,k+1} \times \eta_{max}), \qquad (7.9)$$

where Φ is the set of processor idle time intervals and τ_ε is the processor idle time interval (i.e., the left-hand sum is over all idle time intervals for processors). The chain, X, takes at least $\sum_{k=1}^{x} \tau_k + \sum_{k=1}^{x-1} (c_{k,k+1} \times \eta_{min})$ to finish all tasks in any schedule, i.e.,

$$\omega_{opt} \geq \sum_{k=1}^{x} \tau_k + \sum_{k=1}^{x-1} (c_{k,k+1} \times \eta_{min}) \qquad (7.10)$$

The following inequality is also obvious:

$$\sum_{n_i \in N} \tau_i \leq |P| \times \omega_{opt}. \qquad (7.11)$$

Consequently,

$$
\begin{aligned}
\omega &= \frac{1}{|P|} \left(\sum_{n_i \in N} \tau_i + \sum_{\varepsilon \in \Phi} \tau_\varepsilon \right) \\
&\leq \frac{1}{|P|} \left((2|P| - 1)\omega_{opt} + \sum_{i=1}^{x-1} \left(c_{i,i+1} \times (|P|(\eta_{max} - \eta_{min}) + \eta_{min}) \right) \right) \\
&\leq \left(2 - \frac{1}{|P|} \right) \omega_{opt} + \sum_{i=1}^{x-1} \left(c_{i,i+1} \times \left(\eta_{max} - \left(\frac{|P|-1}{|P|} \right) \eta_{min} \right) \right) . \S
\end{aligned}
$$
$$(7.12)$$

When the number of processors approaches infinite, the performance bound of the TSCC algorithm is within a factor of two times of the optimum scheduled length for general DAGs. When $\eta_{min} = 0$, our performance bound is reduced to the sum of Graham's bound for list scheduling [2]. When $\eta_{min} > 0$, our performance bound is sharper than that in literature.

4. Experimental Results

This section presents experimental results to verify the preceding claims. The feasibility of the proposed algorithm is assessed by evaluating practical applications, such as the FFT, Laplace equation, Fork-trees, Join-trees and 160 randomly generated program graphs, whose graph sizes vary from the minimum of 364 nodes with 363 edges to the maximum of 365 nodes with 606 edges.

We have implemented an evaluation environment that takes SISAL [17] programs as input and evaluates their performance. The optimizing SISAL compiler translates programs to IF1 intermediate files based on the macro-dataflow model. The evaluation environment modifies these IF1 codes based on the paradigm for SCR model. The transformed intermediate files are scheduled by our proposed algorithms and evaluated their performance. The transformation progress does not modify any syntax of IF1; therefore, IF1 could be used as the intermediate code for the SCR model and SISAL compiler could generate executable machine code from it.

Let L_l be 2 cycles/byte, and L_r vary from 4, 8, 16 to 32 cycles/byte. The average communication overhead associated with each edge varies from 32, 64, 128 to 256 bytes. The cost required for each task varies randomly from 1 to 512 cycles. The processor number varies from 2, 4, 8, 16 to 32. The speedup for a scheduling algorithm is defined as

$Speedup = SequentialCompletionTime/ParallelCompletionTime.$

Two algorithms are implemented for comparison. The first, a list scheduling algorithm schedules tasks according to the priority, $est(n_i)+\tau_i+lct(n_i)$. The task with $est(n_i)+\tau_i+lct(n_i)$ is scheduled to a corresponding processor until there is no un-scheduled task. The second, SCH [14] exploits schedule-holes to produce more adequate schedules.

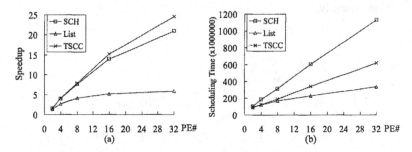

Figure 7.3.   (a)Speedup, (b)Scheduling time vs. number of processors for fork trees.

Figure 7.3 shows the experimental results of 160 fork trees, where "SCH" denotes the SCH algorithm, "List" the list scheduling and "TSCC" the TSCC algorithm. These results indicate that TSCC performs better than others. As the number of processors increases, the difference in speedup between SCH and TSCC also increases. The main explanation is that the little possibility of causing the schedule-holes is due to the structures of fork trees. Figure 7.3(b) confirms the superiority of TSCC in time complexity over the SCH algorithm.

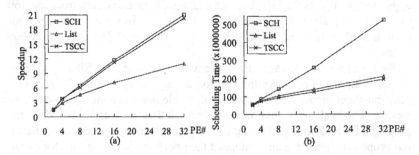

Figure 7.4.   (a)Speedup, (b)Scheduling time vs. number of processors for join trees.

Figure 7.4 shows the experimental results of 160 join trees. These results indicate that SCH performs better than others. However, the average difference in speedup between SCH and TSCC is only about 0.744%, and the time complexity of SCH algorithm was apparently of a high order. The main explanation is that the great possibility of causing the schedule-holes is due to the structures of join trees. Figure 7.4(b) confirms the superiority of TSCC in time complexity over other algorithms.

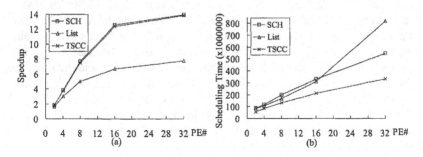

Figure 7.5. (a)Speedup, (b)Scheduling vs. number of processors for random DAGs.

Figure 7.5 shows the experimental results of 160 randomly generated DAGs. Figure 7.5(a) confirms that the speedups increase when the number of processors increases, which corresponds with findings in previous literature. These results also indicate that the performance gain of applying SCH is similar to that of applying TSCC; in fact, the average difference in speedup between SCH and TSCC is only 0.414%. However, the scheduling time of applying TSCC surpasses that of applying the SCH, as shown in Figure 7.5(b). The main reason for the superiority of TSCC in time complexity is that SCH finds the earliest starting time by searching the list of free time slots in each processor.

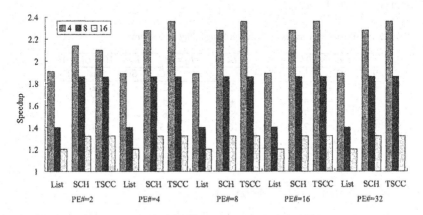

Figure 7.6. Speedup for FFT algorithm.

The example applied here is the classical FFT. The task dependence graph can be considered as the concatenation of two trees: the MERGE tree and

SPLIT tree. We execute this example when $n=2^{16}$. Figure 7.6 shows the speedup for FFT. When the number of processors is 2, the SCH performs better than TSCC. When the number of processors is larger than 2, TSCC is always superior to SCH, as shown in Figure 7.6. These experimental results show that the TSCC algorithm has better performance than that of SCH when the join-degree is equal to the fork-degree within applications. Because TSCC also tries to balance the tradeoff between the resource utilization and the speedup, the optimal parallelism exploitation may not be achieved. The situation is also shown in Figure 7.5. According to the comparison between Figure 7.5 and Figure 7.6, the minor superiority of SCH in Figure 7.5 maybe result from that the number of join-structures is larger than that of fork-structures when we randomly generate the task graphs.

Finally, to show that TSCC is superior in the resource utilization to others, the Laplace Partial-Differential Equation algorithm is evaluated. In such applications, a region is discretized and an iterative method is used to approximate function values within this region. The experimental results for Laplace partial-differential equation are similar to that of FFT. The difference of the performance between TSCC and SCH is very little. As the interprocessor communication latency increases, the difference of the performance between TSCC and SCH increases. However, the resource usage of TSCC is better than that of SCH. In Table 7.1, TSCC is always superior in the resource usage to SCH. This is because that TSCC also tries to balance the tradeoff between the resource utilization and the speedup; the optimal parallelism exploitation may not be achieved. This situation is also shown in previous experimental results. In Table 7.1, the resource usage of applying TSCC is better than that of applying SCH.

Table 7.1. Processor Usages of Different Scheduling Algorithms

PE#	$L_r = 40/L_l = 4$			$L_r = 80/L_l = 8$			$L_r = 160/L_l = 16$		
	SCH	List	TSCC	SCH	List	TSCC	SCH	List	TSCC
2	2	2	2	2	2	2	2	2	2
4	4	4	4	4	4	4	4	3	4
8	8	7	8	8	4	8	8	3	8
16	16	7	15	16	4	15	13	3	8
32	16	7	15	16	4	15	13	3	8

5. Concluding Remarks

This work examines the impact of scheduling tasks to multiprocessor systems by exploiting schedule-holes in schedules with the consideration of the non-negligible intertask communications and the communication contentions. TSCC ensures performance within a factor of two times of the optimum scheduled lengths for general DAGs. We demonstrate the performance of our algorithm by evaluating some practical applications and some randomly generated task graphs. Experimental results demonstrate the superiority of the proposed TSCC algorithm. The scheduling performance depends on the size of the problem, the degree of parallelism and the task graph granularity. The above experiments show that the TSCC can obtain a good performance, if a proper task partitioning is provided. Since exact weight estimation may not be feasible in practice, the experiments show that as long as the task graph is coarse grain, the performance variations are small. Thus, coarse grain partitions with sufficient parallelism are commended.

Acknowledgments

This work was sponsored in part by the National Science Council of the Republic of China under the contract number: NSC89-2233-E-142-002.

References

[1] Data General Corporation, "Standard high volume servers: The new building block."

[2] E.G. Coffman and P.J. Denning,*Operating Systems Theory*. Englewood Cliffs, NJ: Prentice-Hall, 1973.

[3] G.A. Abandah and E.S. Davidson, "Effects of architectural and technological advances on the HP/Convex Exemplar's memory and communication performance," The 25th Annual International Symposium on Computer Architecture, pp.318-329, 1998.

[4] G.C. Sih and L.A. Lee, "A Compile-Time Scheduling Heuristic for Interconnection-Constrained Heterogeneous Processor Architectures," *IEEE Trans. Parallel and Distributed Systems*, vol.4, no.2, pp.75-87, 1993.

[5] G.J. Lai and C. Chen, "Scheduling Parallel Program Tasks with Non-negligible Intertask Communications onto NUMA Multiprocessor Systems," *Journal of Parallel Algorithms and Applications*, vol.12, pp.165-184, 1997.

[6] H. El-Rewini, H.H. Ali and T.G. Lewis, "Task Scheduling in Multiprocessing Systems," IEEE Trans. Computer, 27-37, 1995.

[7] I. Ahmad and Y.-K. Kwok, "On Exploiting Task Duplication in Parallel Program Scheduling," *IEEE Trans. Parallel and Distributed Systems*, vol.9, no.9, pp.872-892, 1998.

[8] I. Ahmad and Y.-K. Kwok, "On Parallelizing the Multiprocessor Scheduling," *IEEE Trans. Parallel and Distributed Systems*, vol.10, no.4, pp.414-432, 1999.

[9] J.-J. Hwang, Y.-C. Chow, F. D. Anger and C.-Y. Lee, "Scheduling Precedence Graphs in Systems with Interprocessor Communication Times," *SIAM Journal of Computing*, vol.18, no.2, pp.244-257, 1989.

[10] J. Laudon and D. Lenoski, "The SGI Origin: A ccNUMA Highly Scalable Server," Proceedings of 24th Annual Int. Symp. On Computer Architecture, pp.241-251, June 1997.

[11] M.A. Palis, J.-C. Liou, and D.S.L. Wei, "Task Clustering and Scheduling for Distributed Memory Parallel Architectures," *IEEE Trans. Parallel and Distributed Systems*, vol.7, no.1, pp.46-55, 1996.

[12] M.-Y Wu and D.D. Gajski, "Hypertool: A Programming Aid for Message-Passing Systems," *IEEE Trans. Parallel and Distributed Systems*, vol.1, no.3, pp.330-343, 1990.

[13] R.M. Wolski and J.T. Feo, "Program Partitioning for NUMA Multiprocessor Computer Systems," *Journal of Parallel and Distributed Computing*, vol.19, pp.203-218, 1993.

[14] S. Selvakumar and C. Siva Ram Murthy, "Scheduling Precedence Constrained Task Graphs with Non-Negligible Intertask Communication onto Multiprocessors," *IEEE Trans. Parallel and Distributed Systems*, vol.5, no.3, pp.328-336, 1994.

[15] T. Lovett and R. Clapp, "STiNG: A CC-NUMA computer system for the commercial marketplace," Proceedings of 23rd Annual Int. Symp. on Computer Architecture, pp.308-317, May 1996.

[16] T. Yang and A. Gerasoulis, "DSC: Scheduling Parallel Tasks on an Unbounded Number of Processors," *IEEE Trans. Parallel and Distributed Systems*, vol.5, no.9, pp.951-967, 1994.

[17] V. Sarkar, *Partitioning and Scheduling Parallel Programs for Multiprocessors*. The MIT Press, Cambridge, MA, 1989.

[18] Y.K. Kwok and I. Ahmad, "Dynamic Critical-Path Scheduling: An Effective Technique for Allocating Task Graphs onto Multi-Processors," *IEEE Trans. Parallel and Distributed Systems*, vol.7, no.5, pp.506-521, 1996.

Chapter 8

ENERGY AWARE SCHEDULING FOR HETEROGENEOUS REAL-TIME EMBEDDED SYSTEMS USING GENETICS ALGORITHMS*

Man Lin* and Sai Man Ng

Department of Mathematics, Statistics and Computer Science,
St. Francis Xavier University
mlin@stfx.ca, x98bld@stfx.ca

Abstract

Many of today's embedded Systems, such as wireless and portable devices rely heavily on the limited power supply. Therefore, energy efficiency becomes one of the major design concerns for embedded systems. Dynamic voltage scaling (DVS) provides the possibility to reduce the power consumption of modern processors. This chapter addresses the problem of static variable voltage scheduling for heterogeneous real-time embedded systems. The aim is to optimize energy consumption while guaranteeing the deadline constraints and precedence constraint of the tasks. The approach is based on Genetic Algorithms. Task mapping, scheduling and voltage selection are integrated in the same phase in our approach in order to achieve lowest energy consumption. The experimental results show that the proposed algorithm is effective and reduces energy consumptions ranging from 20%, up to 90% under different system configurations. We also compare the proposed Genetic Algorithm based algorithm with two list-scheduling-based algorithms and one simulated-annealing-based algorithm. The comparisons demonstrate that the genetic algorithm based algorithm outperformed the other algorithms in terms of finding more feasible schedules and saving more energy.

Keywords: Energy Optimization, Task Scheduling, Real-Time Systems, Embedded Systems, Genetic Algorithms.

*A short version of this chapter appeared in the special issue of Hardware/Software Support for High Performance Scientific and Engineering Computing at Parallel Processing Letters, 2005.
*The author would like to thank NSERC (National Science Engineering Research Council, Canada) for supporting this research.

1. Introduction

Many of today's embedded Systems, such as wireless and portable devices rely heavily on the limited power supply by the battery. Therefore, energy efficiency becomes one of the major design concerns for embedded systems in order to lengthen battery life, to reduce the electricity cost and to improve performance. Reducing the power of CPU is the critical part of energy saving for an embedded system. Dynamic voltage scaling (DVS) [18] is an effective way to reduce energy consumption of a CMOS processor by dynamically changing its supply voltage. Many of today's advanced processors such as those produced by Intel and AMD support DVS technology.

The CPU power consumed per cycle in a CMOS processor can be expressed as $P = C_L F V_{DD}^2$, where C_L is the total capacitance of wires and gates, V_{DD} is the supply voltage and F is the clock frequency. It is obvious that a lower voltage level leads to a lower power consumption. The price to pay for lowering the voltage level is that it also leads to a lower clock frequency and thus slows down the execution of a task. The relation between the clock frequency and the supply voltage is: $F = K * (V_{DD} - V_{TH})^2 / V_{DD}$. As a result, exploiting DVS may hurt the performance of a system. When using DVS in a hard real-time system where tasks have deadlines, we can not lower the voltage levels of the processors too much as we also need to guarantee the deadlines of the tasks be met. Therefore, classic scheduling and DVS has to be addressed together.

Modern embedded systems are often implemented as distributed systems where tasks can be executed in parallel. The tasks need to interact with each other to accomplish a complex job in timely fashion. As a result, the tasks in a distributed hard real-time system often have a deadline and precedence constraints among them. Due to various degree of application parallelism, the processors experience idle intervals. DVS can be exploited to reduce the idle intervals and thus save energy.

In the past few years, there have been a number of algorithms proposed for applying DVS to hard real-time systems [4, 5, 15, 1, 8, 11, 19, 2, 7]. Many previous works of DVS-based scheduling either focus on single processor power conscious scheduling [1, 8, 5, 10] or consider independent tasks only [10, 5]. There is less work done for distributed systems with dependent tasks.

In this paper, we focus on static DVS-based scheduling algorithm for distributed hard real-time systems. The problem of optimally mapping and scheduling tasks to distributed systems has been shown, in general, to be NP-complete [17]. Because of the computational complexity issue, heuristic methods have been proposed to obtain optimal and suboptimal solutions to various scheduling problems. Genetic algorithms have recently received much attention as searching algorithms for scheduling problems in distributed real-time systems [9, 14, 17]. Our DVS-based scheduling algorithm adopts Genetic Algorithms. Different from classic scheduling problem aiming at minimizing execution time, our algorithm takes voltage level as one extra variable and aims at minimizing energy consumption while guaranteeing all tasks meet their deadline. The approach is an integrated method where task assignment (to which processor the tasks will be assigned), task scheduling (when the tasks will be executed) and voltage selection (at which voltage level the tasks will run) are performed at the same phase. Note that we consider multi-voltage DVS processors instead of variable-voltage DVS as real DVS processors show only a limited number of supply voltage levels at which tasks can be executed.

The paper is organized as follows. First, the related works are discussed at Section 2. Then the energy model and the discussion of why using an integrated method are addressed in Section 3. Task Model and schedule model are described in Section 4. After that, The Genetic Algorithm for scheduling with energy level consideration is described in Section 5. Section 6 shows the experiment details and the comparisons of our GA-based approach with other approaches. Finally the conclusions are presented in section 7.

2.   Related Works

Although there have been quite a number of works on applying DVS to real-time systems, there has only been limited works for static power conscious scheduling for dependent real-time tasks on multi-processors[11, 19, 6, 16, 4].

Luo et al. [11] proposed a method to construct power-efficient schedule by combining off-line and on-line schedules. The used heuristic is mainly based on critical path analysis and task execution order refinement.

Zhang et al. [19] studied energy minimization on multiprocessor systems which separates task scheduling from the voltage selection. That is, the algorithm is composed of two phases. The first phase performs task mapping and scheduling and the second phase performs voltage selection based on the existing schedule generated from the first phase. In the second phase, the voltage selection problem is formulated as Integer Programming (IP) problem.

Mishra et al. [16] also proposed a two-phase algorithm for energy aware scheduling. The first phase uses a list scheduling heuristic algorithm to generate static schedules for the tasks on multiple processors. And the second phase focuses on the power management scheme which exploits the static slacks due to the degree of parallelism to slow down some tasks to achieve energy saving.

Gruian [4] proposed a method that uses simulated annealing to find task assignments and constructive heuristic to perform task scheduling. Task assignment and scheduling are performed separately as well. This method is different from the other methods discussed above in that it involves an iterative method to search for a good solution instead of using a pure constructive method.

Our approach uses Genetic Algorithms which integrates task assignment, scheduling and voltage selection in the same phase. Instead of just constructing one optimal solution using a constructive method, we construct and evaluate many different solutions during an iterative process. This is different from Gruian's method [4] where only one solution is considered in one iteration. By exploiting the evolution rules in nature using Genetic Algorithm, betters solution (a solution is a schedule in this case.) can be found as demonstrated by our experiments.

Schmitz et al. [12] had also proposed a method that used Genetic Algorithms. However, their method is non-integrated where task assignment, scheduling and voltage selection are separated, similar to the algorithms in Zhang [19], Mishra [16] and Gruian [4].

The shortcoming of a non-integrated method is that it is not optimal because it is unlikely that the static schedule generated by a list scheduling or other methods is the optimal schedule to begin with for performing voltage scheduling for energy saving. In section 3.3, we will illustrate this using an example. Instead of performing energy minimization based on existing schedules, as done in [4, 16, 19, 12], our algorithm integrates the scheduling problem and energy minimization problem in the same phase. The rational behind the integrated approach is that the energy consumption not only depends on the energy level of each task at each processor, but also depends on how the task is mapped and scheduled in each processor.

Our approach is a static approach where the tasks are assumed to run with the worst case execution time(WCET). In reality, tasks may take less time than their WCET to complete and there will be run-time slacks available. Therefore, further optimization can be done dynamically [2, 4] in run time to lower the voltage level of some processors and to fill the slack as much as possible as long as the constraints of the tasks are met.

3.   Energy Model

3.1   Voltage, speed and energy

The processor energy model used in this paper has been widely described in the literature [18]. For a processor with CMOS circuits, the dominant source of the energy consumption is the dynamic power dissipation, which is:

$$P = C_L * F * V_{DD}^2, \tag{8.1}$$

where C_L is the load capacitance, F is the processor clock frequency and V_{DD} is the voltage supply, respectively. The relationship between operation frequency and the voltage is expressed below.

$$F = K * (V_{DD} - V_{TH})^2 / V_{DD}, \tag{8.2}$$

where k is a constant and V_{TH} is the threshold voltage. We can see from Eq. (8.2), there is an almost linear relationship with the processor speed and the supply voltage. Now we suppose a task t takes M cycles to finish, then the execution time $Exec_t$ required to finish the task will be:

$$Exec_t = M/F, \tag{8.3}$$

and the energy consumed by the task T is given as $E = P * Exec_t$, that is :

$$E = C_L * M * V_{DD}^2. \tag{8.4}$$

From Eq. (8.4) and Eq. (8.3), we can see that if we reduce the voltage by half, the execution time will be double but the energy consumed will just be one-quarter accordingly.

3.2   Energy minimization scheduling example

The goal of using DVS processors is to reduce the total energy consumption by modifying the supply voltage while still guaranteeing tasks meet their constraints. To illustrate how this works, let's consider a very simple scheduling example with three different tasks which are going to be mapped on two identical processors. In this example, we assume that there is no communication time between tasks and the DVS processor takes zero time and zero energy consumption to switch voltage level.

	Length	Deadline
T1	10	20
T2	10	40
T3	10	40

(Voltage = 5.0V)

Figure 8.1.   DAG of a Task Set and the Task Length and Deadline

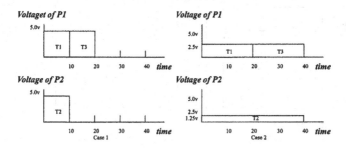

Figure 8.2.   DVS Example

First of all, Figure 8.1 shows the directed acyclic graph (DAG) of the tasks. It also shows the length and deadline of each task when the supply voltage is 5.0V. We assume that the dynamic power dissipation at 5.0V is 4J/s and the CPU speed is 100MHz. Based on Eq. (8.1) and (8.2), the dynamic power dissipation at 2.5V is 0.5J/s (1/8 of 4J/s) and at 1.25V is 0.062J/s (1/8 of 0.5J/s), and the CPU frequency at 2.5V is 50MHz (1/2 of 100MHz) and at 1.25V is 25MHz (1/2 of 50MHz), respectively. Now suppose that T1 and T3 will be executed on processor 1, and T2 will be executed on processor 2, respectively. Case 1 in Figure 8.2 shows the schedule without DVS. In this case, each processor runs at the highest speed with 5.0V voltage supply and the total energy consumption = 4J/s * 10s + 4J/s * 10s + 4J/s * 10s = 120J. Case 2 in Figure 8.2 shows the schedule with DVS. In this case, task T1 and T3 run at voltage 2.5V and they slow down by half and T3 runs at voltage 1.25V and slows down to 1/4. The execution time for T1, T2, T3 are 20s, 20s and 40s, respectively. The total energy consumption in this case is = 0.5J/s * 20s + 0.5J/s * 20s + 0.062J/s * 40s = 22.48J. So we can see by using the DVS processor, the energy consumption reduced up to 80% of the original energy consumption.

3.3   Why using an integrated method?

Next, we will use an example to show the problem of using a non-integrated approach for task assignment, scheduling and voltage selection.

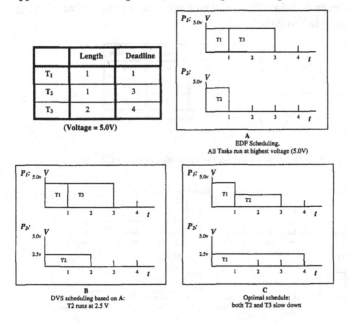

Figure 8.3.   Why an Integrated Method

Let's consider an example where there are three tasks T_1, T_2 and T_3, two processors P_1 and P_2. The tasks' WCET (or length) and deadline are shown in Figure 8.3. Each processor has two voltage levels: 5.0V and 2.5V. A non-integrated method first generates a schedule without considering energy. We choose a commonly used list scheduling algorithm: Earliest-Deadline-First algorithm (EDF). The schedule constructed is shown at Figure 8.3(A). The only possibility for saving energy starting from schedule A is to slow down T_2 (T_2 running at voltage 2.5V as shown at Figure 8.3 (B)). Schedule B is less optimal (consumes more energy) than schedule C where T_3 is mapped to processor P_2 thus allowing both T_2 and T_3 run at voltage 2.5V.

As we have seen, in a non-integrated approach, the schedule produced by the task assignment and scheduling phase might not be the right schedule for the energy optimizer to start with that leads to a final schedule with the least energy consumption. Therefore, we integrate the task assignment, scheduling and voltage selection in the same phase in order to generate an optimal schedule.

4. Task and Schedule Models

We consider the general energy aware scheduling problem for a set of task $T_1, T_2, \ldots, T_N$ on a set of heterogeneous processors $P_1, P_2, \ldots, P_M$ where N is the number of tasks and M is the number of processors. Each processor has a number of voltage levels.

Next, we describe some more detailed notations for the task model.

- Each task has a Worst Case Execution Time (WCET) on each processor for a given voltage level. The worst case execution time of task t on processor p at voltage level l is represented as $w_{t,p,l}$.

- Each task has a deadline. d_i is used to denote the deadline of task i.

- There are precedence constraints among tasks. The precedence constraints among tasks are represented by a directed acyclic graph, $G = (V, E)$, where vertices represent tasks and edges represent dependencies of the tasks. If there exists an edge e: $v_i \rightarrow v_j$ in E, then v_j can only start to execute after v_i finishes. We call v_i a pre-task of v_j.

- The power dissipation for a processor p running at level l is denoted as $POW_{p,l}$.

- Suppose task t is assigned to processor p and run at voltage level l. Then the energy used to execute task t is given by:

$$POW_{p,l} * w_{t,p,l}$$

where $w_{t,p,l}$ is the worst execution time of the task t on the processor p) at voltage supply level l.

- For a set of tasks $T_1, T_2, \ldots, T_N$ scheduling onto the set of processors $P_1, P_2, \ldots, P_M$. Assume T_i is mapped to processor $P(i)$ and runs at level $L(i)$. Then the total energy consumptions can be easily calculated as follows:

$$E_{total} = \sum_{i=1}^{N}(POW_{P(i),L(i)} * w_{T_i,P(i),L(i)})$$

To simplify the energy model, we assume that it takes no time to switch from one voltage level to another and therefore no energy consumed accordingly.

5. Scheduling and Voltage Selection Using GA

Genetic Algorithm (GA) was first invented by John Holland in early 1970's [13]. It is an effective heuristic approach for finding solutions for combinatorial optimization problems [3] with a large search space. The basic component of a genetic algorithm is *chromosomes*. Each chromosome consists of a number of genes. Each chromosome represents one solution for the problem where each gene encodes a particular part of the solution. To find the optimal solution by genetic algorithms, we first generate an initial population which contains a number of chromosomes. Next, by applying two different reproduction methods, *crossover* and *mutation*, to the current population, we can generate a new population. Repeatedly applying the above step for a certain amount of generations, we can find a good solution (near optimal) in the end. Genetic algorithms have been used extensively for task scheduling without energy consideration in the literature [17].

5.1 Schedule representation

A chromosome of our GA algorithm is a schedule. Different from the classic binary string representation for a chromosome, we use a structure representation which is an extension of the schedule representation in [9]. A schedule is represented by an ordered list of genes and each gene contains three data items: the task number, the processor number and the voltage level. The chromosome can be viewed as an $N * 3$ array (see Table 8.1) where N is the total number of tasks. The first row of a chromosome indicates the tasks ordered from left to right. The second row indicates the corresponding processor that each task will be assigned to. And the third row is the voltage level selected for the corresponding processor for each task.

Table 8.1. A Schedule Representation

Task	T_1	T_2	...	T_N
Proc	P_1	P_2	...	P_N
Level	L_1	L_2	...	L_N

In the example shown in table 8.2, tasks t_1, t_2, t_3 and t_4 are to scheduled onto processor p_1 and p_2 where both of the processor have two voltage levels. Task t_2 and t_3 are assigned to process p_2 and runs at voltage level 1 and 2 respectively. Task t_4 and t_1 are assigned to process p_1 and runs at level 2 and 1 respectively.

Table 8.2.   A Schedule Example

Task	2	3	4	1
Proc	2	2	1	1
Level	1	2	2	1

5.1.1   Topological order of genes.   A random order of tasks may result in infeasibility because the precedence constraints might be violated. To avoid such problem, we only allow chromosomes that satisfy topological order [14]. A topological ordered list is a list in which the elements satisfy the precedence constraints. To maintain all the individuals in the populations of any generation to be topological ordered, we adopted the techniques in [14].

- Generate only topological ordered individuals in the initial population (see section 5.2);

- Use carefully chosen genetic operators (see section 5.3).

5.1.2   Calculate the starting time of tasks.   The starting time of a task depends on the earliest available time of the processor it is assigned to and the latest finishing time of all of its pre-tasks.

For a given schedule, the calculation of the starting time of each task is straight-forward. Since each chromosome satisfies topological order, the calculation can be done from left to right. This way, the starting time, and therefore the finishing time of all the pre-tasks for a given task t have been calculated before calculating the starting time of t.

5.2   Population initialization

The population initialization is done by constructing a number of task lists (the first row of the schedules) that satisfy the topological order and randomly assigning processor number and voltage level.

The essence of constructing a topological ordered task list is that a task can be added into the list only if all its pre-tasks have already been added to the list.

To construct the task list that satisfy the topological order, we use a concept defined in [14]: the *in-degree* of a task t. The *in-degree* of a task t is defined as the number of tasks that must be executed before t and have not been put into the list. Note that a task can only start if all its pre-tasks already finish their execution. Therefore, a task is ready to put into the list only when its *in-degree* is zero.

The algorithm to construct a topological list works as follows. First calculate the in-degree for all tasks. Then randomly select a task whose in-degree = 0 and add it to the list. Then remove this task from the task graph and update the in-degree of the tasks in the new task graph. We repeat the above two steps until all the tasks have been added to the list. If a topological order can not be found for a task set, then there will not be any feasible schedule for the scheduling problem under consideration.

Note that the deadline constraint may still be violated even a schedule satisfies a topological order.

We also include two special chromosomes in the initial population to increase the efficiency of our genetic algorithm. The two chromosomes are constructed using earliest-deadline-first heuristic together with the topological ordering. That is, when several tasks can be added to the list (all their pre-tasks are already in the list), the one with the earliest deadline will be selected. The difference of the two chromosomes is that one selects the highest voltage levels for all the processors (the tasks will run fastest, but consume the highest energy) while the other selects the lowest voltage level for all the processors (the tasks will run slowest, but consume the lowest energy).

5.3   Evaluation

The aim of our optimization problem is to minimize the energy consumption of the tasks. The evaluation function of the energy consumption is expressed as follows:

$$E_{total} = \sum_{i=1}^{N}(POW_{P(i),L(i)} * w_{i,P(i),L(i)})$$

where N is the total number of task, $P(i)$ is the processor which task i is assigned to and $L(i)$ is the voltage level used to run task i, $POW_{P(i),L(i)}$ is the power dissipation of the processor running task i with the given voltage level $L(i)$ and $w_{i,P(i),L(i)}$ is the worst case execution time of task i running on processor $P(i)$ with the given voltage level $L(i)$.

However, the individual schedule with smaller E_{total} will not always be considered better. This is because we need to consider one more factor: the deadline constraints (precedence constraints are already encoded into the schedule enforced by the topological order.). Our GA algorithm has been designed in a way that individuals violating the deadline constraints has less chance in getting into the next generation.

5.4   Genetic operators

Genetic Algorithms explore the search space by genetic operators. New individuals are produced by applying crossover operator or mutation operator to the individuals in the previous generation. The probability of the operators indicates how often the operator will be performed. We choose 0.6 as the probability for the crossover and 0.4 as the probability for the mutation.

5.4.1 Mutation. To avoid the solution being tracked into a local solution, mutation operation is used in Genetic Algorithms. The mutation operator creates a new individual with a small change to a single individual. In our approach, we use Processor and/or Level Assignment Mutation. To perform the mutation, we randomly select a range of genes from a chromosome and then randomly change the processor number and/or the level number within this range. Obviously, the mutation operator does not change the order of the tasks. Therefore, the new individual also satisfy the topological order.

5.4.2 Crossover. The crossover operator creates new individuals by combining parts from two individuals. To perform crossover operation, we first randomly pick two chromosomes (as parents) from the current population. Then we randomly select a position where the crossover is going to occur. The first part of child 1 uses the schedule of parent 1 up to the chosen position. The second part of child 1 is constructed by selecting the rest tasks (the tasks not in the first part) from parent 2 in order. The same mechanism also applies to child 2. Below is an example of our crossover operator. Assume we have two individuals as shown in Figure 8.4. Suppose the selected position is 2, then the children will be shown as in Figure 8.5.

Task #	1	5	2	4	3
Processor #	1	2	1	2	1
Level #	1	2	1	2	1
Parent 1					

Task #	5	3	2	1	4
Processor #	2	2	1	1	1
Level #	1	1	2	2	2
Parent 2					

Figure 8.4. Crossover Parents

Task #	1	5	3	2	4
Processor #	1	2	2	1	1
Level #	1	2	1	2	2
Child 1					

Task #	5	3	1	2	4
Processor #	2	2	1	1	2
Level #	1	1	1	1	2
Child 2					

Figure 8.5. Crossover Children

The crossover operator will produce two offsprings that are topological ordered if the parents are topological ordered. The detailed proof can be found in [14].

6. Experimental Results

In this section, we describe the simulation experiments preformed. We first compare our algorithm with one that does not have power management to demonstrate the efficiency of energy reduction of our algorithm. The algorithm we compared is a commonly used List Scheduling method: EDF (Earliest Deadline First). This EDF algorithm does not have power management: all processors run at the highest speed.

We also compare our GA-based approach with three other scheduling algorithms that incorporate power management. The three algorithms are: Longest Task First with Power management (LTFP), Earliest Deadline First with Power management (EDFP) and energy aware Simulated Annealing (SA).

The algorithms are applied to a large number of randomly generated scheduling problems. Next we describe the features of the generated scheduling problems.

6.1   Generating scheduling problems

6.1.1   Task graph.   The tasks to be scheduled in a scheduling problem can be represented as a task graph. We partition the task graph into groups where each group has the same number of tasks and the same number of constraints. The following table shows the number of task and the number of constraints we have considered in our experiments. For each category, 5 task graphs were generated. The result you see later are average result of the 5 problems in each category.

Task #	20	50	100	200
Constraint #	0,10	0,10,25	0,10,25,50	0,10,25,50,100

Beside the task graph, each scheduling problem has one more variable: the number of processors. We have chosen 3, 5, and 10 processors for each task graph.

For simplicity, we assume that each processor only have three different levels of voltage supply. We also assume that there is no communication time between tasks so that each task can be processed immediately after the required resource (CPU) is available. Moreover, we assume that the CPU takes no time to switch from one voltage level to another one.

6.1.2   WCET of tasks.   The worst case execution time (WCET) of the tasks are randomly generated. Note that we consider heterogeneous distributed systems in this chapter. Therefore the execution time for the same task are different on different processors. The variation is within the range of -10% and 10%.

Also note that even though a processor have several voltage levels (and therefore several speed), we only need to generate the execution time for the tasks at the highest voltage supply level of the processor being considered. The execution time for the tasks at other voltage supply levels of the processor can be calculated based on Eq. (8.3).

6.2   Energy reduction rate

The first experiment is to compare the energy consumption of our scheduling algorithm with that of Earliest Deadline First scheduling method which does not have any power management. The experimental results shown at Figure 8.6 indicate the average percentage of the energy reduced for each category.

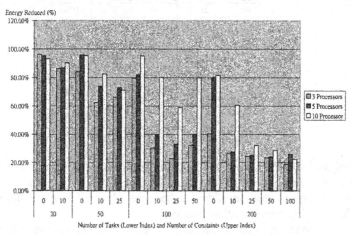

Figure 8.6.   Energy Reduction Rate Chart

By looking at Figure 8.6, we can see that our algorithm can reduce energy ranging from 20%, up to 90%. The smaller task set, the more energy saving can be achieved. Also one interesting result from our experiments is that regardless of the number of tasks, increasing the processor number or decreasing the number of constraints allows more energy saving by our algorithm. This is because the flexibility of a schedule mainly depends on the number of resource it can use or the number of constraints it must satisfy during the scheduling.

6.3   Comparison with other scheduling algorithms

Our second experiment is to compare the GA based algorithm with three other scheduling algorithms with power management: Longest Time First with Power management (LTFP), Earliest Deadline First with Power management (EDFP) and energy-aware Simulated Annealing (SA).

The first two are list scheduling approaches. The general idea of a list scheduling method is that it keeps a list of ready tasks and assigns the tasks to the list based on predefined priorities. A task with a highest priority will be scheduled first. In our experiment, we considered two different priority assignment approaches - Earliest Deadline First and Longer Task First. The first one will place the task with the earliest deadline to the front of the list and

Table 8.3.   Comparison: Percentage of Finding Feasible Solutions

Tasks	Constraints	GA	SA	LTFP	EDFP
20	0	100%	100%	100%	100%
	10	100%	100%	100%	100%
50	0	100%	100%	0%	100%
	10	100%	100%	0%	0%
	25	100%	100%	0%	0%
100	0	100%	33.33%	0%	100%
	10	100%	33.33%	0%	0%
	25	100%	33.33%	0%	0%
	50	100%	33.33%	0%	0%
200	0	100%	0%	0%	0%
	10	100%	0%	0%	0%
	25	100%	0%	0%	0%
	50	100%	0%	0%	0%

the second one will place the task with the longest task length to the list first. The power managements are simple in LTFP and EDFP. Both approaches use random voltage level selection. If the resulted schedule is not feasible, then the highest level will be used for all the processors.

Simulated Annealing (SA) is an iterated search method for optimization problems. The advantage of SA is the ability to avoid being trapped in a local optimum solution as compare to a greedy search method. We consider power management in our SA as follows.

- The initial solution has random voltage levels.

- The neighbors of a solution include not only solutions with small changes in the ordering of tasks or the processors assigned, but also solutions with small changes in the voltage levels.

To run the simulation, we apply all four algorithms to each scheduling problem generated. The results show that GA almost always return the best solutions in terms of the feasibility of the schedules. A schedule is infeasible if the deadline constraints or precedence constraints are violated. In many cases, especially when the task number is large, only GA-based approach can find feasible solutions. The percentage of finding feasible solutions for the four algorithms is shown in the tables 8.3.

The reason that EDFP or LTFP often gets unfeasible solution is that they are one-shot methods with randomly selected voltage levels. SA runs for several iterations, starting from a random schedule. In general, SA is better than EDFP or LTFP, and GA is the best approach in terms of finding feasible solution and saving more energy.

The comparison of the energy saving of SA and GA is shown at the table 8.4. The table shows the average percentage of the energy reduction for GA and SA

Table 8.4. Comparison: Energy Reduction of GA and SA

Tasks	GA	SA
20	91.23%	91.12%
50	78.17%	75.64%
100	78.52%	64.25%
200	36.05%	NF

methods for different task set size. To have a fair comparison, we only consider those problems where both approaches can find feasible solutions.

Note that the LTFP and EDFP are not listed because most of the time they do not find feasible solutions. Both LTFP and EDFP find feasible solutions only when the task number is small (20 in our experiments). The average percentages of energy reduced for LTFP and EDFP for 20 tasks are 60.23% and 59.24% respectively, which are much lower than those of GA (91.23%) and SA (91.12%).

7. Conclusion

We have addressed energy optimization problem in real-time embedded systems in this chapter. A genetic algorithm has been presented for static scheduling for real-time embedded systems that support DVS. The algorithm is designed for heterogeneous systems with tasks that have deadline and precedence constraints among them. The aim is to reduce the energy consumption while satisfying the constraints of the tasks. The algorithm integrates task mapping, scheduling and voltage selection in the same phase instead of adjusting an existing schedule to minimize energy as done in many other methods. A large number of experiments were conducted and the experimental results show that our GA-based approach can reduce the energy consumption of a system ranging from 20%, to 90%. We also compared our GA-based approach with two list scheduling algorithms and the simulated annealing method. The experiments showed that our approach can find better solutions for most scheduling problems in terms of the feasibility of the solutions and the energy saving.

References

[1] F. Yao and A. Demers and S. Shenker. A scheduling model for reduced CPU energy. In *Proceedings of the 36th Annual Symposium on Foundations of Computer Science*, pages 374–382, 1995.

[2] R. Melhem and D. Zhu and B. Childers. Scheduling with dynamic voltage/speed adjustment using slack reclamation in multi-processor real-time systems. In *Proceedings of the 22th IEEE Real-Time Systems Sumposium (RTSS-01)*, pages 84–94, UK, 2001.

[3] F. Glover and M. Laguna. *Modern Heuristic Techniques for Combinatorial Problems.* Blackwell Scientific Publications, 1993.

[4] F. Gruian and K. Kuchcinski. LEneS: Task-scheduling for low-energy systems using variable voltage processors. In *Proceedings of Asia South Pacific-Design Automation Confer-*

ence (ASPDAC-01), pages 449–455, 2001.

[5] Flavius Gruian. Hard real-time scheduling for low-energy using stochastic data and dvs processors. In *Proceedings of the 2001 international symposium on Low power electronics and design*, pages 46–51. ACM Press, 2001.

[6] D. Mosse, H. Aydin, R. Melhem and P. Mejia-Alvarez. Dynamic and aggressive scheduling techniques for power-aware real-time systems. In *Proceeding of The 22th IEEE Real-Time Systems Symposium*, London, UK, December 2001.

[7] G. Qu, M. Potkonjak, I. Hong, D. Kirovski and M. B. Srivastava. Power optimization of variable-voltage core-based ssytems. *IEEE Transactions on Computer-Aided Design of Integrated Circuits and Systems*, 18(12), 1999.

[8] T. Ishihara and H. Yasuura. Voltage scheduling problem for dynamically variable voltage processors. In *Proceedings of International Symposium on Low Power Electronics and Design (ISLPED-98)*, pages 197–202, 1998.

[9] M. Lin and L.T. Yang. Hybrid genetic algorithms for partially ordered tasks in a multi-processor environment. In 1999, *proceedings of the 6th International Conference on Real-Time Computing Systems and Applications (RTCSA-99)*, 382–387.

[10] Y. Liu and A. K. Mok. An integrated approach for applying dynamic voltage scaling to hard real-time systems. In *Proceedings of the 9th Real-Time and Embedded Technology and Applications Symposium*, pages 116–123, Toronto, Canada, May 2003.

[11] J. Luo and N. K. Jha. Static and dynamic variable voltage scheduling algorithms for real-time heterogeneous distributed embedded systems. In *ASP-DAC/VLSI Design 2002*, pages 719–726, Bangalore, India, January 2002.

[12] B. Al-Hashimi, M. Schmitz and P. Eles. Energy-efficient mapping and scheduling for dvs enabled distributed embedded systems. In *Proceedings of 2002 Design, Automation and Test in Europe Conference and Exhibition*, pages 514–521, 2002.

[13] Z. Michalewicz. *Genetic Algorithms + Data Structures = Evolution Programs*. Springer-Verlag, 1994.

[14] J. Oh and C. Wu. Genetic-algorithm-based real-time task scheudling with multiple goals. *To appear on Journal of Systems and Software*, 2002.

[15] Padmanabhan Pillai and Kang G. Shin. Real-time dynamic voltage scaling for low-power embedded operating systems. In *Proceedings of the eighteenth ACM symposium on Operating systems principles*, pages 89–102. ACM Press, 2001.

[16] D. Zhu, D. Mosse, R. Mishra, N. Rastogi and R. Melhem. Energy aware scheduling for distributed real-time systems. In *International Parallel and Distributed Processing Symposium (IPDPS'03)*, Nice, France, April 2003.

[17] N. Beck, T. D. Branun, H. J. Siegel and et. al. A comparison of eleven static heuristic for mapping a class of independent tasks onto heterogeneous distributed computing systems. *Journal of Parallel and Distributed Computing*, 61:810–837, 2001.

[18] A. J. Stratakos, T. D. Burd, T. A. Pering and R. W. Brodersen. A dynamic voltage scaled microprocessor system. *IEEE Journal of Solid-State Circuits*, 35(11):1571–1580, November 2000.

[19] X. Hu, Y. Zhang and D. Chen. Task scheduling and voltage selection for energy minimization. In *Proceedings of Design Automation Conference (DAC-02)*, pages 183–188, New Orleans, Louisiana, USA, June 2002.

Chapter 9

DYNAMIC CLUSTERING OF TASKS AND DCS FOR MULTIPLE TASK ALLOCATION

Deo Prakash Vidyarthi

Department of Computer and Systems Sciences, Jawaharlal Nehru University, Delhi, India

dpv@mail.jnu.ac.in

Anil Kumar Tripathi

Department of Computer Engineering, Institute of Technology, Banaras Hindu University, Varanasi, India

anilkt@bhu.ac.in

Biplab Kumer Sarker

Graduate School of Systems and Information Engineering, University of Tsukuba, Japan

bksarker@kde.is.tsukuba.ac.jp

Laurence T. Yang

Department of Computer Science, St. Francis Xavier University, Canada

lyang@stfx.ca

Abstract   This paper describes how the allocation of stream of tasks, with minimum knowledge, is possible in a distributed computing system . In literature, almost all the task allocation models in a distributed computing system require a priori knowledge of tasks execution time, communication time etc. on the processing nodes. Since the task assignment is not known in advance, this time is difficult to estimate. A cluster-based dynamic allocation scheme is proposed for both the distributed computing system and the tasks that eliminate the execution time requirement. Further, as opposed to a single task, multiple tasks are considered for allocation by the model. For both the task clustering and processor clustering a fuzzy function is used. Clustering and assignment process is used dynamically as it suits the stochastic stream of incoming tasks. Experimental results validate the efficacy of the proposed model.

Keywords: DCS, Task Allocation, Dynamic Task Clustering

1.   Introduction

Distributed Computing System (DCS) provides the platform for parallel/conc-

urrent execution of tasks/modules. A task consists of communicating modules operates (possibly) in parallel. DCS tries to execute incoming stream of tasks allowing their concurrently executable modules to proceed in parallel if computing nodes are available and communication pattern of the hardware/software facilitates the same. When these modules are assigned to the processing nodes, it forms load. A clustered workload assignment algorithm for the tasks in a large heterogeneous DCS is proposed here.

Various task allocation models, discussed in the literature [1]-[15], map the modules of a single task [1]-[2], [4]-[7] or multiple tasks [3] onto the nodes of the DCS. These algorithms have scalability limitations. In general, scalability is a common concern with optimal solutions to task allocation in DCS since the problem is NP-hard [10]. To overcome the scalability limitations, heuristic approaches [11][14] are applied for larger instances of the problem. Based on their performance measures, these approaches can be classified as schedulability-based [12][13] or communication based [14][15]. To reduce the allocation search space, modules of the tasks are clustered into larger units of allocation. Further, allocation effectuate with the resulting module clusters, not individual modules, to available nodes. Various flavor of these are proposed in [14][15]. In general clustering heuristics, such as those in [14], typically require the knowledge of module execution and inter module communication times. These values depend on processor speed and link bandwidth and require a priori knowledge of task to processor assignment. Since the assignment is not known in advance, these heuristics are usually applicable only to a homogeneous system. For large distributed applications, parts of which may span several heterogeneous platforms, this is a serious limitation [9].

The approach, used in this work, differs from other clustering approaches in four respects. First, while in existing approaches clustering is done only once followed by the allocation, a more scalable dynamic approach that iteratively refines the solution is applied in this model. Second, the clustering algorithm proposed can handle heterogeneous systems efficiently. Third, multiple tasks as opposed to a single task is considered unlike most of the allocation models. And finally, the clustering is solely based on the communication aspect of the task and the system. This avoids the priori knowledge of tasks execution times on the nodes of the DCS.

The paper is organized as follows. The next section describes the problem and its possible formulation. Section 3 presents the techniques for cluster formation . Section 4 presents the multiple task allocation (MTA) algorithms. Results of the experimental study are given in section 5 with concluding remarks following in the next section.

2. The Problem

Workload, for a DCS, is composed of a set of tasks T_i, each of which is characterized by a set of modules $M_i \in T_i$. Each module M_i has a worst-case computation requirement e_i measured in processor cycles (or other units independent of processor speed). A module M_i may exchange messages with another module M_j of the same task. The hardware platform on which the application is to be executed is an arbitrary-topology distributed system, composed of several dedicated and shared links. Links may be dedicated (point-to-point) or multiple access (e.g. an FDDI ring). A processor may have access to more than one link. The processors of distributed systems are on the same LAN or many LANs are connected through routers and gateways.

The modules of same task are related and their relation is represented by the task graph. Stream of tasks, arriving for execution in DCS, are disjoint. The task graph considers the precedence and the Inter Module Communication (IMC) among the modules. The tasks that arrives into the DCS is equipped with the following information:

a) IMC between modules m_i and m_j of task $T(c_{ij})$

b) Precedence amongst the modules of the task graph

With this information, object is to find an assignment of modules to processors, in a DCS. Schedule is likely to be found by a suitable clustering (module and processor) and their assignment.

3. Cluster Formations

In a DCS, a sizable fraction of the total time is experienced in the inter module communication. Communication Penalty (CP) experienced by the system is[8].

$$CP = \frac{T_{total}}{T_{comp}} \tag{9.1}$$

Where T_{total} is the time required by the algorithm to solve the given problem and T_{comp} is the time attributed to computation. If T_{comn} is the time involved in communication among different modules of the task, then

$$T_{total} = T_{comp} + T_{comn} \qquad (9.2)$$

As obvious, less communication will reduce the communication penalty. Bandwidth, inter processor distance; links, communication devices etc. affect the communication time amongst the modules. Proposed Cluster formation (both task and processor) considers the above aspect of the communication and aims to reduce the communication penalty.

3.1   Dynamic Cluster Formation

A DCS can be partitioned in different subsystems, called node clusters. A heuristic is used for the cluster formation. Various cluster formation that depends on the network organization of the DCS are depicted below.

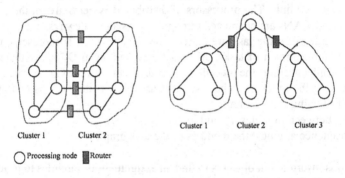

Figure 9.1.   Hypercube and tree structure

Cluster formation takes care of one, the connection among the processors (i.e. if the processors are directly connected, it is better to keep them in the same cluster) and two, the placement of communication devices (routers and gateways). These devices delay the communication and so to exclude them in the clusters formation.

The structure of the cluster changes as per the need and availability of the processing nodes from time to time (Figure 9.1). The examples given in Figure 9.2 and 9.3 elaborate the same.

Clusters of the modules of a task can be formed similarly. Usually the clusters formed for the modules will be fixed throughout their execution i.e. static clusters are formed for the modules of the task.

3.1.1   Processor Clustering.

Processor clustering attempts to identify group of processors that can be treated as a single unit. This group of processors is clustered together. In the present work, attempt is made to form clusters of processors based on the architecture of the DCS and application de-

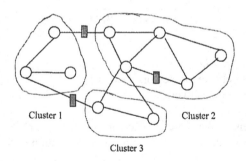

Figure 9.2.   Cluster formation at time T for nonregular network of nodes

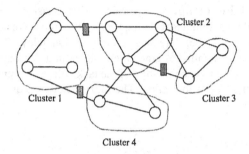

Figure 9.3.   Cluster formation at time $T + t$ for nonregular network of nodes

mand. The nodes in the processor cluster may change dynamically depending on the application requirement.

The aim to have the clustering of processors is to reduce the communication overhead to its possible extent. Thus while forming the clusters, the I/O speed of the processors and the bandwidth of the connecting links are to be considered. Abdelzaher and Shin[9] have defined the attraction force B_{ij} / $i + j$ for the clustering of the processors. Here B_{ij} is the bandwidth of the link connecting two processors P_i and P_j of i and j speed respectively.

Inter processor distance is accounted for the processor cluster formation, here. The communication between two processors, which are not directly connected, incurs more overhead than the communication between two directly connected processors. The more the distance the larger is the communication overhead.

A fuzzy function is applied to define the membership of the processors and is used to form the clusters of the processors. The fuzzy function is to keep those processors in the same cluster that are directly connected or at a little distance. Membership function is defined as follows:

$$\mu(dkl) = \frac{1}{1 + diff(dkl, D)} \qquad (9.3)$$

where, $diff(dkl,D)= |\ dkl - D\ |$
  $dkl=$ the distance between processors P_k and P_l
  $D =$ the diameter of the network

Using the above membership function each processor of the DCS will get a membership value, between 0 and 1, that helps in the formation of the processor clusters.

Processors of other LANs, interconnected via routers, should be excluded in cluster formation as these affect the communication delay.

3.1.2   Module Clustering.

Modules of the task are clustered based on the inter module communication requirements. Highly communicating modules are clustered together to reduce communication delays. The same fuzzy function, as above, is applied to grade the high communicating and low communicating modules. Thus each module of the task will get a membership value, which helps in the cluster formation. The fuzzy function is as below.

$$\mu(c_{ij}) = \frac{1}{1 + diff(c_{ij}, C)} \qquad (9.4)$$

where, $1+diff(c_{ij}, C)= |\ c_{ij} - C\ |$
  $c_{ij}=$ the communication between the modules m_i and m_j
  $C =$ the maximum possible communication between any two modules

4.   Cluster Allocation

This section describes the algorithm, which assigns module clusters to processor clusters. Both the processor cluster and task clusters are formed. Processor cluster may change dynamically, depending upon the availability and needs. Module clusters fit onto the processor clusters according to the following scheduling policies.

a) **Best Fit**: Module cluster is placed in a processor cluster in which it fits almost exactly i.e. it tries to map one to one onto between module cluster and processor cluster as far as possible.

b) **First Fit**: Module cluster is placed in any available processor cluster, which can accommodate it.

c) **Worst Fit**: Module cluster is placed in the processor cluster, which leaves the maximum number of unused processor in the processor cluster.

d) **Reverse Fit**: This mapping is unlike to above three. Here, number of modules in the module cluster is more than the number of processors in the processor cluster.

Obviously worst fit is least desired. Choice is to be made among the best fit, first fit or reverse fit.

In dynamic cluster formation of the processing nodes, the following criterion is adopted for allocation refinement.

i) **Merge**: If the number of modules in the module cluster exceeds the number of processors in a processor cluster, merging of processor cluster may take place depending on the availability of the processors.

ii) **Split**: Similarly splitting the processor cluster can take place if the no. of processor in a processor cluster (P) exceeds the no. of modules in assigned module cluster (T_m). The whole cluster can be spitted into two parts having the unused processor in one cluster and keeping the rest with the other.

4.1 The MTA Algorithm

The mapping of the module clusters to processor cluster takes place according to the following algorithm.

ClusterBased_MTA()
{

1) $PROCESSOR\_CLUSTER()$;

2) **Do**(for all the incoming tasks at hand)

3) Send the task to a computing node for distribution and all the nodes having a task will execute the following steps.

4) $MODULE\_CLUSTER()$;

5) **While** there are module clusters unallocated onto processor cluster use the following scheduling algorithm:
   if BEST FIT
      then EXECUTE()
   else if FIRST FIT
      then SPLIT();
   else if REVERSE FIT
      then MERGE();

6) Subtract the occupied memory from the available memory of the processors.

7) **Else if** memory requirement is not satisfied exclude it from the task queue and enqueue it for the next iteration.

}\\Memory updating is a critical section and is to be taken care of accordingly.

PROCESSOR_CLUSTER();
{

1) Estimate the fuzzy membership value for all the processors with other processors starting with the first processor.

2) Starting from first, cluster those processors that lie in the same and minimum membership value.

3) If there is a communicating device in between two processors, exclude the next processor in the cluster.

4) Do step 2 and 3 for all the remaining processors and if any qualifying processor is already clustered, exclude that processor in the current cluster.
}

MODULE_CLUSTER();
{

1) Estimate the fuzzy membership value for all the modules of the task in respect of IMC starting with the first module.

2) Starting from first module, cluster those module which lie in the same and minimum membership value. Do it for all the remaining modules. If any qualifying module is already clustered, exclude that module in the current cluster.
}

SPLIT();
{

1) Exclude $(P-T_m)$ processors from the processor cluster.
}

MERGE();
{

1) Look for close to (T_m-P) free neighbor processor.

2) Join these processors in the same processor cluster.

3) if none free (T_m-P) neighbor processors. then reallocate (T_m-P) modules on the same processors of the cluster

}\\for P Processors in the cluster T_m modules are allocated

5.   Experiments

The software, for the experimental study of the above algorithm, is developed in Borland C++. Task and processor graphs as well as various communication matrices, for the study, are randomly generated. Three cases are shown here, as other results obtained are similar. For case 2 only, the task graphs and processor graph are shown for easy reference.

Case 1:

Total number of tasks = 3

Total number of processors = 4 of sizes 8, 10, 8, 6
$P\_cluster1$ of P_1, P_2
and $P\_cluster2$ of P_3, P_4 are formed.

Table 9.1.   The results for case 1

Task number 1	Task number 2	Task number 3
Total module 5 of sizes 1,2,1,2,2	Total module 4 of sizes 2,1,2,2	Total module 4 of sizes 1,2,2,1
m_1, m_3 in $T_1\_cluster1$	m_1, m_2 in $T_2\_cluster1$	m_1, m_4 in $T_3\_cluster1$
m_2, m_5 in $T_1\_cluster2$	m_4, m_3 in $T_2\_cluster2$	m_2 in $T_3\_cluster2$
m_4 in $T_1\_cluster3$		m_3 in $T_3\_cluster3$

Mapping:

$T_1\_cluster1 \rightarrow P\_cluster1$
$T_1\_cluster2 \rightarrow P\_cluster2$
$T_1\_cluster3 \rightarrow P\_cluster1$

$T_2\_cluster1 \rightarrow P\_cluster1$
$T_2\_cluster2 \rightarrow P\_cluster2$

$T_3\_cluster1 \rightarrow P\_cluster1$
$T_3\_cluster2 \rightarrow P\_cluster2$
$T_3\_cluster3 \rightarrow P\_cluster1$

Case 2:

Total number of tasks = 3
Total number of processors = 8, Total size = 74
$P\_cluster1$ of P_1, P_2, P_4
$P\_cluster2$ of P_5
$P\_cluster3$ of P_6
and $P\_cluster4$ of P_3, P_7, P_8 are formed.

Table 9.2.   The results for case 2

Task number 1	Task number 2	Task number 3
Total module 10 of sizes 2 each	Total module 8 of sizes 3,5,3,6,2,1,3,2	Total module 6 of sizes 3 each
$m_1 - m_5$ in $T_1\_cluster1$	$m_1 - m_4$ in $T_2\_cluster1$	m_1, m_2, m_3 in $T_3\_cluster1$
m_6, m_7 in $T1\_cluster2$	$m_5 - m_7$ in $T2\_cluster2$	m_4, m_5, m_6 in $T3\_cluster2$
m_8, m_{10} in $T1\_cluster3$	m_8 in $T2\_cluster3$	
m_9 in $T1\_cluster4$		

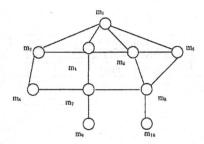

Figure 9.4.   Task graph with corresponding modules for task 1

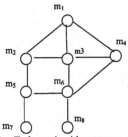

Figure 9.5.   Task graph with corresponding modules for task 2

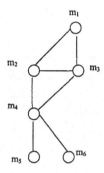

Figure 9.6.   Task graph with corresponding for task 3

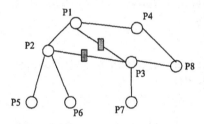

Figure 9.7.   Processor graph for case 2

Mapping:

$T_1\_cluster1 \to P\_cluster1, T_1\_cluster2 \to P\_cluster2$
$T_1\_cluster3 \to P\_cluster3, T_1\_cluster4 \to P\_cluster4$

$T_2\_cluster1 \to P\_cluster2, T_2\_cluster2 \to P\_cluster1$
$T_2\_cluster3 \to P\_cluster4$

$T_3\_cluster1 \to P\_cluster1, T_3\_cluster2 \to P\_cluster2$

Case 3:

Total no. of processors = 5 of sizes 8, 6,4,6,4
$P\_cluster1$ consists of P_1, P_3, P_4
$P\_cluster2$ consists of P_2, P_5

Mapping:

Table 9.3.   The results for case 3

Task no. 1	Task no. 2	Task no. 3	Task no. 4	Task no. 5
Total modules 5 of sizes 1,2,1,2,2	Total modules 6 of sizes 1,2,2,1,2,2	Total modules 4 of sizes 2,2,2,2	Total modules 6 of sizes 1,1,1,1,1,1	Total modules 3 of sizes 2,2,2
Cluster1 m_1, m_3 Cluster2 m_2, m_5 Cluster3 m_4	Cluster1 m_1, m_2, m_6 Cluster2 m_3, m_5 Cluster3 m_4	Cluster1 m_1, m_4 Cluster2 m_2 Cluster3 m_3	Cluster1 m_1, m_5, m_6 Cluster2 m_2 Cluster3 m_3 Cluster4 m_4	Cluster1 m_1, m_3 Cluster2 m_2

$T_1\_cluster1 \rightarrow P\_cluster1, T_1\_cluster2 \rightarrow P\_cluster2$
$T_1\_cluster3 \rightarrow P\_cluster1$

$T_2\_cluster1 \rightarrow P\_cluster1, T_2\_cluster2 \rightarrow P\_cluster2$
$T_2\_cluster3 \rightarrow P\_cluster2$

$T_3\_cluster1 \rightarrow P\_cluster1, T_3\_cluster2 \rightarrow P\_cluster1$
$T_3\_cluster3 \rightarrow P\_cluster1$

$T_4\_cluster1 \rightarrow P\_cluster1, T_4\_cluster2 \rightarrow P\_cluster2$
$T_4\_cluster3 \rightarrow P\_cluster2, T_4\_cluster4 \rightarrow P\_cluster1$

$T_5\_cluster1 \rightarrow P\_cluster1, T_5\_cluster2 \rightarrow P\_cluster2$

6.   Complexity

Cluster formation both module and processor will take constant time. Assume that there are T tasks and their modules are allocated concurrently. Further, let there are m modules in a task T and P node in the DCS. Further, assume that out of m modules mc module clusters and out of P nodes P_c processor clusters are formed. The complexity will be that of first fit, best fit and worst fit and it will be $mc * P_c$. Other timings are considered constant.

7.   Conclusion

The sole objective of the algorithm is to eliminate the necessity of the execution time requirement, yet allocate the tasks efficiently. The results obtained in the experiments claim a good load balance for multiple tasks with the clustering approach. As the algorithm for mapping executes concurrently onto the nodes, it is supposed to be better in terms of efficiency.

The proposed approach has the potential for scalability and support for system heterogeneity. Scalability is achieved by merge and split cluster formation of the processors. The approach considers the communication aspect in the cluster formation and tries to minimize its overhead. This is a realistic approach as the other algorithms, based on the same, uses the priori knowledge of the execution of the modules of the task on the processors of the DCS. The communication bandwidth is known while designing the system, so it is not difficult to measure the IMC requirements for the modules of the task. This work may be a significant move towards the development of task allocator of a DCS, as it eliminates the need of the priori knowledge of execution time of modules of the task.

References

[1] Vidyarthi D P, Tripathi A K (1996) Precedence Constrained Task Allocation in Distributed Computing Systems. *Int J of High Speed Computing* 8(1):47–55

[2] Vidyarthi D P, Tripathi A K, Mantri A N (1996) A Genetic Task Allocation Algorithm for Distributed Computing System Incorporating Problem Specific Knowledge. *Int J of High Speed Computing* 8(4):363–370

[3] Tripathi A K, Sarker B K, Kumar N, Vidyarthi D P (2000) Multiple Task Allocation with Load Consideration. *Int J of Inform and Comp Sci* 3(1):36–44

[4] Kafil M, Ahmed I (1998) Optimal Task Assignment in Heterogeneous Distributed Computing System. *IEEE Concurrency*, July - September:42–51

[5] Chu W W, Lan L T (1987) Task Allocation and Precedence Relations for Distributed Real Time Systems. *IEEE Trans. Computers* C-36(6):667–679

[6] Shatz S M, Wang J P, Goto M (1992) Task Allocation for Maximizing Reliability of Distributed Computer Systems, *IEEE Trans. on Computer* 41(9):1156–1168

[7] Efe K (1982) Heuristic Models of Task Assignment Scheduling in Distributed Systems. *IEEE Computer* June:50–56

[8] Vidyarthi D P, Tripathi A K (1998) A Fuzzy IMC Cost Reduction Model for Task Allocation in Distributed Computing Systems. In: *proc. Fifth Int Sym on Methods and Models in Automation and Robotics*, Poland, August:719–721

[9] Abdelzaher T F, Shin K G (2000) Period-Based Load Partitioning and Assignment for Large Real-Time Applications. *IEEE Tran on Computers* 49(1):81–87

[10] Peng D T, Shin K G (1989) Static Allocation of Periodic Task with Precedence. In: *Proc. Int Conf Distributed Computing Systems*, June :190–198

[11] Hou C J, Shin K G (1994) Replication and Allocation of Task Modules in Distributed Real Time Systems. In:*Proc. 24th IEEE Symp Fault Tolerant Computing Systems*, June:26–35

[12] Shukla S B, Agrawal D P (1994) A Framework for Mapping Periodic Real Time Applications on Multicomputers. *IEEE Tran on Para and Dist Systems* 5(7):778–784

[13] Oh Y, Son S H (1995) Scheduling Hard Real-Time Tasks with Tolerance to Multiple Processor Failures. *Multiprocessing and Multiprogramming* 40:193–206

[14] Tia T S, Liu J W S (1995) Assigning Real Time Tasks and Resources to Distributed Systems. *Int J Mini and Microcomputer* 17(1):18–25

[15] Wu S S, Sweeping D (1994) Heuristic Algorithms for Task Assignment and Scheduling in a Processor Network. *Parallel Computing* 20:1-14

III

NETWORKING, ARCHITECTURES, AND DISTRIBUTED SYSTEMS

Chapter 10

AN AD HOC ON-DEMAND ROUTING
PROTOCOL WITH ALTERNATE ROUTES

Chiu-Kuo Liang and Hsi-Shu Wang

Department of Computer Science and Information Engineering, Chung Hua University
Hsinchu, Taiwan 30067, Republic of China
ckliang@chu.edu.tw, seasu@pdlab.csie.chu.edu.tw

Abstract   Because of node mobility and power limitations, the network topology changes
frequently. Routing protocols plays an important role in the ad hoc network.
A recent trend in ad hoc network routing is the reactive on-demand philosophy
where routes are established only when required. In this paper, we propose a
scheme to improve existing on-demand routing protocols by creating a mesh
and multiple alternate routes by overhearing the data packet transmission. Our
scheme establishes the mesh and alternate routes without transmitting any extra
control message. We apply our approach to the Ad-hoc On-Demand Distance
Vector (AODV) protocol and evaluate the performance improvements by ns-2
simulations.

Keywords: Ad-Hoc, On-Demand, Routing Protocol, Alternate Routes.

Introduction

In a "mobile ad hoc network" (MANET) [1], mobile nodes communicates
with each other using multihop wireless links. There is no stationary infrastructure; for instance, no base stations in the network. Each mobile node (and
associated host) in the network also acts as a router, forwarding data packets
for other nodes. Ad hoc networks consist of hosts communicating one another
with portable radios. These networks can be deployed impromptly without
any wired base station or infrastructure support. In ad hoc mobile networks,
routes are mainly multihop because of the limited radio propagation range, and
topology changes frequently and unpredictably since each network host moves
randomly. Therefore, a central challenge in the design of ad hoc networks,
which also has received interests from many researchers, is the development
of dynamic routing protocols that can efficiently find routes between two com-

municating nodes which are able to route with low overheads even in dynamic conditions. Overhead here is defined in terms of the routing protocol control messages which consume both channel bandwidth as well as the battery power of nodes for communication.

On-demand routing protocols build and maintain only needed routes to reduce routing overheads. Examples include Ad Hoc On-Demand Distance Vector (AODV) [2, 3], Dynamic Source Routing (DSR) [4, 5], and Temporally Ordered Routing Algorithm (TORA) [6]. This is in contrast to proactive protocols (e.g., Destination Sequenced Distance Vector (DSDV) [7]) that maintain routes between all node pairs all the time. In on-demand protocols, a route discovery process (typically via a network-wide flood) is initiated whenever a route is needed. Each node in on-demand routing does not need periodic route table update exchange and does not have a full topological view of the network. Network hosts maintain route table entries only to destinations that they communicate with.

In this paper, we propose an algorithm that utilizes a mesh structure to provide multiple alternate paths to the Ad Hoc On-Demand Distance Vector (AODV) protocol that is one of the on-demand routing algorithms. We construct the mesh structure without producing additional control messages by overhearing the data packet transmission. Since an ad hoc network has limited bandwidth and shared wireless medium, it is critical to minimize the number of packet transmissions. It is beneficial to have multiple alternate paths in MANET due to the wireless networks are prone to route breaks resulting from node mobility, fading environment, single interference, high error rate, and packet collisions.

The rest of the paper is organized as follows. In Section 2, we review the AODV protocol. Section 3 illustrates the protocol operation in detail. Performance evaluation using the ns-2 simulator is presented in Section 4 and concluding remarks are made in Section 5.

1.   Ad Hoc On-Demand Distance Vector Routing

The Ad Hoc On-Demand Distance Vector (AODV) routing protocol described in [2, 3] is built on the DSDV [7] algorithm previously described. AODV is an improvement on DSDV because it typically minimizes the number of required broadcasts by creating routes on a demand basis, as opposed to maintaining a complete list of routes in the DSDV algorithm. The authors of AODV classify it as a pure on-demand route acquisition system, since nodes that are not on a selected path do not maintain routing information or participate in routing table exchanges.

1.1   Construction of AODV

When a source node desires to send a message to a destination node and does not already have a valid route to that destination, it initiates a path discovery process to locate the destination node. It broadcasts a route request (RREQ) packet to its neighbors, which then forward the request to their neighbor, and so on, until either the destination or an intermediate node with a "fresh enough" route to the destination is located. AODV utilizes destination sequence numbers to ensure all routes are loop-free and contain the most recent route information. Each node maintains its own sequence number, as well as a broadcast ID. The broadcast ID is incremented for every RREQ initiated by the node, and together with the node's IP address to uniquely identify an RREQ. Intermediate nodes can reply to the RREQ only if they have a route to the destination whose corresponding destination sequence number is greater than or equal to that contained in the RREQ.

During the process of forwarding the RREQ, intermediate nodes record in their route tables the address of the neighbor from which the first copy of the broadcast packet is received which can be used in establishing a reverse path. If additional copies of the same RREQ are later received, these packets are discarded. Once the RREQ reaches the destination or an intermediate node with a fresh enough route, the destination/intermediate node responds by unicasting a route reply (RREP) packet back to the neighbors from which it first received the RREQ. As the RREP is routed back along the reverse path, the nodes along this path will set up the forward route entries in the route tables, which are pointing to the node from which the RREP came. These forward route entries indicate the active forward route. Associated with each route entry a route timer is set up in order to delete the entry if it is not used within the specified lifetime. Since the RREP is forwarded along the path established by the RREQ, AODV only supports the use of symmetric links. Figure 10.1b shows the process of AODV route discovery. Here is some normal text.

1.2   Maintenance

Routes are maintained as follows. If a source node moves, it is able to reinitiate the route discovery protocol in order to find a new route to the destination. If a node along the route moves, its upstream neighbor will notice the move and propagate a link failure notification message to each of its active upstream neighbors to inform them of the erasure of that part of the route. These nodes in turn propagate the link failure notification to their upstream neighbors, and so on until the source node is reached. The source node may then choose to reinitiate route discovery for that destination if a route is still desired.

An additional aspect of the protocol is the use of hello messages, periodic local broadcasts by a node to inform each mobile node of other nodes in its neighborhood. Hello messages can be used to maintain the local connectivity of a node. Nodes listen for retransmission of data packets to ensure that the next hop is still within reach. If such a retransmission is not heard, the node may use any one of a number of techniques, including the reception of hello messages, to determine whether the next hop is within communication range.

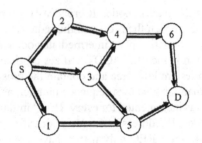

Figure 10.1a. RREQ Broadcast

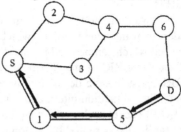

Figure 10.1b. RREP Forwarded Path

The hello messages may list the other nodes from which a mobile has heard, thereby yielding greater knowledge of network connectivity.

2.   The Proposed Protocol

The main purpose of our study is to improve the performance of the Ad Hoc On-Demand Distance Vector (AODV) routing protocol. Therefore, we take advantage of the broadcast nature of wireless communications; a node promiscuously "overhears" data packets that are transmitted by their neighboring nodes. From these packets, a node can obtain alternate path information and become part of the mesh. The operation details of our scheme are described as follows.

2.1   Primary Route Construction

Our algorithm does not require any modification to the AODV's route request propagation process, but instead we slightly modify the AODV's route reply procedure. We add a value called the number of hops to destination (HTD), which is a loose upper bound of the maximal hops to the given destination, into each ROUTE REPLY (RREP) packet.

At the beginning of primary route construction, source S sends ROUTE REQUEST (RREQ) packet to all its neighbors. Every host that receives RREQ for the first time does the same as well. Thus, the RREQ will flood all over the network, and will arrive at destination D eventually (if there is a routing path between S and D). When D receives REEQ packet for the first time, it sends a RREP back with a zero-value HTD to the host (say P) from which the RREQ was sent previously. When P receives RREP, it then creates a route entry for D in its route table. The HTD value of that entry is increased. Host P then propagates RREP, with HTD, to the host from which P receives RREQ for the first time. Every other host receiving RREP will do the same thing as P does. Figure 10.2 shows the process of primary route construction.

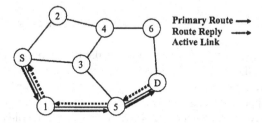

Figure 10.2. AODV route discovery (RREQ Broadcast)

2.2   Alternate Route Construction

The alternate routes are established during the route data delivery phase. We slightly modify data delivery phase to accomplish the task. Taking advantage of the broadcast nature of wireless communications, a node promiscuously "overhears" packets that transmitted by their neighboring nodes. In data delivery phase, we insert a HTD field into common header of data packet. The field can help us to establish a right direction of the alternate route. From these packets, a node obtains alternate path information and becomes part of the mesh as follows. When a node that is not part of the primary route overhears a data packet not directed to it transmitted by a neighbor on the primary route, it does the update alternate route procedure. If there is no alternate route entry or the HTD of data packet is smaller than route entry than it record that neighbor as the next hop to the destination and the HTD in its alternate route entry. By the update alternate route procedure, the nodes that overhear the data packets sending from the nodes on the primary route can choose the smallest HTD among them to update. Nodes that have an entry to the destination in their alternate route table are part of the mesh. The primary route and alternate route together establish a mesh structure (see Figure 10.3).

2.3   Route Maintenance

When a node detects a link break, it changes the common header of data packet to make it forward by the mesh node that not on the primary route. After that the node performs a one-hop data broadcast to its immediate neighbors. Neighbor nodes that receive this data packet unicast the data packet to their

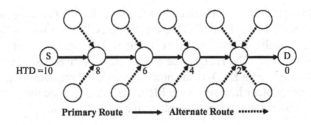

Figure 10.3.   AODV route discovery (RREQ Broadcast)

next hop node only if they have an entry for the destination in their alternate route tables and the HTD in it is smaller than that in the data packet. By this way, data packets can be delivered through one or more alternate routes and will not be dropped when route breaks occur. In order to prevent packet from tracing a loop, every mesh node will forward the data packet only if the packet is not a duplicate and they have the alternate route entry with a smaller HTD than that in the data packet. When a node of the primary route receives the data packet from alternate routes, it operates normally and forwards the packet to its next hop when the packet is not a duplicate. The node that detected the link break also sends a ROUTE ERROR (RERR) packet to the source to initiate a route rediscovery. Due to the purpose of our goal is to build a fresh and optimal route that reflects the current network situation and topology; we reconstruct a new route instead of continuously using the alternate paths. This is also the reason why we choose to overhear the data packet to construct the alternate routes.

A route is timed out when it is not used and updated for certain duration of time in AODV routing protocol. We apply the same technique in our scheme to purge the alternate routes. Nodes that can overhear data packet transmitted through the primary route add or update the alternate route and set up or update it's expire time. If an alternate route is not updated its expired time during the timeout interval, the node removes the path from the alternate route table. In AODV, each RREQ packet has a unique identifier so that nodes can detect and drop duplicate RREQ packets. Our protocol uses this method to help nodes drop duplicate data packets.

2.4   Example

We use Figure 10.4 as an example to show how the mesh and alternate routes are constructed by overhear technique and used in data delivery. When the RREQ reaches the destination node D, the primary route S-1-2-3-D is selected. Figure 10.4(a) show that the destination D set its HTD value to 0 and sends a RREP with increased HTD value 2 to node 3. After receiving this RREP, only node 3 relays the packet to node 2 since it is part of the route. Node 3 also increases the HTD value before it relays the packet. See Figure 10.4(b).

The other node on the select primary route do the same thing until the RREP packet reach the source node S. Figure 10.4(c) shows the HTD state after the primary route was build. Figures 10.4(d), 10.4(e) and 10.4(f) show how the nodes 4 and 5 build the alternate while the data packet transmitting through the primary route. When node S sends the data packet to node 1, nodes 4 and 5, who are within the propagation range of node S, will overhear the data packet but do nothing, since it is useless to record an alternate route to source node S. While node 1 relays the data packet to node 2, nodes 4 and 5 will overhear the packet and add an entry into their alternate route table. Figures 10.4(g) and 10.4(h) show that nodes 6 and 7 will add an entry when node 2 forwards the data packet to node 3. Figure 10.4(i) and 1.4(j) illustrate that nodes 6 and 7 update their route entry since node 3 has a smaller HTD value than their alternate route entries. Besides, nodes 8 and 9 will insert a route entry in their alternate route table. It seems that the alternate route in nodes 8 and 9 is useless. Figure 10.4(k) explains the usage of the alternate routes record in nodes 8 and 9. If the link between nodes 2 and 3 is broken and nodes 6 and 7 are moved out of the propagation range of node 3, node 8 will be moved into the propagation range of node 2 and node 3. We can find an alternate route to salvage the data packets, which is shown in Figure 10.4(l). Notice that the alternate route will be updated when any data packet transmission can be overheard. It makes our alternate route reflects the current network situation and topology.

3.   Simulation Experiments

In this section, we evaluate the performance improvements made by our alternate routing. We compare the simulation results of the AODV protocol with that of AODV protocol that applied our scheme as AODV-AR (AODV with Alternate Routes).

3.1   The Simulation Model

We use a detailed simulation model based on ns-2 [8] in our evaluation. In the recent papers [9, 12, 13], the Monarch research simulation multihop wireless networks complete with physical, data link, and medium access control (MAC) layer models on ns-2. The Distributed Coordination Function (DCF) of IEEE 802.11 [10] for wireless LANs is used as the MAC layer protocol. The radio model uses characteristics similar to a commercial radio interface, such as Lucent's WaveLAN [11]. WaveLAN is modeled as a shared-media radio with a nominal bit rate of 2Mb/s and a nominal radio range of 250m. A detailed description of the simulation environment and the models is available in [8, 9] and will not be discussed here.

The RREQ packets are treated as broadcast packets in the MAC. RREP and data packets are all unicast packets with a specified neighbor as the MAC destination. RERR packets are treated broadcast in AODV. Detect link breaks using feedback from the MAC layer. A signal is sent to the routing layer when

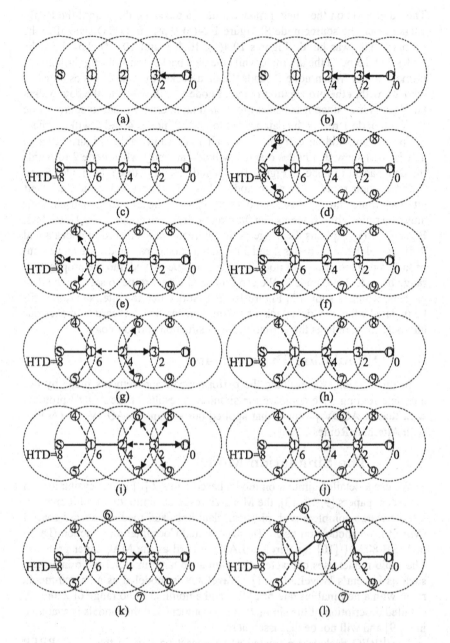

Figure 10.4.   An example how the mesh and alternate routes are constructed by overhear technique and used in date delivery

the MAC layer fails to deliver an unicast packet to the next hop. No additional network layer mechanism such as hello messages [2] is used.

Both protocols maintain a send buffer of 64 packets. It contains all data packets waiting for a route, such as packets for which route discovery has started, but no reply has arrived yet. All packets (both data and routing) sent by the routing layer are queued at the interface queue until the MAC layer can transmit them. The interface queue has a maximum size of 50 packets and is maintained as a priority queue with two priorities each served in FIFO order. Routing packets get higher priority than data packets.

We use traffic and mobility models similar to those previously reported using the same simulator [9, 12, 13]. A traffic generator was developed to simulate continuous bit rate (CBR) sources. The source-destination pairs are spread randomly over the network. The size of data payload was 512-byte.

We use two mobility models, which use the random waypoint model [9] in a rectangular field. In the first experiment model, 50 mobile nodes move around a rectangle region of 1500 meters by 300 meters. The second model, 100 mobile nodes move around a rectangle region of 2200 meters by 600 meters. Each node randomly selects a location, and moves toward that location with a speed uniformly distributed between 0-20 m/s.

Once the location is reached, another random location is targeted after a pause. We vary the pause time, which affects the relative speeds of the mobiles. Simulations are run for 100 s. Each data point represents an average of 100 runs with identical traffic models, but different randomly generated mobility scenarios. Identical mobility and traffic scenarios are used across protocols.

3.2   Performance Results

Figure 5 shows the throughput in packet delivery ratio. The ratio of the data packets delivered to the destination to this generated by the CBR source. Our scheme improves the throughput performance of AODV. We use seven different pause times from 10 sec to 200 sec to measure the influence of mobility. As the pause time gets shorter, the performance gain by alternate routes becomes more significant. Our protocol is able to deliver more packets to the destination than AODV. AODV try to repair the primary route by send RREQ packet while the node is closer to destination node than source node. After a period of time if the node don't get RREP packet the node will drop the data packet. Alternate paths may be broken as well as the primary route because of mobility. Moreover, packets can be lost because of collisions and contention problems.

Average end-to-end delay of data packets - This includes all possible delays caused by buffering during route discovery latency, queuing at the interface queue, retransmission delays at the MAC, and propagation and transfer times. Figure 10.6 and Figure 10.8 show the simulation result. We can find out that at some time AODV-AR has smaller average delay time than AODV. The reason

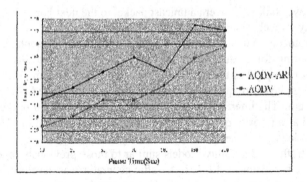

Figure 10.5. Data packet delivery rate (1500m X 300m)

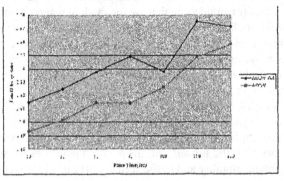

Figure 10.6. Data packet delivery rate (2200m X 600m)

is that AODV try to recover the primary route at the node that near destination, it will cost the time to wait the RREP packet to be sent back from the destination. If our protocol salvages the data packet successfully and AODV fails to recovery the primary route, then the packet's delay time of our protocol will be less than that of AODV.

4.   Conclusion

We presented a scheme take advantage of the broadcast nature of wireless communications to build alternate route without any yield any extra overhead. Our scheme can be incorporated into any ad hoc on-demand unicast routing protocol to improve reliable packet delivery in the face of node movements and route breaks.

In the future, we may try to repair the primary route with alternate route which we build by overhear. In this thesis, the node of main route goes through another node of main route by using backup route only one hop. If we can increase it to two hops or more, then the backup route should be more reliable.

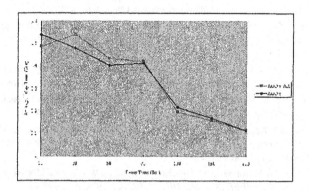

Figure 10.7. Average Delay time (1500m X 300m)

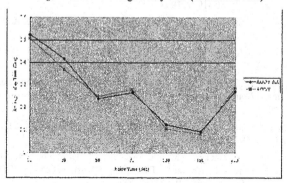

Figure 10.8. Average Delay time (2200m X 600m)

References

[1] J. Macker and S. Corson, "Mobile Ad Hoc Networks (MANET)," IETF WG Charter., http://www.ietf.org/html.charters/manet-charter.htm, 1997.

[2] C. E. Perkins and E. M. Royer, "Ad Hoc On-demand Distance Vector Routing," *Proc. 2nd IEEE Wksp. Mobile Comp. Sys. And Apps.*, Feb.1999, pp.90-100.

[3] C. E. Perkins, E. M. Royer and S. R. Das, "Ad Hoc On-demand Distance Vector (AODV) Routing," IETF, Internet Draft, draft-ietf-manet-aodv-11.txt , June. 2002.

[4] D. Johnson and D. Maltz, "Dynamic Source Routing in Ad Hoc Wireless Networks," T. Imielinski and H. Korth, Eds. *Mobile Computing*, Ch. 5, Kluwer, 1996.

[5] D. Johnson, Dave Maltz, Y Hu, Jorjeta Jetcheva, "The Dynamic Source Routing Protocol for Mobile Ad Hoc Networks (DSR)," IETF, Internet Draft, draft-ietf-manet-dsr-07.txt, February. 2002.

[6] M. S. Corson and V. D. Park, "Temporally Ordered Routing Algorithm (TORA) version 1: Functional specification," Internet-Draft, draft-ietf-manet-tora-spec-00.txt, Nov.1997.

[7] C. E. Perkins and P. Bhagwat, "Highly Dynamic Destination-Sequenced Distance-Vector Routing (DSDV) for Mobile Computers," *ACM SIGCOMM '94*, pp. 234-244.

[8] Kevin Fall and Kannan Varadhan, editors. ns notes and documentation, The VINT Project, UC Berkeley, LBL, USC/ISI, and Xerox PARC, November 1999. Available from http://www-mash.cs.berkeley.edu/ns/.

[9] J. Broch et al., "A Performance Comparison of Multihop Wireless Ad Hoc Network Routing Protocols," *Proc. IEEE/ACM MOBICOM '98*, Oct. 1998, pp.85-97.

[10] IEEE, "Wireless LAN Medium Access Control (MAC) and Physical Layer (PHY) Specifications," IEEE Std. 802.11-1997, 1997.

[11] B. Tuch, "Development of WaveLAN, an ISM Band Wireless LAN," *AT&T Tech. J.*, vol. 72, no. 4, July/Aug 1993. pp. 27-33.

[12] E. M. Royer and C-K Toh, "A Review of Current Routing Protocols for Ad Hoc Mobile Wireless Networks," *IEEE Personal Communication*, pp. 46-55, 1999.

[13] C. E. Perkins, E. M. Royer, S. R. Das, and M. K. Marina, "Performance Comparison of Two On-Demand Routing Protocols for Ad Hoc Networks," *IEEE Personal Communications*, Feb. 2001.

[14] S. Murthy and J. J. Garcia-Luna-Aceves, "A routing protocol for packet radio networks, " *ACM MOBICOM*, 1995, pp. 86-94.

[15] S. Corson and J. Macker, "Mobile Ad hoc Networking (MANET):Routing Protocol Performance Issues and Evaluation Considerations," IETF, Internet Draft,http://www.ietf.org/rfc/rfc2501.txt, Jan. 1999.

Chapter 11

DESIGN OF A VIABLE FAULT-TOLERANT ROUTING STRATEGY FOR OPTICAL-BASED GRIDS

Peter K. K. Loh and W. J. Hsu

School of Computer Engineering

Nanyang Technological University, Nanyang Avenue, Singapore 639798

askkloh@ntu.edu.sg, hsu@ntu.edu.sg

Abstract   This article presents a cost-effective fault-tolerant routing strategy for optical-electronic grids. We propose the design of a fully adaptive, fault-tolerant routing strategy for multi-hop grid networks using wavelength-division multiplexing. The routing strategy is both deadlock-free and livelock-free. Regardless of the number and type of faults and size of the grid network, only three buffer sets and two routing tables of size $O(d)$ are required at each node, where d is the grid dimension. In the absence of faults, minimal paths with the least congestion are used so that latency is minimised. In the presence of faults or congestion, misrouting is constrained selectively to prevent livelock. The routing strategy is local-information based and does not exploit component redundancy or isolation of healthy nodes and links.

Keywords: Optical fault-tolerant routing, wavelength-division multiplexing, grids, deadlock-freedom, livelock-freedom

Introduction

An increased interest has manifested itself in fault tolerance issues in optical-electronic parallel processing systems [1, 5, 6, 8, 10, 11, 19]. Optical-electronic parallel processing systems are multiprocessor systems with electronic processors and communication channels that may be implemented with optical technology. Contemporary technology limits the number of available wavelengths and tunability of optical transceivers, making it difficult to establish a completely optical communications path between all nodes in a large-scale, single-hop *all-optical network (AON)* [3, 7, 9, 16, 17]. In more practical, multi-hop opto-electronic networks, wavelength conversion/amplification at

intermediate nodes along a communication path is carried out [19]. Technological advances in the past decade have made available physically smaller
devices with increased optoelectronic conversion efficiency and lower power
consumption [17]. Some interesting fault-tolerant routing strategies have been
proposed for multi-hop networks based on Wavelength Division Multiplexing
(WDM) [1,5,10-11,19]. In WDM systems, communications on different optical wavelengths may be multiplexed onto an optical fiber. Corresponding
de-multiplexing is then performed at the receiving node.

A fault-tolerant routing scheme is proposed by Bandyopadhyay et al. [1]
for multi-hop networks. In this scheme, each source-destination path is pre-
computed to guarantee message delivery in the presence of faults. All pre-
computed paths are thus deadlock-free and livelock-free. Communication overheads are minimised by specifying an upper bound for the path setup time,
exceeding which the communication is considered blocked. Dynamic faults
that occur during path establishment can be tolerated. Here, it is required that
each fault-free node and its associated router know the routing path to every
other node when the network is fault-free. This may result in a node maintaining complex routing tables that are not cost-effective with increase in network
size. Also, each fault-free router maintains a queue of messages received over
a control channel, which is used for path pre-computation and transmission of
fault information. This, however, requires the need to consider fault tolerance
issues for the control channel as well.

Gerstel et al. [5] proposed a fault-tolerant routing strategy for optical-based,
ring networks. In this strategy, a single fault can be tolerated and alternate
routing may be determined statically. When routing is blocked in a specified direction, rerouting is simply invoked in the opposite direction. In more
complex networks, however, a set of heuristics to provide some adaptivity is
inevitably required to cope with faults.

A fault-tolerant scheme that tolerates only faulty links has proposed by Lalwaney and Koren [10, 11]. The fault model here assumes that a link failure is
caused by an optical transmitter and/or receiver failure. In this scheme, it is
assumed that every node has at least one fault-free tunable transmitter and receiver that can tune to the transmitting and receiving wavelengths of all channels of that node. In the event of a transmitter failure, the fault-free tunable
transmitter alternately switches between its normal operating frequency to that
of the failed transmitter. Both communication streams are time-multiplexed
onto a given link. The use of tunable transmitters and receivers essentially
enables logical reconfiguration of the network topology to bypass link faults.
Contemporary transmitters have, however, limited tuning range that restricts
the types of logical topologies supported [3, 17].

In Shen et al. [19], a fault-tolerant routing strategy has been proposed for
multi-hop, optoelectronic *WDM*-networks of node connectivity $(f + 1)$. Up to
f channel faults may be tolerated provided faults occur before path establishment. This routing model uses a combination of circuit switching to reserve

communication paths and packet switching to physically transmit the messages along these paths. The fault-tolerant routing strategy can handle both optical channel and wavelength conversion faults. Faults that are known before the routing stage, after finding the communication path or after path establishment but before transmission, can be tolerated. However, the strategy requires preprocessing to locate alternate paths during path finding, which increases communication overheads. Despite this, dynamic faults that occur during message transmission are not tolerated as in [12]. Finally, there are no specified mechanisms to tolerate node (processor) failures.

The challenge then is to design a fault-tolerant optical-based routing strategy with the following desired properties:

- For reliability, the strategy should tolerate component (both node and link) faults that may occur not only before but also during message transmission.

- For efficiency, minimal or no preprocessing should be employed. Alternate paths for rerouting should, preferably, be computed "on the fly".

- For cost-effectiveness, existing optical transmitters/receivers should be exploited during the absence and presence of faults with no component redundancy. Local (nearest neighbour) fault information should be used with low complexity routing information that scale slowly with network size. Towards these objectives, the use of communication- and space-efficient schemes [4, 14] becomes an important consideration.

In this section, we propose a fault-tolerant routing strategy for multi-hop *WDM*-based 3-dimensional grid networks, such as [13, 15, 20, 22], with the following attractive properties:

- Adaptive and tolerant to both node and link faults

- Fault detection and handling are performed locally at each node

- Routing strategy is both deadlock-free and livelock-free

- Each node maintains only three buffer sets and two size $O(d)$ routing tables, d is the node degree of the grid

- Spare optical transmitters/receivers are not required

- No computation or broadcast of additional routing information for table updates is needed

The rest of the paper is organised as follows. Section 1 introduces the terminology and notations used in subsequent sections. The design of the routing model is discussed in Section 2 while Section 3 details the proofs for routing properties. The paper concludes with section 4.

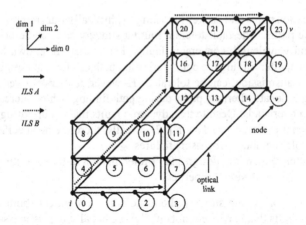

Figure 11.1.   Paths determined by ILS A & B

1.   Preliminaries

A 3-dimensional multi-hop grid (3-D grid) is an m_0 by m_1 by m_2 network containing $N = \prod_{i=0}^{2} m_i$ nodes. Each node, with coordinates (x, y, z), may be addressed as $i = (z * m_0 * m_1 + x * m_1 + y)$, where $0 \leq i < N$. Each node along a dimension d of the grid, may represent a system that comprises a sub-network, and is interfaced to a bi-directional optical link (fiber). Each optical link along a dimension d may be viewed directionally. If the optical link is interfaced to any two nodes along dimension d, $V_a = (a_2, a_1, a_0)$ and $V_b = (b_2, b_1, b_0)\rangle$, we denote the direction along dimension d as F_d, when $b_d > a_d$ or as B_d, when $a_d > b_d$. Finally, each optical link is comprised of multiple channels, with each channel supporting transmission at a unique frequency optical λ. Contemporary technology enables support for 128 different optical frequencies per fiber [3].

2.   Design of the Routing Strategy

In this section, we discuss the design of the routing strategy. We start off with the design of a set of space-efficient routing tables [12]. These tables make use of a variation of the compact labelling scheme known as interval labelling [18, 21].

2.1   Node and Link Labelling Schemes

Nodes and associated links of regular networks like grids can be labelled based on a modified interval labelling scheme for adaptive routing. In an interval labelling scheme (*ILS*), the links of each node may be labelled with an interval, such that the collections of interval sets at any node are disjoint. Messages can only be routed over the link associated with an interval containing the destination address. That is, a link labelled with the interval $[a, b)$ can be used to route messages to destination nodes $\{a, a+1, a+2, \ldots, b-1\}$. To illustrate the modified ILS for adaptive routing, we exemplify the approach with a 4 by 3 by 2 grid, as shown in Figure 11.1. Table 11.1 shows the ILS A for the 3-D grid, where B_d and F_d ($d = 0, 1, 2$) represent the backward and forward directions, respectively, along dimension d of the grid and $\backslash$ is the modulus operator.

Assume that the message at node i is destined for node v. Then, $f(v) = v \backslash m_0$ is computed and the interval associated with a B_0 or F_0 link is first determined. Depending on which interval $f(v)$ falls within, the message is then routed via B_0 or F_0 to the correct dim1-dim2 plane. If $f(v)$ does not fall into an interval, then v is in the same dim1-dim2 plane as the source node. In the second phase, $g(v) = v \backslash (m_0 m_1)$ is computed and compared to intervals assigned to links in dimensions 1 and 2. The message destined for v will be routed along the B_1 or F_1 channel until it reaches the correct row of the destination. Finally, v is compared and the message is routed along B_2 or F_2 to reach the destination node. The bold arrows in Figure 11.1 show the message path taken from source node 0 to destination node 23 using the ILS A.

Table 11.1.   ILS A for 3-D Grids

Direction	Interval
B_0	$[0, i \backslash m_0)$
F_0	$[(i+1) \backslash m_0, m_0)$
B_1	$[0, m_0 * \lfloor i/m_0 \rfloor)$
F_1	$[m_0 + m_0 * \lfloor (i \backslash m_0 m_1)/m_0 \rfloor, m_0 m_1)$
B_2	$[0, \lfloor i \backslash m_0 m_1 \rfloor * m_0 m_1)$
F_2	$[\lfloor (i \backslash m_0 m_1)/m_0 \rfloor * m_0 m_1, m_0 m_1 m_2)$

ILS A defines a minimal path between any two clusters and the routing is in increasing dimension order. Hence, the routing is minimal, deadlock-free and livelock-free in the absence of faults and congestion [2]. In a grid, however, routing can be either in increasing or decreasing dimension order. ILS A, which defines increasing dimension-order routing, determines one path for routing. To handle component faults and congestion, the routing strategy must be able to exploit alternative paths. We define an alternative ILS for decreasing dimension-order routing. Table 11.2 shows ILS B for the grid in Figure 11.1.

ILS B is used in a similar way to ILS A. If the source and destination nodes are not on the same plane, the message is first routed along B_2 or F_2 towards the correct dim0-dim1 destination plane. On the destination plane, the destination address v is compared to the intervals assigned to links in dimensions 1 and 0. Once the message has arrived at the same row as its destination via B_1

Table 11.2. ILS B for 3-D Grids

Direction	Interval
B_0	$[m_0 * \lfloor i/m \rfloor, i)$
F_0	$[i+1, m_0 + m_0 * \lfloor i/m_0 \rfloor)$
B_1	$[\lfloor i/m_0 m_1 \rfloor * m_0 m_1, m_0 * \lfloor i/m_0 \rfloor)$
F_1	$[m_0 + m_0 * \lfloor i/m_0 \rfloor, \lfloor i/m_0 m_1 \rfloor * m_0 m_1 + m_0 m_1)$
B_2	$[0, \lfloor i/m_0 m_1 \rfloor * m_0 m_1)$
F_2	$[\lfloor i/m_0 m_1 \rfloor * m_0 m_1 + m_0 m_1, m_0 m_1 m_2)$

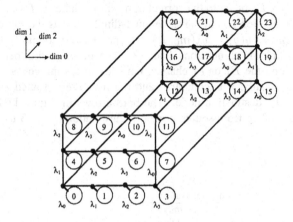

Figure 11.2. Wavelength Allocation for a $4 \times 3 \times 2$ Grid

or F_1, the message is routed to its destination via B_0 or F_0. ILS B thus defines decreasing dimension-order routing. An example applying *ILS B* is shown in Figure 11.1. Dotted arrows represent the message path.

2.2　Wavelength Allocation Scheme

In this section, we describe the wavelength allocation scheme that assigns optical frequencies for reception to each node. That is, a node assigned with an optical frequency of λ receives data destined for it on this frequency. To minimise the number of frequencies to be allocated and indirectly the amount of optical fibre, we cyclically shift the allocated frequencies. In this way, each group of nodes are allocated "unique" frequencies for data reception along a given network dimension. This scheme is adapted from a similar one used by Louri et al. [15] for hypercubes.

Specifically, the number of unique optical frequencies to be assigned is $W = \max(m_0, m_1, m_2)$ for an m_0 by m_1 by m_2 grid network. Assign optical frequencies $\{\lambda_0, \lambda_1, \ldots, \lambda_{W-1}\}$ to nodes of row 0 of dimension d, $\{v_0, v_1, \ldots, v_{W-1}\}$ respectively, where d is the grid dimension with W nodes.

Subsequently, assign $\{\lambda_1, \lambda_2, \ldots, \lambda_{W-1}, \lambda_0\}$ to nodes of the next row of dimension d, and so on. For the next plane of nodes along an orthogonal dimension, assign optical frequencies $\{\lambda_1, \lambda_2, \ldots, \lambda_{W-1}, \lambda_0\}$ to nodes of row 0, and $\{\lambda_2, \lambda_3, \ldots, \lambda_{W-1}, \lambda_0, \lambda_1\}$ to nodes of the next row, and so on. Figure 11.2 illustrates the wavelength assignment for the $4 \times 3 \times 2$ grid network.

Since ILS A or B routes messages along an optical link in dimension order, the optical reception frequency of an intermediate node along each dimension must be determined before routing takes place along that dimension. Consider source node, u, at location (a, b, c) and destination node, v, at location (x, y, z). The optical reception frequency index at v can be computed from the source frequency index $\phi(u)$ by function F as follows:

$$F : (u) \rightarrow \phi(v),$$

where

$$F(\phi(u)) = (\phi(u) + (x - a) + (y - b) + (z - c)) \pmod{W}$$

Note that the wavelength allocation scheme is independent of the routing scheme used. The same optical frequency assignment would apply to the network regardless of whether the routing is based on *ILS A* or *ILS B*. It will become apparent later that the wavelength allocation scheme is also independent of the fault pattern. In the next section, we present the buffer allocation model at each node.

2.3   The Buffer Allocation Scheme

In this section, we present the buffer allocation model at each node. For a 3-D grid, there are a maximum of 6 input and output ports at each node as illustrated in Figure 11.3. Each input port comprises an optical demultiplexer that channels incoming optical frequencies into the W opto-electronic receivers. Each receiver is tuned to a specific frequency and converts that frequency into a corresponding electronic signal. Each output port comprises W opto-electronic transmitters, each of which converts an input electronic signal into a specified optical frequency. A transmitter may be tuned to transmit at more than one frequency. An optical multiplexer then combines up to W different optical frequencies for transmission on the associated optical fiber. The electronic switch between the IO ports is responsible for the routing function, R_{xy}, where x and y denote input and output ports, respectively.

Figure 11.3 shows that there are three input buffers (IB_{0i}, IB_{1i}, and IB_{2i}) associated with each input port i and three output buffers (OB_{0j}, OB_{1j}, and OB_{2j}) associated with each output port j. The number of buffer sets allocated is always three and is independent of the size and dimension of the grid network. Each buffer set constitutes a logical network and supports communications in a specified direction.

Messages in buffer set 0 have the most flexibility, being able to bi-directionally traverse a route along any grid dimension. Messages in buffer set 0 can also

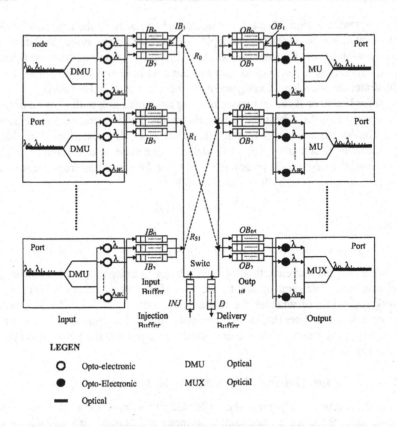

Figure 11.3. Buffer Allocation Model at a Node

switch over to either buffer sets 1 or 2 when certain network or traffic conditions arise. Messages in buffer sets 1 and 2, however, are constrained to route in specified directions. In addition, messages in buffer set 1 are prohibited from using buffer set 2 and vice versa. These constraints are necessary to permit full adaptivity and prevent deadlock as will be proven in the next section. Finally, the injection buffer, *INJB*, holds new packets generated by the local CPU and the delivery buffer, *DB*, holds packets for consumption by the local CPU.

With this design, we are effectively dividing the physical interconnection network into three logical networks, L_0, L_1 and L_2 as illustrated in Figure 11.4. L_0 is connected with L_1 and L_2 through logical links whereas L_1 and L_2 are disconnected. There are at most three logical links for each bi-directional optical link (fiber). The logical links share the bandwidth of the fiber.

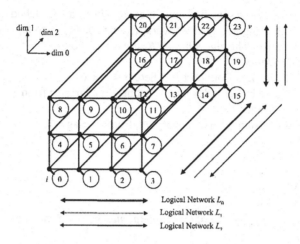

Figure 11.4. Logical Networks (a) L_0 (b) L_1 (c) L_2

2.4 The Fault-Tolerant Routing Algorithm

Here, we present the fault-tolerant routing algorithm, **FTRoute**, in two parts: **AdaptiveRoute** and **LogicalRoute**. Let the locations of the source, current and destination nodes to be at (x_s, y_s, z_s), (x_c, y_c, z_c), and (x_d, y_d, z_d), respectively. For a buffer B, $size(B)$ is the total number of places in the buffer and $hold(B)$ denotes the number of places that are currently occupied by a message. At each node, given the input port and buffer, and the message's destination node, the routing function R specifies the output buffer and port to which the message may be moved. The routing function is defined as R_{ij} : $(i, p) \rightarrow (j, q)$ where i and j are the input and output ports, respectively, $0 \leq i$, $j < 6$ (for a 3-D grid), p and q are the buffer indices at the previous and current nodes, respectively, with $p, q \in \{0, 1, 2\}$. We assume fail-stop faults. The failure of an optical receiver may be assumed to be detected at the sending opto-electronic transmitter [11, 19]. Thus, a faulty receiver may be treated as a faulty transmitter for analysis purposes (see Section 4).

Definition of Dimension Reversal, DR : The dimension reversal number, DR, of a message is the number of times a message has been routed from a dimension m to a neighbouring node in a lower dimension, $n < m$. Essentially, DR is used to control the extent of misrouting or non-minimal routing that the message undergoes. DR is assigned to each message header as follows:

1) Every new message is initialized with a DR of 0.

2) Each time a message is misrouted from an input buffer IB_{mi} in any node to an output buffer OB_{nj} in the same node, the DR of the message is incremented if $m > n$.

3) If a message is routed along a minimal path, the DR is not incremented.

When *DR* reaches a specified limit, messages in L_0 are switched to L_1 or L_2. A message travelling in logical network, L_1, cannot switch to logical network, L_2, and vice versa. The algorithm *FTRoute* is as follows:

AdaptiveRoute

INPUT *message* from port i , where $0 \le i < 6$

GET source buffer index p and destination address v from message header

GET dimension reversal count, *DR*, from message header

IF destination v reached

  STOP

ELSE

  RESET bit i in mask vector

  IF ($p = 1$ or 2) call *LogicalRoute(p, message)*   /* message in L_1 or L_2 */

    ELSE   /* message in L_0 */

     IF (dimension reversals $DR <$ reversal limit RL)

      Select primary output port s based on *ILS A*

      Select alternative output port t based on *ILS B*

      IF *hold(OB$_{0s}$)* $<$*size(OB$_{0s}$)* **OR** *hold(OB$_{0t}$)* $<$*size(OB$_{0t}$)*

      select(OB$_{0j}$) $= min$(*hold(OB$_{0s}$)*, *hold(O$_{0t}$)*)

        ELSE   /* fault encountered or traffic congestion */

        IF *first(hold(OB$_{0k}$)* $<$*size(OB$_{0k}$)*), where $0 \le k < 6$ and $k \ne s$ or t

        select(OB$_{0j}$) $= OB_{0k}$

        IF ($k < i$) increment *DR*

        ELSE discard and retransmit message $<$**EXIT**$>$

    ELSE IF (($y_d < y_c$) **AND** ($z_d \ge z_c$)) **OR** (($y_d \le y_c$) **AND** ($z_d > z_c$))

     call *LogicalRoute(1,message)*

        ELSE IF (($y_d > y_c$) **AND** ($z_d \le z_c$)) **OR** (($y_d \ge y_c$) **AND** ($z_d <$ z_c))

          call *LogicalRoute(2,message)*

            ELSE discard and retransmit message $<$**EXIT**$>$

/* Output message to transmitters at port j */

$R_{ij} : (i, p) \rightarrow (j, q)$ /* establish switched links */

GET local node's reception wavelength $\phi(c)$

COMPUTE $\phi(v) = F(\phi(c))$ /* compute destination node reception frequency */

IF NON-FAULTY(transmitter($\phi(v)$)

 send(message, $\phi(v)$)

ELSE *send(message, g(v))*   /* $g(v)$ is frequency of 1st non-faulty transmitter */

LogicalRoute(p,message)

IF ($x_d < x_c$)   /* In logical network, L_1 */

  IF ($y_d = y_c$) **AND** ($z_d = z_c$)

$select(OB_{1j}) = OB_{10}$
ELSE IF $(y_d < y_c)$ **AND** $(z_d = z_c)$
$select(OB_{1j}) = min(hold(OB_{10}), hold(OB_{12}))$
ELSE IF $(y_d = y_c)$ **AND** $(z_d > z_c)$
$select(OB_{1j}) = min(hold(OB_{10}), hold(OB_{15}))$
ELSE IF $(y_d < y_c)$ **AND** $(z_d > z_c)$
$select(OB_{1j}) = min(hold(OB_{10}), hold(OB_{12}), hold(OB_{15}))$
ELSE IF $(x_d > x_c)$
IF $(y_d = y_c)$ **AND** $(z_d = z_c)$
$select(OB_{1j}) = OB_{11}$
ELSE IF $(y_d < y_c)$ **AND** $(z_d = z_c)$
$select(OB_{1j}) = min(hold(OB_{11}), hold(OB_{12}))$
ELSE IF $(y_d = y_c)$ **AND** $(z_d > z_c)$
$select(OB_{1j}) = min(hold(OB_{11}), hold(OB_{15}))$
ELSE IF $(y_d < y_c)$ **AND** $(z_d > z_c)$
$select(OB_{1j}) = min(hold(OB_{11}), hold(OB_{12}), hold(OB_{15}))$
IF $(x_d < x_c)$ // In logical network, L_2 //
IF $(y_d = y_c)$ **AND** $(z_d = z_c)$
$select(OB_{2j}) = OB_{20}$
ELSE IF $(y_d > y_c)$ **AND** $(z_d = z_c)$
$select(OB_{2j}) = min(hold(OB_{20}), hold(OB_{23}))$
ELSE IF $(y_d = y_c)$ **AND** $(z_d < z_c)$
$select(OB_{2j}) = min(hold(OB_{20}), hold(OB_{24}))$
ELSE IF $(y_d > y_c)$ **AND** $(z_d < z_c)$
$select(OB_{2j}) = min(hold(OB_{20}), hold(OB_{23}), hold(OB_{24}))$
ELSE IF $(x_d > x_c)$
IF $(y_d = y_c)$ **AND** $(z_d = z_c)$
$select(OB_{2j}) = OB_{21}$
ELSE IF $(y_d > y_c)$ **AND** $(z_d = z_c)$
$select(OB_{2j}) = min(hold(OB_{21}), hold(OB_{23}))$
ELSE IF $(y_d = y_c)$ **AND** $(z_d < z_c)$
$select(OB_{2j}) = min(hold(OB_{21}), hold(OB_{24}))$
ELSE IF $(y_d < y_c)$ **AND** $(z_d < z_c)$
$select(OB_{2j}) = min(hold(OB_{21}), hold(OB_{23}), hold(OB_{24}))$

3.   Proofs of Routing Properties

In this section, we present the development of proofs for the fault-tolerant routing strategy. In order to achieve deadlock-free routing based on ILS A and ILS B, the following routing rules must be satisfied:

1) A new message enters the network if and only if there exists an OB, such that $hold(OB) < (size(OB) - 1)$. This leaves at least one space for transit messages.

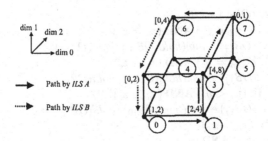

Figure 11.5. Communications cycle exists with ILS A & B

2) A transit message has higher priority than a new (entry) message.

3) Messages arriving at the same time are handled in a round robin fashion to ensure fairness and avoid channel starvation.

4) If $hold(DELB) = size(DELB)$, then $select(OB) = \min(hold(OB_{jq}))$, where $0 \leq j < 2d$ and $q \in \{0, 1, 2\}$. Message is re-injected into the network when the delivery buffer is full.

5) If $hold(OB_{iq}) = size(OB_{iq})$, $select(OB_{jq}) = min(hold(OB_{jq}, 0 \leq j < 2d, q \in \{0, 1, 2\}$ and $j \neq i)$. When $\|select(OB)\| > 1$, one is chosen randomly.

6) Rate of message consumption exceeds rate of message injection [2].

Lemma 1:
Routing with *FTRoute* is minimal and adaptive.
Proof:
Routing using either ILS A or ILS B is deterministic, dimension-ordered and the corresponding route produced for any source-destination node cluster pair is the shortest. At any node, either ILS A or ILS B may be used. ■

Lemma 2:
Routing with ILS A and ILS B alone is not deadlock-free.
Proof:
Use of ILS A and ILS B alone creates a communications cycle. Consider the 2 by 2 by 2 grid in Figure 11.5. At cluster 0, a message destined for cluster 7 is routed over the path determined by ILS A. At cluster 3, a message intended for cluster 6 is routed over a path determined by ILS B. Cluster 7 sends to cluster 2 via ILS A. Finally, at cluster 6, a message destined for cluster 1, is routed along the path determined by ILS B. Since there is a cycle of communication requests, deadlock can arise. ■

Prevention of deadlock requires adherence to the above specified routing rules as well as the routing directions specified by the logical networks. To prove deadlock-freedom in *FTRoute*, we must prove deadlock-freedom in *AdaptiveRoute* as well as in *LogicalRoute*.

Theorem 1:

Routing phase *AdaptiveRoute* is deadlock-free.

Proof:

We will prove this by contradiction. Assuming *AdaptiveRoute* is not deadlock-free with source and destination clusters u and v, respectively. Then, a cycle of full IO buffers will exist, (R_{ij} such that $hold(OB_{pi}) = size(OB_{pi})$ and $hold(OB_{qj}) = size(OB_{qj})$), at all nodes, inclusive of u and w, in the communication path. Assume that w is a neighbouring node of v in the communication path. This implies that either Rule 6 (v is not receiving the message) or Rule 1 is violated. If $hold(OB_{qk}) = (size(OB_{qk}) - 1)$, no new message can be injected but transit messages are not prohibited. A transit message then moves towards v in the opposite direction to the movement of the empty buffer place. In either case, a deadlock cannot exist. ■

Lemma 3:

Routing phase *AdaptiveRoute* is fully adaptive.

Proof:

Messages first attempt to follow the minimal paths defined by ILS A or ILS B. Misrouting is used when these minimal paths are congested or faulty. This is evident from the routing algorithm where any OB can be used at some point. Specifically, a message may be routed in L_0 starting with any dimension and in any direction along a specified dimension. ■

Theorem 2:

Routing phase *AdaptiveRoute* is not livelock-free in an d-D grid.

Proof:

By Lemma 3, *AdaptiveRoute* is fully adaptive. There exist some clusters such that $hold(OB_{qj}) = size(OB_{qj})$ for $j = 0, 1, ..., d - 1$ (minimal paths) and $hold(OB_{qj}) < size(OB_{qj})$ for $j = d, d+1, ..., 2d-1$ (non-minimal paths). In such a situation, misrouted messages follow other paths that never reach their destinations. ■

Although routing phase, *AdaptiveRoute*, achieves deadlock-freedom and adaptivity, livelock may occur. To prevent livelock, we make use of *Dimension Reversal, DR*, defined previously. After a new message enters the network, it is first routed in L_0. The message is initialized with a DR of 0. DR is used to constrain misrouting and prevent livelock as follows.

Once DR reaches RL, the reversal limit, the message must use minimal routing by invoking **LogicalRoute**. In a m_0 by m_1 by m_2 grid, we let RL = $max\{m_0, m_1, m_2\}$. For increased misrouting, RL may be set higher. In **LogicalRoute**, however, misrouting is not allowed. When minimal paths are congested or faulty, messages have to wait instead of being routed along other paths. Here, messages are routed in either L_1 or L_2. The message being routed in L_1 or L_2 cannot be switched back to L_0. Since L_1 and L_2 are disconnected, messages cannot switch between L_1 and L_2.

Theorem 3:
Routing phase **LogicalRoute** is deadlock-free and livelock-free.
Proof:
Since logical networks, L_1 and L_2, are disconnected, routing in the physical network is deadlock-free if routing in each logical network is deadlock-free. From Figure 11.4, it is evident that the permissible routing directions defined for the L_1 logical network do not contain any cycles and is deadlock-free. A message from any cluster in the dim0-dim2 plane, traversing dimension 1, can not return since the defined message paths are unidirectional in dimension 1. Since dimension 2 message paths are also unidirectional, no cycles of buffer requests can develop in the dim0-dim2 plane as well. Deadlock-freedom in the L_2 logical network can be proven similarly (see Figure 11.4). In either L_1 or L_2, routing is minimal and every step taken by a message is closer to its destination. This is evident from the routing algorithm, **LogicalRoute**. Hence, it is livelock-free. ■

Theorem 4:
FTRoute is fully adaptive, deadlock-free and livelock-free.
Proof:
DR does not restrict the use of any particular set of output buffers and by Lemma 3, routing phase one, **AdaptiveRoute**, is fully adaptive. Routing phases one and two of **FTRoute** are deadlock-free by Theorems 1 and 3, respectively. In phase one, when DR constrains misrouting and when its value reaches the upper bound RL, a message is switched to either L_1 or L_2. The routes used in L_1 or L_2 are minimal. Phase two of **FTRoute** is livelock-free by Theorem 3. Hence, **FTRoute** is livelock-free. ■

Theorem 5:

FTRoute guarantees message delivery in a connected d-dimensional grid only if the number of faulty opto-electronic transmitters are upper bounded by $(W - 1)(RL + d)$.

Proof:

In the worst case, in a connected d-dimensional grid, there is only one surviving input and surviving output port at each node on the message path. At each output port, up to $(W - 1)$ opto-electronic transmitters can be faulty. The longest message path involves up to RL misroutes (see algorithm *AdaptiveRoute* and definition of DR). In either L_1 or L_2, *LogicalRoute* prohibits misrouting (by Theorem 3) and the message may be successfully delivered in a maximum of d hops (where d is the dimension of the grid). Hence, the length of the longest message path traverses $(RL + d)$ nodes before reaching the destination and the claim follows. ∎

4. Conclusion

In this paper we have presented a fully adaptive, deadlock-free and livelock-free fault-tolerant routing strategy for low-dimensional opto-electronic grids. Our strategy is cost-effective and supports fault-tolerant routing with moderate amounts of resources. Only three logical networks, L_0, L_1 and L_2, and two routing tables of size $O(d)$ are needed (d is the maximum degree of a processor) regardless of network size. Future work will proceed to extend the routing model to other regular networks.

5. Acknowledgements

This research is supported in part by the Academic Research Fund administered by the Ministry of Education and Nanyang Technological University, Singapore.

References

[1] S. Bandyopadhyay, A. Sengupta, and A. Jaekel, "Fault-tolerant routing scheme for all-optical networks", *Proceeding of SPIE - All-Optical Networking: Architecture, Control and Management Issues*, Vol. 3531, Nov. 1998, pp 420-431.

[2] W. J. Dally and C. L. Seitz, "Deadlock-free Packet Routing in Multiprocessor Interconnection Networks", *IEEE Transactions on Computer*, Vol. 36, No. 5, May 1987, pp.547-553.

[3] C. DeCusatis, E. Maass, D. P. Clement, and R. C. Lasky (Editors), *Handbook of Fiber Optic Data Communication*, Academic Press, 1998.

[4] G. N. Frederickson and R. Janardan, "Space-Efficient and Fault-Tolerant Message Routing in Outerplanar Networks", *IEEE Transactions on Computers*, Vol. 37, No. 12, December 1988, pp 1529-1540.

[5] O. Gerstel, R. S. Ramaswami, and H. Galen, "Fault tolerant multiwavelength optical rings with limited wavelength conversion", *IEEE Journal on Selected Areas in Communications*, Vol. 16, No. 7, Sep 1998, pp. 1166-1178.

[6] M. Guizani, M. A. Memon, and S. Ghanta, "Optical Design of a Fault-Tolerant Self-Routing Switch for Massively Parallel Processing Networks", in the *Proceeding of 2nd International Conf. On Massively Parallel Processing Using Optical Interconnections (MMPOI'95)*, 1995, pp 246-253.

[7] O. Kibar, P. J. Marchand, and S. C. Esener, "High-Speed CMOS Switch Designs for Free-Space Optoelectronic MIN's", *IEEE Transactions on VLSI Systems*, Vol. 6, No. 3, Sept. 1998, pp 372-386.

[8] H. Kirkham and E. Hsu, "AbNET, a fault-tolerant fiber optic communication system", *Proceeding of the IEEE International Workshop on Factory Communication Systems (WFCS'95)*, 1995, pp 175-181.

[9] W. S. Lacy, J. L. Cruz-Rivera, and D. S. Wills, "The Offset Cube: A Three-Dimensional Multicomputer Network Topology Using Through-Wafer Optics", *IEEE Transactions on Parallel and Distributed Systems*, Vol. 9, No. 9, September 1998, pp 893-908.

[10] P. Lalwaney and I. Koren, "Fault tolerance in optically interconnected multiprocessor networks", in the *Proceeding of Conf. On Fault-Tolerant Parallel and Distributed Systems*, 1995, pp 91-98.

[11] P. Lalwaney and I. Koren, "Fault tolerance schemes for WDM-based multiprocessor networks", *Proceeding of 2nd International Conf. On Massively Parallel Processing Using Optical Interconnections (MMPOI'95)*, 1995, pp 90-97.

[12] P. K. K. Loh and W. J. Hsu, "Performance Analysis of Fault-Tolerant Interval Routing", *11th International Conference on Parallel and Distributed Computing Systems*, Chicago, Illinois, USA, 4th September 1998.

[13] P. K. K. Loh and W. J. Hsu, "A Viable Optical Bus-Based Interconnection Network", *2nd International Conference on Information, Communications & Signal Processing*, December 1999.

[14] P. K. K. Loh and V. Hsu, "A Genetics-Based Fault-Tolerant Routing Strategy for Multiprocessor Networks", *Future Generation Computer Systems*, Vol. 17, No. 4, 2001, pp 415-423.

[15] A. Louri, B. Weech, C. Neocleous, "A Spanning Multichannel Linked Hypercube: A Gradually Scalable Optical Interconnection Network for Massively Parallel Computing", *IEEE Transactions on Parallel and Distributed Systems*, Vol. 9, No. 5, May 1998, pp 497-512.

[16] G. C. Marsden, P. J. Marchand, P. Harvey, and S. C. Esener, "Optical Transpose Interconnection System Architectures", *Optics Letters*, Vol. 18, No. 13, pp 1083-1085, July 1993.

[17] R. Ramaswami and K. N. Sivarajan, *Optical Networks: A Practical Perspective*, Morgan Kaufmann Publishers, 1998.

[18] N. Santoro and R. Khatib, "Labelling and implicit routing in networks", *The Computer Journal*, Vol. 28, February 1985, pp 5-8.

[19] H. Shen, F. Chin, and Y. Pan, "Efficient Fault-Tolerant Routing in Multihop Optical WDM Networks", IEEE Transactions on Parallel and Distributed Systems, Vol. 10, No. 10, October 1999, pp 1012-1025.

[20] T. Szymanski, "Hypergrids: Optical Interconnection Networks for Parallel Computing", Journal of Parallel and Distributed Computing, Vol. 26, pp 1-23, 1995.

[21] J. van Leeuwen and R. B. Tan, "Interval Routing", *The Computer Journal*, Vol.30, No.4, 1987, pp 298-307.

[22] J. Wu, "Fault-Tolerant Adaptive and Minimal Routing in GridConnected Multicomputers Using Extended Safety Levels", *IEEE Transactions on Parallel and Distributed Systems*, Vol. 11, No. 2, February 2000, pp 149-159.

Chapter 12

INFORMATION HIDING SYSTEM STEGOWAVEK FOR IMPROVING CAPACITY

Young-Shil Kim
Dept of Computer Science & Information, Daelim College
526-7 Bisan Dong, Dongan-gu, Anyang-si, Kyungki-do, Korea
pewkys@daelim.ac.kr

Young-Mi Kim, Jin-Yong Choi
Dept of R&D, CEST .LTD
Hyocheon B/D, 1425-10, Secho-Dong, Secho-Gu, Seoul,Korea
rose@cest.co.kr, cjng96@hanmail.net

Doo-Kwon Baik
College of Information & Communication, Korea University
5 Ga, Anam-Dong, Sungbuk-Gu, Seoul, Korea
baik@software.korea.ac.kr

Abstract   Steganography was designed to get users harder to find out the data through hiding data in forms of various materials such as text, image, video, and audio. The most generalized Audio Steganography technique is Lowbit Encoding which insert one bit of Mask to the last bit. Attacker has the disadvantage where attack was able to do the Mask which was easily concealed in case of Lowbit Encoding. Also capacity of Stego-data is low. To improve low capacity, we embed more than one bit in every sixteen bit. But the attacker easily filters Mask when inserted bit is equally bits in every sixteen bits. It is proposed that the Mask should be inserted in forms of sign curve with changing the number of bits. We apply new method with CDMA to level up information hiding.

Keywords: Information Hiding, Encryption, Decryption, Steganography, CDMA.

1.   Introduction

Steganography was designed to get average users(not specialized ones) harder to find out the data through hidden data in forms of various materials such as text, image, MPEG, and audio. If some secret message were encrypted, the security level could go higher. Though some attacker might find out the coded secret data, the attacker had to decoding the data. According to the size of Mask, the size of Cover-data should be decided. Therefore Mask must be condensed to be hidden in the Cover-data. At present the most highly developed Steganography is the one with using image technique; the most heated Steganography is the one with using audio technique. Steganography was designed to get average users(not specialized ones) harder to find out the data through hidden data in forms of various materials such as text, image, MPEG, and audio. If some secret message were encrypted, the security level could go higher. Though some attacker might find out the coded secret data, the attacker had to decoding the data. According to the size of Mask, the size of Cover-data should be decided. Therefore Mask must be condensed to be hidden in the Cover-data. At present the most highly developed Steganography is the one with using image technique; the most heated Steganography is the one with using audio technique.

2.   File Encryption Algorithm

Encryption algorithm is divided into two algorithms, Private-key encryption and Public-key encryption algorithm. Private-key encryption algorithm is called Symmetry key encryption algorithm, too. This algorithm is the same as session key used for encryption and decryption. For creating session key, random number generator is generally used or user could create the needed key by himself. A way to using a random number generator will make it difficult to infer session key though has a strong in a dictionary attack method. On the contrary, it is easy remember the way which a user creates a key to want directly but it is weak in a dictionary attack. DES one of Symmetric key algorithm is faster than RSA one of Public-key algorithm approximately $1000\widetilde{1}0000$ times in hardware process speed and about 100 times if implemented with software comparatively [5][6]. We propose improved file encryption algorithm that can improve the problem that showed a specific pattern in addition to encrypt of a file to raise a level of security. The proposed method is composed of following steps. First is the applying stage which employs AES algorithm to enhance over one step level of encryption. AES has variable key length of 128 bits, 192 bits, 256 bits at a variable length block of 128 bits, 192 bits, 256 bits. Therefore, safety of data is improved. Second is hiding the structure and form of encrypted Ciphertext for removing some particular patterns which could be appeared in encrypted Ciphertext. And it is applied to the MBE(Modified Block Encryption) which encrypts Ciphertext using the key based on this after generating random number of Ciphertext blocks.

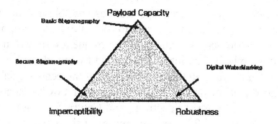

Figure 12.1.   Steganography and Digital Watermarking [3]

3.   Steganography

Steganography means "Covered Writing" coming from Greek language. This is to hide some secret message between sender and receiver who are two subjects in telecommunication. This method aims at concealing the fact that an ordinary message has some secret contents by a third person [8][9]. Currently disputable Steganography techniques are ones developed being based upon digital environment.

3.1   Difference of Steganography and Watermarking

It is a purpose that data conceal hidden fact as for the Steganography but watermarking is a purpose to do in order to be able to give no transformation to the data that it is not a purpose to hide data. Because Watermarking is the give proof of ownership of digital data by embedding copyright statements [2]. But it is limited which degree size of the data can embed in a wave file of approximately 4 minutes play quantity to work in case of Watermarking. Therefore, it cannot embed data of large size. A purpose of Steganography is not recognize the fact which has hidden data in Stego-data. So Steganography is that actual attacker can embed data of large size within the range that data do not know embedded fact. And Steganogrphy is usually not robust against modification of the data, or has only limited robustness but Watermarking is not.

3.2   Audio Steganography

Audio Steganography is developed upon the theory secret data would be easily transported if message could be hidden in audio files. Low-Bit Encoding, Phase Encoding, Spread Spectrum, and Echo Data Hiding are all the methods that make it possible to do audio Steganography [4][11][12]. Lowbit Encoding method is the simplest one to insert data into different data structure. This method is to substitute the secret data with the last bit of sampling one by binary stream. The phase coding method works by substituting the phase of an initial audio segment with a reference phase that represents the data. Spread Spectrum is that most communication channels try to concentrate audio data in as narrow a region of the frequency spectrum as possible in order to conserve bandwidth and power. When using a spread spectrum technique, however, the encoded data is spread across as much of the frequency spectrum as possible Echo data hiding embeds data into a host signal by introducing an echo. The data are embedded by varying three parameters of the echo: initial amplitude, decay rate, and offset, or delay. The Capacities of Lowbit Encoding, Echo Hiding, Phase Coding, Spread Spectrum, and Ceptral Hiding are 44100 bps, 16 bps, 20 bps, 4 bps, and 20 bps. Assuming music is played for 1 minute, users can store 846000 bits using lowbit encoding, 960 bits using echo hiding, 1200 bits using phase coding, 240 bits using spread spectrum, or 1200 bits using central hiding. In other words, all techniques suggested except Lwbit Encoding are strong against attacks such as compression, but can store only small amount of data and have to support synchronization to reproduce signals. Also, to insert and extract hidden data as in the original status before the message was hidden, additional techniques must be used [21][22]. These techniques are not appropriate to hide general documents, but instead, they are mostly used for copyrights protection. Therefore, a technique that does not have good stability but has high capacity must be selected to hide and extract data without any loss.

4.   StegoWaveK Model

StegoWaveK is a model that uses the 2-Tier file encryption in order to raise a security level of the data which are going to embed the audio Steganography system that can hide Mask of various banishments and encoded. Commercialized Audio Steganography software has greatly two problems. First, is taking the Low-Bit Encoding way that is the simplest application way of audio Steganography. By listening to a wave file or watching wavelength type simply, users or listeners did not know that information is embedded, but there is the important thing that information embedded by attacker has a problem for a filtering to be able to easily work. Second, we need the Cover-data of 16 times for Mask file arithmetically. It makes difficulties for choice of the Cover-data. Therefore, development of the technology that can embed of large size Mask is necessary.

4.1   Design of StegoWaveK Model

In order to solve a problem that is able to have been easily analyzed structure and a characteristic of a file because general file encryption algorithm shows a specific pattern and that a filtering can easily work in attacker, and capacity was low because Commercialized Audio Steganography let the last 1 bit of 16 bit hiding data, this paper proposes StegoWaveK. Figure 12.3 is a StegoWaveK model to be composed of a level to insert secrete message in Cover-data by compression, encryption and embedding.

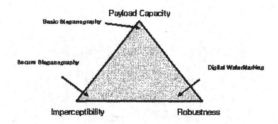

Figure 12.2. Flowchart of Message Encryption in StegoWaveK

4.2   2-Tier File Encryption

2-Tier file encryption is the file encryption that can improve the problem that showed a specific pattern in addition to encrypt of a file to raise a level of security. 1-Tier is the applying stage which employs AES algorithm to enhance over one step level of encryption. AES has variable key length of 128 bits, 192 bits, 256 bits at a variable length block of 128 bits, 192 bits, 256 bits. Therefore, safety of data is improved.

2-Tier hides structure and form of secondly encrypted Ciphertext for removing some particular patterns which could be appeared in encrypted Ciphertext. And it is applied to the MBE(Modified Block Encryption) which encrypts Ciphertext using the key based on this after generating random number of Ciphertext blocks. MBE algorithm circulates 255 keys which it has sequential created from image key and carries out each block and XOR operation. The following is MBE algorithm to have applied to 2-Tier.

4.3   Message Embedding Algorithm

The most generalized audio Steganography technique is Low-Bit Encoding which insert one bit of Mask to the last bit. In the Commercialized system, it embeds Mask only to the most right digit from the 16 bit of wave file. But the most reliable Steganography technique is the Cepstral Hiding, it's storing capacity is very low. It is very hard to embed all different size of Mask. The proposed algorithm in this paper is revised Low-Bit Encoding method, and improves the two types of problems, which is low capacity and easy filtering in Commercialized Audio Steganography. First, in order to insert bigger size of Mask to the limited size of Cover-data, we embed more than one bit in every sixteen bit. Figure 12.3 shows result from opinion of 100 students listening Stego-data hiding as 1 bit, 2 bit, 4 bit, and 6 bit. The student listened to music using a speaker. All students were not able to distinguish between Stego-data and Cover-data. Therefore, we used headphones for a precision analysis. Most of student do not feel the difference of Cover-data and Stego-data. But if we increase the number of bit to insert unconditionally, then there is significant difference of the two data. Since Cover-data is injured, listener is aware of information embedding. Thus we know how about the damage of Cover-data

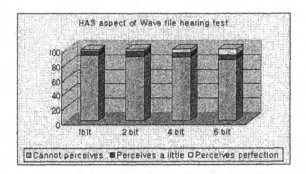

Figure 12.3.   Flowchart of Message Encryption in StegoWaveK

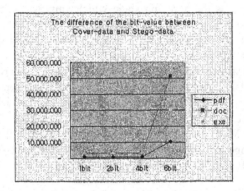

Figure 12.4.   Flowchart of Message Encryption in StegoWaveK

is reduced as to 1 bit, 2 bit, 4 bit, and 6 bit, and how about difference in the these Stego-data and Cover-data is showed by file structure aspect. Figure 12.4 shows the discrepancy of values of weighted bit between Stego-data and Cover-data.

In Figure 12.6, the difference of the bit-value which is inserted to Mask bit from 1 bit to 4 bit to Stego-data is not significant. However, for the data inserted more than six bit, we get the information that there are significant difference of the bit value. From this fact, we could conclude that the ideal number of insertion bit is from 1 bit to 4 bit in order to minimize changing between Cover-data and Stego-data, and evaluate the efficiency of Capacity. In Figure 12.6, the difference of the bit-value which is inserted to Mask bit from 1 bit to 4 bit to Stego-data is not significant. However, for the data inserted more than six bit, we get the information that there are significant difference of the bit value. From this fact, we could conclude that the ideal number of insertion bit is from 1 bit to 4 bit in order to minimize changing between Cover-data and Stego-data, and evaluate the efficiency of Capacity.

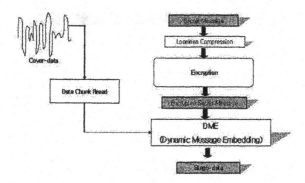

Figure 12.5. Flowchart of Message Encryption in StegoWaveK

In order to prove there in no meaningful difference between Cover-data and Stego-data inserted by 1 bit, 2 bit, 4 bit, and 6 bit, we use Cover-data having format of 16 bit PCM Wave file. We transfer 16 bit segment to decimal number and select three thousand of decimal values to analyze. The Correlation Analysis is performed to know what difference is between Cover-data and Stego-data. In the analysis result, since correlation coefficient of relation between Stego-data and Cover-data is close to 1, we know the fact that Stego-data obtains properties of Cover-data. But in the case of 6 bit Stego-data, correlation coefficient is 0.9996 and thus some properties of Cover-data is dropped. The Attacker easily filters Mask when inserted bit is equally 2 bit, 3 bit, or 4 bit. To improve this problem, we propose the method that bits of Mask is inserted in forms of sign curve with changing the number of bits, not inserted by regular rate per 16 bit of Cover-data. As a result of Correlation Analysis for Cover-data and 1 bit Stego-data, we can know that high correlation relationship appears between Stego-data with a 1 bit sign curve and Cover-data. In insertion of Mask, we use sign curve and can keep a characteristic of Cover-data. In the Dynamic Message Embedding (DME) module, the secret message is inserted into a certain critical value, not the lowbit as long as characteristics of the cover-data are maintained. For the critical value, features of the cover-data and the secrete message are analyzed and processed. Also, the most suitable algorithm is selected to insert the secret message from the algorithm that hides one bit and the algorithm that improves capacity by the sine curve form.

In the pre-processing, the sound volume of the cover-data that is a wave file is analyzed and distribution of the sound volume of the wave file is studied. Then, referring to the ratio with the next secret message, the critical value to hide the secret message is decided. After the location to hide the secrete message is decided, the message embedding algorithm is decided Basically, Fmt chunk (the header of the wave file) size is 18 bytes. Last 2 bytes of these 18 bytes describe the size of extension information. However, if extension information is not included, remaining 16 bytes is designed as Fmt chunk. Actually,

Figure 12.6.   Example of First Step in StegoWaveK

in most cases, Fmt chunk is designed to be 16 bytes. In the commercialized audio steganography software, only the wave file with the data chunk identifier in 4 bytes from the 37th byte (the location defined assuming that Fmt chunk of the wave file is 16 bytes) is recognized as a wave file. In other words, the commercialized audio steganography software does not recognize 18 byte wave files. Especially, when MP3 music files are converted into wave files, mostly they have 18 byte or 14 byte Fmt chunk, which is not supported by the commercialized audio steganography software. To solve this problem, the Chunk Unit Read (CUR) module processing according to the chunk of the wave file has been designed. In the CUR module, data characteristics are not judged by reading fixed location values, but instead, the wave file is processed according to the chunk. Therefore, not only the wave file with 18 byte Fmt chunk (the basic format) but also wave files with 16 byte and 14 byte Fmt chucks can be used as the cover-data.

5.   Performance Evaluation of StegoWaveK

In this section, StegoWaveK that has been implemented by VC++.Net is compared with Invisible Secretes 2002 (hereinafter to be referred to as "CS I") and Steganos Security Suite 4 (hereinafter to be referred to as "CS II") that have been commercialized and in use now. According to [36], in steganography analysis, visual, audible, structural, and statistical techniques are used. Therefore, the comparison and the analysis in this study were based on criteria of the Human Visible System (HVS), Human Auditory System (HAS), Statistical Analysis (SA), and Audio Measurement (AM). Since the HAS can be relatively subjective, audio measurement analysis was added to more objectively analyze and compare the stego-data and the cover-data. For comparison and analysis data, PopSong by Kim Min Song was used. In experiments with other genre music, similar results were gained.

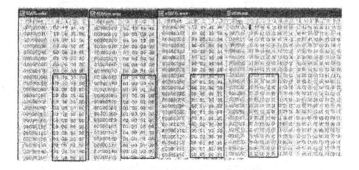

Figure 12.7. waveform of the stego-data

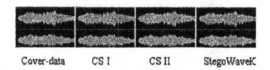

Cover-data   CS I   CS II   StegoWaveK

Figure 12.8. Hexa-decimal values of Cover-data and Stego-data

5.1 Human Visible System (HVS) Criteria

According to the waveform analysis result of the stego-data created by Invisible Secrets 2002 and StegoWaveK using an audio editor, CoolEditor, it is hard to visually tell the difference due to HVS characteristics. Figure 12.8 shows waveform of the stego-data captured by CoolEditor and Figure 12.9 shows hexa-decimal code values of cover-data and stego-data.

5.2 Human Auditory System (HAS) Criteria

To analyze and compare the suggested system with the existing system on criteria of the Human Auditory System (HAS), 13 messages with different sizes and 4 wave files were selected as cover-data. We played the stego-data where the message is hidden through CS I and CS II using lowbit encoding and the stego-data where the message is hidden through StegoWaveK system to 100 students. Although it could be subjective, most students could not tell the difference between the cover-data and the stego-data. Following Figure 12.14 shows the experiment results.

5.3 Statistical Analysis (SA) Criteria

In the following, correlations between the cover-data and the stego-data created by the CS I, and between the cover-data and the stego-data where the

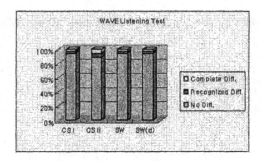

Figure 12.9.   Hearing results of many Stego-data

	Cover-data	CS I
Average	0.00964	0.00965
Variance	0.223003	0.222976
Obs	9143	9143
DF	9143	9142
F ratio	1.00012	
P(F<=f) one-tailed test	0.497721	
F threshold: one-tailed test	1.35007	

Figure 12.10.   Results of one-way analysis of variance

	Cover-data	StegoWaveK
Average	-0.00964	-0.00988
Variance	0.223003	0.221045
Obs	9143	9143
DF	9143	9142
F ratio	1.008957	
P(F<=f) one-tailed test	0.336674	
F threshold: one-tailed test	1.035007	

Figure 12.11.   F-Test StegoWaveK and Cover-data

secret message was hidden through StegoWaveK are analyzed by extracting characteristics from stego-data. In the result, we can find the stego-data have similar characteristics to the cover-data in both cases.

Treatments	Obs.	Sum	mean	Variance
Cover-data	9143	-88.177	-0.00964	0.223003
CS I	9143	-88.218	-0.00965	0.222976
StegoWaveK	9143	-90.315	-0.00988	0.221045

Analysis of variance						
Source	Sum of square	DF	Mean square	F ratio	P-value	P threshold
Treatments	0.00037	3	0.000123	0.000555	0.999982	2.605148
Error	8136.622	36568	0.222507			
Total	8136.623	36571				

Figure 12.12.   Results of one-way analysis of variance

Variable	N	Average	Standard Deviation	Sum
Origin	9144	-0.00949	0.47221	-86.77300
CS I	9144	-0.00964	0.47221	-88.17800
StegoWaveK	9144	-0.00965	0.47218	-90.21500

Simple Statistics

Variable	Min	Max
Origin	-1.37000	2.10600
CS I	-1.37000	2.10600
StegoWaveK	-1.37000	2.10600

Pearson Correlation Coefficient N=9144

	CS I	StegoWaveK
Origin	0.99952	0.99952
	<0.0001	<0.0001

Figure 12.13.   Correlation Analysis of Cover-data and Stego-data

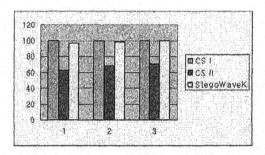

Figure 12.14. Comparison of SNR(dB) between Cover-data and Stego-data

5.4   Audio Measurements (AM) Criteria

Audio measurement and analysis includes frequency response, gain or loss, harmonic distortion, intermodulation distortion, noise level, phase response, and transient response. These parameters include the signal level or phase and the frequency. For example, the Signal to Noise Ratio (SNR) is a level measurement method represented by dB or ratio. The quality of the stego-data where the message is hidden was measured using SNR. SNR represents ratios of relative values [15, 16]. The following graph shows SNRs between the cover data and the stego-data created by the CS I, the CS II, and StegoWaveK. The SNR of the stego-data created by the suggested system is not significantly different from that of the stego-data created by the CS I. However, the SNR of the stego-data created by the CS II is relatively different from that of the stego-data created by the suggested system.

6.   New Approach with CDMA

We introduce new approach to hide data and this method use CDMA process. We explain CDMA encoding procedure. Precondition is that source is digital data. The following shows an example of 8 bit PN code generation.

$$(1, 1, 1, 1, 1, 1, 1, 1)$$

$$(1, 1, 1, 1,-1,-1,-1,-1)$$

$$(1, 1,-1,-1, 1, 1,-1,-1)$$

$$(1, 1,-1,-1,-1,-1, 1, 1)$$

$$(1,-1, 1,-1, 1,-1, 1,-1)$$

$$(1,-1, 1,-1,-1, 1,-1, 1)$$

$$(1,-1,-1, 1, 1,-1,-1, 1)$$

$$(1,-1,-1, 1,-1, 1, 1,-1)$$

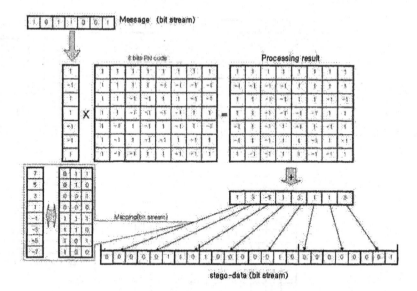

Figure 12.15. Encoding process using by CDMA

By this PN code, we represent and encoding 10110010. We replace 0 with -1 and 10110010 is (1,-1,1,1,-1,-1,1,-1). The following shows of multiplication of PN code and this data

$$(1) * (1, 1, 1, 1, 1, 1, 1, 1) = (1, 1, 1, 1, 1, 1, 1, 1)$$

$$(-1) * (1, 1, 1, 1,-1,-1,-1,-1) = (-1,-1,-1,-1, 1, 1, 1, 1)$$

$$(1) * (1, 1,-1,-1, 1, 1,-1,-1) = (1, 1,-1,-1, 1, 1,-1,-1)$$

$$(1) * (1, 1,-1,-1,-1,-1, 1, 1) = (1, 1,-1,-1,-1,-1, 1, 1)$$

$$(-1) * (1,-1, 1,-1, 1,-1, 1,-1) = (-1, 1,-1, 1,-1, 1,-1, 1)$$

$$(-1) * (1,-1, 1,-1,-1, 1,-1, 1) = (-1, 1,-1, 1, 1,-1, 1,-1)$$

$$(1) * (1,-1,-1, 1, 1,-1,-1, 1) = (1,-1,-1, 1, 1,-1,-1, 1)$$

$$(-1) * (1,-1,-1, 1,-1, 1, 1,-1) = (-1, 1, 1,-1, 1,-1,-1, 1)$$

The next step is sum of resulted data by position and we get (0, 4,-4, 0, 4, 0, 0, 4). This data is transformed to bit stream. The number of real occurrence is 9(these are -8, -6, -4, -2, 0, 2, 4, 6, 8). We need memory to present 9, and 8 * 4 = 32 bits to encode 8 bit by 8 bit PN code. The following figure shows process on codes.

Decoding is executed by specified PN code and we explained the fifth bit extraction. In the following figure, we divide bit stream into three bit unit.

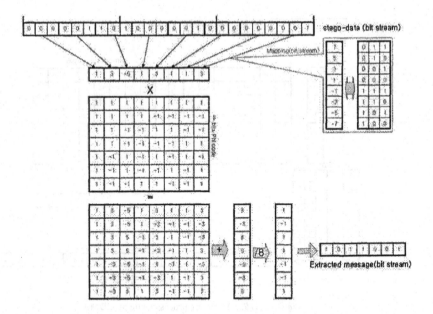

Figure 12.16. Decoding process using by CDMA

After mapping this data, we obtained (1,3,-5,1,3,1,1,3). Multiply this by the fifth PN code (1,-1,1,-1,1,-1,1,-1) in order.

$$(1,3,-5,1,3,1,1,3) * (1,-1,1,-1,1,-1,1,-1) = (1,-3,-5,-1,3,-1,1,-3)$$

Sum result of (1,-3,-5,-1,3,-1,1,-3) is $1 - 3 - 5 - 1 + 3 - 1 + 1 - 3 = -8$. Devide this number by 8, we obtain -1 and extracted bit is 0.

We insert new type identifier(code 0xFFFFFFFF) into file extension. In decoding process, to compare between existed data and new type data, we insert 4 byte identifier in new type data. To solve the problem that make difference between StegoWaveK and CDMA method, we need following steps.

1) In cover-data, we extract on bit.

2) If previous two byte of extracted data is not 0xFFFF, then this data is existed type and process is continued.

3) If previous two byte of extracted data is 0xFFFF, we start to extract two new bit from data.

4) If previous four byte of extracted two bit data is 0xFFFFFFFF, then this is new type data and we apply proper method to data procesing.

5) If previous four byte of extracted two bit data is not 0xFFFFFFFF, this is incorrect data type and send the error message.

We experiment many data by new method, compare exited method by five criteria. We modify the process to level up information hiding.

7.   Conclusion

The audio steganography that hides data uses the wave file as cover-data; the cover-data has the same size as the size of the stego-data file in the suggested system; and most listeners and users do not tell any difference in the sound quality. Therefore, they cannot recognize that data is hidden in stego-data. Also, none of the HVS system or the HAS system can analyze the wavelength that had been analyzed through a simple audio editing tool in an intuitive way. Therefore, it can be useful to send secret data. The commercialized steganography software uses only certain types of wave files as the cover-data. As one bit of the secret message is inserted into the Lowbit of the cover-data, the cover data can be easily filtered. Also, as one bit is inserted to hide the secrete message, the cover-data size increases. StegoWaveK model suggested in this study has been specially designed for Korean users to improve problems of existing commercial audio steganography softwares have. Firstly, to solve the problem that the secret message can be hidden only in the wave file of which Fmt Chuck is composed of 16 bytes, StegoWaveK model processes the wave file by Chunk. Secondly, to improve the capacity of the cover-data and to prevent the attacker from filtering the cover-data, the writer designed and implemented DME module and applied it. With DME module, users can decide the critical value and the insertion algorithm to hide the secret message based on the cover-data and characteristics of the secret message. This will make it difficult to tell whether there is hidden data as in the case of the open key steganography, although the suggested model uses the private key steganography. Thirdly, in StegoWaveK model, encoding is performed to prevent the attacker from visually checking characteristics of the secret message before the secret message was hidden and to prevent the attacker from checking contents of the secret message even if he/she might succeed in gaining the secret message from the stego-data and the cover-data. Lastly, while data is only visually hidden through characteristics of the file in Windows O/S, StegoWaveK model hides data in the audio data that is often used. Although the hidden data does not exist in the computer any longer, the user can extract data whenever he/she wants without any loss of the hidden data. Therefore, StegoWaveK model can be useful to hide important design drawings, program files, and confidential documents. More studies shall be performed relating to migration to the embedded system in the future. By introducing new methods suggested in [37], or by using loss-free compression programs such as TIFF with high performance, it would be possible to improve performance of StegoWaveK system. More researches shall be made also to develop more convenient user interfaces. With StegoWaveK system, it is possible to hide personal information of multimedia content users at the cyber training and various kinds of other information that can be used by the evaluation system. StegoWaveK model can be also utilized as a multi-level personal information protection system that can protect personal information at several levels. We try to apply, experiment, and evaluate new mrthod in order to level up information hiding.

References

[1] J.Zollner, H.Federrath, H.Klimant, A.Pfitzmann, R.Piotraschke, A.Westfeld, G.Wicke, G.Wolf. (1998). *Modeling the security of steganographoc systems.* 2nd Workshop on Information Hiding, Portland, LNCS 1525, Springer-Cerlag, pp.345-355.

[2] Stegan Katzenbeisser, Fabien A.P Petitcilas. (2000). *Information Hiding Technique For Steganography and Digital Watermarking* Artech House, pp. 97-98.

[3] http://www.crazytrain.com/monkeyboy/mde_johnson_gmu2001_stegob.pdf

[4] http://www.cbcis.wustl.edu/~adpol/courses/cs502/project/report/node1htm

[5] Raymond G. Kammer. (1999). *DATA ENCRYPTION STANDARD* Federal Information Processing Standards Publication.

[6] http://www.securitytechnet.com.

[7] http://www.softforum.co.kr/learningcenter/learningcenter_04.html

[8] Korea National Computerization Agency. (2000). *A Study on the Information Hiding Techniques and Standardization for the Protection of Intellectual Property Right.* Korea National Computerization Agency, pp.19-41.

[9] Ross J. Anderson, and Fabieb A.P. Petitcolas. (1998). *On The Limits of Steganography.* IEEE Journal of Selected Areas in Communication, 16(4):474-481.

[10] G. J. Simmoms. (1984). *The Prisoners' Problem and the Subliminal Channel.* Proceeding of CRYPTO '83, Plenum Press, pp.51-68.

[11] http://www.cs.uct.ac.za/courses/CS400W/NIS/papers99/dsellars/stego.html

[12] S.K. Pal, P.K. Saxena, and S.K. Muttoo, *The Future of Audio Steganography.*

[13] http://www-ccrma.stanford.edu/CCRMA/Courses/422/projects/WaveFormat

[14] http://www.wisdom.weizmann.ac.il/~itsik/RC4/rc4.html

[15] http://burtleburtle.net/bob/rand/isaac.html

[16] Richard C. Cabot, P.E., Bruce Hofer, and Robert Metzler, Chapter 13.1 Audio Measurement and Analysis,

[17] http://www.tvhandbook.com/support/pdf_files/audio/Chapter13_1.pdf

[18] http://211.38.132.225/new_b24.htm

[19] J.D.Gordy and L.T.Bruton. (2000). *Performance Evaluation of Digital Audio Watermarking Algorithms.* IEEE MWSCAS.

[20] Stefan Katzenbeisser, and Fabien A.P.Petitcolas. (2000). *Information hiding techniques for steganography and digital watermarking.* Artech House Publishers.

[21] BenZamin Arazi. (1986). *A Commonsense Approach to the Theory of Error Correcting Codes.* MIT Press.

[22] http://debut.cis.nctu.edu.tw/~yklee/Reaserch/Steganography/Qalter_Bender/IHW96.pdf

[23] Peter Wayner. (2002). *Disappearing cryptography Information Hiding: Steganography & Watermarking.* second edition, chapter 17, Morgan Kauffman.

Chapter 13

TOWARD A COMPREHENSIVE SOFTWARE BASED DSM SYSTEM

Michael Hobbs, Jackie Silcock and Andrzej Goscinski

School of Information Technology Deakin University, Geelong, Australia 3217

{ mick,jackie,ang } @deakin.edu.au

Abstract   Software based Distributed Shared Memory (DSM) systems have been the focus of considerable research effort, primarily in improving performance and consistency protocols. Unfortunately, computer clusters present a number of challenges for any DSM systems that are not solvable through consistency protocols alone. These challenges relate to the ability of DSM systems to adjust to load fluctuations, computers being added/removed from the cluster, to deal with faults, and the ability to use DSM objects larger than the available physical memory. We present here a proposal for the Synergy Distributed Shared Memory System and its integration with the virtual memory, group communication and process migration services of the Genesis Cluster Operating System.

Keywords: Distributed Shared Memory, Cluster Computing, Operating Systems

1.   Introduction

Traditionally, parallel processing has been the monopolised by the supercomputer and MPP machines, architectures that have been shown to be too expensive and very difficult to scale. The cluster is an architecture that is proving to be an ideal alternative to the supercomputer. A dedicated cluster is generally built using commodity components, such as using fast computers and interconnected with fast networks. The success of this architecture for building very high performance parallel machines is shown by the (increasing) number of the world's fastest computers that are built using the cluster architecture [22]. On the other hand, non-dedicated clusters based on common PCs and networks are widely available in many organisations. These clusters form a valuable and inexpensive resource that is not being taken advantage of.

DSM is a parallel programming model that can be easily employed to harness the computational resources of a cluster. This is achieved by making the memory resources on each (distributed) computer available to the other computers in the cluster. In the ideal case of a DSM system, programmers only need to focus on the computation to be performed and synchronisation issues. The DSM system ensures the memory is consistent between all computers, by communicating changes between the shared DSM memory objects.

The area of software DSM has been the focus of considerable research for many years, in particular in the mid to late 1990s. Unfortunately, the primary thrust of this work has only been with the execution performance and protocols employed to maintain consistency between the shared DSM objects [9] [4][11]. We identified a need for addressing not only high performance but also ease of programming, ease of use and transparency and developed a software DSM system within an operating system (rather than as middleware) this offers services that satisfy these requirements [19]. A need for a more integrated approach to building DSM system was also advocated in [9]. A strong assessment of software DSM was presented in [6]. Our response, based on our research, to that assessment is the subject of another paper. Here we address technological issues of software DSM, which will be used later to specify our response.

The major technological problems that exist with currently available software DSM systems are:

- DSM systems are difficult to program and use, and do not support transparency;

- DSM objects are fixed to a computer and unable to be moved, leading to load imbalances;

- Poor (practically no) support for virtual memory;

- Poor support from fault tolerance services such as check-pointing; and

- Poor use of group communication in consistency protocols.

The culmination of these problems is that many DSM systems are inflexible in their operation and are unable to benefit from the advanced services available in some modern operating systems. A common cause for this is that many DSM systems are implemented at the user level not fully integrated with the operating system.

The goal of this paper is to present the design of the Genesis Synergy Distributed Shared Memory System, an advanced DSM system that addresses these problems. This paper is structured as follows. Section 2 presents related work in the area of DSM, especially those systems that address some of the problems identified. Section 3 introduces the cluster architecture, DSM and parallel processing. Sections 4 and 5 present the Genesis Cluster Operating Systems developed and the design of the Genesis Synergy Distributed Share Memory System (SDSM), respectively. Section 6 summarises our work and details our future work.

2. Related Work

Much of the effort in software DSM research has concentrated on improving performance of the systems, rather than reaching a more integrated DSM design [9]. The well known DSM systems, Munin [4] and TreadMarks [15], have neglected ease of use, availability, transparency and fault tolerance. Both of them were developed based on the middleware approach.

User friendliness has not been addressed in either system. Application developers using Munin or TreadMarks must have significant understanding of both the application they are developing and the DSM system. In Munin programmers must label different variables according to the consistency protocol they require and in both systems they are required to have substantial input into the initialisation of DSM processes. Programmers must either enter the number of computers required to execute an application including the names as command line arguments or create a computer list file that contains a list of the computers that comprise the cluster [15], [4].

Many DSM implementations only support the running of applications in which the problem size is limited to that which will fit into the memory on the local machine. One exception is JIAJIA [18], a software based DSM which uses Scope Consistency, which is one of the few DSM systems which discusses the use of Virtual Memory to increase the size of DSM applications to larger than the size of local memory. Virtual memory is implemented in JIAJIA but the performance tests carried out are for application sizes which did not use the virtual memory facility so the influence of virtual memory is never actually tested. This still makes the use of virtual memory open.

Research has been carried out on Network RAM [16] which uses DSM-type mechanisms to cache pages selected for replacement in the memory of remote computers rather than writing them to disk [13]. The purpose of this research was not to measure the performance of the applications but to examine the problems of fault tolerance when using remote computers memories as caches. Similarly, BFXM is a parallel file system model based on the mechanism of DSM that links the memory of all computers into a large cache reducing the need to save pages to disk [12]. A spin-off from this project might be to use these mechanisms to improve the fault tolerance and execution speed of non-DSM applications.

Load balancing in DSM systems has been presented in [23], thread migration and loop scheduling in [17] [10] [21] [8], migrating or replicating pages in [2] [5], migration and replication of objects in [3]. In [8] the work described involves the comparison of performance between the migration of threads and data in the MCRL multithreaded DSM multiprocessor system. Many existing DSM systems allow users to create a set of DSM processes on designated computers. The set of processes remain on these computers until they exit [4] [11] [18].

The need for availability, transparency and fault tolerance in DSM-based clusters has been strongly advocated in [14]. However, availability and transparency are still not provided and fault tolerance is poor. A variety of techniques for detecting and correcting faults are presented, however, their implementation is so difficult that they are not in place [20]. Application developers experience difficulties using checkpoint systems, they must port library code and applications, there are restrictions imposed by these libraries, and their applications must be recompiled or relinked. Because of these difficulties, only few developers employ checkpointing in their applications [1].

3.   Cluster Architecture

We introduce in this section the characteristics of a computer cluster, parallel applications and their relationship to DSM.

3.1   Cluster Types

Computer clusters fall into two broad classes, dedicated and non-dedicated. Dedicated cluster are specifically built to execute applications in a batch manner, where a given application is allocated the whole or subset of the cluster to solely execute on until completion. Only a single process runs on a computer. In non-dedicated clusters applications are able to share constituent computers within the cluster with other separate applications.

3.2   DSM and Parallel Processing on Clusters

Parallel processing can be divided into the initialisation, execution and termination phases. The initialisation phase involves mapping processes to computers, instantiation of these processes on these computers, and, in the case of DSM, the creation and initialisation of sharable objects. The execution phase involves a set of processes executing in parallel. During execution it may be necessary to reallocate parallel processes to improve the overall execution performance and utilisation of resources. The co-ordination role of DSM parent process ends after the initialisation phase. During the execution and termination phases it performs in the same way as a child [19]. Finally, in the termination phase each parallel process completes the work and blocks at a barrier.

3.3   Effects of Non-dedicated Clusters on DSM

A non-dedicated computing cluster has a number of characteristics that have a considerable impact on the execution performance and flexibility of DSM based parallel applications. A primary cause of this impact is due to the shared nature of a non-dedicated cluster.

The structure and configuration of clusters can be complex and dynamic, as computers are added or removed. Programmers and users of DSM applications rely on this configuration information in the development and execution of their programs. This adds to the burden of the DSM programmer and user.

The load of shared clusters can fluctuate dramatically, especially with a high number of interactive users who log in and out. This can result in the cluster having highly overloaded computers, whilst often there exists lightly loaded, or idle, computers within the cluster. If not corrected, these load imbalances can lead to the processes executing on the overloaded computers experiencing unacceptable low levels of performance; thus slowing down the overall execution of the parallel application.

The sharing of computers within a non-dedicated cluster increases the competition for resources, primarily memory resources. Although the memory resources of modern computers (PCs) are considerable, the secondary storage space available on these computers is often many orders of magnitude larger. Therefore it is desirable to support virtual memory; enabling physical memory resources to be shared efficiently between the most active processes. In terms of DSM, this would also allow the allocation of shared DSM objects that exceed (in size) the amount of physical memory available on a given computer.

Faults (hardware/software) can cause the termination of DSM (or any) applications running on a non-dedicated cluster (although, dedicated cluster also suffer from this). With the increasing scale of clusters, the potential for faults, both hardware and software, also increases. In the case of non-dedicated clusters, interactive users increase the chance of causing errors through software faults, as well as user error such as turning off a computer.

Non-dedicated clusters often rely on commodity networks for the interconnection the computers. Compared with specialised high performance (and expensive) networks, the data rates and latencies of the commodity networks are significantly worse. Adding to this basic problem, non-dedicated clusters executing multiple applications on shared computers can substantially increase the load on the network. The network load has a negative impact on the protocols used to maintain consistency of DSM objects.

4. The Design of the Genesis DSM

4.1 Genesis Overview

Genesis is microkernel based operating system specifically designed and developed for the management of a computer cluster [7]. In this section we briefly discuss those components that are directly related to DSM, as shown in Figure 13.1.

4.1.1 Microkernel. The microkernel is a small section of code that provides the bare minimum set of services needed to support the execution of processes. These services include handling of interrupts and exceptions, low level page management, scheduling and context switching of processes, as well as local inter-process communication. The remaining services normally

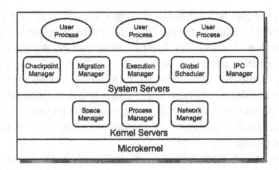

Figure 13.1.   Cluster Architecture

provided by an operating system are provided by the kernel and system servers and form the core of Genesis.

4.1.2   Kernel Servers.   The primary resources of a computer are managed and controlled in Genesis by a set of privileged, cooperating kernel server processes called managers. Those directly related to DSM include:

- Space Manager   a space is a region of memory, thus the role of this server is to manage the allocation, sharing and revocation of memory resources. It also supports virtual memory by mapping memory pages to disk. DSM is a component of the Space Manager.

- Process Manager   manages the information related to process control, execution and relationships.

4.1.3   System Servers.   The highest level management processes in the Genesis system are the system servers. The system servers that affect the proposed SDSM include:

- Migration Manager   coordinates the movement of an executing process from one computer to another. Process migration is an advanced service that enables dynamic load balancing as well as fault recovery (restoring checkpointed processes and moving processes of failing computers).

- Execution Manager - creates a process from a file (similar to the fork() and exec() combination in Unix) and duplicates a process either a heavy-weight or medium-weight (similar to fork() in Unix). In particular, it coordinates the single, multiple and group creation and duplication of processes on both local and remote computers, as directed by the Global Scheduler.

- IPC Manager   supports remote inter-process communication through the discovery and re-direction of messages to processes located on remote computers. It also supports group communication within sets of processes.

- Global Scheduler supported by the Execution and Migration Managers is able to provide load balancing decisions at the instantiation of a process (initial placement decisions) as well as during the execution of processes (dynamic load balancing and load sharing). These services are critical in spreading the computation load evenly over the cluster.

- Checkpoint Manager enables checkpoints (by exploiting process duplication carried out by the Execution Manager) of processes to be taken, cooperates with other Checkpoint Managers to synchronise the building of a coordinated checkpoint for the whole parallel application, and storage of the checkpoint. In the event of a fault, the checkpoint can be restarted using services provided by the Migration Manager.

4.1.4   User Processes.   User processes form the remaining entities in Genesis and access the services provided through the system servers, kernel servers (via RPCs) and the microkernel (via system calls). User applications are built to execute on the cluster as a whole and are unaware of which workstation they are executing on. This is achieved by making every resource in Genesis uniquely identifiable over the entire distributed cluster.

4.2   Genesis DSM

We decided to embody DSM within the operating system in order to create a transparent, easy to use and program environment and achieve high execution performance of parallel applications [19]. Since DSM is essentially a memory management function, the Space Manager is the server into which the DSM system was integrated. This implies that the programmer is able to use the shared memory as though it were physically shared; hence, the transparency is provided. Furthermore, because the DSM system is in the operating system itself and is able to use the low level operating system functions high efficiency can be achieved.

In order to support memory sharing in a cluster, which employs message passing to allow processes to communicate, the DSM system is supported by the IPC Manager. However, the support provided to the DSM system by this server is invisible to application programmers. Furthermore, because DSM parallel processes must be properly managed (including their creation, synchronisation when sharing a memory object, and co-ordination of their execution) the Process and Execution Managers support DSM system activities. The placement of the DSM system in Genesis and its interaction with the basic servers are shown in Figure 13.2.

When an application using DSM starts to execute, the parent process initialises the DSM system with a single primitive function. This function creates

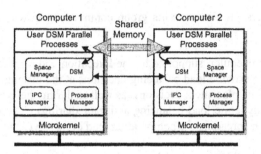

Figure 13.2. Genesis DSM Architecture

shared DSM objects and a set of processes. The latter operation is performed by the Execution Managers of remote computers, selected by the Global Scheduler based on the system load information.

The granularity of the shared memory object is an important issue in the design of a DSM system. As the memory unit of the Genesis Space is a page, it follows that the most appropriate object of sharing for the DSM system is a page.

The Genesis DSM system employs release consistency model (the memory is made consistent only when a critical region is exited), which is implemented using the write-update model [19]. Synchronisation of processes that share memory takes the form of semaphore type synchronisation for mutual exclusion. The semaphore is owned by the Space Manager on a particular computer which implies that gaining ownership of the semaphore is still mutually exclusive when more than one DSM process exists on the same computer. Barriers are used in Genesis to co-ordinate executing processes. Processes block at a barrier until all processes have reached the same barrier; the processes then all continue execution. Barriers are also controlled by the Space Manager but their management is centralised on one of the computers in the cluster.

In code written for DSM as in code written for execution on any shared memory system a barrier is required at the start and end of execution. Barriers can also be used throughout the execution whenever it is necessary that processes have completed a particular phase of the computation before the start of the next one.

5.   Genesis Synergy DSM

We claim that the facilities provided by Genesis, such as virtual memory, process migration and process check-pointing; can be combined with the Genesis DSM facility to form an advanced Synergy DSM (SDSM) service. The SDSM addresses many of the problems traditional DSM systems experience on non-dedicated clusters (as described in Section 3.3). Our previous research [19] has shown the advantages of providing a DSM service fully integrated into the operating system. In this section we describe the design of the Genesis Synergy DSM system.

5.1 Easy to Program and Use DSM

The first problem addressed by the Genesis SDSM relates to the role of the programmer/user. Genesis transparently supports the addition and deletion of computers from a cluster. The user is not required to identify available computers to run their application. This operation is performed automatically by the operating system, which hides from the user the individual computers and presents a view of single large virtual computer. By hiding the architectural details of the cluster, this greatly reduces both the programming and execution burden of the user. DSM processes of a parallel application are created concurrently on available computers by the Execution Manager thus improving the initialisation performance.

Coding of DSM applications has been made very easy as the semaphore-based mutual exclusion approach is in use to achieve synchronisation of shared DSM objects. The programmer is only required to add one statement into code of a parent and another statement into code of a child to allow the system to initialise parallel applications on a cluster.

5.2 DSM and Load Balancing

The second problem area addressed by the design of the Genesis SDSM is that of load imbalances between computers of the cluster which causes a reduction in the overall performance. Genesis supports process migration, enabling processes from over loaded computers to be moved to idle or lightly loaded computers; dynamically balancing the load over the cluster or load sharing by using idle computers. The Global Scheduler and Process Migration Manager are the kernel server processes that provide this service.

To support the migration of processes accessing shared DSM objects, the process migration service must also support the movement of the shared DSM objects. Two issues are introduced here, the movement of a process and its DSM object to a computer that is currently not being used by another process of the DSM parallel application; and when the destination computer already has one (or more) of the processes of the DSM parallel applications and thus, already has a DSM object on that computer. In the first instance, the DSM object is simply migrated to the destination computer, updating the DSM data structures in the Space Manager to reflect this change. In the second instance, since the DSM object is a copy of the same data on both computers it is not necessary to migrate the DSM object to the destination computer, just the process. The migrated process, once on the destination computer, can then physically share the original DSM object. This actually requires the migration of less data than in the first case. Figure 13.3 demonstrates this situation, where user process 2 is migrated to a computer already executing a process of the same parallel application.

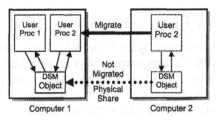

Figure 13.3. DSM and Process Migration

5.3   DSM and Virtual Memory

Virtual memory is a service which improves the utilisation of physical memory resources by writing infrequently used memory pages to disk, thus freeing these pages to be used by other processes. Another benefit allows processes to use spaces whose size exceeds the amount of physical memory within a given computer.

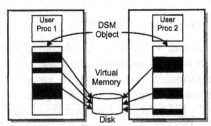

Figure 13.4. DSM and Virtual Memory

It is possible for a shared DSM object to use the services of virtual memory, thus gaining the benefits of an overall improvement of memory utilisation and the use of very large DSM objects. To achieve this, the DSM system can mark a page to be flushed to disk. Before this page can be written to disk, it must be synchronised with the other DSM objects; this is a normal part of the DSM consistency operation. Once made consistent, it can be then put to disk; this status is then recorded in the DSM data structures (held within the Space Manager). This is a simple extension to the currently available consistency protocols, where a page is either owned locally, or owned remotely. Where a page is located on disk, it is as if the page is remote to all of the DSM objects. Figure 13.4 pictorially represents the mapping of portions of DSM spaces to disk, where the disk can either be local (to each computer) or a remote shared disk.

5.4 DSM and Fault Tolerance

As the number of computers within a cluster and the execution time of the parallel application increases, the probability that an error will occur (hardware or software) also increases. It is not satisfactory to simply restart a parallel application in event of a fault, therefore a mechanisms is required to recover from this situations. A common method used to provide a level of fault tolerance is that of process checkpointing and recovery.

Genesis uses coordinated checkpointing that requires that non-deterministic events such as process interacting with each other or with the operating system are prevented during the creation of checkpoints. The messages used for the interaction are then included in the checkpoints of the sending process. The checkpointing facility provides high performance and low overhead by allowing the processes of a parallel application to continue their execution during the creation of checkpoints.

The creation of checkpoints is controlled by the Checkpoint Manager that is located on each computer of a cluster, and invokes the kernel servers to create a checkpoint of processes on the same computer. Furthermore, one Checkpoint Manager (coordinating manager) located on the computer where the parallel application was created coordinates the blocking of non-deterministic events, creating checkpoints for an application, and releasing the non-deterministic events. The coordinating Checkpoint Manager directs the creation of checkpoints for a parallel application by sending requests to the remote Checkpoint Managers to perform operations that are relevant to the current stage of checkpointing.

Applications are recovered form faults by restoring checkpointed processes. The Migration Manager is employed to provide this service.

5.5 DSM and Group Communication

Genesis also supports group communication services, where a single message can be delivered to multiple destinations, greatly reducing the load on the network. This enables fast and efficient communication of DSM update information, as needed by the consistency protocols. In Genesis, rather than to save checkpoints on a central disk, they are stored in memories of some computers of the cluster. For this purpose at-least-k delivery semantics of group communication is used to deliver the checkpoint data to remote computers.

To track the DSM processes of a parallel application, group membership management mechanisms are used. This is achieved by creating and managing a process group on behalf of the application. The application processes are then enrolled in this process group as they are created and withdrawn when they exit.

6.   Summary and Future Work

We illustrate in this paper the detailed design of an advanced, dynamic and adaptive distributed shared memory system called the Genesis SDSM. The design of this system is an outcome of our identification and investigation of problems that are present in existing software based DSM systems. We realised that many of these issues could be addressed by combining and integrating into the existing DSM system the services that are provided by the Genesis cluster operating system.

The Genesis SDSM system provides a distributed shared memory system that is easy to program and use; has DSM processes that can be migrated from heavily loaded to idle or lightly loaded computers; supports the creation and use of DSM objects that are larger than the amount of physical memory available on the computers; supports the checkpointing of DSM process and recovery from faults; and finally, possesses the ability to improve consistency protocols and execution performance of checkpointing through the use of group communication mechanisms. These advanced features combine to form a unique DSM system that is fully transparent, reliable and able to support the execution of high performance parallel applications on non-dedicated (shared) computer clusters.

Currently the Genesis cluster operating system executes on both the Sun3/50 and Intel x86 platforms. Individually, the advanced services of DSM, process migration, load balancing, virtual memory, check-pointing and group communication have all been implemented and tested [7]. We are at the stage of integrating the DSM system with the virtual memory and modifying the consistency code to utilise group communication and to support the migration of DSM spaces.

Acknowledgments

The authors would like to thank the other members of the Genesis group for their comments and suggestions.

References

[1] Agbaria, A. and Plank, J. (2000). Design, implementation, and performance of check-pointing in netsolve. In *International Conference on Dependable Systems and Networks*, pages 49–55, New York, New York. IEEE Computer Society.

[2] Amza, C., Cox, A., Dwarkadas, S., Keleher, P., Lu, H., Rajamony, R., Yu, W., and Zwaenepoel, W. (1996). Treadmarks: Shared memory computing on networks of workstations. *IEEE Computer*, 29(2):18–28.

[3] Bal, H., Kaashoek, F., and Tanenbaum, A. (1992). Orca: A language for parallel programming of distributed systems. *IEEE Transactions on Software Engineering*, 18(3):190–205.

[4] Carter, J., Bennett, J., and Zwaenepoel, W. (1995). Techniques for reducing consistency-related communication in distributed shared-memory systems. *ACM Transactions on Computer Systems*, 13(3).

[5] Dwarkadas, S., Hardavellas, N., Kontothanassis, L., Nikhil, R., and Stets, R. (1999). Cashmere-vlm: Remote memory paging for software distributed shared memory. In *13th International Parallel Processing Symposium and 10th Symposium on Parallel and Distributed Processing*, pages 153–159, San Juan, Puerto Rico. IEEE Computer Society.

[6] Gharachorloo, K. (1999). The plight of software distributed shared memory. In *1st Workshop on Software Distributed Shared Memory (WSDSM '99)*, Rhodes, Greece.

[7] Goscinski, A., Hobbs, M., and Silcock, J. (2002). Genesis: An efficient, transparent and easy to use cluster-based operating system. *Parallel Computing*, 28(4):557–606.

[8] Hsieh, W. (1995). *Dynamic Computation Migration in Distributed Shared Memory Systems*. PhD thesis, Massachusetts Institute of Technology.

[9] Iftode, L. and Singh, J. (1999). Shared virtual memory: Progress and challenges. *Proc. of the IEEE*, 87(3).

[10] Ioannidis, S. and Dwarkdas, S. (1998). Compiler and run-time support for adaptive load balancing in software distributed shared memory systems. In *Fourth Workshop on Languages, Compilers, and Run-time Systems for Scalable Computers (LCR '98)*, pages 107–122, Pittsburgh, Philadelphia. ACM.

[11] Keleher, P. (1996). The relative importance of concurrent writers and weak consistency models. In *16th International Conference on Distributed Computing Systems (ICDCS-16)*, pages 91–98, Hong Kong. IEEE.

[12] Li, Q., Jing, J., and Xie, L. (1997). Bfxm: A parallel file system model based on the mechanism of distributed shared memory. *Operating Systems Review*, 31(4):30–40.

[13] Markatos, E. and Dramitinos, G. (1996). Implementation of a reliable remote memory pager. In *1996 Usenix Technical Conference*, pages 177–190, San Diego, CA. Usenix.

[14] Morin, C., Lottiaux, R., and Kermarrec, A.-M. (2001). A two-level checkpoint algorithm in a highly-available parallel single level store system. In *Workshop on Distributed Shared Memory on Clusters (CCGrid-01)*, Brisbane, Australia.

[15] Parallel-Tools (1994). Concurrent programming with treadmarks. User manual, Parallel Tools L.L.C.

[16] Pnevmatikatos, D., Markatos, E. P., Magklis, G., and Ioannidis, S. (1999). On using network ram as a non-volatile buffer. *Cluster Computing*, 2(4):295–303.

[17] Shi, W., Hu, W., Tang, Z., and Eskicioglu, M. (1999). Dynamic task migration in home-based software dsm systems. In *8th IEEE International Symposium on High Performance Distributed Computing*, Redondo Beach, California.

[18] Shi, W. and Tang, Z. (1998). Intervals to evaluating distributed shared memory systems. *IEEE TCCA Newsletter*, pages 3–10.

[19] Silcock, J. and Goscinski, A. (1998). The rhodos dsm system. *Microprocessor and Microsystems*, 22(3-4):183–196.

[20] Stelling, P., Foster, I., Kesselman, C., Lee, C., and Laszewski, G. v. (1999). A fault detection service for wide area distributed computations. *Cluster Computing*, 2(2):117–128.

[21] Thitikamol, K. and Keleher, P. (1999). Thread migration and load balancing in non-dedicated environments. In Dwarkadas, S., editor, *3rd Workshop on Runtime Systems for Parallel Programming*, San Juan, Puerto Rico. Lecture Notes in Computer Science, Springer-Verlag.

[22] Top500 (2002). Worlds top 500 computer systems. ¡http://www.top500.org¿. Web Site Last accessed 6th December, 2002.

[23] Zoraja, I., Rackl, G., and Ludwig, T. (1999). Towards monitoring in parallel and distributed systems. In *Conference on Software in Telecommunications and Computer Networks (SoftCOM '99)*, pages 133–141.

Chapter 14

RELIABILITY OF A DISTRIBUTED SEARCH ENGINE FOR FRESH INFORMATION RETRIEVAL IN LARGE-SCALE INTRANET

Nobuyoshi Sato, Minoru Udagawa, Minoru Uehara

Department of Information and Computer Sciences, Toyo University, 2100 Kujirai, Kawagoe City, Saitama 350-8585 Japan

{ jju, ti980039 } @ds.cs.toyo.ac.jp, uehara@cs.toyo.ac.jp

Yoshifumi Sakai

Graduate School of Agricultural Sciences, Tohoku University

1-1 Tsutsumidori-Amamiyamachi, Aoba-ku, Sendai City, Miyagi 981-8555 Japan

sakai@biochem.tohoku.ac.jp

Hideki Mori

Department of Information and Computer Sciences, Toyo University, 2100 Kujirai, Kawagoe City, Saitama 350-8585 Japan

mori@cs.toyo.ac.jp

Abstract   We have developed distributed search engine, called Cooperative Search Engine (CSE), in order to retrieve fresh information. In CSE, a local search engine located in each Web server makes an index of local pages. And, a meta search server integrates these local search engines in order to realize a global search engine. However, in such a way, the communication delay occurs at retrieval time. So, it is thought to be difficult to search fast. However, we have developed several speedup techniques in order to realize real time retrieval. By the way, distributed search engines such as CSE are essentially fault tolerant. However, the meta server is single point of failure in CSE. So, we propose redundancy of meta search servers in order to increase availability of CSE. In this paper, we describe reliability of CSE and their evaluations.

Keywords: Cooperative Search Engine, WWW, Redundant Meta Search Servers

1.   Introduction

Search engines are very important for Web page retrieval. Typical search engines employ a centralized architecture, in which a robot collects Web pages and an indexer makes an index of these pages so that they can be searched quickly. The update interval is defined as the period between which a page is published and when it first becomes available to be searched. A centralized architecture has the problem that this update interval is very long. As an example, Google used to have an update interval of 2 to 3 months[1], and currently it is still approximately 2 or 3 weeks[2]. We developed a distributed search engine, called Cooperative Search Engine (CSE)[3] [4] , in order to reduce this update interval.

In CSE, a local search engine located in each Web server makes an index of local pages. Furthermore, a meta search engine integrates these local search engines in order to realize a global search engine. Although this mechanism reduces the update interval, the communication overhead increases. As a result, CSE is currently available for intranet information retrieval in small-scale networks that consist of less than 100 servers. However, large international enterprises often have more than 100 servers in their domain.

In order to improve the scalability of CSE, we have developed several techniques such as Score based Site Selection (SbSS)[8], and the Persistent Cache [10] method. In SbSS, when a second or subsequent page is retrieved in a "Next 10" search, a client sends a query to at most the top 10 sites having the highest rank scores of all servers. As a result, CSE can realize this scalability on retrieving the second or subsequent pages of a search result. The Persistent Cache method keeps valid data after it is updated and thus realizes the scalability once the same page is retrieved again.

Another problem existing with centralized search engines is that they have a single point of failure. In such engines, the whole system stops when a server stops. On the other hand, in a distributed search engine, the whole system can continue to function even if a few servers stop working. In this sense, distributed search engines are more reliable than centralized search engines.

In CSE, a local native search engine is running on each web server. These engines are integrated by a single meta search server, called a Location Server. The Location Server selects suitable sites using Forward Knowledge, and queries are then sent on to these sites. There is only one Location Server in CSE making it a potential point of failure as if the Location Server stops, no documents can be searched for. In this paper, we propose a new reliable architecture for CSE based on increasing the redundancy of the Location Servers.

The remainder of this paper is organized as follows: We present an overview of CSE and describe its behavior in Section 2. We propose reliable architecture in Section 3, and evaluate it in Section 4. In Section 5, we survey the related works on distributed information retrieval. Finally, we summarize conclusions and future works.

2. Cooperative Search Engine

In this section, we explain the basic idea of CSE. In order to minimize the update interval, every web site creates indices via a local indexer. In order for the sites to be cooperative, each site sends the information about what (i.e. which words) it knows to the manager. This information is called Forward Knowledge (FK), and is Meta knowledge indicating what each site knows. FK is the same as Forward Information (FI) used in Ingrid[13]. When searching, the manager informs the client of which sites have documents containing any word in the query, and the client then sends the query to each of those sites. As a result of this two-pass communication when searching, the retrieval time of CSE is longer than that of a centralized search engine.

CSE consists of the following components (see see Figure 14.1).

Location Server (LS): this manages FK exclusively. Using FK, LS performs Query based Site Selection as described later. LS also has a Site selection Cache (SC) which caches the results of site election.

Cache Server (CS): this caches FK and retrieval results. LS can be thought of as the top-level CS. It realizes "Next 10" searches by caching retrieval results. Furthermore, it realizes a parallel search by calling LMSE, mentioned later, in parallel. CS has two sorts of caches. One is a Retrieval Cache (RC) which caches the retrieval results of some specific queries. The other is a Site selection Cache (SC). This has the same function as SC of LS. SC of CS is a partial and/or incomplete copy of SC of LS

Local Meta Search Engine (LMSE): this receives queries from a user, sends them to CS (User I/F in Figure 14.1), and performs the local search process by calling LSE which is mentioned later (Engine I/F in Figure 14.1). It works as the Meta search engine that abstracts the difference between LSEs.

Local Search Engine (LSE): this gathers documents locally (Gatherer in Figure 14.1), makes a local index (Indexer in Figure 14.1), and retrieves documents using this index (Engine in Figure 14.1). In CSE, Namazu [5] can be used as an LSE. Furthermore we are currently developing an original indexer designed to realize high-level search functions such as parallel search and phrase search.

Namazu is widely used as the search service on various Japanese sites.

Next, we explain the update process. In CSE, the Update I/F of LSE carries out the update process periodically, and the algorithm for this process is as follows.

1) Gatherer of LSE gathers all the documents (Web pages) in the target Web sites using direct access (i.e. via NFS) if available, using archived

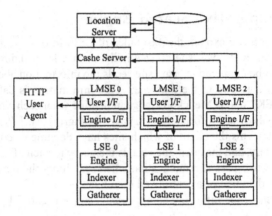

Figure 14.1. The Overview of CSE

access (i.e. via archiving CGI) if it is available but direct access is not available, and using HTTP access otherwise.

In archived access, a special CGI program that provides mobile agent place functions is used. A mobile agent is sent to that place. The agent archives local files, compresses them and sends back to the gatherer.

2) Indexer of LSE makes an index for the gathered documents using parallel processing based on the Boss-Worker model.

3) Update phase 1: Each $LMSE_i$ updates as follows.

    (a) Engine I/F of $LMSE_i$ obtains from the corresponding LSE the total number N_i of documents, the set K_i of all the words appearing in all documents, the number $n_{k,i}$ of documents containing the word k, and the value $TF_{k,i} = \max_{d \in D} tf(d, k)$ for each $k \in K_i$, where D is the set of all the documents. This information is then sent to CS along with the URL of the sending sLMSE.

    (b) CS then sends the contents received from each $LMSE_i$ to the upper-level CS and also caches this information. The transmission of the contents is terminated when it reaches the top-level CS (namely, LS).

    (c) LS calculates the value of $idf(k) = \log(\sum N_i / \sum n_{k,i})$ from $N_{k,i}$ and N_i for each word k.

4) Update phase 2: Each $LMSE_i$ updates as follows

    (a) $LMSE_i$ receives the set of Boolean queries Q which has been searched and the set of idf values from LS.

    (b) Engine I/F of $LMSE_i$ obtains from the corresponding LSE the highest score $\max_{d \in D} S_i(d, q)$ for each $q \in \{Q, K_i\}$, $S_i(d, k)$ is a

Table 14.1. The Evaluation of Update Times

	Gathering	Indexing	Transfer Index	Total	
Namazu full	0:25:50	0:20:32	0:00:00	0:46:22	[h:m:s]
Namazu	0:19:51	0:01:27	0:00:00	0:21:18	[h:m:s]
CSE	0:00:09	0:01:27	0:00:18	0:01:54	[h:m:s]
Parallel CSE	0:00:02	0:00:37	0:00:11	0:00:50	[h:m:s]

score of document d containing k, D is the set of all the documents in the site, and sends to CS all of them together with its own URL.

(c) CS sends all the contents received from each $LMSE_i$ to the upper-level CS. The transmission of the contents is terminated when they reach the top-level CS (namely, LS).

Note that the data transferred between each module are mainly used for distributed calculation to obtain the score based on the $tf \cdot idf$ method. We call this method the distributed $tf \cdot idf$ method. The score based on the distributed $tf \cdot idf$ method is calculated at the search process. So we will give the detail about the score when we explain the search process in CSE.

As an experiment, homepages (8000 files, 12MB) of about 2000 users were moved from a server of computer center of our school to a PC (Celeron 300MHz, 128MB of memory, FreeBSD), and parallel processing is performed with two PCs (A PC same as above and Celeron 400MHz dual, 128MB of memory, FreeBSD). The result of this experiment is shown in Table 14.1, where following 4 cases are used for comparisons: Full update with wget and Namazu, Simple update with wget and Namazu, CSE without parallel processing and CSE with parallel processing. As a result, simple update greatly shortens the index update time compared with full update, direct access greatly shortens the document collection time compared with HTTP access, and the parallel processing reduces the total updating time to about a half.

The performance of the search process in CSE is sacrificed in order to improve the performance of the update process. This search process is explained below.

1) When $LMSE_0$ receives a query from a user, it sends the query to CS.

2) CS obtains from LS all the LMSEs expected to have documents satisfying the query.

3) CS then sends the query to each of the LMSEs obtained.

4) Each LMSE searches for documents satisfying the query using LSE, and the results are returned to CS.

5) CS combines all of the results received from the LMSEs, and returns them to $LMSE_0$.

6) $LMSE_0$ then displays the search results to the user.

Under this search process, the communication delay increases, slowing the retrieval response of CSE. This problem is alleviated using the following techniques.

Query based Site Selection (QbSS) [6] CSE supports Boolean search based on Boolean formulae. The operators "and," "or," and "not" are available, where "not" does not mean negation but rather the binary operation that represents the difference between two objects. Let S_A and S_B be the set of target sites for search queries A and B, respectively. Then, the set of target sites for queries "A and B", "A or B", and "A not B" are $S_A \cap S_B$, $S_A \cup S_B$, and S_A, respectively. This form of selecting target sites, can reduce the number of messages required in the search process.

Look Ahead Cache in "Next 10" Search [7] To shorten the delay of the search process, CS prepares in the background the next results for a "Next 10" search. That is, the search result is divided into page units, and each page unit is cached in advance by a background process without increasing the response time.

Score based Site Selection (SbSS) [8] In a "Next 10" search, the score of the next ranked document in each site is gathered in advance, and requests to sites with low-ranked documents are suppressed. This suppression means the network traffic does not increase unnecessarily. For example, there are more than 100,000 domain sites in Japan. However, using this technique, approximately ten sites are sufficient to handle requests on each continuous search.

Global Shared Cache (GSC) [9] When an LMSE sends a query to the nearest CS, many CSs may send the same requests to LMSEs. Therefore, in order to globally share cached retrieval results among CSs, we proposed a Global Shared Cache (GSC). In this method, LS records the authority CS_a of each query, which is the CS that initially accepted a specific query and sent it to LS. The LS then informs the other CSs that CS_a is the retrieval target site instead of the LMSEs. The other CSs then cache the cached contents of CS_a.

Persistent Cache [10] There is at least one CS in CSE in order to improve the retrieval response time. However, the cache quickly becomes invalid because the update interval is very short, and the valuable first page is also lost. Therefore, we need a persistent cache, which holds valid cache data before and after updating.

These techniques are applied to the following cases.

```
if (it's the first page of "Next 10" search)
    if (its query contains operators "and" or "not")
        if (it has been searched once)
            if (searched before update)
                Persistent Cache
            else                          // searched after update
                Global Shared Cache
            fi
        else                              // it has not been searched yet
            QbSS
        fi
    else                                  // query does not contain "and" or "not"
        SbSS
    fi
else                                      // 2nd or later page
    LAC
fi
```

QbSS can reduce a set of LMSEs to 40% theoretically, and to less than theoretical value if documents are not balanced among LMSEs. In our experiments, QbSS has reduced it to about 10%.

Next, we describe about the efficiency of score based site selection. We evaluated the performance of score based site selection with three PCs (Pentium3 1GHz, 256MB of memory PC for CS and LMSEs, Pentium3 933MHz dual, 1GB of memory PC and Pentium3 1.13GHz dual, 1GB of memory PCs for LMSEs. FreeBSD is installed into all PCs.). The result of this evaluation is shown in Figure 14.2. In Figure 14.2, there are 4 lines as follows; the retrieval time of 1st page without score based site selection, the retrieval time of second or later page without score based site selection, the retrieval time of first page with score based site selection, and the retrieval time of second or later page with score based site selection. Here, note that these retrieval times are normally hidden seemingly because CS retrieves in background, in order words, during users brows previous retrieval results. As shown at Figure 14.2, score based site selection is effective when retrieving second and later pages.

Next, we evaluate the effect of Global Shared Cache (GSC). Table 14.2 shows the response times of GSC and without GSC. In case of without GSC, the response time is shortest if hit, however, the response time is longest if not hit. In case of GSC, if GSC is introduced by a LS, the response time is much shorter than the longest one.

Then, we describe the evaluation of persistent cache. To compare the retrieval times between before update and after update, we compared the retrieval times between normal cache and persistent cache in case of 20 sites of LMSEs. Here, "A and B" is used as a conjunctive query, QbSS could not select sites since all sites have documents which contain keyword A and B. Furthermore,

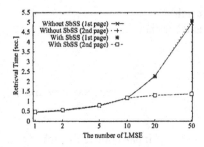
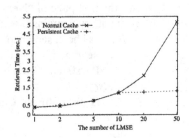

Figure 14.2. The Evaluation of Score Based Site Selection

Figure 14.3. The Scalability of Normal Cache vs. Persistent Cache at Retrieval

Table 14.2. The Response Time of Global Shared Cache

	Without GSC (Hit)	Without GSC (No Hit)	GSC
Response Time [sec]	0.45	4.67	0.66

since the highest score of A and B is the same in these 20 sites, SbSS could not select these sites. In addition, assume that the number of retrieval results in a page is 10. It means that the request is sent to only 10 sites in persistent cache. In normal cache, however, the request must be sent to all 20 sites. Figure 14.3 shows the scalability of normal cache and persistent cache. If the number of sites is increased to 50, normal cache spends more than 5 seconds. However, persistent cache spends only the same time as the case of 10 sites.

3. Reliability

Here, we describe the design of reliable architecture. First, we define types of faults as silent failures of both nodes and links in this paper. These failures occur at run time. If something is repaired, it is regarded as adding new one.

In distributed systems, a link fault cannot be different from delay caused by a node fault. If a failed link exists, though a node is not actually failed, it may seem failed. However, there may be another route to deliver messages. In such a situation, it is possible to increase reliability by forwarding messages. As such a system, there is P2P network. We employ basic mechanism of P2P network.

As described in previous section, LS is single point of failure in CSE. So, LS must be redundant. CS need not be redundant because at least one unfailed CS is needed. LMSE cannot be redundant because LMSE is depended on each Web server. Even if a LMSE has failed, CSE does not stop searching documents except a part of documents. In addition, a reference to LS group must be redundant. The relationship among these components is shown as Figure 14.4.

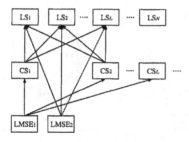

Figure 14.4. The Relationship among Components

A LMSE selects a CS from multiple CSs and sends a query to it. A LMSE selects a LS from multiple LSs and sends an update message to it. A LS broadcasts update messages to other LSs. When new LS begins to run, its reference is notified to other LSs by broadcasting. Here, there are two kinds of reliable group communication. One is anycast in which a message is sent to one of multiple servers. Another is broadcast (or multicast) in which a message is sent to all servers.

Anycast is realized as repeating unicasts until a message is sent successfully.

The way of broadcasting is dependent on the number of LSs, topology (i.e. rank, the number of links), routing and so on. There are two kinds of routing methods: breadth first routing and depth first routing. Furthermore, breadth first routing is dependent on Time-To-Live (TTL).

Depth First Routing (DF) In DF, a node receives a message including the list of visited nodes, and adds itself to the list, and forwards that modified message to unvisited nodes. Therefore, DF is suited when there are few nodes.

Breadth First Routing with $TTL = 0$ (BF0) In BF0, a node sends a message to other nodes directly. BF0 is the best way when there is no link fault.

Breadth First Routing with $TTL = L$ (BFL) In BFL, when a node has received a message with TTL $= L$, a node broadcasts a message with TTL $= L - 1$ to all neighbor nodes if TTL > 0. BFL is available even if there are many nodes. However, in BFL, the number of messages exponentially increases.

Link faults may cause to divide a network into some sub networks. In disconnected networks, meta index can be shared by using broadcast. In order to solve this problem, we employ the following way. At updating time, a LMSE sends meta index to a CS. A CS sends meta index, which is received from multiple LMSEs, to a LS at once. A LS forwards meta index to other LSs by broadcasting. A LS replies the list of LSs that have received meta index to the

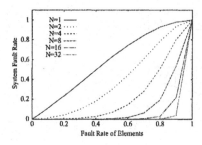

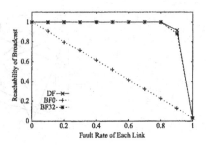

Figure 14.5. The Relationship of System Fault Rate to Fault Rate of Nodes in Case of $M = 2N$

Figure 14.6. The Relationship of Reachability to Link Faults

CS. The CS searches a CS which can deliver a message to undelivered LSs, and delegates that CS to deliver a message to undelivered LSs. Since the number of CSs is larger than the number of LSs, the possibility that a message is delivered to all LSs is thought to be high.

4. Evaluations

First, we discuss only node fault.

When the number of LSs N is equivalent to the number of links L, the system does not stop while either at least one LS is running or at least one CS is running. Therefore, system fault rate F is defined as follow:

$$F = f^N + f^M - f^{N+M}$$

where f is fault rate of elements (LS or CS), N and M are the number of LS and CS respectively.

We show the relationship of system fault rate to fault rate of nodes in case of $M = 2N$ as Figure 14.5. Since this relationship is independent on routing, the relationships of DF, BF0, and BF32 are equivalent to Figure 14.3. If N is greater than or equal to 32, then system fault rate is less than 0.1. Therefore, the scale of system is enough when $N = 32$.

Next, we discuss only link fault. We show the relationship of reachability to fault rate of links in case of $N = 32$ as Figure 14.6. Here, we define the reachability as the rate of nodes which have received a broadcast message. In BF0, there are many nodes which cannot receive a message. Next, we show the relationship of the number of messages to fault rate of links in case of $N = 32$ as Figure 14.10. The number of messages in DF is nearly equal to the number of messages in BF0, and it is very smaller than the number of messages in BF32. Therefore, DF is the best.

The relationship between the fault rate and L (when $N = 16$) is shown in Figure 14.7. The larger L is, the higher the reliability of the system becomes. Moreover, the relationship between the fault rate and L in the case of $N =$

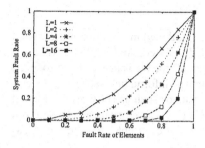

Figure 14.7. The Relationship of Fault Rates to L ($N = 16$)

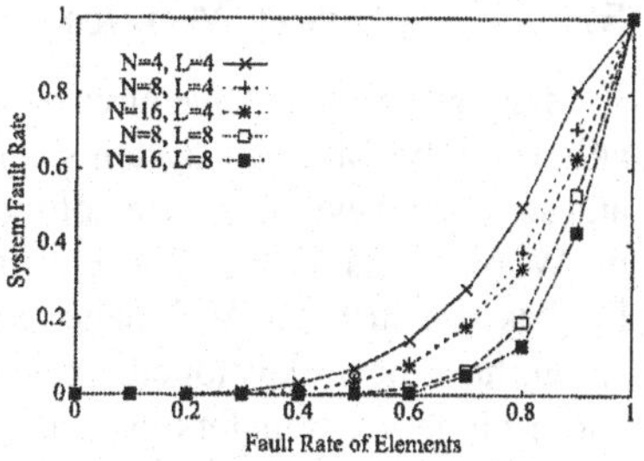

Figure 14.8. The Relationship of Fault Rates to L ($N = 4, 8, 16$)

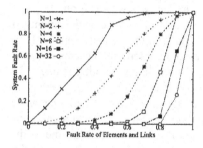

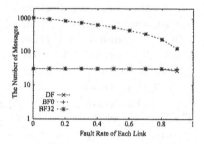

Figure 14.9. The Relationship of Node and Link Faults to System Fault Rate

Figure 14.10. The Relationship of the Number of Messages to Link Faults

$4, 8, 16$ is shown in Figure 14.8. It is clear that the system fault rate depends more heavily on L than it does on N. It is therefore unnecessary to increase N in order to increase the system reliability. Although increasing N is useful for load balancing, it also increases the number of messages. We conclude that N should be less than or equal to 16 and L should be equivalent to N.

Next, we discuss both node fault and link fault. We show the relationship of system fault rate to fault rate of elements (nodes and links) as Figure 14.9. In case of $N = 32$, if fault rate of each element is less than 0.9, then system fault rate is also less than 0.25. This result is worse than Figure 14.3 because link faults prevent CS from communicating with LS. Although we can think the way that CS communicates with LS through other CSs, it is impossible because CS must communicates with LS in order to communicate with other CSs. Therefore, when both nodes and links are failed, CSE can search documents if and only if there is at least one pair of CS and LS, which can communicate with each other.

5.   Related Works

Many researchers have already studied distributed information retrieval and as a result the following systems have been developed: Archie, WAIS, Whois++, and so on, however these are not search engines for Web pages. FK, introduced by Whois++, is a basic concept in distributed information retrieval. Several FK-based distributed Web page retrieval systems such as Harvest, Ingrid, and so on, have been developed. In Whois++[11], FKs are grouped as a centroid and each server transfers queries using FK if it does not know their destinations. This technique is known as query routing.

In Whois++, FKs are grouped as a centroid and each server transfers queries using FK if it does not know their destinations. This technique is known as query routing.

The most famous research on distributed information retrieval is Harvest [12]. Harvest consists of Gatherer and Broker components. A Gatherer collects documents, summarizes them in Summary Object Interchange Format (SOIF), and transfers them to a Broker. SOIF is the summary of a document, which consists of the author's name, the title, key words and so on. In practice, a Gatherer needs to send almost the full text of all collected documents to a Broker, because the full text must be included in the SOIF to support Harvest's full text search. A Broker makes an index internally, accepts a query, and retrieves the requested information by cooperating with other Brokers. In Harvest, both Glimpse and Nebula are employed as search engines in the back end of the Brokers, which effectively perform the indexing and searching tasks. The index size of Glimpse is very small and Nebula can search documents very quickly. In Harvest, the Gatherer component itself can access documents directly. However, because Gatherer does not make an index, it needs to send the index to a Broker. Therefore, Harvest cannot reduce the update interval more effectively than CSE.

Ingrid[13] is the information infrastructure developed by NTT, which aims to realize topic-level retrieval. Ingrid links collected resources to each other, making an original topology, and FI servers manage this topology. The Ingrid navigator communicates with the FI servers in order to search the way to a specific resource. Searching the way in Ingrid is equivalent to determining the LMSEs to be searched in CSE. Ingrid is flexible but its communication latency is long because searching the way is carried out sequentially. In CSE, only LS performs the searching, so although it may become a bottleneck its communication latency is short.

In distributed systems, there are two kinds of faults. The first is a fail-silent fault, and the other is a Byzantine fault. In the case of a Byzantine fault, it is well known that a 1-fault tolerant algorithm does not exist theoretically[14]. However, if the semantics of the correctness for the algorithm are redefined, several algorithms such as Perry's global coin toss[15] and so on are available. Unfortunately, these methods are not well suited for CSE because they are not scalable. Another approach is fault avoidance by voting outputs of redundant modules[16]. However, in this approach, we need more than 3 tasks that process the same work and hence the resources are not used efficiently.

In group communication, ISIS[17] is well known. ISIS supports several atomic broadcast communication methods: ABCASTCBCAST and so on. However, with these methods the slowest site becomes the bottleneck. We do not employ group communication because such a bottleneck is not feasible for CSE.

P2P networks also realize fault tolerant communication. Napster, Freenet [18], gnutella, JXTA[19] and so on are well known P2P systems. In particular, gnutella is a pure decentralized file sharing system. However, such P2P systems are not efficient because the number of messages is very large. Furthermore, in P2P, consistency is not always guaranteed because the reachable area of a message is eliminated with TTL (Time-To-Live). The completely connected network we employed in this paper does not realize the best performance but it maintains consistency.

6. Conclusions

In this paper, we describe scalability and reliability of CSE. In order to increase scalability, we employ several techniques, especially SbSS and persistent cache. SbSS realizes scalable retrieval of second or later pages. The persistent cache realizes scalable retrieval of first page after updating once. Furthermore, in order to increase reliability, we employ redundant location servers, depth first message routing, multiple links of LS in both CS and LMSE in order to increase availability of CSE. As this result, for an instance, when the system consists of 32 LSs with their fault rate 90%, fault rate of the whole system is about 25%. Therefore, we conclude that our method realizes enough availability.

Acknowledgment

This research was cooperatively performed as a part of "Mobile Agent based Web Robot" project in Toyo University and a part of "Scalable Distributed Search Engine for Fresh Information Retrieval (14780242)" in Grant-in-Aid for Scientific Research promoted by Japan Society for the Promotion of Science (JSPS). The INOUE ENRYO Memorial Foundation for Promoting Sciences in Toyo University gave the support to this project. Finally, we thank the office of the Foundation in Toyo University.

References

[1] Yamana, H., Kondo, H., "Search Engine Google," *IPSJ MAGAZINE*, Vol.42, No.8, pp.775–780 (2001)

[2] Google, "Google Information for Webmasters," http://www.google.com /webmasters/

[3] Sato, N., Uehara, M., Sakai, Y., Mori, H., "Distributed Information Retrieval by using Cooperative Meta Search Engines,"in *proc. of the 21st IEEE International Conference on Distributed Computing Systems Workshops (Multimedia Network Systems, MNS2001)*, pp.345–350, (2001)

[4] Sato, N., Uehara, M., Sakai, Y., Mori, H., "Fresh Information Retrieval using Cooperative Meta Search Engines," in *proc. of the 16th International Conference on Information Networking (ICOIN-16)*, Vol.2, 7A-2, pp.1–7, (2002)

[5] The Namazu Project, "Namazu," http://www.namazu.org/

[6] Sakai, Y., Sato, N., Uehara, M., Mori, H., "The Optimal Monotonization for Search Queries in Cooperative Search Engine," in *proc. of DICOMO2001, IPSJ Symposium Series, Vol.2001*, No.7, pp.453–458 (2001) (in Japanese)

[7] Sato, N., Uehara, M., Sakai, M., Mori, H., "Fresh Information Retrieval in Cooperative Search Engine," in *proc. of 2nd International Conference on Software Engineering, Artificial Intelligence, Networking & Parallel/Distributed Computing 2001 (SNPD'01)*, pp.104–111, Nagoya Japan (2001)

[8] Sato, N., Uehara, N., Sakai, Y., Mori, H., "Score Based Site Selection in Cooperative Search Engine," in *proc. of DICOMO'2001, IPSJ Symposium Series*, Vol.2001, No.7, pp.465–470 (2001) (in Japanese)

[9] Sato, N., Uehara, M., Sakai, Y., Mori, H., "Global Shared Cache in Cooperative Search Engine," in *proc. of DPSWS 2001, IPSJ Symposium Series*, Vol.2001, No.13, pp.219–224 (2001) (in Japanese)

[10] Sato, N., Uehara, M., Sakai, Y., Mori, H., "Persistent Cache in Cooperative Search Engine," in *proc. of The 4th International Workshop on Multimedia Network Systems and Applications (MNSA2002)*, pp.182–187, Vienna, Austria (2002)

[11] Weider. C., Fullton, J., Spero, S., "Architecture of the Whois++ Index Service," RFC1913 (1996)

[12] Bowman, C.M., Danzig, P.B., Hardy, D.R., Manber, U., Schwartz, M.F., "The Harvest Information Discovery and Access System," 2nd WWW Conference, http://www.ncsa.uiuc.edu/SDG/IT94/Proceedings/Searching /schwartz.harvest/schwartz.harvest.html

[13] Nippon Telegraph and Telephone Corp., "Ingrid", http://www.ingrid.org/

[14] Fischer, M.J., Lynch, N.A., and Paterson, M.S., "Impossibility of distributed consensus with one fault process," *Journal of ACM* Vol.32, No.2, pp.3740–382 (1985)

[15] Perry, K.J., "Randomized Byzantine agreements," *IEEE Transaction of Software Engineering* SE-11, No.6, pp.539–546 (1985)

[16] Uehara, M., Mori, H., "Fault Tolerant Computing in Computational Field Model," in *proc. of IEEE Conf. ECBS'97*, pp.34–37 (1997)

[17] Birman, K.P. "The Process Group Approach to Reliable Distributed Computing," *Commun. of the ACM*, vol.36, pp.36–53, Dec. (1993)

[18] Clarke, I., Miller, S.G, Theodore W. Hong, Oskar Sandberg, Brandon Wiley, "Protecting Free Expression Online with Freenet," *IEEE Internet Computing*, Jan./Feb. pp.40–49 (2002)

[19] Project JXTA, "JXTA," http://www.jxta.org/

Chapter 15

INDEPENDENT GLOBAL SNAPSHOTS IN LARGE DISTRIBUTED SYSTEMS

M.V. Sreenivas

Lucent Technologies India Private Ltd.
Building 372/2/B North Main Road, Koregaon, Pune, India
mandalam@hotmail.com

S. Bhalla

Database Systems Laboratory
University of Aizu, Aizu-Wakamatsu, Fukushima, 965-8580, Japan
bhalla@u-aizu.ac.jp

Abstract   Distributed systems depend on consistent global snapshots for process recovery and garbage collection activity. We provide exact conditions for an arbitrary checkpoint based on independent dependency tracking within clusters of nodes. The method permits that nodes (within clusters) can independently compute dependency information based on available (local) information.

   The existing models of global snapshot computations provide the necessary and sufficient conditions. But, these require expensive global computations. The proposed computations can be performed by a node to identify existing global checkpoints. The nodes can also compute conditions to make a checkpoint, or conditions, such that a collection of checkpoints, can belong to a global snapshot.

Keywords: Consistent global state, distributed systems, garbage-collection, global check-pointing, process recovery, process failure.

1.   Introduction

   In centralized systems, checkpoints and process restart, provide fault tolerance against process crashes [28]. In contrast, distributed systems consist of a collection of processes. These communicate with each other by exchanging messages. As a result, a process state often becomes dependent on another process. In cases of failures, the states of dependent processes are likely to become inconsistent, due to failures and restarts.

Consider that, a process sends a message and fails. Due to recovery from a checkpoint, it loses knowledge of the message sent. Such a message is called an **orphan message** and the receiving process, an **orphan process**. To overcome the inconsistency, the change resulting from the receipt of such a message must be undone. In a similar manner, a restart may cause a process to lose some messages received before the failure. Such messages are known as **lost messages**. In order to get the lost messages, the senders must be made to restart from an earlier checkpoint. In both cases, a non-fail process rolls backwards, so that the system state becomes consistent. Sometimes the state of a process transitively depends on the state of another process. Also considering a failure and subsequent roll backs, an attempt to recover may result in unbounded cascading of process roll backs. This problem is referred to as domino effect [27, 29] .

Distributed systems use process recovery mechanisms for recovery from transient failures. The mechanisms need to be based on periodic creation and saving of **globally consistent snapshots** [19]. Many applications including parallel debugging, distributed simulation, and fault tolerant computing also rely on globally consistent snapshots of the system state [4, 6, 18, 23]. A global snapshot is a collection of checkpoints, one for each process. It is consistent, if all the (process) checkpoints occurred simultaneously, or have the potential to occur simultaneously. If any of the local checkpoint happens before another, the snapshot looses consistency and is rejected. In some situations, the rejection may lead to rollback propagation, and may force the processes to start execution from the beginning [37].

The necessary and sufficient conditions based on 'happens before' relation are well defined [19, 21, 24]. However, the computation procedure involves complex global calculations that make online detection of global snapshot difficult [22, 23, 24, 36].

New studies corroborate the necessity of incorporating missing message dependencies, in addition to sender dependencies [15, 34, 3]. In [16] a algorithm based on pessimistic message logging has been presented. However, failures occur rarely. Based on this assumption, we consider optimistic message logging, in which messages are logged asynchronously, and not frequently [7].

By using an improved criterion for independent dependency tracking, the generation of insignificant checkpoints can be prevented [24]. The recovery process is also freed of chances of repeated roll backs, by virtue of a consistent snapshot. The computation facilitates an improved garbage collection mechanism [34]. It evolves the necessary and sufficient conditions for independent recovery [3, 35]. The proposed technique has been shown to compare well with other studies (please see section on "A Comparison with Previous Studies").

The present proposal is based on the hypothesis that the recovery model for a distributed system with n processes, should be identical to a system with one process. That is, as in the case of a one process system, each process should track its total dependencies, at all times. For this purpose, we propose to eliminate the anomaly caused by **orphan messages** and **lost messages**, by introducing total dependency tracking (TDT). The TDT is based on tracking **sender dependencies** and **receiver dependencies** for each process, against each acknowledged message. Conventional proposals based on [19] consider sender messages and acknowledgments, but do not introduce tracking receiver dependencies, as an initial step to include least overheads. However, sufficient conditions need additional dependency tracking [24]. The additional tracking of receiver dependencies, serves to eliminate the occurance of **lost messages**, at the onset. Further, it solves the problems associated with checkpoints, [39] namely :

1) Optimal process recovery considering current states of non-failed processes, and recoverable states of failed processes;

2) generating a consistent global snapshot of system state, given a target set of local checkpoints;

3) given a process finding (minimum, maximum) consistent global checkpoints that are consistent with respect to a given state of this process;

4) Independent and autonomous calculation of recoverable state, or snapshots by any process; and

5) allow decentralized calculations in a mix of piece-wise deterministic and non-piece-wise deterministic executions, by forcing processes to take select checkpoints.

Our study is aimed at minimizing overheads, the number of roll backs [10, 32], at generating distributed recovery mechanisms [33], and recovery among network clusters. The contents of the paper are organized as follows. The next section outlines the recovery models that deal with domino effect. Section 3 introduces the model of recovery and the total dependency graph. Sections 4 discusses the algorithms for process recovery. In section 5, a comparison is made between the algorithm and other related techniques. Section 6 contains performance considerations and comparisons. In section 7, as an application of the recovery model, a large network of processes, has been considered for recovery from failures. In section 8, based on the new model, the garbage collection procedures are presented. Finally, section 9 consists of summary and conclusions.

2. Background

In techniques based on asynchronous message logging, messages are stored in a volatile log. At irregular intervals, each process saves its log on a stable storage [9, 26] . On recovery from a failure, a process restores its status to the latest checkpoint and replays the logged messages to roll forward. This technique is called optimistic message logging. Models based on optimistic message logging can be found in [8, 10, 12, 13, 32, 33] . In such an approach, the recovery mechanism detects and eliminates the orphan and lost messages, on recovery [2, 25, 17].

The recovery mechanisms restore the state of the system in the event of a failure by using check-pointing and message logging [8, 10, 12, 13, 26, 32, 33]. A checkpoint stores the state of the system in stable storage. As checkpoints incur a significant overhead within the system, these are supplemented by asynchronous message logging. In case of asynchronous message logging, messages are stored in volatile storage (buffer). Occasionally, the contents are transferred to stable storage, before the buffer is full. A failed process recovers by restoring its status to an appropriate check-point and replaying the messages logged in stable storage. Since a number of messages are exchanged by processes while executing a task, it is necessary to contain the number of messages stored at various sites. This requires identifying messages which are no longer needed for process recovery. This identification and deletion of these messages is termed as **garbage collection**.

In recovery models proposed by [10, 12, 13], the authors have presented garbage collection mechanisms as a part of the process recovery mechanism. Also, these are centralized in nature, and use coordinator-based garbage collection and recovery. Other mechanisms of process recovery also perform garbage collection [33, 32]. The proposed model does not depend on a coordinator.

2.1 Global Snapshot Algorithms for Large Networks

There are two existing models for adoption of a global recovery model for large distributed systems. In the first model, each process attaches a vector of size 'n' to its messages, where 'n' is the number of processes in the system. At every instant of time, a process knows (also declares) its dependencies with respect to each of the other processes. After a failure, a globally consistent state of processes is computed and restored [8, 32, 34, 35, 33]. In the second model, each process keeps track of its dependencies with respect to its communicating set of neighbors. The processes attach a single integer to outgoing messages indicating their current level of messages received. But this model requires coordinated recovery in the event of a failure [10].

With the increase in the number of processes in the system, attaching a vector of size 'n' introduces an initial overhead. Also, the coordinated recovery is costly. In addition, the probability of a failure in the system increases, this makes the use of these models difficult to manage as the system may end up in recovery phase most of the time. For this reason, most of the computations initiated by a group of processes need to be confined to a specific set of processes, when the system is large [8, 14, 20]. The processes are often organized as clusters in large distributed systems to increase fault-tolerant capability [14]. Thus, a system can be viewed as non-overlapping clusters of nodes. Communication between these clusters is not ruled out.

An abstract model for recovery among clusters is presented by Lowry, et al. [20]. However, it causes false dependencies, leading to unnecessary roll-backs in the system. To avoid false dependencies, the authors have proposed the use of pessimistic gate ways, and dependency tracking. This model is similar to the concept of "out side world" as proposed by Strom and Yemini [33]. A model of the system is presented in section 8, using the proposed total dependency tracking.

3. System Model

In the proposed technique, each node maintains information related with sender dependencies which are transitive. This is a common feature of conventional recovery techniques. In addition, in the proposed approach, the receiver dependency information is also maintained in the same fashion. This combination facilitates independent recovery for the participating nodes in the event of a failure. A brief description of the model is presented in the following sections.

A distributed system consists of a collection of processes. There is no sharable memory or universal clock in the system. The communication channels are assumed to be first in first out (FIFO). That is, the messages are received by a site B are always in the same order in which these have been sent by the sender site A. In addition, we assume that the channels are reliable, and these do not loose messages. Also, processes in the system are fail-stop processes [30, 31]. That is, if a process fails, it stops and does not feed erroneous information into the system.

3.1 Message Dependencies

The period of execution of a process is divided into intervals, called states of a process. Each state is a count of messages received by it. In a state, a process can send any number of messages to other processes. The state is initialized to '0' at the beginning. Thus, when a process pi, receives a message, the state of process pi changes as, state(pi) = state(pi) + 1. We represent any state 'j' of process pi as P_j^i. Continuation of P_j^i depends on the following factors:

1) forward continuation of the state of any process px, which has sent a message to pi (sender dependency); and

2) forward continuation of new states of all the processes which have acknowledged messages sent by process pi (receiver dependency).

Any failures and recovery for any of the processes, makes it necessary that process pi rolls back to adjust its own state.

3.1.1   Sender Dependency.

In Figure 15.1 (casual ordering), the process state P_1^1 depends on P_1^3, on account of a state change by message m3. In the event of failure of process p3, if p3 restarts from state '0', p1 becomes an **orphan process**. Similarly, P_1^3 depends on P_1^2. Thus, P_1^1 transitively depends on P_1^2. This is termed as *transitive sender dependency.*

3.1.2   Receiver Dependency.

In Figure 15.1(Zig zag ordering), the process state P_1^1 depends on P_1^2 because of message m2. On failure of process p2, m2 becomes a **lost message**. Process p1 should roll back and send the message m2 again. Similarly, P_1^2 depends on P_1^3. This implies P_1^1 transitively depends on P_1^3. This is termed as *transitive receiver dependency.*

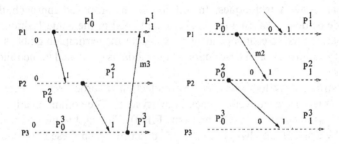

Figure 15.1.   A. Messages in Casual Ordering.   B. Messages in Zig Zag Ordering.

3.2   Recoverable States of a Process

Each process stores the received messages in a volatile storage. At irregular intervals, the process transfers the messages to a stable storage. Any message 'm' is called a logged message, if and only if, its data, information about the new state dependencies (sender and receiver), and the sequence number have been transferred to stable storage. This is denoted by logged(pi,j).

Definition 1. *Inconsistent State of a Process.* Any process state that depends (directly or transitively) on an unlogged process state (or a lost state of a failed process) is called an inconsistent state.

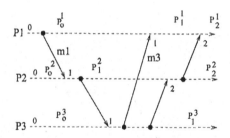

Figure 15.2. Interacting processes.

Definition 2. *Current Stable State of a Process.* The most recent state of a process (or a recent message) stored in stable storage is the current stable state of the process.

All processes independently take a checkpoint at the beginning and many times during execution. When process pi recovers from a failure, it restores its status to the latest checkpoint taken in say state 'j-a'. Further, it replays the messages logged and regains state 'j'.

The system state in case of failure free execution, is a collection of all the process states in the system. It is termed as the global state. After all the messages (still in the channels) are delivered to their destinations, and all acknowledgments are delivered to the respective senders, the global state is a consistent system state. The system state in case of failures, is the state to which the processes in the system are restored. Such a system state is consistent, if the system is free from orphan messages and lost messages [2]. Models to deal with orphan messages are discussed in [1, 5].

When a process fails, the messages in its volatile log are lost. It leads to lost messages. After recovering from a failure, the recovered state of a process, does not depend on any failed state of other processes. In the following subsections, we present a method for identifying dependencies of state among processes, as described in **Definition 1**.

3.3 Dependency Graph of the System State

Consider the Figure 15.2, messages have been sent with acknowledgments received. Process state P_1^1 depends on P_1^3(sender dependency due to message m3). As per the notion, it also depends on its own previous state, P_0^1. Similarly, P_1^1 depends on P_1^2 (receiver dependency due to message m1). Dependencies of various states are progressively determined by taking cumulative sum of previous dependency with existing dependency, as is described in section 4 and

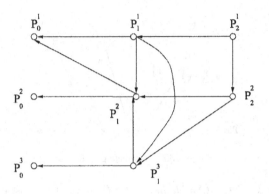

Figure 15.3.   Total Dependency Graph.

Appendix.

Definition 3. *Total Dependency Graph (TDG).* A dependency graph is a digraph G = (V,E), where V is the set of nodes labeled P_j^i. Consider E as a set of directed edges (P_j^i, P_l^k), such that P_j^i directly depends (sender/ receiver) on P_l^k. Also, E contains the pair (P_{j+1}^i, P_j^i), for all $j \geq 0$. In Figure 15.3 a TDG of the communicating processes of Figure 15.2 is shown. (Please also see the notion of R graph in [39])

From the TDG, it can be observed that P_2^1 depends (directly) on P_1^1 and P_2^2. Also, P_1^1 depends on P_1^3(sender dependency), P_1^2 (receiver dependency), and P_0^1 (its own previous state).

Reachability (R). If node P_j^i depends directly (or transitively) on P_y^x, then there is an edge (or a path) from P_j^i to P_y^x in the dependency graph represented by $R(P_j^i, P_y^x)$.

Reachability Graph (RG). Reachability graph $RG(P_j^i)$ of a node P_j^i is a graph containing P_j^i and a set of reachable nodes V' ($V' \leq V$) and edges E' , such that there are no outgoing edges to $RG(P_j^i)$ from $(G-RG(P_j^i))$. Note that $RG(P_j^i)$ includes all nodes $P_{j'}^i$, where $j' \leq j$. In Figure 15.4., graphs GI and GII are two examples of $RG(P_2^2)$.

Definition 4. *Minimum Reachability Graph (MRG).* The reachability graph $RG(P_j^i)$ with least number of nodes is called the minimum reachability graph, $MRG(P_j^i)$.
In Figure 15.4, the graph GII is a $MRG(P_2^2)$. Thus, no node within the graph

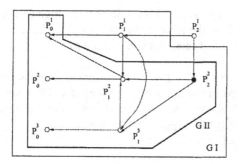

Figure 15.4. Minimum Reachability Graph.

$MRG(P_j^i)$ is dependent on any node within $(G - MRG(P_j^i))$.

Given $MRG(P_j^i)$, If there exists $R(P_j^i, P_y^x)$, such that P_y^x is the earliest state that is lost due to a failure, then for all 'i' and 'j', P_j^i is an inconsistent state.

Looking at Figure 15.3, if P_2^1 becomes a lost state (or an inconsistent state), no other process state depends on it directly (also indirectly). The MRGs of other process states do not include the node P_2^1. Similarly, if P_1^2 is lost, the process state that has an edge, or a path (**reachability**) directed at this node will become an inconsistent state. Thus, the following nodes that include P_1^2 in their MRGs, will become inconsistent.

$P_1^1, P_2^1, P_2^2, P_1^3$

Definition 5. *Consistent System State* (after recovery from a failure). The consistent system state after a failure is represented by Minimum Reachability Graph at each node P_y^x, such that,

$MRG(P_y^x)$ does not contain any of the lost or failed states.

4.   Independent Node Recovery After a Failure

On detecting a system failure each process transfers its current state logs to stable storage. In order to achieve a state that will be a part of **consistent global state**, each process examines, if its highest state is a consistent state. If the highest state is found to be consistent, no process roll-back is necessary. Otherwise, the next highest process state is tested for consistency (by comparing its MRG with the known lost states). That is

$\forall px \wedge y, MRG(P_y^x)$ does not contain a lost state.

Definition 6. *Recoverable Process State* . The highest state of process pk, P_l^k in the graph G is the recoverable state of pk. That is, P_{l+1}^k is either an inconsistent state, a lost sate, or a non-existent state.

The highest state 'l' of a process pk in graph G is the **optimal recovery state** of process pk. In order to restore status after the event of a failure, the site restores its status to a checkpoint C (taken before the recoverable process state P_l^k) and replays the logged messages to recover upto P_l^k. This is termed as **process rollback** .

4.1   System Recovery Computation

After a failure in state 'j', a process pi recovers to a state $j'(j' \leq j$) depending upon its stable state (recent checkpoint and logged state). Process pi send a recovery message with new state j', to all other processes in the system. Each process attempts to find its states that are consistent with respect to j'. Appendix describes the procedure that generates a cumulative dependency vector, giving for each process state the highest state of other processes that exist on a reachability path.

Thus, given j', the process px identifies its highest state 'y' that does not depend on any lost state of pi. The process px rolls back to the state 'y', such that (please also see appendix)

$$(T_y^x[i]) \leq j'.$$

Referring to Figure 15.A.3, if P_2^2 is a failed state and on recovery process P2 recovers as P_1^2 based on an earlier log(or Checkpoint), the recovery algorithms at P1 roll-backs, process P1 to P_1^1. Process P3 continues without a roll-back as P_1^3

4.2   Proof of Correctness

Theorem 2.0 . The algorithm results in consistent system state.
Proof . We prove this by considering the following contradictions:

- on recovery from a failure, an orphan message (Mo) exists within the system;

- on recovery, the system state results in a lost message(Ml).

Case 1 : Let P_j^i be a state formed on receipt of message Mo sent in P_y^x. Assume Mo is an orphan message. Due to the existence of Mo, an edge (P_j^i, P_y^x) exists in the dependency graph. The edge (P_j^i, P_y^x) must belong to MRG(P_y^x). Hence, P_j^i is a lost state and can not be a part of process recovery state of pi.

Case 2 : Let process pi in state 'j' have a lost message Ml, sent by process px (in state 'y'). Because of Ml, there exists an edge (P_{y+1}^x, P_j^i). This edge must belong to MRG(P_j^i). Hence, P_{y+1}^x is an inconsistent state and cannot be part of process recovery state of pi.

5. A Comparison with Previous Studies

The proposed approaches require computation of dependency information and maintenance of status vector. Although, most of the other existing approaches do not use the dependency graphs, the related dependency information is captured in different forms and data structures [17].

Drawbacks associated with conventional dependency tracking are highlighted by Netzer [24]. A notion of **zigzag path** has been introduced, that can capture the transitive receiver dependencies. This is shown to be a necessary modification for the exiting dependency tracking mechanisms. The existing use of casual paths to define **happens before** relationship as a notion, only captures - transitive sender dependencies.

Earlier Dependency Graph Approaches : Casual dependency tracking (as described above) by attaching the current state of the sender to each message, and maintaining dependency vectors is proposed by Johnson and Zwaenepoel [11]. By replaying the messages logged in stable storage, a process can achieve a maximum recoverable system state. The recovery model requires logging the dependency vector and also the messages. An alternate method of dependency tracking by including the full dependency vector with each message sent has been introduced by Strom and Yemini [33].

Sistla and Welch [32] have proposed two alternative recovery algorithms. The first algorithm tags each message sent with a transitive dependency vector, as also in the Strom and Yemini [33] model. The second algorithm tags each message with the sender's current state interval index, its message logging progress. Also, to find out the current recovery state, each process exchanges additional messages, in order to distribute the complete transitive dependency information.

Johnson and Zwaenepoel [10] base their recovery on a central coordinator. The dependency vector and log information is sent to the coordinator, by each process. A recent survey of recovery techniques can be found in [23].

6.   Performance Study and Related Work

Lemma 1 . The system recovery requires (n-1) messages for each process's recovery after its failure.

Proof . When a process recovers from a failure, it informs all other (n-1) processes of its recovery state. Each process independently rolls back to a recoverable process state. If k processes fail, the number of messages generated in the system will be k(n-1).

The technique can be compared with other similar techniques. Strom and Yemini [33] have proposed a model of decentralized recovery. In this model, each process keeps track of the number of messages it has sent to the other processes in the system. In the worst case, a process may undergo $O(2^n)$ rollbacks. The number of messages generated can be as high as $(n2^n)$ during the recovery process. Sistla and Welch [32] have proposed a recovery model, which generates $O(n^2)$ messages, when $O(n)$ extra information is attached to a message. It generates $O(n^3)$ messages, if $O(1)$ information is attached with the message.

The model by Johnson and Zwaenepoel [10] is a centralized recovery model. Also, it takes into account the stable states of non-failed processes rather than current states in determining the system state. Thus, the maximum recoverable system state is not optimal. The sender appends each message with an $O(1)$ extra information, containing its status. During recovery the centralized controller generates $O(n)$ messages. Juang and Venkatesan [12] use a model in which an $O(1)$ extra information is attached to each message, but a process failure may generate $O(n^2)$ messages in worst case. A process in the worst case undergoes 'n' roll-backs. Another model proposed by Juang and Venkatesan [13], generates messages of the order of $O(V . E)$, where V is the number of processes and E the number of communication links in the system. The number of messages generated is $O(n^2)$ in best case, when the network is tree connected, and $O(n^3)$ when the network is fully connected. Each process undergoes 'n' roll-backs during recovery.

Table 1.1 compares the message complexities of various techniques. The cost of processing within the proposed model is the least of all, and compares well with the centralized recovery technique [10]. Further, in case of Johnson and Zwaenepoel [10], each process periodically sends the dependency vectors and new log information to the central controller to determine the recoverable system state.

Time Complexity : Assume that, the messages take one unit time to traverse through a link. The message processing time at each site is negligible.

Table 15.1. Comparison of Recovery Techniques

Model	Size of Vector attached to a message	Messages generated during recovery	Number of roll-backs	Need a Coord-inator to re-cover	Added over-head depend-ency	Optim-ality: (Reco-very State
Strom and Yemini	$O(n)$	$O(n2^n)$	2^n	no	no	current states [33]
Sistla and Welch	1. $O(n)$ 2. $O(1)$	$O(n^2)$ $O(n^3)$	1 1	no no	no yes	stable states [32]
Johnson and Zwaenepoel	$O(1)$	$O(n)$	1	yes	yes	stable states [10]
Juang and Venkatesan	$O(1)$	$O(n^2)$	n	yes	no	stable states [12]
Juang and Venkatesan	nil	$O(n^3)$	n	yes	yes	stable states [13]
Proposed Model	$O(n)$	$O(n)$	1	no	no	current states [3]

The failed process, on recovery needs to send its recovery state to all the processes in the system. The time required for this purpose, is the time required to inform the farthest process in the system. Assuming 'd' as the diameter of the system, the time complexity of the proposed algorithm for general networks is $O(d)$. For tree networks, the time complexity is $O(h)$, where 'h' is the length of the longest branch or height of the tree. For ring networks the time complexity is $O(n)$, where 'n' is the number of processes in the ring.

7.   System Recovery Within Large Networks

The system recovery after a failure is carried out within a cluster, where optimistic message logging and check-pointing are used. For messages passing across the cluster boundary, the pessimistic message logging and check-pointing are used, to avoid propagation of process dependencies.

7.1   Recovery Within a Cluster

The recoverable state of a cluster is the union of recoverable states of all processes within the cluster.

7.2   Recovery Across Cluster Boundaries

Assume that, process pi in state 'j' (in cluster A) has sent a message 'm' to process px in state 'y-1' (in cluster B). The new state of process px is 'y'. Since inter-cluster communication is pessimistic, process pi makes states in $MRG(P_j^i)$ stable before it sends a message in state 'j'. Also, the receiving process px, on receiving the message, makes its new state 'y' recoverable by making states in $MRG(P_y^x)$ stable. So, the inter cluster message can never be an orphan or lost message. In this way, a failure in a cluster does not affect the states of processes in other clusters. So, the processes in the system do not need to keep track of dependencies with respect to processes in other clusters.

7.3   An Example

Consider a four process distributed system in which there are two clusters A and B. In Figure 15.5, message 'm' represents a inter cluster message. Before process pA2 sends message 'm' to process pB1 in cluster B, it makes all nodes in $MRG(PA_1^2)$ stable. Thus, PA_1^2 becomes a recoverable process state (Figure 15.6). On receiving the message, process pB1 processes the message and determines the new state PB_2^1. Before sending an acknowledgment it makes the states in $MRG(PB_2^1)$ stable, so that it becomes a recoverable process state. Thus, the message 'm' can not be a orphan message or a lost message in the event of a failure of any process in any of the two clusters.

7.4   Global Recovery From Failures

As processes fail inside a cluster, message dependencies do not propagate across cluster boundaries. After a failure in state 'j', a process pi restores its status to the latest checkpoint (say 'C'), replays messages logged to regain some state (say j') such that $j' \leq j$. Process pi sends a recovery message with new state j' to all other processes in the cluster.

Each process finds its states which are consistent with respect to j'. For a given j', the process px identifies its highest state 'y' that does not depend on a failed state, such that,

$$T_j^i \leq j'$$

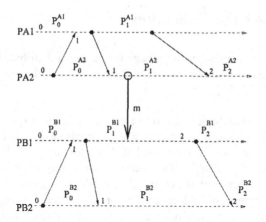

Figure 15.5. Messages in Clusters A and B.

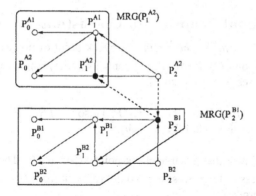

Figure 15.6. Dependency Tracking Across Clusters A and B.

In order to restore its state to 'y', process px initially restores its status to the highest checkpoint 'C' taken before the state 'y', replays the logged messages (if any), and rolls forward to state 'y'.

Lemma 2. The model generates (n-1) messages for each failure within a cluster.

Proof. When a process recovers from its failure, it informs all the other (n-1) processes in the cluster of its recovery state. It sends one message to each process, which is the minimum overhead for communicating a recovery after a failure. Each process independently determines its latest recovery state. Each process rolls back to this state by using its own checkpoints and message logs.

8.   Garbage Collection

Most existing approaches to garbage collection in distributed systems are ad hoc approaches and exist as a related component of the process recovery techniques [10, 33, 38].

Conventional Garbage Collection : In a model of garbage collection proposed by Venkatesan and Juang [38], two proposals have been introduced for garbage collection. In the first proposal, if all stable storage is full, all processes in the system are forced to fail. On system recovery, each process identifies the latest recovery checkpoint and clears of the earlier checkpoints and messages. In the second approach, each process is forced to take a checkpoint and log messages to generate a globally check-pointed state (stable check-point).

The proposed technique incurs least amount of overheads for implementing garbage collection by using dependency tracking in the background. It supports independent garbage collection without global synchronization activity.

8.1   Global Snapshot of Consistent System State

Definition 7.   *Stable Checkpoint.* A check-point of process P_j^i is called a stable check-point C_j^i, if MRG (P_j^i) contains nodes, which represent stable states of processes (at various sites).

$$\forall P_y^x that \in MRG(P_j^i), \quad the\ MRG(P_y^x)\ also \in MRG(P_j^i)$$
(by the definition of **reachability graph**).

Theorem 1.0 Given that a stable check-point exists at P_j^i. Then, P_j^i is a recoverable process state. process pi need not rollback from P_j^i in the event of a failure of any process.

Proof. For process pi to rollback from state P_j^i, there are two possibilities. Either P_j^i is a lost state, or it depends on a lost state of some other process.

- P_j^i can not be a lost state as it is a stable state.

- Assume that, it depends on a lost state P_y^x (say). This implies that there exists a path from P_j^i to P_y^x in the total dependency graph. Therefore, MRG (P_j^i), includes the node P_y^x. Hence, P_y^x is a stable state and not a lost state.

Assume that P_j^i is the latest stable state of pi, for which a stable check-point C_j exists. In the event of a failure of process pi, it will start again from checkpoint C_j and replay the later messages stored in stable storage to attain the state P_j^i. Thus, all the messages received and the check-points taken before C_j

are no longer needed for recovery, and can be declared as **garbage**. These can be deleted.

8.2 Garbage Collection Algorithm

This approach is more suitable for applications in which message transfer costs are high. Also, in some environments, there can be a large number of active processes that compute over a long period of time. Also, the volume of messages exchanged between processes can be high.

> **procedure** GARBAGE-COLLECT(P_j^i);
> **begin**
> **for all** 'k' $(1 \leq k \leq j)$ **do**
> check if, process states in MRG(P_k^i) are stable (belong to
> the state **status vector**);
> **if** 'yes' **then**
> IDENTIFY latest check-point taken before P_k^i and
> the corresponding state k' ;
> DECLARE messages and check-points
> corresponding to states $\leq k'$, as GARBAGE
> **else** exit.
> **end**;

Figure 15.7. Garbage collection algorithm.

In this approach, no additional messages are generated for check-points and garbage collection. It is assumed that, garbage collection is performed during the idle time by a process. Processes are made to attach the state number, corresponding to the latest message logged in stable storage, to each message. Based on this information, each process maintains a stable state **status vector** of size 'n' which stores the latest stable states of other processes (upto as far as is known), through messages received from processes. From the status vector, a process can determine, whether the process states included in the MRG (P_j^i), are stable states or are not stable states. For any P_j^i, if all components of MRG (P_j^i) are stable states, then for pi, the system can identify the messages and check-points that are no longer required for recovery. The highest state j, for which a 'stable check-point' exists, is used to delete all the previous check-points and messages.

Thus, the routine message transfer activity also carries stable state information as logged at a sender site, concerning other processes. An algorithm to carry out garbage collection is shown below (Figure 15.7).

9. Summary and Conclusion

A model of recovery has been presented to provide independent and consistent snapshots based on local computations. These system are divided into non-overlapping clusters of nodes to localize the effects of failures. Within a cluster, asynchronous message logging and check-pointing is used. A distributed approach for recovery from failures within a cluster is examined. Message logging is used for inter cluster communication to isolate the failures inside individual clusters. A method for independent recovery by nodes within clusters has been studied. A computing process using dependencies among communicating processes has been described from the point of view of implementation.

References

[1] D.H. Abawajy, Orphan Problems and Remedies in Distributed Systems, *Operating Systems Review*, vol. 27, no. 1, 1993, pp. 27-32.

[2] M. Ahuja, A.D. Kshemkalyani and T. Carlson, A Basic Unit of Computation in Distributed Systems, In *Proceedings of 10th Int. Conference on Distributed Computer Systems*, 1990, pp. 12-19.

[3] S. Bhalla, and M.V. Sreenivas, Independent Node and Process Recovery in Message Passing Distributed Systems, *Proceedings of the 3rd International Conference on High Performance Computing*, Trivandrum, IEEE Computer Society Press, December 1996, pp. 283-288.

[4] B. Bhargava and S.R. Lian, "Independent checkpoint and Concurrent Rollback for Recovery - An Optimistic Approach", in *Proceedings of IEEE Symposium on Reliable Distributed Systems*, 1988, pp 3-12.

[5] A.D. Birrel and B.J. Nelson, Implementing Remote Procedure Calls, *ACM Transactions on Computer Systems*, vol. 2, no. 1, 1984, pp. 39-58.

[6] K.M. Chandy, and L. Lamport, Distributed Snapshots: Determining global states of Distributed Systems, *ACM Transactions on Computer Systems*, vol. 3, no. 1, 1985, pp. 63-75.

[7] E.N. Elnozahy, D.B. Johnson, Y.M. Wang, "A Survey of Rollback-Recovery Protocols in Message-Passing Systems," technical report CMU-CS-96-181, Carnegie Mellon University, USA, 1996, pp. 1-46.

[8] A.P. Goldberg, A. Gopal, A. Lowry and R. Strom, Restoring Consistent Global States of Distributed Computations, In *Proc. of the ACM/ONR Workshop on Parallel and Distributed Debugging*, Santa Cruz, CA, 1991, pp. 144-154.

[9] J. Gray, Notes on Database Operating Systems, Operating Systems: An Advanced Course, *Lecture Notes in Computer Science LNCS 60, Springer-Verlag*, 1978, pp. 393-481.

[10] D.B. Johnson, and W. Zwaenepoel, Recovery in Distributed Systems Using Optimistic Message Logging and Check-pointing, *Journal of Algorithms*, 11, 1990, pp. 462-491.

[11] D.B. Johnson, and W. Zwaenepoel, Recovery in Distributed Systems Using Optimistic Message Logging and Check-pointing, *Proceedings of ACM Symposium on Principles of Distributed Computing*, 1988, pp. 171-180.

[12] T. Juang and S. Venkatesan, Efficient Algorithms for Crash Recovery in Distributed Systems, *Lecture Notes in Computer Science LNCS 472*, Springer-Verlag, 1990, pp. 349-361.

[13] T. Juang and S. Venkatesan,, Crash Recovery with Little Overhead, In *Proceedings of the 11th International Conference on Distributed Computing Systems*, 1991, pp. 454-461.

[14] S. Hariri and A. Choudhary, Architectural Support for Designing Fault-Tolerant Open Distributed Systems, *IEEE Computer*, June, 1992, pp. 50-62.

[15] J.-M. Helary, R.H.B. Netzer, and M. Raynal, "Consistency Issues in Distributed Checkpoints," *IEEE Transactions on Software Engineering*, Vol. 25, No. 2, March-April 1999.

[16] J.-M. Helary, A. Mostefaoui, and M. Raynal, "Communication-Induced Determination of Consistent Snapshots," *IEEE Transactions on Software Engineering*, Vol. 25, No. 2, March-April 1999.

[17] J.L. Kim and T. Park, "An efficient Protocol for Checkpointing Recovery in Distributed Systems", *IEEE Transactions on Parallel and Distributed Systems*, vol. 4., no. 8, pp. 955-960, August 1993.

[18] R. Koo, and S. Toueg, Checkpointing and Rollback Recovery for Distributed Systems, *IEEE Transactions on Software Engineering*, vol. SE-13, no. 1, 1987, pp. 23-31.

[19] L. Lamport, "Time, Clocks, and the Ordering of Events in a Distributed System", *Communications of ACM*, vol. 21, no. 7, pp. 558-565, July 1978.

[20] A. Lowry, J.R. Russell and A.P. Goldberg, Optimistic Failure Recovery for Very Large Networks, *Proceedings of 10th Symposium on Reliable Distributed Systems*, 1991, pp. 66-75.

[21] F. Mattern, "Efficient Algorithms for Distributed Snapshots and Global Virtual Time Appriximation", *Journal of Parallel and Distributed Computing*, August 1993, pp. 423-434.

[22] D. Manivannan, R.H.B. Netzer and M. Singhal, "Finding Consistent Global Checkpoints in a Distributed Computation", *IEEE Transactions on Parallel and Distributed Systems*, vol. 8, No. 6, June 1997, pp. 623-627.

[23] C. Morin, and I. Puaut, "A Survey of Recoverable Distributed Shared Virtual Memory Systems", *IEEE Transactions on Parallel and Distributed Systems*, vol. 8, No. 9, September 1997, pp. 959-969.

[24] R.H.B. Netzer and J. Xu, "Necessary and Sufficient Conditions for Consistent Global Snapshots", *IEEE Transactions on Parallel and Distributed Systems*, vol. 6, no. 2, Feb 1995, pp. 165-169.

[25] M.T. Ozsu, and P. Valduriez, *Principles of Distributed Database Systems*, New Jersey : Prentice Hall, 1990.

[26] M.L. Powell and D.L. Presotto, Publishing: A Reliable broadcast Communication Mechanism, *Proc. of 9th ACM Symposium on Operating System Principles*, October 1983, pp. 100-109.

[27] B. Randell, System Structure for Software Fault Tolerance, *IEEE Transactions on Software Engineering*, SE-1, no. 2, 1975, pp. 220-232.

[28] B.Randell, P.A.Lee and P.C. Treleaven, Reliability Issues in Computing Systems Design, *ACM Computing Surveys*, vol. 10, no. 2, June 1978, pp. 123-166.

[29] D.L. Russell, State Restoration in Systems of Communicating Processes, *IEEE Transactions on Software Engineering*, SE-6, no. 2, 1980, pp. 183-194.

[30] R.D. Schlichting, and F.B. Schneider, Fail-Stop Processors : An approach to Designing Fault-Tolerant Distributed Computing Systems, *ACM Transactions on Computer Systems*, vol. 1, no. 3, 1983, pp. 222-238.

[31] F.B. Schneider, Byzantine Generals in Action : Implementing Fail-Stop Processors, *ACM Transactions on Computer Systems*, vol. 2, no. 2, 1984, pp. 145-154.

[32] A. Sistla and J. Welch, Efficient Distributed Recovery Using Message Logging, In *Proc. of ACM Symposium on Principles of Distributed Computing*, 1989, pp. 223-238.

[33] R.E. Strom, and S. Yemini, Optimistic Recovery in Distributed Systems, *ACM Transactions on Computer Systems*, vol. 3, no. 3, August 1985, pp. 204-226.

[34] M.V. Sreenivas, and S. Bhalla, Garbage Collection in Message Passing Distributed Systems, in *Proceedings of International Symposium on Parallel Algorithms / Architecture Synthesis*, March 1995, IEEE Computer Society Press.

[35] M.V. Sreenivas, and S. Bhalla, Independent Global Snapshots in Large Distributed Systems, *Proceedings of the 4th International Conference on High Performance Computing*, Banglore, IEEE Computer Society Press, December 1997, pp. 462-467.

[36] G. Tel, "Introduction to Distributed Algorithms", on Snapshots, chapter 10, *Cambridge University Press*, 1994.

[37] K. Venkatesh, T. Radhakrishnan and H. Li, Optimal Checkpointing and Local Recording for Domino-free Rollback Recovery, *Information Processing Letters*, 25, 5, 1987, pp. 295-304.

[38] S. Venkatesan, and T. Juang, Efficient Algorithms for Optimistic Crash Recovery, *Distributed Computing*, Volume 8, No. 2, pp. 105-114, Springer-Verlag, 1994.

[39] Yi-Min Wang, "Consistent Global Checkpoints that Contain a Given Set of Local Checkpoints" *IEEE Transactions on Computers*, Vol. 46, No. 4, April 1997, pp. 456-468.

Appendix: Implementation Details

1. An Algorithm to Compute Recovery State

A dependency graph is made to capture the transitive dependency information, as described earlier (Definition 1, and Definition 4).

1.1 Data Structures

1.1.1 Message Transfer.

Message dependencies of a process state are represented as sender and receiver dependencies. For P_j^i, the dependencies are represented by dependency vectors $S_j^i[1,n]$ and $R_j^i[1,n]$, respectively.

$$S_j^i[1,n] = (s1,s2,s3,\ldots,sn)$$
$$R_j^i[1,n] = (r1,r2,r3,\ldots,rn)$$

where 'n' is the total number of processes in the system. Depending upon the exchange of messages, Component 'sx' of S_j^i is set to the maximum level of the state of process px (the sender), on which P_j^i depends. In the absence of any messages, If state(pi) does not depend on any state of process px, then sx is set to '-'. The value of '-' is kept less than zero for sake of comparison. Similarly, the values of R_j^i are also maintained.

The message losses owing to asynchronous message logging, and duplicate messages need to be taken care by application programs [25]. Therefore, each process appends a sequence number to the message to be sent. Also, each message is attached with a vector T, which is a combination of S and R vectors of the sender. This total dependency vector is determined by taking the piece-wise maximum of sender and receiver dependency vectors.

$$T_j^i = max(S_j^i, Rj^i), \ \forall i, j.$$

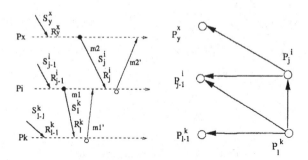

Figure 15.A.1. Random Messages and Total Dependency Graph .

1.1.2   State Vector .

Each process maintains a vector of size 'n', say M[n], in which the 'i'th element contains the highest sequence number of the message received from process pi. In case of a duplicate message, the receiver sends an old copy of the acknowledgment, with the corresponding (previous) dependency vectors, from its message log.

1.1.3   Log Status Vector.

In addition to this state vector, each process also maintains a *Log Status Vector* that indicates the known stable state of any process pi, as its 'i'th element.

1.2   The Algorithm

Each node in the system, maintains dependency vectors S and R. These vectors are updated with each message exchange. At any moment, T_j^i vector for a process pi indicates existence of a path between P_j^i and states of other processes in the system.

1.2.1   Normal Process Execution .

Consider the system shown in Figure 15.A.2. The message transmission is shown by using dark lines with acknowledgments sent through dashed lines. Let process pi send a message 'm1' to process pk. On receiving the message, process pk determines its new state 'l' and its new dependency vectors S_l^k and R_l^k, and appends the total dependency vector to the acknowledgment $m1'$. Process pi collects the acknowledgment for the messages sent and computes the dependency vectors in volatile storage. The receiver dependency is established, at the time at which the acknowledgment is received.

Let us assume that process pi in state 'j-1' receives a message 'm2'. As a result, process pi changes its current state to 'j'. P_j^i directly depends on P_y^x (sender dependency) and P_l^k (receiver dependency). The elements of **sender dependency vector**, S_j^i, for the new state 'j' are computed by taking piecewise maximum of

1) sender dependency vector of its previous state, S_{j-1}^i; and

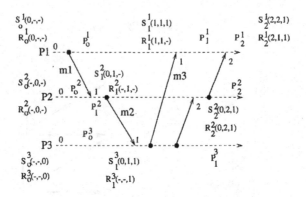

Figure 15.A.2. Interacting Processes.

2) total dependency vector of the sender process px, T_y^x

$$S_j^i[t] = \begin{vmatrix} max(S_{j-1}^i[t], T_y^x[t]), \ \forall t = 1, \cdots, n \wedge t \neq i \\ j, \ for \ t = i \end{vmatrix}$$

where, $S_j^i[t]$ = state(pt) on which P_j^i depends. The **receiver dependency vector** R_j^i can be constructed by taking piecewise maximum of

1) receiver dependency vector of its previous state, R_{j-1}^i ; and

2) total dependency vectors of all the receivers of messages from which acknowledgments have been received by process pi in its last state, 'j-1', say, for all k, T_l^k .

$$R_j^i[t] = \begin{vmatrix} max(R_{j-1}^i[t], T_l^k[t]), \ \forall t = 1, \cdots, n \wedge t \neq i, \\ \forall k, \ni pi \ in \ state \ 'j-1' \ received \ acknowledgment \ from \ pk. \\ j, \ for \ t = i. \end{vmatrix}$$

where, $R_j^i[t]$ = state(pt) on which P_j^i depends. Also, as mentioned earlier, the **total dependency vector** can be determined as follows.

$$T_j^i = max(S_j^i, Rj^i), \ \forall i, j.$$

Messages and acknowledgments carry the **total dependency vector** indicating the state in which the message has been sent. The dependency graph is also given in Figure 15.A.1.

1.3   Case Example

Let us consider system consisting of three processes p1,p2 and p3 and several messages, m1 to m5 (Figure 15.A.2). For each message, the sender and receiver dependencies can be constructed by using the following steps.

Event 1 : Process p2 receives m1 with dependency vector T_0^1.
S_1^2 = max (S_0^2, T_0^1) and $R_1^2 = R_0^2$
new state(p2) = 1; $S_1^2[1]$= 1; $R_1^2[1]$= 1
Process p2 sends acknowledgment to process p1 by attaching the vector $T_1^2 = (0,1,-)$.

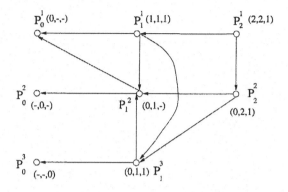

Figure 15.A.3.   Total Dependency Graph with Cumulative State Dependencies

Event 2 : Process p3 receives message m2 with dependency vector T_1^2.
$S_1^3 = \max(S_0^3, T_1^2)$ and $R_1^3 = R_0^3$
new state(p3) = 1; $S_1^3[3] = 1$; $R_1^3[3] = 1$
Process p3 sends an acknowledgment to p2 by attaching dependency vectors $T_1^3 = (0,1,1)$.

Event 3 : Process p1 receives a message m3 with dependency vector T_1^3 . Also, Process p1
has received acknowledgments to its message from processes p2 in state '0'.
$S_1^1 = \max(S_0^1, T_1^3)$ and $R_1^1 = \max(R_0^1, T_1^2)$
new state(p1) = 1; $S_1^1[1] = 1$; $R_1^1 = 1$
The process attaches $T_1^1 = (1,1,1)$ to the acknowledgment.

In Figure 15.A.3, the total dependency graph of Figure 15.A.2 is shown along with total
dependency vectors.

IV

APPLICATIONS

Chapter 16

INTERACTIVE DATA MINING BASED ON PC CLUSTER ENVIRONMENT

Zhen Liu
Faculty of Human Environment,
Nagasaki Institute of Applied Science, 536 Aba-machi, Nagasaki 851-0193, Japan
liuzhen@cc.nias.ac.jp

Minyi Guo
Department of Computer Software,
The University of Aizu, Aizu-Wakamatsu City, Fukushima 965-8580, Japan
minyi@u-aizu.ac.jp

Abstract   In order to realize high performance and high effectiveness data mining, not only a parallel and distributed environment, but also an interactive and dynamic visual data mining support are necessary. In this chapter, a scheme of interactive data mining support system in high performance parallel and distributed computing environment is proposed. The overall architecture and the mechanism of the system are described.

Keywords: Data mining, Visualization, Interactive, Parallel and distributed processing, PC cluster

1.   Introduction

The quantity of data has been increasing at a high speed along with the progress of database technology and data collection technology. It has been estimated that the amount of data in the world double every 20 months. The size and number of databases probably increase even faster [1]. Enterprises store more and more data in data warehouse for decision support purposes. It is not realistic to expect that all these data can be carefully analyzed by human analysts and users due to the increasing of large amount of data.

The huge size of real-world databases systems brings the following problems in data using, and creates both a need and an opportunity for a partially-automated form of data mining: (1) Data quantitative problem, (2) Data qualitative problem, and (3) Data presentation problem.

The data quantitative problem causes the decline of the processing speed having to do with a system that the accumulated amount of data becomes enormous too much. Also, there is a limit in the judgment and the ability to process. To solve this, it is necessary to develop the technique to improve processing efficiency. And the system that facilities the processing of data and judgment for the human being must be developed too. The data qualitative problem occurs because the complicated relation exists between the attributes or the data in the large-scale databases. The near combinations exist infinitely as the relations of data, attributes of data and the combinations of them are very complicated. As it is impossible to verify all of them, it is necessary to improve the processing efficiency. Also, when the pattern among the detected data is too complicated, the thing that one finds some meaning from there becomes difficult. This is the data presentation problem. It is necessary to provide a complicated detection result in the form which is easy for the human being to understand to cope with this. It can expect the squeeze of further data, a new discovery and so on.

An effective way to enhance the power and flexibility of data mining in data warehouses and large-scale databases is to integrate data mining with on-line analytical processing (OLAP), visualization and interactive interface in a high performance parallel and distributed environment.

2.   Related Technologies of Effectiveness Data Mining

2.1   Parallel and distributed processing technology

Parallel and distributed processing are two important components of a successful large-scale data mining application because that the computation requirements are very large, and the enormity of data or the nature of data collections often requires that the data be stored across multiple storage devices.

A distributed application can be viewed as a collection of objects (user interface, databases, application modules, users). Each object has its own attributes and has some methods which define the user behavior of the object. For example, an order can be viewed in terms of its data and the methods which create, delete, and update the order object. Interactions between the components of an application can be modeled through "messages" which invoke appropriate methods.

Parallel processing is performed by simultaneous use of more than one CPU to execute a program. Ideally, parallel processing makes a program run faster because there are more engines running it. Most computers have just one CPU, but some models have several. With single-CUP computers, it is possible to perform parallel processing by connection the computers in a network. For example, some parallel data mining researches are doing on PC/WS (Personal Computer/Work Station) clusters [5][6]. In recent years, more and more works are focused on paralleling data mining. The study field is wide-ranging from the designing of parallel processing system to the parallel realizing of various data mining algorithms [4][5][6][7].

2.2   On-Line Analytical Processing

OLAP was introduced by E. F. Codd [8][9], the father of relational databases in 1993. He came to the conclusion that relational databases for OLTP (On-Line Transaction Processing) had reached the maximum of their capabilities in terms of the views of the data they provided the user. The problem stemmed principally from the massive computing required when relational databases were asked to answer relatively simple SQL queries. He also came to the view that operational data are not adequate for answering managerial questions. He therefore advocated the use of multi-dimensional databases. His conversion to the DSS/EIS viewpoint gave legitimacy to the data warehouse based concepts. The basic idea in OLAP is that managers should be able to manipulate enterprise data across many dimensions to understand changes that are occurring.

As the facility of powerful multidimensional analysis for data warehouse, it is necessary to adopt on-line analytical processing technology in data warehouse and large-scale database. OLAP provides such facilities as drilling, pivoting, filtering, dicing and slicing so the user can traverse the data flexibly, define the set of relevant data, analyze data at different granularities, and visualize the results in different forms. These operations can also be applied to data mining to make it an exploratory and effective process. Together with OLAP, data mining functions can provide an overview of the discovered knowledge such that the user can investigate further on any interesting patterns or anomalies. Because with OLAP operations, the size of the data set is relatively more compact. So that, the mining integrated with OLAP technology can do insure faster response than mining in the raw data directly.

2.3   Visualization technology and interactive interface

Visualization is to display data successfully in the screen of the computer for grasping the nature of the enormous data intuitively. In the past, so-called scientific visualization which deals with a great deal of numerical data such as the simulation result was to do mainstream being if saying visualization.

Numerical data are rarely comprehensive in raw forms: tables of numbers tend to confuse the content and hide the essential patterns present without the data. In addition, for many applications each data point has associated with it more attributes than can be adequately described by the standard row and column. A multi-dimensional data enables each data point to be characterized by a potentially unlimited number of patterns, visualization technology used in data mining can lead itself to slicing and pivoting among multiple dimensions to display the data in any number of forms.

Visualizing data helps user quickly determine what the data really mean; it literally transforms data into information. Visualization becomes even more powerful as the amount of raw data increase, especially if the visualization in interactive. The purpose of visualization is to transform data into information that forms a critical component within the decision making process.

3.　　Interactive Data Mining Scheme

3.1　　Key technologies

In order to develop an interactive data mining support system in high performance parallel and distributed computing environment successfully, the following key problems must be considered firstly: (1) On-line data mining, (2) Data parallelism, (3) Visual data mining, and (4) Interactive interface.

Data mining and OLAP are all analytical tools, but obvious differences exist between each other. The analysis process of data mining is completed automatically. It is only needed to extract hidden patterns, and predict the future trends and behaviors without giving exact query by user. It is of benefit to finding unknown facts. While OLAP depends on user's queries and propositions to complete analysis process. It restricted the scope of queries and propositions, and affects the final results. On the other hand, to data, most OLAP systems have focused on providing access to multi-dimensional data, while data mining systems have deal with influence analysis of data along a single dimension. It is an effective way to enhance the power and flexibility of data mining in data warehouse by integrating data mining with OLAP to offset their weaknesses [10].

Data parallelism refers to the execution of the same operation or instruction on multiple large data subsets at the same time. This is in contrast to control parallelism, which refers to the key idea in data parallelism is that the whole data set is partitioned into disjoint data subsets, each of them allocated to a disjoint processor, so that each processor can apply the same operation only to its local data. From the point of view of the application programmer, automatic parallelization is an important advantage of data parallelism. In the control-parallelism paradigm the application programmer is in charge of all inter-processor communication and synchronization, which makes programming a time-consuming, error-prone activity. A major advantage of the data parallelism is machine-architecture independence. Data parallelism should be possible to add a number of processor nodes (CPU+RAM) to the system proportional to the amount of data increase, to keep the query-response time nearly constant, although there will be some increase in query-response time due to the increase in inter-processor communication time caused by adding more processors to exploit data parallelism.

Visual data mining is different from scientific visualization and it has the following characteristic: (1) wide range of users, (2) wide choice range of the visualization techniques, and (3) important dialog function. The users of scientific visualization are scientists and engineers who can endure the difficulty in using the system for little at most. However, a visual data mining system must have the possibility that the general person uses widely and so on easily. It is almost that the simulation results are represented in 2D or 3D visualization. However, it is more ordinary that the objects are not actual one in the information visualization. Moreover, it is possible to make a completely different expression form, too. The purpose of the information visualization becomes a point with important dialogs such as repeating data more in another visualization by changing the way of seeing data and the technique of the visualization and squeezing it because it is not visualization itself and to be in the discovery of the information retrieval and the rule is many.

The idea of the interactive data mining support system is based on the following viewpoints: (1) data mining is a multi-step process, and (b) the human user must be allowed to be front and center in the mining process. In the interactive data mining support system, data mining is performed not by one-sidedly on the side of the system by the algorithms, but showing it by the visualization in the form for which it is easy to judge a temporary processing result for the human being and feeding back the judgment and the knowledge of the human being into the side of the system.

3.2   The overall architecture and mechanism

The architecture of the interactive high performance data mining support system is suggested as shown in Figure 16.1. It mainly consists of:

1) Parallel database: the platform of the on-line analytical data mining;

2) Parallel database server: a horizontal-partitioning;

3) Data Mining Agent: performing analytical mining in data cubes aided by OLAP engine;

4) OLAP Engine: providing fast access to summarized data along multiple dimensions;

5) PGUI (Parallel Graphic User Interface): transforming multidimensional data into understandable information and providing parallel data mining visualization.

6) Applications Programming Interface (API): aggregation of instructions, functions, regulations and rules for on-line data mining, supporting interactive data mining.

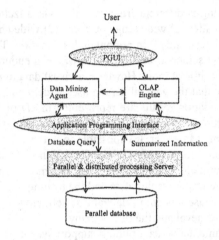

Figure 16.1.   Overall architecture of the system

The system has both of on-line data mining and parallel data mining features. Mainly components of the system is parallel database sever, API and PGUI which will be illustrated in the following subsections.

Data mining agent performs analytical mining in data cubes with the aid of OLAP engine. Data mining agent and the OLAP engine both accept user's on-line queries through the user interface and work with the data cube through the applications programming interface in the analysis. Furthermore, data mining agent may perform multiple data mining tasks, such as concept description, association, classification, prediction, clustering, time-series analysis, etc. Therefore, data mining agent is more sophisticated than the OLAP engine since it usually consists of multiple mining modules which may interact with each other for effective mining.

Since some requirements in data mining agent, such as the construction of numerical dimensions, may not be readily available in the commercial OLAP products, particular mining modules should be built in model base. Although, data mining agent analysis may often involve the analysis of a large number of dimensions the finer granularities and thus require more powerful data cube construction and accessing tools than OLAP analysis, there is no fundamental difference between the data cube required for OLAP engine and that for data mining agent. Since data mining agent is constructed either on customized data cubes which often work with relational database systems, or on top of data cubes provided by the OLAP products, it is suggested to build on-line analytical mining systems on top of the existing OLAP and relational database systems, rather than from the group up.

3.3   Parallel database server

Generally, there are two types of parallel database server, specialized hardware parallel database server and standard hardware parallel database server. The major types of the former are Intelligent Disks, Database Filters and Associative Memories. The major types of the later are Share-memory, Shared-disk, and Shared-nothing [12].

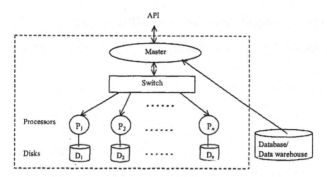

Figure 16.2.   Parallel and distributed processing server.

The parallel and distributed processing server is a cluster of shared-nothing multiprocessor nodes as shown in Figure 16.2. The main memory is distributed among the processors, and each processor manages its own disk. In the architecture, all processors can access their corresponding disks in parallel, minimizing the classical I/O bottleneck in database systems. Each processor can independently process its own data, and the processors communicate with each other via the Master only to send requests and receive results. This avoids the need for transmitting large amounts of data through the Master. It takes advantages of high-performance, low-cost commodity processors and memory, and it fit to be realized with PC/WS cluster.

3.4   Interactive interface

Numerical simulation and analysis usually consistent of three main stages: (1) generating computational grids, (2) solving physical equations, and (3) visualizing the result data. As the rapid arising of the process capability of computers, the computational grid is becoming more and more complicated, and the data amount of computational result is becoming large and large. The parallel visualization subsystem offers an effective visualization platform and an interactive exploration for various types datasets arising from parallel data mining for users. The framework of the parallel visualization subsystem is shown in Figure 16.3.

The concurrent visualization with calculation on the high performance parallel and distributed system is supplied with the parallel visualization subsystem. It outputs to clients graphic primitives rather than resulting images. On each client, the users can set viewing, illumination, shading parameters, and so on, and display the graphic primitives.

The parallel visualization subsystem also provides the follows features for users.

1) Data partition visualization,

2) Dynamic communication traffic visualization, and

3) Dynamic visual presentation of parallel data mining process.

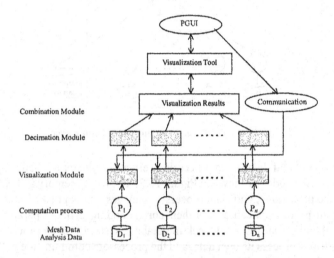

Figure 16.3.   Parallel visualization subsystem.

Basing on parallel visualization subsystem, an interactive Application Programming Interface (API) is provided. The basic function of the API is that of a PGUI (Parallel Graphic User Interface). It includes direct operation, dynamic search, continuous operation, and reversible operation, and so on.

The interactive dialog will be realized with a GH-SOM (Growing Hierarchical Self-Organization Map) model. SOM (self-Organization Map) is an artificial neural network model that proved to be exceptionally successful for data visualization applications where the mapping from a usually very high-dimensional data space into a two-dimensional representation space is required. The GH-SOM was proposed by Dittenbach [12]. It uses a hierarchical structure of multiple layers where each layer consists of a number of independent self-organization maps. One SOM is used at the first layer of the hierarchy. For every unit in this map a SOM might be added to the next layer of the hierarchy. This principle is repeated with the third and further layers of the GH-SOM. Each layer in the hierarchy consists of a number of independent self-organizing maps which determine their size and arrangement of units also during the unsupervised training process. The GH-SOM model is especially well suited for application which have large-scale dataset. It will be applied in a high performance parallel and distributed computing environment.

Acknowledgments

This work is supported by The Telecommunications Advancement Foundation, Japan.

References

[1] Frawley, W., Piatetsky-Shapiro, G., and Matheus, C, "Knowledge Discovery in Databases: An Overview, Knowledge Discovery in Databases", eds. G. Piatetsky-Shapiro and W. Frawley, 1- 27, Cambridge, *Mass.: AAAI Press / The MIT Press*, 1991.

[2] Masato Oguchi, Masaru Kitsuregawa, "Data Mining on PC Cluster connected with Storage Area Network: Its Preliminary Experimental Results", *IEEE International Conference on Communications*, Helsinki, Finland ,2001.

[3] Masato Oguchi and Masaru Kitsuregawa, "Using Available Remote Memory Dynamically for Parallel Data Mining Application on ATM-Connected PC Cluster", *Proc. of the International Parallel and Distributed Processing Symposium, IEEE Computer Society*, 2000.

[4] C.C. Bojarczuk, H.S. Lopes, A.A. Freitas. "Genetic programming for knowledge discovery in chest pain diagnosis", *IEEE Engineering in Medicine and Biology magazine - special issue on data mining and knowledge discovery*, 19(4), July/Aug. 2000.

[5] Mohammed J. Zaki, "Parallel Sequence Mining on Shared-Memory Machines", *Journal of Parallel and Distributed Computing*, 61, 2001.

[6] Diane J. Cook, Lawrence B. Holder, Gehad Galal, and Ron Maglothin, "Approched to Parallel Graph-Based Knowledge Discovery", *Journal of Parallel and Distributed Computing*, 61, 2001.

[7] Sanjay Goil, "PARSIMONY: An Infrastructure for Paralle Multidimensional Analysis and Data Mining",*Journal of Parallel and Distributed Computing*, 61, 2001.

[8] E. F. Codd, E. S. Codd and C. T. Salley, "Beyond Decision Support", *Computerworld*, Vol.27, No.30, July 1993.

[9] Qing Chen, "Mining Exceptions and Quantitative Association Rules in Olap Data Cube", *IEEE Transactions on Knowledge and Data Engineering*, 1999.

[10] Liu Zhen and Guo Minyi, "A Proposal of Integrating Data Mining and On-Line Analytical Processing in Data Warehouse", *Proceedings of 2001 International Conferences on Info-tech and Info-net*, 2001

[11] A.A.Freitas, Generic, "Set-Oriented Primitives to Support Data-Parallel Knowledge Discovery in Relational Databases Systems", thesis of the doctoral degree, Department of Computer Science, University of Essex, 1997.

[12] M. Dittenbach, D. Merkl, A. Rauber, "The Growing Hierarchical Self-Organization Map", *Proceeding of the international Joint Conference on Neural Networks*, July, 2000.

Chapter 17

LONG-TERM MAIL ADDRESS TRANSITION IN THE MOBILE INTERNET UNDER UNSOLICITED BULK EMAIL

Toshihiko Yamakami

Research and Development Division

ACCESS 2816 Sarugakucho, Chiyodaku, Tokyo, JAPAN

yam@access.co.jp

Abstract   The mobile Internet penetrates into the every day life in a drastic pace. This emergence of new technologies easily triggered the new social problems like unsolicited bulk email. The author analyzes the mobile Internet transition from the social process viewpoint. A 2-year analysis of mobile email transition observed on a commercial mobile web service shows the two-staged transition to cope with the bulk email problems. Changing the Internet identity such as email address has cognitive and social aspects. From the results, the author proposes an identity transition factor model to describe the social process of the forced email address changes in the mobile Internet.

Keywords: Mobile Internet, Unsolicited bulk mail, long-term transition

1.   Introduction

The mobile Internet penetrates into the every day life in a drastic pace. In the last five years, significant efforts were devoted to ensure interoperability in the mobile handsets [1] [5]. A growing number of information appliances, especially mobile handsets, appear with Internet capabilities. The number of so-called non-PC Internet-enabled devices like mobile handsets and game consoles is expected to reach a billion in 2006 [2]. The market penetration rate of cellular telephones has reached 80% or higher in many parts of Asia and Europe. In Japan, the market penetration rate of Internet-enabled mobile handsets in the total mobile handsets reached 84% in June 2003. It is reported that there were 64 million Internet-enabled mobile handset users. This emergence of new technologies easily triggered the new social problems like UBE(Unsolicited Bulk Email). The PC Internet users have experiences with UBE from early days of the Internet. However, the emerging new users in the mobile Internet were shocked with these unsolicited attacks from strangers. In the mobile Internet, due to the display and storage limitations, UBE causes serious problems for end users. In addition, people in the early days of the mobile Internet were unprepared against the UBE attacks. It accelerated the UBE attacks in some cases. In the PC Internet, it is common to filter or ignore the UBE messages. In the mobile Internet, the burden for these routine works is prohibiting. This causes the frequent mobile Internet email address changes for mobile Internet users. The identity change forced by the uncomfortable experience is a significant step for end users. It impacts their social lives in the mobile Internet. The research about the identity transition is an important research source to understand the fundamental aspects of the mobile Internet. UBE in the mobile Internet is rarely studied because it is hard to store all UBE evidence and analyze them in the handset. In this study, we call the Internet users using micro-browsers on a mobile handset as mobile Internet users.

2.   UBE in the Mobile Internet

UBE is very common in PC Internet users [3] [4]. It was called as spam mail in the slang. It is commonly unsolicited mail delivery originated from strange mass advertisers. Over a span of time, various techniques like Internet search, aggregating mail exploder addresses, common name guessing, virus-based personal information search and brute-force trials. The struggle against UBE in the PC Internet continues in spite of the social awareness against UBE. There are some techniques to block UBE like white-list-filtering or black-list-filtering, which are not perfect. When the mobile Internet emerged, the users were unprepared against UBE attacks. Due to the input limitations, the shorter names were preferred. In addition, as the identity cognition, the telephone number was preferred as the main part of the email address because they were easy to memorize for people. The mobile telephone number is 11-digit long in Japan. However, the first 3 digits are used for the mobile carrier identification code. Therefore, it had the same strength as the 8-digit number. It was vulnerable to the attacks. These considerations for the mobile Internet characteristics were volatile against the UBE attacks. In the early days, some mobile carriers set the initial email address as identical as the telephone number except the mail domain name. It was easy to memorize, however, very vulnerable to UBE attacks The fixed-length numeric characters are easy to generate and test for brute force attacks. The brute force attack is to try all potential addresses including telephone numbers, and store the delivery results on a database. The unique features of the mobile Internet make the social impact distinguished. There are three social issues in UBE in mobile Internet. First, the mobile Internet has an always-on feature. Therefore, UBE is more intruding for the end users. Second, the mobile handsets are poorly equipped with anti-UBE facilities. The feature and user interface is limited by CPU power, available storage, and battery power. The manual sorting and filtering needs more cognitive cost for end users in the limited user interface environment like mobile handsets. Third, in many cases, the mobile carriers charge every packet to the end users. The charges outrage the users who pay for the unsolicited mail. It causes economic damages. These three factors impacted the end users, gradually forced them to change their identity, the email address in the mobile Internet. In addition, the mobile UBE have hidden effects. It causes the problems of the gateway between the Internet and the mobile carriers because the attacks come from the Internet side. This leads to the delays of the mail exchange between the mobile carrier and the Internet.

During the mobile Internet emergence, the strong market growth attracted many UBE-based underground advertisement business as well as common content providers. In Japan, the harms done by mobile Internet UBE became apparent in the spring of 2001. People witnessed the forced email address change because many people received more than 100 UBE messages every month. This UBE phenomenon is based on a guess on mail address and brute force attacks. Gradually, end users change their mail addresses in order to escape from the uncomfortable experience. It is recommended to use a mixed character mail address with alphabets, numbers and special characters like a period or an underscore. In addition, it is recommended to use a longer email address that is robust against brute force attacks. The suggested length was increased against stronger brute force attacks evolved. Now, the recommended length of mail address is more than 12. In a side effect, mobile Internet content providers lost a lot of customer email addresses, which are crucial in mobile e-commerce to ensure the interactions with close end-user contacts. The author performed a preliminary analysis on the email address change in the mobile Internet in 2001-2002 [7]. In this preliminary study, the author found that the drastic email address changes in a short span of time under the UBE in the mobile Internet.

3. Mobile Internet Identity

The significance of the mobile Internet identity depends on the mobile Internet life style. In the early stage of the mobile Internet, it was apparent that the mobile Internet email address was not an integrated part of personal identities. It is not used in the real world communication. When it had some problems, it was easy to change. When the mobile Internet penetrates into the every-day world, it increased the significance and relations to the social contexts. First, it is the 24-hour contact point for people. Second, it is troublesome to notify the new email address for people to communicate by email. Another issue is UBE awareness. Without UBE threats, it is uncommon to include various special characters in the email address for robustness. When the people depend on the mobile email and are aware with the UBE threats, they will use the longer and complicated email address and change it less frequently.

The first template for the mobile Internet email addresses is either telephone number or PC-world familiar email address. Under the UBE threats, the users are forced to have a very artificial identity for their personalized communication life. This complicates the cognitive aspect of the email address transition in the mobile Internet. The change frequency and choice of email address complexity are the indicators about the people's experience of the mobile Internet and UBE.

4.   Long-term Address Transition Analysis

The author analyzes the email address transition analysis on the commercial charged service provided for the two different carriers. The carrier A charged by per-packet base, and the carrier B did not charge on the incoming mail. The target service is a business-oriented information service listed on the mobile carrier official site in both carriers. There is a news alert service. For this service, one third of the users registered their mobile handset email addresses. There are two logs for the mail address, one for the mail registration log, and the other from the alert sending log. The author examines the mail registration logs for the service in the carrier A from August 2000 to July 2001 and one in the carrier B from October 2000 to July 2002. In addition, the author examines the alert mail origination log for the comparison between the static registration-based analysis and the dynamic active sending-based analysis. The purpose of the study includes:

- Monthly transitions of the mail address patterns,

- Comparison of the carrier A user behavior and the carrier B user behavior, and

- Comparison of the static mail address pattern analysis and the dynamic mail address pattern analysis.

The author is engaged in the mobile web side user behavior studies since 2001 [6] in order to the user identifier-based tracking analysis. On the transition analysis, the author performs the monthly transition over a span of time on

- Mail address length, and
- Mail address character pattern.

In character patterns, the addresses are categorized in the four patterns:

- Numeric only,
- Combination of alphabet and numeric characters, and

- Other patterns including three common punctuation characters(".", "_", "-").

Originally, the initial mail address was all numeric, which was identical to the user's telephone number. The new system to use more robust initial mail addresses started in July 2001 after the significant damages cased by mobile BSE.

5.   Case Studies in the mobile email addresses

There are three case studies. The first one is the study for monthly logs for mail registration in the carrier A. It outlines the general trend for new mail address registration/update. The second one is the study for real origination use log every month. The valid addresses used for the notification service is analyzed. It outlines the active user mail address behavior. The third one is the mail registration every month for the carrier B. It outlines the inter-carrier difference on the UBE attack impact. The average mail address length did not show the significant change over a span of period. The length of telephone numbers is 11. Usually, the alphabetic address is shorter than that. The average length is almost stable during the period in this observation.

The registration mail address patterns are easier to analyze because each user registers only once. The average length transition from August 2000 to July 2002 is depicted in Figure 17.1.

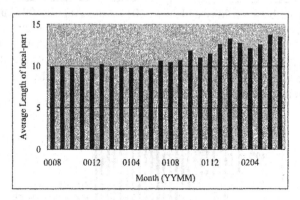

Figure 17.1.   Average Length of local-part in the service A registration from August 2000 to July 2002

The mail address length range is moving to the longer one. The length range transitions in "len < 8", "8 ≤ len < 12", "12 ≤ len < 16", and "len ≥ 16", where len denotes the length of the local-part email address, are presented in Figure 17.2. The longer addresses increase. The numbers of users in the "12 ≤ len < 16" range increased significantly in May and June 2001 and continued to increase until February 2002. On the contrary, the "len < 8" range was stable until October 2001. During the period between October 2001 and July

2002, the range shows decrease with some fluctuation. The "len <8" range is a mail address similar to the PC Internet. The range "$8 \leq$ len < 12" includes the telephone number-based 11-digit numeric addresses. It shows the constant decrease trend from 70% to 30%.

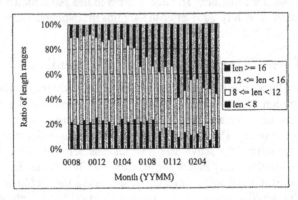

Figure 17.2.　Local-part Length Ranges in the service A registration from August 2000 to July 2002

The character patterns in mail addresses are depicted in Figure 17.3. In the year 2000, the trend was stable. 80-85% of users used numeric only addresses. 10-15% of users used alphabet only addresses. This trend drastically changed in the period between May and July 2001. After August 2001, the numeric only is stable. Now two thirds of users use some special characters like ".", "_", and "-" in their addresses. Also, it should be noted that the initial mail address has been not in numeric only since July 2001. However, the increase showed in May 2001. Therefore, it can be observed that the user behavior to change their addresses against UBE influences the trend.

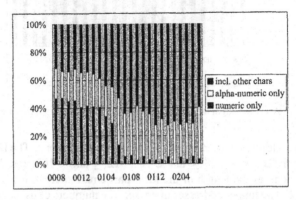

Figure 17.3.　Local-part Character Patterns in the service A registration from August 2000 to July 2002

A comparison study is done on another carrier, the carrier B. This carrier has the special charging policy that the incoming mail communication fee is free. The mail address relatively shorter addresses in the similar transition pattern. In the carrier B, no alert service is provided and the users are voluntarily asked to register their email addresses. One fifth of the users registered their email. However, the low use of the registered address shows the instability of the registered address patterns.

The average length from November 2000 to July 2002 is shown in Figure 17.4.

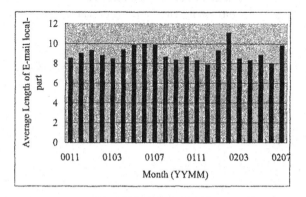

Figure 17.4. Average Length of local-part in the service B during Nov 2000 and July 2002

The local-part length ranges are shown in Figure 17.5. The address range transition is depicted in Figure 17.5. It is not stable, however, it should be noted that the shorter addresses are unchanged or even increased. These results indicates the sensitivity of the address transition patterns. However, the firm statistic results cannot be obtained due to the different contexts in the two services.

The local-part character patterns are shown in Figure 17.6. The drastic address change occurred in June and July 2001, slightly later than the previous case studies.

The registration can partially capture the user behavior when users newly register or update their mail address updates. The commercial service observed in this study provides the mail alert service. It is an optional service. In this service, the users can receive notification mail every time a new content with the user's registered keywords. This provides the email addresses used in this notification service. It means the active mail addresses, because it is necessary to update the current mail address to enjoy the notification function. It reflects the current mail addresses, and also is influence by the active users' behavior. The registration mail addresses may be unchanged during the user's update of mail addresses to avoid junk mail when the user does not subscribe this particular notification service. The length ranges transition is presented in

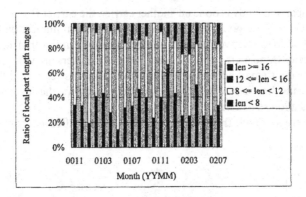

Figure 17.5. Local-part Length Ranges in the service B registration during Nov 2000 and July 2002

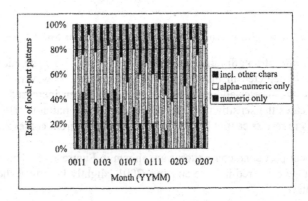

Figure 17.6. Local-part Character Patterns in the service B registration during Nov 2000 and July 2002

Figure 17.7. The average length monthly transition is depicted in Figure 17.9. Finally, the mail address patterns transition is depicted in Figure 17.8. Compared to the registration, the origination log has the tendency that the address pattern changes are observed slightly delayed. One of the reasons include that the UBE forced the user to change their addresses, however, it gave the reconsideration opportunity for end users in the current subscription services. Therefore, the sudden rise of UBE impacted the precious resource of the mobile web content providers. The result shows that the registration-based metrics are more sensitive in the heavy UBE condition.

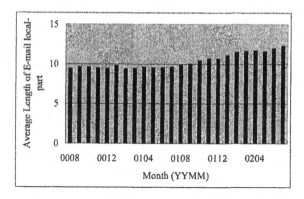

Figure 17.7. Average Length of local-part in the service A alert mail origination log from August 2000 to July 2002

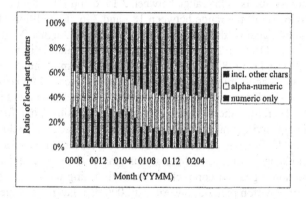

Figure 17.8. Local-part Character Patterns in the service A alert mail origination log from August 2000 to July 2002

6. Evaluation

6.1 Findings

In order to test the changes of the average length of the local-part email addresses, the author performs the Student's t-test with Welch's approximation method assuming that the mother standard deviation is unknown. It tests the difference of the average mail address length chosen in the different stages Each month's average length of the mail addresses for the mail alert service origination log is tested against the first month data in August 2000, and the last month data in July 2002. The origination log is used because it reflects the real active mail address use. The degree of the freedom is significantly larger than 20, therefore, the t-distribution is close to the normal distribution. In the confidential interval with 0.05, the null hypothesis against the same average length with July 2002 is denied in the range of August 2000 and January

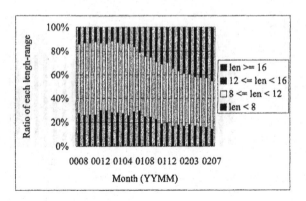

Figure 17.9. Local-part Length Ranges in the service A alert mail origination log from August 2000 to July 2002

2001 where t-value is in the range between 3.1416 and 6.1708 with the degree of the freedom is in the range between 186 and 346. In addition, the similar null hypothesis against the same average length with August 2000 is denied in the range of October 2001 to July 2002 where t-value is in the range between 2.1257 and 6.1708 with the degree of the freedom in the range between 189 and 286. The average length grows gradually over a long span of time. This statistic significance of the length transition was not found in the preliminary study. Therefore, there are two stages for the transition, one for character pattern change and the other for length change. The latter takes longer to be realized. The BSE impacted the choice of the address length. It is a statistically significant change over a more-than-a-year span of time. The registration log and origination log is not completely identical. Using the similar t-test with Welch approximation method, the August 2000 data has the t-value = 2.4668 with the degrees of freedom = 510. The July 2002 data has the t-value = 1.3773 with the degrees of freedom = 105. In the July 2002 data, the null hypothesis is not denied, however, the null hypothesis is denied in the case of August 2000. Evaluation on the case studies are categorized in the three aspects:

- Long-term address pattern transition,

- Inter-carrier comparison on the traffic charging policy, and

- Evaluation of the mail log analysis on anti-UBE behaviors.

The mail address length is not sensitive to the mobile UBE attacks. The 11-digit telephone number address is already too long to make it longer for end users. It is clear that users adopt special character patterns in addresses to prevent brute force attacks. The mobile handset mail characteristics may have some implications on this forced behavior. More than 50% of users use non-alphanumeric characters in their addresses. In the low UBE environment, the ratio was under 10%. The transition took two to three months. The social process to propagate the criteria of the robust email address choice is interesting and for further studies. About the methodology, the mail address observation captures the user behavior diffusion in mail address changes. The mail log is commonly available on most systems. Therefore, it is easy to use for the first step study without intrusion to mobile users. The mail registration and real mail use are different aspects of the mobile mail services. This study shows little difference between these two factors. It is easier to analyze the mail address transition at the mail registration base when there are millions of users that are not uncommon in the top mobile content providers.

6.2   Limitations

To evaluate the limitations of this study, the following three aspects should be considered:

- Fairness in the case study samples,

- Fairness about the inter-carrier comparisons, and

- Social processes for the propagation of the renewed criteria for email address choice.

The first limitation is the evaluation of the samples. The case studies in this study focused one particular commercial mobile service due to the log availability. The second limitation is the bias in the inter-carrier comparisons. The study shows the impact of the charging policy on the email address transition patterns. It needs more studies to make further conclusion.

This study examines the result of the user behavior, not the behavior itself. The social aspects of the email address transition like know-how propagation, education and interactive processes are for further studies. Further research topics include the following issues:

- User cognitive difference between PC-based Internet UBE and mobile UBE,

- User mental model about changing mail addresses in different stages, and

- Social effects for mail address change behavior diffusion under UBE attacks.

The tradeoff between the UBE attack damage and the forced mobile Internet identification update is an interesting topic. The long-term observation is impacted by the carrier policy to enforce certain types of email address choices. The consistent observation over multiple years is difficult to design.

6.3   An Identity Transition Factor Model

The change of the mobile Internet identity depends on both of cost models and cognitive models. An identity transition factor model is depicted in Figure

17.10. From the finding in the address transition, the identity transition has two phases, one for the complexity and the other for the longer address. The choice criteria in the email address are a combination of the wider choice of characters and the length of the address. This reflects the cost aspects and the cognitive and social aspects of the address choice criteria. The choice criteria reflect the culture and economic environment. This study shows that the charge policy may impact the choice of the address. It can indicate the know-how and awareness propagation, educational efforts by carriers, cost consideration, and the UBE threat strength.

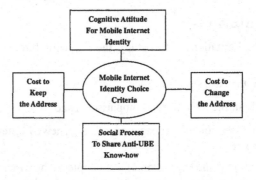

Figure 17.10.   An Identity Transition Factor Model

7.   Conclusions

The author notices the importance of the identification of the mobile Internet characteristics. In this study, the author uses long-term transition analysis on the mobile Internet email address statistics. The author performs the analysis on the registered email address in several commercial mobile Internet web sites for 2 years. The analysis is based on the static one with registration log and the dynamic one with origination log. The observation indicates the two-stage changes of the mobile Internet email address choice by end users. As a methodology, email address transition analysis is general and applicable to the wide range of email based mobile web services. The dynamic aspect from origination log and the static aspect from registration log show slightly different side of the email address transition. The email address transition is a mixture of the cost, cognitive and social aspects of the UBE situation. An identity transition factor model is proposed. The mobile Internet diffusion is a global phenomenon. Therefore, the email address transition may reveal different cultural aspects of the mobile Internet identity in the virtual world. The further studies will include user mental and social model of the email choice behaviors in the mobile Internet. The issues around the mobile Internet identity including email address choice include research topics about the user behavior on the 24-hour virtual society. The author expects that a simple methodology like the address transition analysis will reveal the variety of the cultural and social aspects of the mobile Internet that will emerge in a worldwide manner in the near future.

References

[1] Baker, M., Ishikawa, M., Matsui, S., Stark, P., Wugofsky, T., and Yamakami, T. (2000). XHTML™ basic. W3C Recommendation 19 December 2000. http://www.w3.org/TR/xhtml-basic.

[2] Cerf, V. (2001). Beyond the post-PC internet. *CACM*, 44(9).

[3] Cranor, L. F. and LaMacchia, B. A. (1998). Spam! *CACM*, 41(8):74–83.

[4] Denning, P. J. (1982). electronic junk. *CACM*, 25(3):163–165.

[5] Kamada, T. (1998). Compact html for small information appliances, W3C Note, 9 Feb. 1998.

[6] Yamakami, T. (2001). Unique identifier tracking analysis: A methodology to capture wireless internet user behaviors. In *IEEE ICOIN-15*, pages 743–748, Beppu, Japan.

[7] Yamakami, T. (2003). Impact from mobile spam mail on mobile internet services. In *Parallel and Distributed Processing and Applications, ISPA2003*, pages 179–184. Springer Verlag. LNCS 2745.

GLOSSARY

UBE   Unsolicited mail sent from a stranger as a part of mass mailing. Junk mail. Unsolicited Bulk Commercial mail (UBC). Spam mail in the slang.

Chapter 18

ALGORITHMS FOR THE VISUALIZATION OF FUNCTIONALLY DEFINED OBJECTS ON DISTRIBUTED SYSTEMS

Pierre-Alain Fayolle, Tsuyoshi Yamamoto, Carl Vilbrandt

Department of Computer Software, University of Aizu, Aizuwakamatsu, Japan

p.fayolle@free.fr, udauki@topaz.plala.or.jp, vilb@u-aizu.ac.jp

Philippe Perrin

philiperrin@free.fr

Abstract   This chapter presents two approaches for an efficient polygonal approximation on distributed computers of surfaces defined by the Function Representation model. The first algorithm uses a dynamic distribution of the geometric grid elements to allow maximum efficiency on grid of computers. The second algorithm targets parallel computers and cluster of computers and tries to minimize communications by distributing the geometric grid elements statically. Potential applications for these software algorithms are rendering in CAD system, and computer graphics animation for solids with complex surfaces.

Keywords: Function Representation, HyperFun, parallel processing, polygonization, rendering

1.   Introduction

A new shock wave of technological advances denoted by digitally enhanced processes and devices is increasing the need for computational resources, a need that may be answered by grids of computational clusters called *computational farms*. Sudden advances in technology such as volumetric scanning will thrust digital modeling representation forward beyond virtual surfaces of polygons to functionally based synthetic objects requiring also more and more intensive processing.

So called Function Representation (F-Rep), introduced by [7], and its associated modeling language HyperFun, introduced by [8], are promising applications for modeling complex shapes and solids. Rendering and visualization of F-Rep synthetic objects, as well as simulation involving such objects are time consumming processes but these time performances can be greatly improved on distributed or parallel environments.

Parallel processing for efficient rendering in computer graphics has been often considered in the past: [9], and [10], suggested parallel algorithms to compute radiosity, [11], and [12], parallel algorithms for ray tracing, finally [13], and [14], proposed parallel processing for global illumination model.

Parallel rendering of shapes defined by Function Representation has been considered by [4]; they discussed the parallel implementation of a ray tracer using a shared memory approach with the network system Linda. [5], and [6], considered static and dynamic load balancing implementations for the original polygonizer of [1]. The implementation targeted a network of computers hooked on a Local Area Network (LAN), like the ones available in a university.

This chapter presents two approaches for an efficient polygonization of HyperFun models on distributed architectures. One relies on dynamic load balancing, the other one on static load balancing. Both approaches uses a message passing interface for the communication between the nodes.

The approach using dynamic load balancing targets cluster of heterogeneous computers and more generally heterogeneous computers hooked on a LAN. With dynamic load balancing the application may be able to adapt if the workload of some of the computers evolve during runtime, which may happen when using for example computers from an university, or if the application wants to use free CPU cycles from hooked computers.

The second approach uses a semi-static load balancing (it is not fully static since there is a rebalancing before the computation of triangle patches) and tries to minimize the number of communications between the node for maximal speed of execution. It targets parallel computers or cluster of computers dedicated for this task, which means that the application has not been designed for handling runtime modification of the workload for some of the nodes. What is more, the application has been designed to take into consideration heterogeneousity of computers, and to adapt the distribution of the computing according to the computational power of each nodes.

2.   Polygonal approximation of F-Rep objects

Given a F-Rep object F, the problem is stated to approximate its implicit surface (the locus of points for which the F-Rep is null), by a set of polygons. The main points of the implicit surface piecewise analytical description method proposed by [2], and [1], are reminded here. First, the location of the vertices are computed, then they are connected together to form a triangle.

A parallelepiped containing the object is given in the three dimensional Euclidean space; by introducing a regular point grid the parallelepiped is represented as a set of $G_x \times G_y \times G_z$ cells.

The polygonal approximation of the surface can be obtained by visiting all cells and finding all the surface patches belonging to an individual cell.

2.1   Finding the vertices

A three dimensional array M of size $G_x \times G_y \times G_z$ is filled with the value of F at each node of the grid. The detection of a sign change between two adjacent nodes indicates the existence of a vertice on the edge of the cell joining the two nodes; its approximate position on the edge is obtained by a linear interpolation. See Figure 18.1 for an illustration of these ideas.

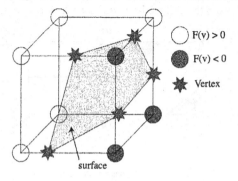

$\bigcirc$ F(v) > 0

$\bullet$ F(v) < 0

$\ast$ Vertex

surface

Figure 18.1.   Detected vertices with sign changes on the grid

2.2   Creation of the triangles

The vertices need to be connected to form a triangular patch of the surface using a connectivity graph in each cells of the grid. Such a graph has twelve nodes (one for each edges of the cell) and is created by considering for each of the six faces of a cell the three following possible cases:

- no vertex on the face.

- two vertices on the edges of the face.

- four vertices on the edges of the face.

The last case is ambiguous because there are two possible ways to connect the edges, as shown in Figure 18.2. The ambiguity is overcome by using the bilinear contour method as proposed in [2], [1], and [3]. The contours of the connection can be represented locally by parts of an hyperbola. An ambiguous face corresponds then to the case when both parts of the hyperbola intersect a face. In that case, the hyperbola is of type: $v = \frac{a+bu}{e+du}$, with $\frac{b}{d} \in [0,1]$ and

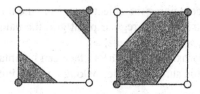

Figure 18.2. An ambiguous face

$-\frac{e}{d} \in [0, 1]$. The correct choice for the connections is made by comparing the abscissa u for which $v = 1$, with the abscissa of the center of the hyperbola, given by $-\frac{e}{d}$ If u is bigger than the threshold, then the orientation A is used, otherwise orientation B is used. The Figure 18.3 shows the corresponding orientations. From the connectivity graph a set, of disconnected non planar

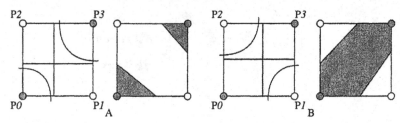

Figure 18.3. Bilinear contours method

polygons approximating the implicit surface can be produced. It is straightforward to obtain a mesh of triangles by creating fictuous edges.

2.3   Computing normals and triangle orientation

In order to obtain smoother surface on a display, normals at each vertices of the triangle may be required. At one vertex, the normal is obtained by computing the normalized gradient of the function F. The gradient is usually obtained numerically by finite differences.

All the triangles need also to have the same orientation (clockwise or counterclockwise) for avoiding problems with illuminations while visualizing the mesh. The average of the normals at the vertices is computed and compared with the normal computed from the vertex coordinates (in the triangle (A, B, C) the normal is given by $\vec{AB} \wedge \vec{AC}$). If they have a different orientation, the triangle is reversed by exchanging two vertices.

3. A dynamic load balancing approach for the polygonization of functionally defined objects

3.1 Overview

A dynamic load balancing approach has been considered for a distributed polygonization of the shape of functionally defined objects. Such an approach targets more specifically dedicated cluster of heterogeneous computers or heterogeneous computers hooked on LAN, like for example computers on a network university. This distributed approach extends the original polygonization algorithm with two steps, the distribution of element of the grid scene between the workers, and the gathering of the elements computed by each workers.

The original grid is broken into some cubic blocks, distributed over the nodes. The size of the blocks is a parameter left to the control of the user and should be such that the computational time on the slowest machine would not exceed the length of the average computational time for all the others.

Each nodes do the computation on its own blocks exactly in the same way as it was done with the single processor version of the polygonizer of HyperFun and creates some parts of the polygonal mesh. Finally, the server node gathers all the parts, patches them and creates the final polygonal mesh.

3.2 The distribution of the blocks

One of the important issues to parallel performance is load balancing. If the distribution of work is not balanced, nodes which do not have enough computation finish their tasks earlier than nodes with heavy computation, and these lighter, early nodes must wait for the overloaded, late ones. This imbalance is a waste of computing resources and causes a decline in performance.

In case of the polygonization of implicitly defined surfaces, the number of computed elements, such as vertices or triangles, is different in each block and difficult to anticipate before calculation. As a consequence the workload differs between the nodes when they are processing blocks of the same size. In order to avoid some nodes remaining idle, we used a server with a pool of blocks to which each idle workers make requests, after having finished their previous tasks. Therefore the block distribution is dynamically balanced among the nodes during runtime.

Such a dynamic distribution presents other advantages: it makes possible to add new nodes during runtime. It makes also possible to use efficiently the system on a network of computers whose workload may evolve during runtime, like for instance when using the computers from the network of a university.

3.3 Gathering Parts of the Mesh

The computed mesh data uses a simple data structure in order to reduce the cost of transporting and translating the data:

- vertices,which have an index number

- normals for each of the vertices

- triangle data, which are represented by an index of a set of three vertices

One of the problems, in gathering parts of the mesh to the master node is the numbering of the vertices index, because, before gathering, the index of vertices is local to each node and not independent of the vertices of other nodes. Vertices are distributed on each node and the local index number is changed to a global index number. Each node, $P_1, P_2, \cdots P_n$, builds an index of the array of vertices it owns and broadcasts this index to other nodes by turns. Each node changes its local index number to a global index number as:

$$(\text{index in } P_i \text{ array}) + \sum_{k=1}^{n-1}(\text{size of array } P_i) \tag{18.1}$$

3.4   Test Environment and Result

The tests with the dynamic load balancing approach were done on a set of 40 Sun workstations (Fujitsu GP 400S model 10) connected by Ethernet.

Figure 18.4.   Screenshot of "Core" with a $100 \times 100 \times 100$ grid

To make the test, two HF models, the model called "noisy-sphere" and the more complex one called "core" (see Figure 18.4), were polygonized with $100 \times 100 \times 100$ resolution grid. The timing results for these different objects with different numbers of nodes are shown in Figure 18.5.

Using the distributed approach, the speed of polygonization of models is increased. The time to polygonize was reduced from 147 seconds (1 node) to 9 seconds (40 nodes) in the case of "noisy-sphere," and from 382 seconds (1 node) to 15 seconds (40 nodes) in the case of "core."

Then, the speed up of polygonization is considered. The relative speed up with N nodes $S(N)$ is defined as:

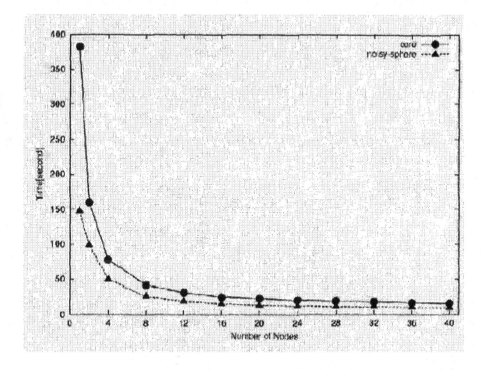

Figure 18.5. Execution time in function of the number of nodes

$$S\ (N) = T_1/T_N$$
$$T_1\ :\quad \text{Time with 1 node} \tag{18.2}$$
$$T_N\ :\quad \text{Time with } N \text{ nodes}$$

The desired speed up using N nodes is N times. The relative speed up graph of each model and a desired linear speed up are shown in Figure 18.6

In the case of "noisy-sphere", the speed up increases with the number of nodes like the theoretical $y = x$ linear ratio, when the number of nodes is below 16. For a number of nodes above 16, the speed up is still increasing linearly with the number of nodes, but with a smaller coefficient. In the case of "core", the speed up increase is even closer to the theoretical expectations when the number of nodes is less than 16; when the number of nodes is more than 16, the speed up keeps increasing linearly with the number of nodes, but with a smaller coefficient. The speed up with 40 nodes is 15 times (37.5% of desired linear) in the case of "noisy-sphere", and 25 times (62.5% of desired linear) in the case of "core."

These results show that the approach is effective to speed up the polygonization of HyperFun models. It is even more effective if the model is complex.

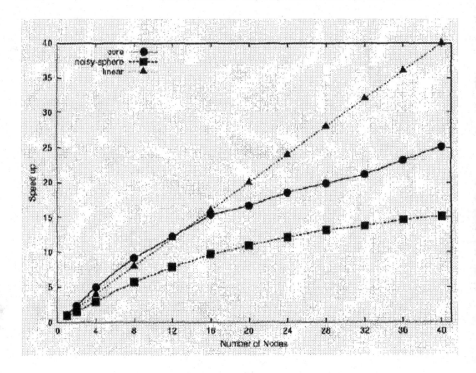

Figure 18.6.   Speed up in function of the number of nodes

4.   A parallel algorithm for the polygonization of functionally defined objects

4.1   Overview

This section describes a parallel version with a quasi static load balancing of the algorithm reminded in section 2. Remember that the analyzed space is divided by a finite tridimensional grid, thus forming naturally "elementary cells". The basic idea is that each processor will be provided with a pool of these cells (illustrated by Figure 18.7), and compute, for each of them, the in-bound vertices and triangles. The cells assigned to a processor are said to "belong" to it, as well as the in-bound vertices and triangles. Finally, these computed data will be sent back to the master.

Another important aspect of the problem is that each processor has a local numbering of vertices, and that we must create a global numbering for dealing with shared vertices.

We will discuss the following points:

- dispatching the cells among processors,
- determining the ownership of shared vertices,

■ converting the local numbering of vertices to a global one.

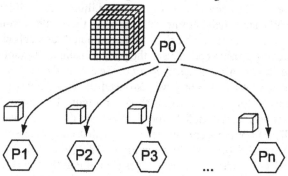

Figure 18.7. The master delivers cells to the slaves

4.2 Initialization

The processors are organized in a Master - Slave architecture: P_0 is the master, and $P_1, \ldots, P_n$ are the slaves. P_0 sends some information to each of them:

w_i: the weight of the current processor,

pw: the sum of the weights of the previous processors,

tw: the sum of the weighs of all processors,

c: the number of cells (in fact, the grid dimensions $G_x \times G_y \times G_z = c$).

The notion of weight has been introduced for the case when the system is used on a cluster of heterogeneous computers. The amount of work of each node should be proportional to its computational power. The problem of assigning a correct weight to each of the nodes has been solved by running a test function on all the nodes during a small amount of time (usually from 30 to 60 seconds) and see how many time this function has been computed.

In the following algorithm, every processor, *including the master P_0* will run what we call "the worker's algorithm" described in the next subsection 4.3. With the informations received, each processor can find the cells assigned for his work. The cells of the scene (corresponding to the grid) are implicitly numbered: each worker P_i will initially own $c \times \frac{w_i}{tw}$ cells, starting from the cell number $c \times \frac{pw}{tw}$. Actually, this cell dispatching makes each processor own "slices" of the grid (mostly contiguous cells).

4.3 Worker's algorithm

Finding vertices. Every worker will now consider each of the $c \times \frac{w_i}{tw}$ cells assigned to it. For each of them, it will compute the function values of the F-Rep object at the 8 corners, in order to detect sign changes on each edge (as described in [1], reminded in section 2 and illustrated on Figure 18.1 page 269). Actually, since neighboring cells are used, the 8 values won't have to be computed every time for each cell: a value computed for a cell will be re-used for the next neighboring cell. This is the point of using contiguous cells.

Now the slave considers the 12 edges of the cell, and detects if they support vertices or not. What is more, we also need the coordinates of all vertices. Since an edge belongs to 4 cells (as shown in Figure 18.8 page 276), a vertex located on it will be detected 4 times. In order to determine which processor has to really compute its coordinates (we say that this processor *owns* it), we set up an ownership rule. As shown in Figure 18.9 (left part), for each cell, we systematically consider the same 3 edges (in bold on the figure), and they are said to belong to the processor computing this cell. In that way, a processor detecting a vertex on an edge will immediately know if it belongs to itself or not (in fact, by knowing that this edge is among the 3 owned segments or not). As shown in the right half of Figure 18.9 (case of a $2 \times 2 \times 2$ grid), this will determine the ownership of almost every edge. Some of the edges on the scene's faces will be "forgotten" (those not in bold on the figure). This problem is solved by making the last slave going through those segments for finding vertices. If a vertex is detected on an edge owned by a processor, its coordinates will be computed. Otherwise, the processor simply knows that it exists, without knowing its coordinates.

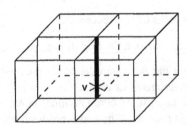

Figure 18.8.   Ownership of a vertex among 4 cells

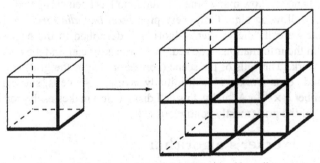

Figure 18.9.   Ownership of edges determined by cells

Guessing the number of triangles.   At the same time, while finding vertices inside the cells, each worker guesses how many triangles can be formed inside it. It finally sums these numbers, thus knowing approximately the number of triangles to be found inside all its cells (as well as the individual numbers for each of them).

Re-dispatching cells.   Now that all workers have detected the vertices inside their owned cells, we must reconsider the cell dispatching. Remember that the cells were initially distributed in a very basic way: each processor received "slices" of the model. This implies that some of them (like those in the middle of the scene) found many more vertices than others (like those on the edges of the scene). Therefore, before going on with the algorithm, we have to redistribute the cells so that all processors will probably find the same number of triangles in the next stage (the notion of weights, as described in 4.2, is also used for redistributing cells according to the computing power of each processor).

To achieve this redistribution, all slaves send their approximate number of triangles to the master. It now has to compute a set of *(sendingWorker, receivingWorker, numTriangles)* triplets, representing the cell transfers among workers: this means that for each triplet, the processor $P_{sendingWorker}$ must send enough of its own cells to $P_{receivingWorker}$ so that $numTriangles$ will be transferred inside them. The master forms a table of these triplets, and sends them to all slaves.

Now each slave reads this table and acts as the master decided. When a worker sends a cell to another, it sends:

- the cell coordinates,

- the coordinates of the owned vertices inside this cell (they are 3 at most),

- the list of the other vertices on the cell edges (they are 12 at most).

A worker that sends a cell has to "forget" it (it doesn't own it any more): it has transfered all the information related to it to a new worker, which is now its new owner.

At the end of this re-dispatching step, many cells are transfered to new workers, so that the number of triangles inside them is approximately the same. For a worker, there is no distinction between the cells it owned since the beginning of the algorithm (those of the "slice" initially assigned) and those it received from other workers (if any).

Finding triangles.   Then each slave goes through its owned cells (the initial and the newly acquired ones). The detected vertices inside them are grouped in triangles. A "triangle" is composed of 3 vertices: a "vertex" is referenced by the cell edge it is located on. Each processor builds a triangle table (3 columns, for storing these edge numbers) and a vertex table (4 columns:

the edge number of the vertex and its 3 coordinates). The vertex table must be sorted by increasing number of their edges, and contains only the vertices owned by the processor.

Note that for the moment, vertices are referenced by the segments of the grid where they are located. This represents a first global numbering, but we can not keep it: we want a new numbering in order to avoid the numbers of the segments supporting no vertex. The aim of this final numbering is that triangles should store the 3 vertex numbers, that we could use for directly accessing their coordinates in a contiguous array.

Computing normals.   If the user asked for it, each worker goes through its owned vertices, and computes the normals of the F-Rep at these points. These normal coordinates are stored with the vertex coordinates themselves, and are part of the output.

Global numbering of vertex.   Now each processor has a sorted table of its own vertices; these $n + 1$ tables are disjointed and each row contains 4 fields: the global number of the edge supporting the vertex, and the 3 coordinates. The processors also have disjointed triangle lists, each row containing the 3 edge numbers corresponding to the vertices on them.

The vertices have to be numbered globally, instead of the current edge-numbering; this operation will be distributed. Each worker $P_0, P_1, \ldots, P_n$ builds an array of integers containing the sorted global edge numbers of the vertices it owns. Then it broadcasts this array to the others (first P_0 then $P_1\ldots$). This helps making a global implicit numbering of vertices: each vertex (belonging to P_i) whose global edge number was broadcasted by P_i will have the final global vertex number:

$$(index\ in\ P_i's\ array) + \sum_{k=0}^{i-1}(size\ of\ P_k's\ array)$$

When a worker receives such a table, it goes through its own triangle table, and replaces the edge numbers by the global vertex numbers (they are easy to find because the global edge numbers were sorted), as described above.

At the end of this renumbering step, appending the vertex tables (in the order $P_0 \ldots P_n$) would create a global vertex array, where their indices would be the numbers stored in the triangle tables. This is what we aimed at.

4.4   Sending the vertices and triangles to the master

Gathering results.   The master P_0 is the processor that initiated the algorithm, and that must gather the results from the slaves. For the moment, P_0 has its local table of triangles (like all other workers), where the vertices are indexed by the final global numbering (some of these vertices are owned by the master itself, the others by other workers). Each slave has to send its local vertex table to the master, sorted by their global edge numbers (these tables contain only locally owned vertices). The master appends each of them at the end of its own vertex table. In this way, the indices of the vertices in this final whole table will be the same as the global numbers used in the triangle tables.

Lastly, every slave sends its triangle table to P_0, sequentially. The master appends these arrays, starting with its own local triangles.

At the end of this step, P_0 has the global triangle array, containing the global vertex numbers (set by the other workers).

Orienting the triangles.   If the polygonizer was asked to compute the normals associated to the vertices, the triangles are oriented according to the average of the normals of the 3 vertices. This means that the master goes through the triangle array, and swaps two vertices among the three if the triangle was not correctly oriented. This step proved to be very fast compared to the total execution time, in spite of the scalar products, and therefore could be left to the master.

4.5   Results

Now here are the results of a distributed polygonization with an increasing number of processors. The model *core.hf* (see Figure 18.4) was polygonized with a 100 grid on a set of heterogeneous Sun systems (half Sun Ultra Sparc 5, and half Sun Blades 100). The hosts involved in polygonization were connected on a 100Mb/s commuted LAN (using switches instead of hubs reduces collision during the cell re-balancing stage). See Figure 18.10 for the graph obtained (polygonization time in function of the number of processors).

The two isolated symbols at the beginning of the graph (labeled *1F* and *1S*) represent the execution time with only 1 CPU. The first one (*1F*) is for the case of a "Fast" processor (a Sun Blade 100, whose time is 97.5 seconds); the second one (*1S*) is for the case of a "Slow" processor (a Sun Ultra Sparc 5, whose time is 139.0 seconds). All the next measures correspond to pools where these two types of processors are equally mixed.

The graph looks very much like a $y = 1/x$ function. This means that to divide execution time by 2 or 3, you should multiply the number of processor by 2 or 3. What is more, the graph is quite smooth: distributing work among heterogeneous processors does not cause irregularities.

5.   Conclusion

Function Representation (F-Rep) and its associated language HyperFun are promising for modeling complex shapes and solids. The rendering of such objects can be made by polygonization of the surface, but is an intensive com-

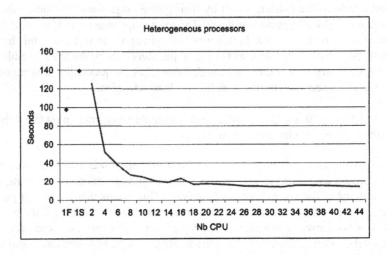

Figure 18.10.   Execution times in function of processing power

putational process. Fortunately, the algorithm for polygonization of the surface is based on independent computations on a geometric grid, and thus can naturally be distributed over computers.

Two implementations have been explored for more efficient rendering by distributing the cells of the geometric grid between computers. The first method uses dynamic load balancing: a server keeps a pool of the available cells and receive requests from the different workers for sending blocks. Then each node processes the blocks like in the single processor algorithm. By using a dynamic distribution of blocks, this implementation is effective on grid of heterogeneous computers. A modification in the runtime workload of the nodes (other users) can be handled, it is also possible to add new nodes during the processing.

The second implementation targets parallel computers and dedicated cluster of computers (with homogeneous or heterogeneous nodes). The number of communication has been minimized to decrease the communication overhead.

Both implementations present interesting results for practical efficient rendering of complex F-Rep objects. They also suffer from some drawbacks due to the way they have been designed. The static approach does not support new nodes being added on the fly. It will also behave badly on a network, where the workload of some computers will be modified during runtime, like for instance if someone planned to use the application on the network of a university when some other users may also use the computing ressources. The dynamic approach will handle it correctly, but may suffer from a bigger communication overhead and thus may be less efficient in time. Also the efficiency of the dynamic approach deeply relies on the size of a block, which is difficult to estimate and may depend on the model being rendered; if the size of a block is too small it could cause a huge communication overhead, inversely if the size of a block is too big then the implementation will behave like the static approach and loose its advantages.

References

[1] Pasko A.A., Pilyugin V.V., Pokrovskiy V.V. "Geometric modeling in the analysis of trivariate functions", *Computers and Graphics*, vol.12, Nos.3/4, 1988, pp.457-465.

[2] Pasko A.A., Pilyugin V.V., Pokrovskiy V.V. "Geometric modeling in the analysis of trivariate functions", *Communications of Joint Institute of Nuclear Research*, P10-86-310, Dubna, USSR, 1986 (in Russian).

[3] Gregory M. Nielson and Bernd Hamann, "The asymptotic decider: Resolving the ambiguity in the marching cubes", *Proceedings Visualization '91* - sponsored by the IEEE Computer Society, pages 83–91, 1991.

[4] Sedukhin I., Sedukhin S., Pasko A., Savchenko V., Mirenkov N., Parallel rendering of functionally represented geometric objects with the network Linda system, Technical Report 95-1-001, University of Aizu, Japan, 1995, 15 p.

[5] Savchenko V., Pasko A., Parallel polygonization of implicit surfaces on transputers: algorithm, time performance evaluation and rendering results", in Transputer Research and Applications 7, H.Arabnia (Ed.), NATUG-7, *Proceedings of the Seventh Conference of the North American Transputer Users Group*, IOS Press, 1995, pp. 22-30.

[6] Ten S., Savchenko V., Pasko A., Time performance evaluation of implicit surfaces polygonization on distributed systems, in Parallel Computing: Technology and Practice, PCAT-94, *Proceedings of the 7th Australian Transputer and Occam User Group Conference*, J.P.Gray and F.Naghdy (Eds.), IOS Press, 1995, pp.183-193.

[7] Pasko A., Adzhiev V., Sourin A, and Savchenko V., Function representation in geometric modelling: concepts, implementation and applications, *The visual computer* 11 (1995), 429-446.

[8] Adzhiev V., Cartwright R., Fausset E., Ossipov A. , Pasko A., and Savchenko V., HyperFun project: language and software tools for FRep shape modeling, *proceedings of Eurographics/ACM SIGGRAPH Workshop Implicit Surfaces 1999*.

[9] Baum D.R., and Winget J.M., Real time radiosity through parallel processing and hardware acceleration, Computer Graphics, *SIGGRAPH 90 Proceedings*, vol.24, no.4, pp.67-75, 1990.

[10] Singh J., Holt C., Totsuka T., Gupta A. and Henessy J., Load balancing and data locality in adaptive hierarchical N-body methods: Barnes-hut, fast multipole, and radiosity, *Parallel and Distributed Computing*, vol.27, pp.118-141, 1995.

[11] Nishimura H. et al., LINKS-I: A parallel pipelined multimicrocomputer system for image creation, *Proceedings of ISCA* 83, pp.387-394, 1983.

[12] Badouel D., Bouatouch K., and Priol T., Distributing data and control for ray tracing in parallel, *IEEE CG and Application*, vol.14, no.4, pp.69-77, 1994.

[13] Kobayashi H., and Nakamura T., A massively parallel processing approach to fast photorealistic image synthesis, in *Communicating with Virtual Worlds*, ed. D.T. Nadia Magnenat Thalmann, pp. 497-507, CG International, 1993.

[14] Kobayashi H., Yamauchi H., Toh Y., and Nakamura T., MPI2: A hierarchical parallel processing system for a global illumination model, *IEICE Trans. Inf. and Syst.*, vol.E79-D, no.8, pp.1055-1064, 1996.

Chapter 19

AUTOMATED DIGITAL IMAGE REGISTRATION AND ITS PARALLEL IMPLEMENTATION

Gui Xie and Hong Shen
Graduate School of Information Science
Japan Advanced Institute of Science and Technology
g-xie@jaist.ac.jp, shen@jaist.ac.jp

Abstract   Digital image registration is a fundamental task in image processing, which is concerned with establishment of correspondence, particularly geometric correspondence, between two or more pictures taken, for example, at different times, from different sensors or from different viewpoints. Because of the variety of the gray levels in images, it's very difficult to match them automatically with a satisfactory accuracy. In this chapter, we address the problem of geometric registration, in which a spatial transformation is needed to remove the variations of the misaligned images. This geometric registration problem is discussed in a theoretical modal first, and then a novel efficient geometric registration algorithm based on the shape of the closed-regions is presented. Experiments have verified the advantages of this algorithm, but shown that the performance of its sequentially execution depends too much on the size of the input images. Its time complexity increases exponentially as image size increases, so finally we extend the sequential algorithm to a parallel scheme to perform the registration task more efficiently.

Keywords: Images registration, geometric transformation, shape-specific points, differential operators, closed-regions, matching degree, parallel execution

1.   Introduction

Image registration is used to match two or more pictures by establishing the relationship between the variations in the images, which is a significant component in a wide range of applications such as matching a target with a real-time image of a scene for target recognition, monitoring global land usage using satellite images, matching stereo images to recover shape for autonomous navigation, and aligning images for different medical modalities for diagnosis. Three major types of variations are distinguished[1]. The first type are the variations due to the differences in acquisition which cause the images to be misaligned geometrically. To register these images, a spatial transformation is needed to remove the variations. The second type of variations are those which are also due to differences in acquisition, but cannot be modelled easily such as lighting and atmospheric conditions. This type usually effects intensity values, but they may also spatial, such as perspective distortions. The third type of variations are differences in the images that of interest such as object movements, growths, or other scene changes. Variations of the second and third type of variations are not directly removed by registration. This chapter addresses the first type of variations, i.e., geometric registration problem.

Geometric registration or alignment of remote sensing images with the same target or scene accurately is a fundamental task in numerous applications in 2-D remote-sensing images processing[1][2]. For example, in the fusion of remote-sensing images[3], the accuracy of the images registration must reach the pixel or sub-pixel level; otherwise it is impossible to continue the consequent process of images fusion. Generally, images registration is to compute the parameters of geometric transformation between a pair of images, such as rotation, scaling and translation. These images with same targets are taken at different times, from different sensors, or from different viewpoints.

Many different registration algorithms have been presented[4][5][6], which can be loosely divided into the following classes: algorithms that use image pixel values directly, e.g. correlation methods; algorithms that use frequency domain, e.g. FFT-based methods; algorithms that use low-level features such as edges and corners, e.g. features-based methods; and algorithms that use high-level features such as identified objects or relations between features, e.g. graph-theoretical methods. Cross-correlation is the basic statistical approach to registration, which gives a measure to evaluate the degree of similarity between an image and a template. By the convolution theory, we can use the products of Fourier transforms to compute correlation. An important reason why this metric has been widely used is that it can be implemented by using the Fast Fourier Transform (FFT). For an input image with large size, it can be implemented efficiently. Template matching using correlation has many variations[7]. If the allowable transformations include rotation or scale, for example, multiple templates can be used. As the number of template grows, however, the computational costs quickly become unmanageable. Moreover, using correlation has a main limitation of inability to deal with dissimilar images since the gray-level characteristics of images are quite different. For this reason, feature-based techniques[8][9][10], which match features extracted from images, are more preferable, if images are acquired under different circumstances, e.g. varying lighting or atmospheric conditions. Among them, the control-points-based mapping techniques are the primary approach currently taken to register images. The general control-points-based method consists of three stages. In the first stage, features in the image are extracted. In the second stage, feature points in the reference image, often referred to control points, are mapped with the correspondent feature points in the data image. In the last stage, the parameters of the transformation are computed by the mapped pairs of the features points in the two images. Control-points-based methods are very efficient for registration and applied widely in the registration field. However choosing appropriate feature points are very difficult for computers and mapping the feature points in two images usually needs human's help. Moreover, feature points are too sensitive to noise. Sometimes it's impossible to get valid control points. So some other features in the image, which are not sensitive to noise, are more preferred to be used in registration. Among them, contours are widely used, because they are not only insensitive to noise, but also very easy to extract. In[11], closed boundaries are extracted and used as matching primitives. Another contour-based method for registering Spot and Seasat images is proposed in[8]. The authors in[12] present two contour-based images registration algorithms: a basic contour matching scheme and an elastic contour-matching scheme for optical-to-SAR images registration. The basic algorithm presented in[12] uses chain code correlation to match the contours between two images. It doesn't work well for image pairs in which the contour information is not well preserved. Moreover, chain code is very sensitive to noise. The computational cost on computing the chain code correlation increases rapidly as the complexity of the contours grows. As for the elastic contour-matching scheme given in[12], it just works well when optical and SAR images have been coarsely aligned.

In this chapter we present a new registration algorithm that takes full advantage of shape information of the closed-regions bounded by contours in images, which is used to register general remote-sensing images without other constraint on the image types. Moreover it can perform the registration task automatically and accurately. A preliminary version of our algorithm was pre-proposed in [13].

Experiments have validated the algorithm. The results of experiments also showed that if we execute the registration algorithm sequentially, the performance decreases exponentially as the size of input images increases. So based on the principle of the new registration algorithm given in this paper, we present a scheme to execute our algorithm in parallel on a modified PRAM model, which is a theoretical model that plays a central role in studying the parallel algorithms. A PRAM[14] is a set of synchronous processors connected to a shared memory, whose main feature is the capability for different processors to simultaneously access the shared memory. There are several variations of PRAM introduced in the literature[14][15]. The parallel computational scheme presented here makes a little modification of the PRAM model and adds a controller processor into the model to supervise the progress of the registration task.

In Section2, the geometric registration is discussed in theory. In Section3, the principle of the algorithm is introduced and also the method to get the closed-regions in the images is given. More details about how to detect and link edges to construct closed boundaries are discussed in Section4. The method to match the closed-regions is discussed in Section5. In Section6, we give the results of experiments to validate the new registration algorithm. And then we propose a parallel computation scheme to extend the algorithm in Section7. In Section8 how to use feedback technology to improve the registration accuracy is discussed. In the last section, we summarize this chapter.

2.   Theoretical Modal of Geometric Registration

Geometric image registration is defined as a mapping between two images by a geometric affine transformation and an intensity transformation. The goal of the registration is to maximize a predefined metric that measures the similarity of the registered images. If we let two images to be registered be $2D$ arrays denoted by their intensity matrices $I_1(x,y)$ and $I_2(x,y)$, then the geometric registration of these two images can be expressed as this mapping:

$$I_2(x,y) = g(I_1(f(x,y))) \qquad (19.1)$$

where f is a $2D$ affine spatial-coordinate transformation and g is a $1D$ intensity transformation. An affine transformation composed of a combination of rotation, scaling and translation is a linear rigid mapping such that straight lines remain straight and parallel lines remain parallel, but rectangles become parallelograms. It maps two spatial coordinates x and y, to new coordinates x' and y' using four parameters t_x, t_y, s and θ as follows:

$$\begin{pmatrix} x' \\ y' \end{pmatrix} = \begin{pmatrix} t_x \\ t_y \end{pmatrix} + s \begin{pmatrix} \cos\theta & -\sin\theta \\ \sin\theta & \cos\theta \end{pmatrix} \begin{pmatrix} x \\ y \end{pmatrix} \qquad (19.2)$$

where (x', y') is the position after (x, y) is shifted by t_x in the horizontal direction and t_y in the vertical direction, rotated by the degree of θ and scaled by the factor of s. This can be rewritten as follows:

$$\vec{p_2} = \vec{t} + sR\vec{p_1} \qquad (19.3)$$

where $\vec{p_1}$, $\vec{p_2}$ are the coordinate vectors of the two images, $\vec{t}$ is the translation vector, s is a scale factor and R is the rotation matrix.

Given two matching pairs of points between the reference and data images denoted by $(x_1', y_1') = f(x_1, y_1)$ and $(x_2', y_2') = f(x_2, y_2)$, we can determine the parameters of the affine transformation as follows:

$$\theta = \arctan(\frac{y_2 - y_1}{x_2 - x_1}) - \arctan(\frac{y_2' - y_1'}{x_2' - x_1'}) \qquad (19.4)$$

$$s = \frac{\sqrt{(x_2' - x_1')^2 + (y_2' - y_1')^2}}{\sqrt{(x_2 - x_1)^2 + (y_2 - y_1)^2}} \qquad (19.5)$$

$$\begin{pmatrix} \Delta x \\ \Delta y \end{pmatrix} = \begin{pmatrix} x'_1 \\ y'_1 \end{pmatrix} - s \cdot \begin{pmatrix} \cos\theta & \sin\theta \\ -\sin\theta & \cos\theta \end{pmatrix} \begin{pmatrix} x_1 \\ y_1 \end{pmatrix} \qquad (19.6)$$

Finding the above four parameters of the optimal affine spatial transformation is generally the critical phase to the geometric registration problem because the intensity transformation g is not always necessary, and often a simple lookup table determined by sensor calibration techniques is sufficient.

It is very difficult, if not possible, to match the images in the initial domain of the pixels because of the variety of gray levels. Therefore, two images $I1$ (reference image) and I_2 (data image) are usually transformed to the feature domain by an extraction process, where it is easier and more reliable to compute the parameters for the registration. The following figure illustrates a general model to be used in our registration algorithm.

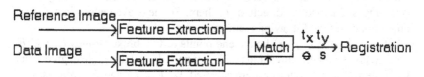

Figure 19.1. A general geometric registration model

3. Principle of the New Algorithm

Control-points-based methods can perform the registration task between images accurately, but it's very difficult to choose appropriate control points in images by computers because there is little shape information in points. The closed-regions bounded by contours contain so many points from which sufficient shape information can be extracted. Moreover, choosing and matching closed-regions can be done by computers automatically without any human's help. So instead of using control points, we take full advantage of the closed-regions to perform the registration task. The main steps of this algorithm are listed as follows:

1) Edges are detected and linked in the reference image **R** and data image **I** respectively.

2) Valid closed-regions are selected to construct two closed-region set corresponding to the reference and data images respectively.

3) Identify an appropriate closed-regions between the above two sets.

4) Based on the matched closed-regions, compute the parameters of the affine transformation.

5) Register the images by the affine transformation we found.

The data image is the image we want to match with the reference image. As shown in the above flow chart, firstly, the algorithm detects and links edges in the input images. Secondly, we choose the regions bounded by the closed contours, which are called closed-regions in this paper. So we get two sets of closed-regions, one of which is obtained from the reference image **R** and the other from the data image **I**. After having obtained the two sets, the original input images can be discarded in the following steps of the algorithm. Using the technique of matching the closed-regions, which will be discussed in detail in Section5. we can easily compute parameters of images registration such as the degree of rotation, the factor of scaling and the distances of shifting.

For detecting the edges in the input images **R** and **I**, we can use some differential operators[16][18][17] such as Robert operator, Prewitt operator and Sobel operator. By these gradient operators, we get not only the magnitudes of the edges, but also the directions of them. So the broken edges in a contour can be linked by the following method.

Let (x_1, y_1) and (x_2, y_2) be the end points of two broken edges E_1 and E_2 respectively. Given the thresholds of the magnitude and the angle degree T and A . If the following conditions are satisfied, we link E_1 and E_2 from (x_1, y_1) to (x_2, y_2).

$$|\nabla f(x_1, y_1) - \nabla f(x_2, y_2)| \leq T$$
$$|\varphi(x_1, y_1) - \varphi(x_2, y_2)| \leq A \qquad (19.7)$$

where f denotes the grayscale distribution of the remote-sensing images, ∇ is the gradient operator we choose to detect edges, and $\varphi(x_i, y_i)$ denotes the angle of the gradient's direction at a given point (x_i, y_i). After all the end points of broken edges have been checked by the above method, we pick up the regions encircled by the closed contours into two sets of closed-regions from images **R** and **I** respectively.

4.   Edge Detection and Linking

This section introduces edge detection and linking technology in more detail because this process is critical for our proposed algorithm. As the above section described, edges can be detected by some gradient operators. A gradient operator is the first-order derivative operator. For an image of the intensity distribution function $f(x, y)$, its gradient at the position of (x, y) is expressed as

$$\Delta f(x, y) = [G_x \quad G_y]^T = [\frac{\partial f}{\partial x} \quad \frac{\partial f}{\partial y}]^T \qquad (19.8)$$

where G_x, G_y are the components corresponding to the horizontal and vertical directions respectively. Δf is a vector with the magnitude:

$$\Delta f = mag(\Delta f) = (G_x^2 + G_y^2)^{(1/2)} \qquad (19.9)$$

and angle:

$$\phi(x, y) = \arctan(G_y/G_x) \qquad (19.10)$$

Eq.19.9 is computed using the modulo 2. Another two common computation methods use modulo 1 and ∞:

$$\Delta f_{(1)} = |\frac{\partial f}{\partial x}| + |\frac{\partial f}{\partial y}| \qquad (19.11)$$

$$\Delta f_{(\infty)} = \max\{|\frac{\partial f}{\partial x}|, |\frac{\partial f}{\partial y}|\} \qquad (19.12)$$

In practice, the above partial derivation in the gradient operator is approximated by the convolution using some local templates. Both of G_x and G_y need templates, so each gradient operator consists of two templates. According to the size and elements of the templates, numerous gradient operators have been proposed, which have different performance in different applicatons. Among them, three most useful operators are Roberts cross operator, Prewitt operator and Sobel operator which are illustrated in Figure19.2.

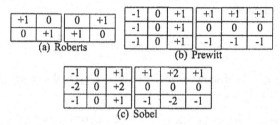

Figure 19.2. The templates of some commonly used gradient operator

Applying a gradient operator on an image results in three images, i.e., the edge image whose gray levels reflect the gradient magnitudes of their corresponding pixels, the binary edge image showing only the location of the edge points, and the directional edge image that encodes the direction of the edge (angle of the gradient). In general, an edge image shows each object outlined in edge points. Since these edges seldom form closed, connected boundaries that are required for our algorithm, edge linking is a necessary process that associates nearby edge points so as to create a closed, connected boundary. A simple linking method based on the magnitude and angle of the gradient has been introduced in the previous section to fill the small gaps on the boundaries. More sophisticated methods such as heuristic search, curve fitting and hough transform can also be applied to achieve better performance.

5. Matching between the Closed-Regions

We develop an efficient method to match the closed-regions by shape-specific points. From the matched pairs, we can compute the parameters of image registration.

We first give the definition of shape-specific points, which plays a key role in our algorithm. Given a closed region R, which contains some discrete points denoted by $\{(x_i, y_i)|i = 1, 2, ..., N\}$. Let T be a geometric transformation operated on R. Assume $R' = T(R)$, which means R' is a new closed region after transforming R by operator T. Given a function f, whose input is a set of points and output is one point. Denote two points by p and p', which satisfy $p = f(R)$ and $p' = f(R')$. We say p is a shape-specific point if and only if $p' = T(p)$.

According to the above definition of the shape-specific points, if we let the transform T be rotation, scaling, translation or their combinations, it is easy to prove that the following points computed by following functions are shape-specific points:

- Center point

$$x_A = \frac{\sum_i x_i}{N}, \quad y_A = \frac{\sum_i y_i}{N} \qquad (19.13)$$

- Centroid point

$$x_B = \frac{1}{W} \sum_i \omega_i x_i, \quad y_B = \frac{1}{W} \sum_i \omega_i y_i \qquad (19.14)$$

where ω_i is the distance from the point (x_i, y_i) to the center point (x_A, y_A) and $W = \sum_i \omega_i$.

Then using the shape-specific points of the closed-regions, we compute the parameters of the geometric transformation for a registration. The procedure is illustrated in Figure19.3. As Figure19.3 shows, let T be the combination of these operations that rotates the closed-region clockwise by a degree of θ, scales it α times and translates horizontally and vertically by the distances Δx and Δy. We get a new region $r' = T(r)$. Let A, B, A' and B' be the shape-specific points of the two regions respectively, whose coordinates are (x_A, y_A), (x_B, y_B), $(x_{A'}, y_{A'})$ and $(x_{B'}, y_{B'})$ as illustrated in the figure. The parameters of the geometric transformation can be computed as follows:

- the degree of rotation

$$\theta = \arctan(\frac{y_{B'} - y_{A'}}{x_{B'} - x_{A'}}) - \arctan(\frac{y_B - y_A}{x_B - x_A}) \qquad (19.15)$$

- the factor of scaling

$$\alpha = \frac{\sqrt{(x_{B'} - x_{A'})^2 + (y_{B'} - y_{A'})^2}}{\sqrt{(x_B - x_A)^2 + (y_B - y_A)^2}} \qquad (19.16)$$

- the distances of translation

$$\begin{pmatrix} \Delta x \\ \Delta y \end{pmatrix} = \frac{1}{\alpha} \cdot \begin{pmatrix} \cos\theta & \sin\theta \\ -\sin\theta & \cos\theta \end{pmatrix} \begin{pmatrix} x_{B'} \\ y_{B'} \end{pmatrix} - \begin{pmatrix} x_B \\ y_B \end{pmatrix} \qquad (19.17)$$

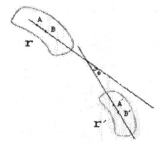

Figure 19.3. Computing the parameters of the geometric transformation based on shape-specific points

After edges are detected and linked, we get two sets of closed-regions, denoted by RS_R and RS_I from the two input image R and I. If we can find a matched pair of closed-regions $r \in RS_R$ and $r' \in RS_I$ satisfying $r' = T(r)$,the parameters of the geometric transformation T can be computed from the above procedure.

To find the matched pairs between two sets of closed-regions, we give a method to measure the matching degree between any two closed-regions. Using this measurement, we can evaluate whether two closed-regions are a matched pair.

Given two closed-regions r_1 and r_2, we compute the matching degree denoted by $M(r_1, r_2)$ between the two regions as following steps:

1) Firstly, compute the parameters of a geometric transformation T between the closed-regions r_1 and r_2 based on their shape-specific points as illustrated in Figure19.3.

2) Secondly, transform r_2 by the operator T with the parameters we've got in the above step. Denote the outcome of the transformation by $r_3 = T(r_2)$. r_3 is the transformed version of r_2.

3) Finally, compute the normalized matching degree between r_1 and r_3 as follows.

Suppose r_1 and r_3 are located in two bounded rectangles $M_1 \times N_1$ and $M_3 \times N_3$ as shown in Figure19.4. Let $M = \max(M_1, M_3)$ and $N = \max(N_1, N_3)$. Define two functions as

$$R_1(m, n) = \begin{cases} 1 & (m, n) \in r_1 \\ 0 & (m, n) \notin r_1 \end{cases} \qquad (19.18)$$

$$R_3(m, n) = \begin{cases} 1 & (m, n) \in r_3 \\ 0 & (m, n) \notin r_3 \end{cases} \qquad (19.19)$$

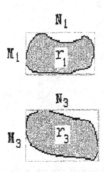

Figure 19.4.   Bounded rectangles of the closed-regions

We let the normalized correlation coefficient between the regions r_1 and r_3 be the matching degree $M(r_1, r_2)$ between r_1 and r_2, which is computed as

$$M(r_1, r_2) = \sqrt{\frac{[\sum_{n=1}^{N} \sum_{m=1}^{M} R_1(m, n) R_3(m, n)]^2}{[\sum_{n=1}^{N} \sum_{m=1}^{M} R_1^2(m, n)][\sum_{n=1}^{N} \sum_{m=1}^{M} R_3^2(m, n)]}} \quad (19.20)$$

Obviously, $M(r_1, r_2)$ is in the range of $[0, 1]$. If (r_1, r_2) is a matched pair of closed-regions which satisfies $r_1 = T(r_2)$, $M(r_1, r_2)$ equals 1. If they are not a matched pair, the matching degree between them is less than 1. So we can use this quantity to evaluate whether two close-regions are a matched pair.

However, in practical applications of registration, $M(r_1, r_2)$ cannot reach the ideal value of 1 because of the distortion in interpolation and quantization. So we give an efficient way to do the matching work. Given a closed-region $r_1 \in RS_R$, let r_1' be a closed-region in the set RS_I. We say that (r_1, r_1') is a matched pair if and only if the matching degree $M(r_1, r_1')$ is greater than any other pairs (r_1, r_2'), where $r_2' \in RS_I$ and $r_2' \neq r_1'$.

After we evaluate the matching degrees between closed-regions, we obtain some matched pairs of closed-regions between two input images. Assume several matched pairs are got by evaluating their matching degrees. From each of them, we can compute a group of geometric parameters using the specific-points. The average of them are the registration parameters we want to compute.

6.   Experiments

We give two experiments to validate the new registration algorithm. One is an experiment of computer simulation and the other is an experiment of registering two practical remote-sensing images.

Figure 19.5(b) is a geometric transformed version of Figure 19.5(a). The transformation includes rotating clockwise by 10°, scaling to 80% of the original size and no translation. We register Figure 19.5(a) to Figure 19.5(b) by the presented algorithm.

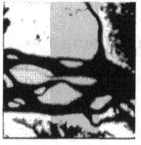

(a) The reference image   (b) The data image

Figure 19.5.   Test images in the simulation

Figure19.5(a) shows Using Sobel operator to detect and link the edges, after which a set of closed-regions is formed. To avoid the interference of noise, we just keep large closed-regions, whose sizes exceed a threshold. Similarly process Figure19.5(b). We get two sets of closed-regions from two input images respectively. For simplicity of discussion, we assign numbers to the closed-regions as illustrated in Figure19.6(a) and Figure19.6(b).

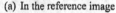

(a) In the reference image   (b) In the data image

Figure 19.6.   Extracted closed-regions

By evaluating matching degrees among the closed-regions, we obtain the four matched pairs such as $(1,6)$, $(2,7)$, $(3,8)$ and $(4,9)$. From each matched pair, we compute a group of parameters of the geometric transformation. Averaging over them, we get the parameters of the geometric transformation for registering the input images as follows

1) Rotation degree

$$\theta = \frac{1}{4}(10.7778 + 9.8654 + 9.5037 + 11.4381)$$
$$= \quad 10.3963 \approx 10 \tag{19.21}$$

2) Scaling factor

$$\theta = \frac{1}{4}(0.8178 + 0.8436 + 0.8031 + 0.7646)$$
$$= \quad 0.8071 \approx 0.8$$

(19.22)

3) Translation distances

$$\Delta x \approx 0 \qquad \Delta y \approx 0$$

(19.23)

we can see, the accuracy of the new registration algorithm is excellent.

Note that the closed-regions 5 and 10 are a matched pairs, but our algorithm doesn't find them. The reason is that the two regions are circular symmetric and the two shape-specific points given in Section5 converge into one point. For this case, we cannot evaluate the matching degree between them. But losing some matched pairs of closed-regions has no effects on the outcomes of our algorithm if we get enough matched pairs. Sometimes, we can register images accurately even by one matched pair of closed-regions.

The second experiment is to register two practical remote-sensing images by our algorithm. In Figure19.7(a) and Figure19.7(b) are the remote-sensing images with the same region captured by Landsat and SPOT respectively. The

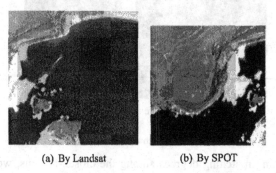

(a) By Landsat   (b) By SPOT

Figure 19.7.   Remote-sensing images registration

parameters of the geometric transformation computed by the new algorithm are listed as follows:

1) Rotation $\theta \approx -0.2183$

2) Scaling $\alpha \approx 1.2087$

3) Translation distances $\Delta x \approx -169$ (horizontal shift); $\Delta y \approx 22$ (vertical shift)

The registered image is illustrated as the following figure:

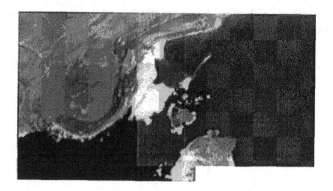

Figure 19.8. The registered image

7. Parallel execution

The time complexity of the proposed geometric registration algorithm depends a lot on the size of input images. Through the above experiments, we can find that 95% of the time is spent on detecting and linking edges. When the size of images exceeds $1024 * 1024$, the performance of sequentially executing the registration algorithm is very bad, sometimes intolerable. So we design a scheme to execute the registration algorithm in parallel.

We first decompose a large image into some small sub-images and assign each of them one process to detect and link edges. A controller process is used to supervise the progress of the whole scheme, which links the contours on the borders between the sub-images, form the set of closed-regions after all the sub-processes finish their tasks in their correspondent sub-images, computes the parameters of the registration. The structure of the parallel scheme is illustrated in Figure19.9 .

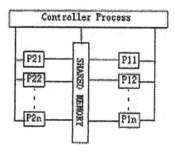

Figure 19.9. The distribution scheme

The two input images we want to register are stored in a shared memory. As shown in Figure19.10, the controller process decomposes the input two images into n sub-images with same size respectively and creates a sub-process for each sub-image.

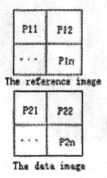

Figure 19.10.   The decomposed images

The following steps give the flow of the controller process:

1) Start all the sub-processes and wait until all of them finish their tasks.

2) When all the sub-processes stop, link the contours on the borders between the sub-images.

3) Combine all the closed-regions in different sub-images into two set of closed-regions correspondent to two input images respectively.

4) Computing the registration parameters and register the two input images.

Each sub-process executes the same task as follows:

1) Detect and link the edges.

2) Form the closed-regions in the current sub-image.

We know from experiments that the computational time denoted by T_c of detecting and linking edges takes more than 95% of the total time denoted by T_s of executing the original algorithm sequentially. In the extension scheme, this most time-consuming task is distributed on $2N$ processors. Let T_r be the other part of the total time T_s. Denoting the computational time spent on executing the parallel scheme by T_d, we have

$$T_s = T_c + T_r \tag{19.24}$$

$$T_d = \frac{T_c}{2N} + T_r \tag{19.25}$$

where N is the numbers of sub-images in each input image. Because $T_c \gg T_r$, we get

$$\frac{T_d}{T_s} = \frac{\frac{T_c}{2N} + T}{T_c + T_r} \simeq \frac{\frac{T_c}{2N}}{T_c} = \frac{1}{2N} \tag{19.26}$$

which means the performance of the parallel scheme is about 2N times that of the sequential algorithm .

8.   Registration by Feedback

This section gives a brief discussion on how to increase the registration accuracy by incorporating the feedback technique into our algorithm. The feedback technique has been developed successfully for registration based on rigid and affine transformation.

Obviously, our new algorithm depends on the integrity of the extracted closed-regions, but sometimes automatically acquired contours are ambiguous or invalid. For these cases where feature detection and feature matching are difficult, the use of feedback between the stages of constructing the closed-regions and finding the optimal affine transformation can significantly improve the registration accuracy.

For our algorithm, let T denote the set of thresholds that control the process of constructing the closed-regions, and M the measure of how well the reference and data images are registered so far. Then we can use the relaxation technique over the set T in order to maximize M. M can be computed as the normalized correlation between the overlapped regions in the reference and data images after registration. Each possible match for a set of thresholds defines a displacement which is measured by the function M giving a rating according to how closely the reference and data images are registered. Each match whose displacement is close to the actual displacement will tend to have a higher rating. Adjust the set of thresholds to try another match. The procedure is iterated adjusting the set of thresholds based on the ratings until the optimal transformation resulting in the maximized rating is found.

9.   Summary

The geometric image registration was addressed in this chapter. A new algorithm of remote-sensing images registration was presented in this paper, which takes full advantage of shape information of the closed-regions in images. With this algorithm, we can perform the registration task automatically and accurately. Experiments validated the proposed algorithm. Moreover, we extended it to a parallel scheme and got much better performance. The performance of our algorithm depends on how the contours are reserved in images. How to efficiently detect and link edges is an important topic in the future research. Also future work could be on how to incorporate the new algorithm into other existing registration schemes.

References

[1] L. Brown. *A survey of Images registration Techniques*. ACM Computing Surveys, vol.24, no.4, 1992: 325-376.

[2] J. Le Moigne et al. *First Evaluation of Automatic Images registration Methods.* IGARSS'98, July 1998.

[3] C.Pohl, J.L. Van Genderen. *Image Fusion in Remote Sensing: Concepts, Methods and Applications.* Intern. J. Rem. Sens., vol.19, 1998.

[4] B.J. Devereux, R.M. Fuller, L. Carter, and R.J. Parsell. *Geometric Correction of Airborne Scanner Imagery by Matching Delaunay Triangles.* Int'l J. Remote Sensing, vol.11, no.12, 1990: 2,237-2,251.

[5] B.S. Reddy and B.N. Chatterji. *An FFT-Based Technique for Translation, Rotation, and Scale-Invariant Images registration.* IEEE Trans. Image Processing, vol.3, no.8, Aug. 1996: 1,266-1,270.

[6] J.P. Djamdji, A. Bijaoui, and R. Manjere. *Geometrical Registration of Images: The Multiresolution Approach.* Photogrammetric Eng. And Remote Sensing J., vol.59, no.5, 645-653.

[7] W.K. Pratt. *Digital Image Processing.* John Wiley & Sons, Inc., NY 1978.

[8] Y. Wu and H. Maitre. *A multiresolution approach for registration of a spot image and a SAR image.* Proc. Int. Geosci. Remote Sensing Symp., May 1990, pp. 635-638.

[9] E. Rignot et al. *Automated multisensor registration: Requirements and techniques.* Photogrammetric Eng. Remote Sensing, vol. 57, pp. 1029-1038, Aug. 1991.

[10] A. Ventura, A. Rampini, and R. Schettini. *Images registration by recognition of corresponding structures.* IEEE Trans. Geosci. Remote Sensing, vol. 28, pp.305-314, May 1990.

[11] A. Goshtasby, G. Stockman, and C. Page. *A region-based approach to digital images registration with subpixel accuracy.* IEEE Trans. Geosci. Remote Sensing, vol. 24, pp. 390-399, May 1986.

[12] Hui Li, B.S. Manjunath, and Sanjit K. Mitra. *A contour-based approach to multisensor images registration.* IEEE Trans. On Image Processing, vol. 4, no. 3, March 1995.

[13] Gui Xie and Hong Shen. *Automatic remote-sensing images registration by matching closed-regions.* International Symposium, ISPA 2003 Proceedings.

[14] Karp, R. M. and Ramachandran. *Parallel algorithms for shared-memory machines* in Handbook of Theoretical Computer Science, V1990, ed. J. Van Leeuwen, pp. 869-941. Amsterdan:Elsevier Science Publishers.

[15] Jaja. *An introduction to parallel algorithms.* Reading, Mass.:Addison-Welsey. 1992.

[16] Zhang Yujin. *Image Segmentation.* ISBN-7-03-007241-3, Beijing: Science Publishing Company, 9-19,2001.

[17] Marr D, Hildreth E. *Theory of edge detection.* Proceedings of R. Soc. London, 1980, B207:187-217.

[18] Zhang Yujin. *Image processing and analysis.* Beijing: Tsinghua Publisher,1999.

Chapter 20

A MULTIAGENT INFRASTRUCTURE FOR DATA-INTENSIVE GRID APPLICATIONS

Maria S. Pérez
DATSI. FI. Universidad Politécnica de Madrid. Spain
mperez@fi.upm.es

Jesús Carretero, Félix Garcia
Departamento de Informática. Universidad Carlos III de Madrid. Spain
jcarrete@arcos.inf.uc3m.es, fgarcia@arcos.inf.uc3m.es

José M. Peña, Victor Robles
DATSI. FI. Universidad Politécnica de Madrid. Spain
jmpena@fi.upm.es, vrobles@fi.upm.es

Abstract   Grid constitutes a new computing paradigm, which inherits a great number of its features from distributed systems. This new paradigm enables resource-sharing across networks, being data one of the most important ones. Data-intensive grid systems are grid applications, whose major goal is to provide efficient access to data. Existing data-intensive applications have been used in several domains, such as physics, climate modeling, biology or visualization. The I/O problem is not completely solved in this kind of applications. This chapter presents MAPFS as a flexible and high-performance platform for data-intensive applications and, more specifically, for data grid applications.

Keywords: Data grid, multiagent architecture, I/O optimizations, dynamic reconfiguration.

1.   Introduction

Grid computing has become one of the most important topics appeared and widely developed in the computing field in the last decade, together with the agent technology.

The terminology *grid* was used by first time in the middle 1990's for naming a distributed infrastructure, dedicated to scientific research and advanced engineering, making usage of Internet [7]. Unlike the conventional networks, which are focused on the communication between devices, grid computing takes advantage of the low-load periods of all the computers connected to a network, making possible computing resources sharing.

On the other hand, there is a growing interest in the development of high-performance Input/Output systems, because the I/O phase has become a bottleneck in the computing systems due to its poor performance. The increasing importance of the I/O systems can be observed in the names of the different periods of the computer science. The period between the 1960's and 1980's was named *computing revolution age*. However, the period beginning in the 1990's is named *information age*. This change of mentality has allowed the information and I/O systems to take a main role in the computing field.

Nevertheless, improvements in disk access times have not been proportional to the increase of processors performance, which have been enhanced more than 50% per year. Despite disk capacity has drastically increased [14], reducing the transference time between 60% and 80% per year, the total access time has only been reduced 10% per year, due to its dependence on mechanical systems. Amdahl's law states that the speedup obtained from computers is limited by the slowest system component. Thus, it is fundamental to improve I/O systems performance with the aim of enhancing the whole system. This limitation is more relevant in applications creating and operating on large amounts of data. Nowadays, there is a huge number of such applications, e.g. data mining systems extracting knowledge from large volumes of data. Existing data-intensive applications have been used in several domains, such as physics [13], climate modeling [17], biology [31] or visualization [10].

One of the major goals of grid computing is to provide efficient access to data, being data-intensive grid applications (or data grids, in short) one of the most relevant grid architectures. Data-intensive grid applications try to tackle problems originated by the needs of a performance-full I/O system in a grid infrastructure. In these architectures, data sources are distributed among different nodes. Also, a typical data grid requires access to terabyte or higher sizes datasets. For example, high-energy physics may generate terabytes of data in a single experiment. Accesses to data repositories must be made in an efficient way, in order to increase the performance of the applications using the grid. Furthermore, data-intensive grid applications have several functional requirements and access patterns.

Therefore, the I/O system must be flexible enough to match these demands. The usage of hints, caching and prefetching policies or different data distribution configurations are optional features, which can reduce latency and increase I/O operations performance. In order to integrate all these functionalities in the storage system, it is possible to use different distributed systems technologies. Agents technology is very appropriate because of its adaptability to different domains. Furthermore, the usage of agents provides additional features, such as autonomy, reactivity and proactivity [30].

Currently, there are different systems that offer services to access resources in a data grid. Accessing heterogeneous resources with interfaces and different functionalities is solved, in the majority of the cases, by means of new services that offer a uniform access to different types of systems. Examples of this kind of systems are Globus [28], Storage Resource Broker (SRB) [2], DataCutter [4], DPSS [27] and BLUNT [18]. All these systems use replication to improve the I/O performance and reliability.

Many efforts have been made in order to design and implement an integrating data grid infrastructure [5]. The data access API of this general architecture involves a standard interface to storage systems. Nevertheless, this API does not support the usage of high-performance I/O operations.

This chapter presents MAPFS, a multiagent architecture, whose goal is to allow applications to access data repositories in an efficient and flexible fashion, providing formalisms for modifying the topology of the storage system, specifying different data access patterns and selecting additional functionalities.

The outline of this chapter is as follows. Section 2 presents MAPFS as a flexible infrastructure for data-intensive grid applications. Section 3 describes MAPFS architecture, indicating how MAPFS can interact with other data grid infrastructures. Section 4 shows the results obtained for the evaluation of applications using MAPFS. Section 5 shows the related work. Finally, section 6 summarizes our conclusions and suggests further future work.

2.   MAPFS as a Data-Intensive Grid Infrastructure

The previous section states that a key feature of data grids infrastructures is the flexibility. MAPFS [24] is a multiagent architecture, which supplies this property through several approaches:

- System topology configuration: Ability to change system topology, setting the I/O nodes and their relationships. This feature is achieved through the usage of **storage groups**.

- Access pattern specification: Although MAPFS is a general purpose I/O system, it can be configured in order to adapt to different I/O access patterns. The main configuration issues of the MAPFS system are: (i)I/O caching and prefetching, approach that increases the I/O operations efficiency, because of the optimal usage of disk caches and (ii)usage of hints on future access patterns. MAPFS offers an independent API, different from I/O operations, that allow applications to configure access patterns, which are translated into hints by the I/O system. All these features can be configured through the usage of **control user operations**.

- There are different reasons to allow some functionalities (such as caching or prefetching) to run in parallel on different nodes and even in the data servers. Moving executions to data servers may reduce network latency and traffic. The **agent** technology is a suitable framework for integrating these functions in the storage system, because of its adaptability to different domains and its capability to provide autonomy to the processes.

2.1   Storage Groups as Data Resource-sharing

A *storage group* is defined in MAPFS as a set of servers clustered in groups. These groups take the role of data repositories. Therefore, storage groups contain a set of files, which is distributed among their nodes. These groups can be built applying several policies, trying to optimize the accesses to all the storage groups. Some significant policies are:

- Grouping by server proximity: Storage groups are built based on the physical distribution of the data servers. Storage groups are composed by servers in close proximity to each other. This policy optimizes the queries addressed to a storage group because of the similar latency of messages sent to servers.

- Grouping by server similarity: Storage groups are composed of servers with similar processing capacity. This policy classifies storage groups in different categories, depending on their computational and I/O power.

These two policies are the most appropriate polices in a grid infrastructure, because of the geographical and technical differences of the nodes that belong to such infrastructure. However, it is possible to extend these policies with new ones and use them for building storage groups.

Storage groups allow MAPFS to reconfigure dynamically data storage servers. If the system topology is changed, data must be reconstructed in the new layout, degrading the performance of the I/O system. In order to avoid data reconstruction, MAPFS defines two types of storage groups: (i)main storage groups, which constitute current layouts; and (ii)secondary storage groups, which are used for storing old layouts.

This approach schedules data reconstruction until the system runs a defragmentation operation, which is used for deleting secondary groups and simplifying the storage system description, or when a server or storage group is deleted. In this way, storage system description is composed by main storage groups, until a new topology change is made in the system.

2.2   Control User Operations as Applications Access Pattern Specifications

Hints are structures known and built by the I/O system, which are used for improving the read and write operations performance. MAPFS uses these hints

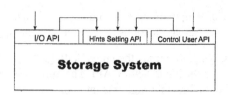

Figure 20.1. Storage System API

to access data. For example, storage systems using hints may provide greater performance because they use this information to decrease cache faults and to prefetch the data most probably used in next executions. In other words, the more information it has been used, the less uncertainty in the future access guesses and, therefore, the better prefetching and caching results.

In MAPFS, hints can be obtained in two ways:

1) Given by the user, that is, the user application provides the necessary specifications to I/O system;

2) Built by the multiagent subsystem. In fact, one of the characteristics of agents is their capacity of *learning*. The creation of hints dynamically can be possible due to this feature. If this option is selected, the multiagent system must analyze the access pattern of the applications in order to build hints improving data access. This feature can be achieved using statistical and AI methods on historical logs.

If hints are provided by the user application, it is necessary for the system to provide syntactic rules for setting the system parameters, which configure the I/O system. On the other hand, if the multiagent subsystem creates the hints, it is also necessary to store them in a predefined way. In any case, lexical and syntactic rules must be introduced in the system.

The system is configured through several operations, which are independent of the I/O operations, although these last ones use the former operations. The configuration operations are divided into:

- Hints Setting Operations: Operations for establishing the hints of the system. Therefore, they can set and get the values of the different fields of the hints.

- Control User Operations: Higher level operations that can be used directly by the user applications to manage system performance.

Figure 20.1 shows the three levels in which the Storage System API is divided.

As can be seen in the figure, there are three ways of accessing the Hints Setting Module:

1) The I/O operations may ask for hint values and even modify them.

2) The control user operations may modify the hints. This is the usual method for the user applications to interact with hints.

3) To make the system flexible, the Hints Setting Module may be accessed directly through the Hints Setting API. The multiagent system may build and modify these hints through this interface.

2.3   Agents as Resource Integrators

The nature of the problem of the creation of a data grid can be solved in a more natural way through a distributed system. A multiagent system is inherently distributed. Moreover, the integration between such system and a data grid can take advantage of all the features of the agent technology.

The multiagent system consists of a set of agents, with the following features: (i)autonomous behavior, that is, they are able to act theirselves and on behalf of other systems, (ii)reactivity, that is, they perceive the changes of the environment and they act according to this, (iii)proactivity, that is, the ability of foreseeing future needs and acting with the aim of solving them and (iv)intelligence, because agents attempt to act intelligently on behalf of the user or another system.

MAPFS uses an agent hierarchy, which solves the information retrieval problem in a transparent and efficient way. This hierarchy is composed of:

- Extractor agents: They are responsible for information retrieval, invoking parallel I/O operations.

- Distributor agents: They distribute the workload to the extractor agents. These agents are placed at the higher level of the agents hierarchy.

- Caching and prefetching agents: They are associated with one or more extractor agents, caching or prefetching their data.

- Hints agents: They study applications access patterns to build hints improving data access.

A key point in the deployment of these functionalities to a grid infrastructure is the need of addressing the problem of the **security**. Owing to the global and wide scope of such infrastructures, security and authorization must be supported.

These capabilities are implemented in MAPFS through a new agent subsystem, named security subsystem. This subsystem interact with distributor agents in order to authorize a concrete user the usage of the system. Thus, once a distributor agent is authorized on behalf of a user, the rest of the hierarchy is allowed to be used within this session. The beginning and end of the sessions are established through the usage of two MAPFS primitives, in a similar way to the sessions in a sequential file system. This subsystem uses a concrete security policy, which defines the authorization and access controls to

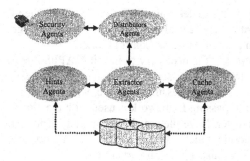

Figure 20.2. Taxonomy of agents used in MAPFS

be used for client access to MAPFS. Different security policies may be used through the implementation of suitable security modules.

Figure 20.2 represents the relation among all MAPFS agents. Nevertheless, the taxonomy of agents can be extended to provide additional functionalities.

Through the usage of the agent hierarchy, MAPFS evolves to a service oriented architecture, providing the following services (related to the different kind of agents): (i)caching and prefetching services, with the aim of increasing the performance, (ii)security service, in order to give credentials and guarantee access rights and denial to the information and (iii)hint service, for providing intelligence and learning capacity to the process of accessing data.

This feature is desirable in grid infrastructures, because user are mainly interested in services. Indeed, the future of the Grid and Web services seems to go hand-in-hand to develop an integrated framework [8]. Global Grid Forum is currently concerned about the Web-Grid integration in the form of the Open Grid Services Interface Working Group [23].

3. MAPFS Architecture

Besides of the flexibility, another desirable feature of data grids is that they must be able to use heterogeneous data servers. MAPFS is based on a client-server architecture using general purpose servers, providing all the MAPFS management tasks as specialized clients.

In the first prototype, we use NFS server. NFS [21] has been ported to different operating systems and machine platforms and is widely used by many servers worldwide. Therefore, it is very easy to add new data repositories to the data grid infrastructure. The only requirement of these data servers is to use NFS and export a directory tree to data grid users. Data is distributed through the servers belonging to a storage group, using a stripe unit. Additionally, data servers must be authorized by the security subsystem for all the users of such repository. Security subsystem may use several authentication and authorization mechanisms. MAPFS has configuration information that determines the type and level of security services required for a storage group. MAPFS uses these security services to determine user identity. Once the identity and authorization information has been obtained, security subsystem grants or denies the access based on an ACL (Access Control List).

On the client-side, it is necessary to install MAPFS client, which provides a parallel I/O interface to the servers. This module is implemented with MPI [19], the standard message passing interface, widely used in parallel computing. This message-passing framework is used with the aim of connecting several nodes in a cluster. Nevertheless, this technology is not valid for connecting clusters with internal nodes[1]. In order to provide a global space and dynamic resource sharing, we use a grid infrastructure.

One of the major goals of a data grid infrastructure is to provide access to a huge number of heterogeneous data sources. In this sense, it is important that MAPFS can interoperate with other grid architectures and give access to their data repositories. Because MAPFS is implemented with MPI, its integration with other grid infrastructures is relatively simple, through the usage of MPICH-G2, [6] a grid-enabled implementation of the MPI, which makes possible running MPI programs across multiple computers at different sites. MPICH-G2 is the second generation of the library MPICH-G. This library extends the Argonne MPICH using services from the Globus Toolkit. MPICH-G2 automatically converts data in messages sent between machines of different architectures and supports multiprotocol communication.

Therefore, MAPFS can be used in two different modes: (i)applications can use MAPFS as the main infrastructure, accessing to data from the storage groups defined in this system and (ii)applications can use MAPFS together with other grid architectures. In this case, it is possible to extend the storage groups with other nodes accessible through the Globus services. Concretely, the Global Access Secondary Storage (GASS) service [3] is used to stage executables to remote machines and to support efficient communication in dynamic grid environments. The integration between MAPFS and GASS is not redundant, because GASS does not provide the full functionality of a parallel file system. MAPFS provides a rich parallel interface, which can be used in wide area computing with the aid of GASS and other Globus services.

On the other hand, additional multiagent subsystems, such as security subsystem, provide several functionalities and they are executed on different nodes. The most usual configuration is to run these subsystems in data servers, helping to reduce network traffic.

4.   MAPFS Evaluation

In order to validate our implementation, it is necessary to evaluate its performance. Experiments were run in two different storage groups, which use the server similarity grouping policy, because of the technical differences of both groups. The first storage group (G_1) is composed of four nodes Athlon 650MHz, with 256 MB of RAM memory, connected by a Gigabit network.

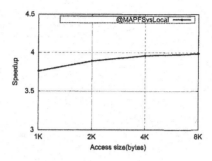

Figure 20.3.   Speedup of the MAPFS solution (group G_1) versus Local solution

The second storage group (G_2) has six nodes Intel Xeon 2.40GHz, with 1GB of RAM memory with a Gigabit network. The storage group G_2 provides better performance. Nevertheless, the storage group G_1 offers higher storage capacity. These two storage groups constitutes our initial trial data grid. Our experiment consists in a process per node running a multiplication of two matrices, where the matrices are stored in the grid, using MAPFS as underlying platform. The resultant matrix is also stored in a distributed fashion. A prefetching multiagent subsystem is used, which is responsible for prefetching rows and columns of the matrices. In this case, hints provided by the applications are the indexes of the matrix row and the matrix column of the element calculated in every iteration. Hints are used as data tags for processing the elements in an efficient manner, skipping non-related elements in the cache.

This experiment was compared to another one, which consists in multiplying the same matrices stored in the local disk through the usage of a traditional I/O system. The size of the matrices is 100 MB.

Figure 20.3 shows the speedup of the MAPFS solution for the group G_1 versus local solution, varying the access size used in the I/O operations. As can be seen, the speedup is very close to 4, the number of nodes, which is the maximum speedup, limited by the "Amdahl law".

Figure 20.4 represents the execution time of the groups G_1 y G_2 for the matrix multiplication. As we previously mentioned, the storage group G_2 provides better results.

In this scenary, we add two servers to the storage group G_2, modifying the topology of the storage groups. These two servers form a new secondary group, G_3. The storage group G_2 becomes a secondary group. The group G_4 is the new main storage group with all the nodes from G_2 and G_3.

If we use the new group G_4, the results of the multiplication improve, because the system takes advantage of a higher parallelism (higher number of nodes). Figure 20.5 shows this comparison.

A defragmentation operation involves the reconstruction of the secondary storage group G_2 over the main storage group G_4. If the access size is 16K and

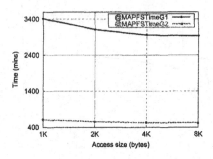

Figure 20.4. Comparison between the different storage groups

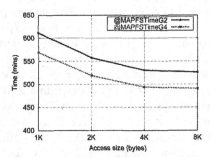

Figure 20.5. Improvement of the multiplication adding two servers to the storage group

the group G_2 has 50 GB-size files, the time necessary for the reconstruction is around 30 minutes. This operation must be made in low-load periods.

5.   Related Work

Grids are persistent frameworks that enable applications to integrate resources managed by diverse organizations in widespread ubications.   Some of the most known grid applications are the *Search for Extraterrestrial Intelligence (SETI@Home)* project [15], which analyzes data obtained from telescopes in order to explore and explain the origin of life in the universe, or *Great Internet Mersenne Prime Search (GIMPS)* [12], whose goal is discovering the highest prime number. As we can observe, grid computing is used in the analysis of different sources of data, taking advantage of computing cycles in idle nodes.

Grid computing focuses on the remote access to computational resources. This paradigm is not linked to a concrete technology. Nevertheless, there is a *de facto* standard, Globus.

Globus is a grid framework proposed by Globus Alliance [11]. Its main purpose is the creation of fundamental technologies behind the Grid, which lets applications share computing, data and tools resources through secure communication channels, without sacrificing local autonomy. The Globus Toolkit includes open-source software services for resource monitoring, discovery, and management, in addition with security and file management.

On the other hand, several researchers and commercial companies are investigating topics related to data-intensive grids and I/O systems used in computational grids. The problems tackled by these research lines are similar to those discussed in this chapter.

Armada [22] is a framework that allows grid applications to access datasets that are distributed across a computational grid. Applications combine modules called *ships* into graphs called *armadas*. These armadas provide a path for the application to access data.

The Remote I/O (RIO) library [9] is a tool for accessing to files located on remote file systems. RIO follows the MPI-IO interface and allows any application that uses MPI-IO to operate unchanged in a wide area environment. MAPFS provides this feature for MPI programs.

SRB [2] provides a UNIX-style file I/O interface for accessing heterogeneous data distributed over wide area nodes. SRB uses replication to improve data availability and performance.

Kangaroo [26] belongs to the Condor grid project [16] and it is a reliable data movement system that keep applications running. Kangaroo service continues performing I/O operations even if the process that initiated these requests fails.

Legion [20] is an object-oriented infrastructure used in distributed computing. LegionFS [29] provides UNIX-style I/O operations, using Legion services such as naming or security.

GridFTP [1] is an extension of the standard FTP protocol, providing secure and efficient data management in grid architectures. In order to exhibit this behaviour, GridFTP includes among others: (i)Kerberos support, (ii)parallel and striped data transfer, (iii)support for reliable and restartable data transfer and (iv)instrumentation and monitoring tools.

Unlike SRB and LegionFS, MAPFS provides a rich parallel I/O interface, with operators like collective I/O and non-blocking I/O mechanisms. MAPFS also allows applications to access remote data in an efficient way. Moreover, using MPICH-G, it is possible to access to storage groups belonging to other data grids. Furthermore, the data access patterns configuration provides flexibility to applications using MAPFS. This characteristic is different from the rest of the systems previously described.

6.   Conclusions and Future Work

In this work we have presented MAPFS, a new infrastructure for data-intensive grid applications, which takes advantage of the parallel I/O field and distributed systems. MAPFS provides a parallel and high-performance multiagent platform for data access with the following properties: (i)system topology configuration; (ii)access patterns specifications by applications; (iii) I/O caching and prefetching features and (iv)execution of specific functionalities on other nodes than the clients. The same application has been evaluated with and without MAPFS and the resultant speedup is very close to the maximum one. Furthermore, the performance of the system has been evaluated with several storage groups, measuring the effects of a topology change.

This first data grid version uses NFS as storage server file system. However, this fact constitutes the major weakness of this version, because NFS is a stateless protocol, which has no representation of the system calls open and close. For this reason, the I/O system does not provide semantics significantly different than those provided by NFS. Furthermore, NFS interface does not show any binding between individual operations and processes that initiate them. For this reason, security issues have to be performed by another module, that is, the security subsystem.

We consider that using a most appropriate storage file server may improve the performance and usability of the global infrastructure. Thus, we are studying different alternatives as future storage file systems. Nevertheless, the factibility of using NFS on the server-side, keeping the desirable features of MAPFS, shows the robustness of our design.

Finally, it would be interesting to build and evaluate additional subsystems with other functionalities, e.g. fault tolerance.

Notes

1. We consider internal nodes those nodes with a private IP address

References

[1] Allcock, B., Bester, J., Bresnahan, J., Chervenak, A.L., Foster, I., Kesselman, C., Meder, S., Nefedova, V., Quesnal, D., and Tuecke, S. (2002). Data management and transfer in high performance computational grid environments. *Parallel Computing Journal*, 28(5):749–771.

[2] Baru, C., Moore, R., Rajasekar, A., and Wan, M. (1998). The SDSC storage resource broker. In *Proceedings of CASCON'98*, Toronto, Canada.

[3] Bester, Joseph, Foster, Ian, Kesselman, Carl, Tedesco, Jean, and Tuecke, Steven (1999). GASS: A data movement and access service for wide area computing systems. In *Proceedings of the Sixth Workshop on Input/Output in Parallel and Distributed Systems*, pages 78–88, Atlanta, GA. ACM Press.

[4] Beynon, M.D., Ferreira, R., Kurc, T., Sussman, A., and Saltz, J. (2000). DataCutter: Middleware for filtering very large scientific datasets of archival storage systems. In *Proceedings of the 2000 Mass Storage Systems Conference*, pages 119–133, College Park, MD. IEEE Computer Society Press.

[5] Chervenak, A., Foster, I., Kesselman, C., Salisbury, C., and Tuecke, S. (1999). The data grid: Towards an architecture for the distributed management and analysis of large scientific datasets. *Network and Computer Applications*.

[6] Foster, I. and Karonis, N. (1998). A grid-enabled MPI: Message passing in heterogeneous distributed computing systems. In *Proceedings of SC'98*. ACM Press.

[7] Foster, I. and Kesselman, C., editors (1999). *The Grid: Blueprint for a New Computing Infrastructure*. Morgan Kaufmann.

[8] Foster, I., Kesselman, C., Nick, J., and Tuecke, S. (2002). The physiology of the grid: An open grid services architecture for distributed sustems integration.

[9] Foster, IanT., Kohr, David, Krishnaiyer, Rakesh, and Mogill, Jace (1997). Remote I/O fast access to distant storage. In *Proceedings of the IOPADS 1997*, pages 14–25.

[10] Freitag, LoriA. and Loy, RaymondM. (1999). Adaptive, multiresolution visualization of large data sets using a distributed memory octree. In *Proceedings of SC99: High Performance Networking and Computing*, Portland, OR. ACM Press and IEEE Computer Society Press.

[11] Globus.www. The Globus Project. *http://www.globus.org*.

[12] Hajratwala, Nayan (2002). *GIMPS Finds First Million-Digit Prime*, chapter Computation Nations and Swarm Supercomputers. Perseus Publishing. Article belonging to [25].

[13] Holtman, K. (2000). Object level physics data replication in the Grid. In *Proceedings of ACAT'2000*, pages 244–246.

[14] Hugues, GordonF. (2002). Wise drives. *IEEE Spectrum*.

[15] Korpela, E.J., Heien, E.M., and Werthimer, D. (2000). Pulse detection algorithms for use in seti@home. *Bulletin of the American Astronomical Society*.

[16] Litzkow, M., Livny, M., and Mutka, M. (1988). Condor: A hunter of idle workstations. In *Proc. of the 8th International Conference of Distributed Computing Systems*, pages 104–111.

[17] Lyster, P.M., Ekers, K., Guo, J., Harber, M., Lamich, D., Larson, J.W., Lucchesi, R., Rood, R., Schubert, S., Sawyer, W., Sienkiewicz, M., daSilva, A., Stobie, J., Takacs, L.L., Todling, R., and Zero, J. (1997). Parallel computing at the NASA data assimilation office (DAO). San Jose, CA. IEEE Computer Society Press.

[18] Martinez, M.R. and Roussopoulos, N. (2000). MOCHA: A self-extensible database middleware system for distributed data sources. In *Proceedings of the ACM SIGMOD International Conference on Management of Data*, Dallas, TX.

[19] MPI-1-94 (1994). *MPI: A Message-Passing Interface Standard*. Message Passing Interface Forum.

[20] Natrajan, Anand, Humphrey, MartyA., and Grimshaw, AndrewS. (2001). Capacity and capability computing using Legion. *Lecture Notes in Computer Science*, 2073.

[21] NFSPSSpec (1989). *NFS: Network File System Protocol Specification*. Network Working Group. RFC 1094.

[22] Oldfield, Ron and Kotz, David (2002). Armada: a parallel I/O framework for computational grids. *Future Generation Computer Systems*, 18(4):501–523.

[23] open-grid-service.WWW. Open Grid Service Interface Working Group, Global Grid Forum. *http://www.gridforum.org/ogsi-wg*.

[24] Prez, MaraS., Garca, Flix, and Carretero, Jess (2001). A new multiagent based architecture for high performance I/O in clusters. *2001 International Conference on Parallel Processing Workshops*.

[25] Rheingold, Howard (2002). *Smart Mobs: The Next Social Revolution*. Perseus Publishing.

[26] Thain, Douglas, Basney, Jim, Son, Se-Chang, and Livny, Miron (2001). The Kangaroo approach to data movement on the grid. In *Proceedings of the Tenth IEEE Symposium on High Performance Distributed Computing*.

[27] Tierney, B., Lee, J., Johnston, W., Crowley, B., and Holding, M. (1999). A network-aware distributed storage cache for data-intensive environments. In *Proceedings of the Eighth IEEE International Symposium on High Performance Distributed Computing*, pages 185–193, Redondo Beach, CA.

[28] Vazhkuda, S., Tuecke, S., and Foster, I. (2001). Replica selection in the Globus data Grid. In *Proceedings of the International workshop on Data Models and Databases on Clusters and the Grid (DataGrid2001)*. IEEE Computer Society Press.

[29] White, BrianS., Walker, Michael, Humphrey, Marty, and Grimshaw, AndrewS. (2001). LegionFS: A secure and scalable file system supporting cross-domain high-performance applications. In *Proceedings of the IEEE/ACM Supercomputing Conference (SC2001)*.

[30] Wooldridge, Michael and Jennings, NicholasR. (1995). Intelligent agents: Theory and practice. *Knowledge Engineering Review*.

[31] Young, S.J., Fan, G.Y., Hessler, D., Lamont, S., Elvins, T.T., Hadida, M., Hanyzewski, G., Durkin, J.W., Hubbard, P., Kindlmann, G., Wong, E., Greenberg, D., Karin, S., and Ellisman, M.H. (1996). Implementing a collaboratory for microscopic digital anatomy. *Supercomputer Applications and High Performance Computing*, 10(2/3):170–181.

Chapter 21

MODELING ANALYSIS OF KEY MESSAGE APPROACH ON CLUSTERS

Ming ZHU
Dept. of Electrical and Computer Engineering
Drexel University, Philadelphia, PA 19104
zhuming@cbis.ece.drexel.edu

Wentong CAI, Bu-Sung LEE
School of Computer Engineering, Nanyang Technological University, Singapore 639798
aswtcai@ntu.edu.sg, ebslee@ntu.edu.sg

Laurence T. YANG
Department of Computer Science
St. Francis Xavier University, Antigonish, NS, B2G 2W5, Canada
lyang@stfx.ca

Yang WANG
Department of Computing Science University of Alberta Edmonton, Alberta T6G 2E8
ywang@cs.ualberta.ca

Abstract   Research on cluster/distributed computing has been fueled by the availability of cost-effective workstations and high performance networks. Many parallel programming languages and related programming models have become widely accepted. However, the high communication overhead is a major problem of running parallel applications in cluster/distributed computing environments. To reduce the communication overhead and thus the completion time of a parallel application, this paper introduces and analyzes an efficient Key Message (KM) approach to supporting parallel computing in cluster environments. The approach includes the application model and communication model. The application model adopts a DAG (*directed acyclic graph*) task graph to abstract a parallel application. The communication model presents a priority-based M/M/1 queue to analyze the communication delay. Then, with these fundamental models and assumptions, an analytical method is presented to verify the performance of the approach. It demonstrates that when the network background load increases or the computation to communication ratio decreases, the analysis results show a significant improvement on communication of a parallel application over the system which does not use the KM approach.

Keywords: Cluster Computing, Key Message Approach, Communication Optimization, Parallel Programming, Modeling Analysis.

1.   Introduction

Cluster computing systems have become increasingly popular not only because of the benefit from the high volume economy of existing commodity components, but also because they provide the potential to exploit parallelism for high performance computing. However, this potential is compromised by the underlying high communication overhead, especially with the rapid advances in hardware and software. The reasons lie in several facts. Firstly, the improvement of network bandwidth lags behind that of the overall performance of workstations, relatively speaking. Secondly, the underlying communication protocols are not amenable to high performance computing. A typical example is the TCP/IP protocol stack, which has been proved to be the bottleneck in communication that introduces a major delay in the message-passing in a parallel application. Finally, the topology of the communication network is not optimized for high performance computing. Under these limitations, the current development of the cluster computing systems is usually oriented to a class of coarse-grained parallel applications. Thus, to expand clusters to other applications, removing the performance barrier of communication systems is crucial.

To reduce the communication overhead, current efforts generally fall into three areas. The first is to design a new communication system from scratch with an attempt to exploit the special characteristics of the underlying communication hardware[1, 2, 3, 18]. The second is to optimize the existing protocols to improve the communication performance in cluster environments such as Active Message[12],Fast Message[13] and Fast Socket [14]. Although these approaches are quite impressive in communication overhead reduction, they suffer from the same limitation of not differentiating the types of messages. Consequently, all messages transmitted in the network have the same priorities. However, under heavy network traffic load conditions, an important message may experience a significant delay due to all earlier unimportant messages that are competing for the same communication channel.

To address this problem, the third effort exploits high-level application information to facilitate the optimization of message passing[16, 19]. Compared to the previous approaches, this optimization is independent of the underlying hardware and communication libraries, and hence enjoys the advantage of high portability and easy implementation.

A typical study following this dimension is *Key Message* approach[10]. Based on its application and communication models, a kernel algorithm is applied to a DAG(i.e., directed acyclic graph) task graph[11] to optimize the communication time for its original and potential critical paths. Thus, shortened communication time of a critical path results in a reduction of its completion time. This means that the overall execution time of the parallel application is reduced. The philosophy of this optimization is from the observation that under networks with heavy traffic, a message generated in the critical path of a parallel application (the Key Message) may suffer a significant delay since it has to wait until all earlier (possible unimportant) messages are processed. Therefore, there may be a performance benefit from the introduction of a priority queue into the communication system to serve the Key Message first before any low priority messages in the queue.

The benefit of Key Message has been verified on the IBM SP2 and reported in [10]. However, it still lacks an accurate modeling analysis through which a deep insight into its potential can be gained. The objective of this paper is to compensate for this shortage.

The rest of this paper is organized as follows. Section 2 introduces the related work. Section 3 briefly describes the KM approach and illustrates the KM algorithm. The performance preliminary modeling analysis is given in Section 4. Conclusions and some future directions are presented in Section 5.

2. Related Work

The concepts of critical paths and priorities are certainly not new. However, to our knowledge, there are no existing communication libraries like KM that integrate these two concepts to optimize communication time of a parallel application in clusters.

Kale et al. [9] proposed to use the priority-based process scheduler provided by the operating system to speedup the processing of parallel tasks. In their approach, tasks of a parallel application are assigned higher priority than other tasks on a node. However, the underlying communication in these tasks is not prioritized. Communication generated by a parallel application and sequential tasks on the same node still have the same priority.

Kwok and Ahmad[4] studied the static scheduling algorithms for allocating task graphs to fully -connected multiprocessors. Their proposed algorithm, which is called the *Dynamic Critical-Path* (DCP) scheduling algorithm, uses the critical path concept to prioritize the tasks so as to avoid scheduling less important tasks before the more important ones. To capture the changes in the relative importance of tasks, their priorities can be determined dynamically during the scheduling process. Although this algorithm integrates the concepts of critical path and priorities, it only focuses on the task scheduling without considering the communication optimization.

In addition to the task scheduling, a number of research efforts target the communication scheduling in various software systems by employing priority approaches.

S. Karlsson et al[19]. investigated message behaviors in software *Distributed Shared Memory* (DSM) systems and found that performance critical messages can be delayed behind less important messages by the enqueuing behavior in the communication libraries, thus limiting the DSM performance. To address this problem, they advocated the use of message priorities to reduce the latency of performance -critical control messages such as those involved in cache coherent protocol. More specifically, messages with a high priority, e.g. control messages, are transferred before messages with lower priority, say data messages. Obviously, in their model, the control message corresponds roughly to our Key Message, but it has no related concept of a critical path. All the data messages such as page migration have the same priority and are scheduled on a First-Come-First-Serve (FCFS) policy.

GM [15] is a message-passing system which provides two levels of message priority for Myrinet networks. In GM, message sending is regulated by a simple token-passing mechanism to prevent GM's bounded-size internal queues from overflowing. Typical GM applications use only one GM priority. The high priority channel is usually used for control messages or for single-hop message forwarding. Communication in GM is "connectionless". There is no need for client software to establish a connection with a remote port in order to communicate with it: the client software simply builds a message and sends it to any port in the network. Message order is preserved only for messages of the same priority, from the same sending port, and directed to the same receiving port. Messages with differing priorities never block each other. Consequently, low priority messages may pass high priority messages, unlike in some other communication systems. GM is only available over Myrinet networks.

Dong et al.[16] studied the communication prioritization in a network of workstations. Communication generated by parallel applications was given higher priority than those generated from sequential application. Only SPMD parallel applications were studied. Effectiveness of their optimization was demonstrated by a simulation. The Key Message approach proposed in this paper differs from Dong's optimization technique in that messages generated from a parallel application are put at different priority levels. The objective of our optimization is to shorten the execution time of critical paths in a parallel application by identifying key messages that need higher priority in transmission. In addition, our approach can be applied to SPMD as well as MPMD parallel applications.

Unlike the previous research which prioritizes different types of messages for scheduling, Surma et.al[8] studied the message scheduling problem from a different angle by employing a priority scheme. The problem they considered was how to improve the communication performance by reducing message collisions under tightly-coupled architectures such as a two-dimensional mesh processor network utilizing XY-routing. Message collisions resulted from two or more parallel messages competing for the same communication channel. As a result, one had to be scheduled before the other. The scheduling strategy may had a great impact on the final completion time of the application. To solve this problem, they proposed a static-dynamic hybrid approach that utilized known information about message traffic patterns to determine priorities for each individual message that strictly signified the ordering of message transmissions. The goal of this approach is to minimize the processing time of all the messages. However, it is possible to delay the critical path messages due to the avoidance of message collisions.

Although critical path is useful for message optimization, its identification is not trivial in practice because of its space requirements and adverse impact on application performance, especially for large, long running programs. Hollingsworth[5] studied this problem for message passing and shared-memory programs and proposed a runtime, nontrace-based algorithm to compute the critical path profile of executions. Its online version for a variant of critical path, called *critical path zeroing*, is also introduced with its measurements of the reduction of application execution time. Other related work on this aspect can be found in [7, 6]

3.   Key Message Approach

The Key Message approach consists of a fundamental *Key Message model*, the underlying *Key Message algorithm* and *Key Message runtime system*. In this approach, a parallel application is pre-processed to generate a task graph. Then, the Key Message algorithm is applied to the task graph, which uses the current network load to identify communication that needs to be optimized and generates an augmented task graph. Next, using the Key Message APIs, an optimized parallel application is generated based on the augmented task graph. Finally, the modified parallel application is compiled and linked with the Key Message library to generate the executable that could be executed on top of the Key Message runtime system. The KM algorithm is the central part of the approach. This paper focuses on the modeling analysis of the algorithm based on Key Message model which illustrates a parallel application and an underlying communication system.

3.1   Key Message Model

As presented, the essence of Key Message algorithm is built on top of its Key Message model, which is further divided into an *application model* and a *communication model*. The application model is represented by a weighted DAG task graph, an abstraction of a parallel application. Its weighted node signifies the task with computation time, and its directed weighted edge in-

	non-preemptive	preemptive-resume
level 1, t_{d1}	$1/\mu + (\lambda_1 + \lambda_2)/((\mu - \lambda_1)\mu)$	$1/(\mu - \lambda_1)$
level 2, t_{d2}	$1/\mu + (\lambda_1 + \lambda_2)/((\mu - \lambda_1)(\mu - \lambda_1 - \lambda_2))$	$\mu/((\mu - \lambda_1)(\mu - \lambda_1 - \lambda_2))$

Table 21.1. Average Total Delay per Packet Using Priority Policies: λ_1 is the arrival rate of level 1 (high priority) packets and λ_2 the arrival rate of level 2 (low priority) packets, μ service rate.

dicates the number of packets sent from source task to destination task. The communication model is established with a single connection that connects a set of processing nodes. The tasks are assumed to be mapped to the nodes and enter the task queues located at the nodes. The communication among tasks is through message passing, which is abstracted as a queueing system with a single server, multiple queues. Therefore, message transmission delay can be obtained following a M/M/1 queue model. In addition to task queue, each node also possesses a message queue to receive messages, and each message queue has two levels of priorities. Messages from a critical path enjoy a high priority when entering the queue, whereas the background traffic messages which are assumed to be generated by a *Possion process* and non-critical-path messages are put directly in the message queue with low priorities. The transmission policy at each node is on a priority basis.

3.2   Illustrating Key Message Algorithm

The basic idea of the Key Message algorithm is to prioritize the messages that are generated in the critical paths of a parallel application. It consists of several optimization steps on a task graph. In each step, the algorithm finds a critical path in the task graph and optimizes the message passing in the critical path by adjusting the edge cost (communication cost) using the total delay formulas for priority policy (Table 21.1). Messages that are identified to be on a critical path are put in high priority (level 1) and all other messages are in low priority (level 2). However, after these steps, the original critical path is shortened, and other non-critical paths may become critical. So this algorithm is iterative until no more messages need optimization. The algorithm detail can be found in[10]. A concrete example of this algorithm is shown in Figure 21.1. It describes how to use Key Message algorithm to optimize communication for an application. Definitions used in the illustration are as follows:

- Optimization ratio is defined as the ratio between the number of Key Message paths and the total number of paths in a task graph.

- Improvement ratio is defined as the ratio between the original maximum path completion time and the optimized maximum path completion time after applying the Key Message algorithm.

To simplify the explanation, one task is mapped to one node. In this example, there are nine tasks. Thus, there are nine nodes. The task weight equals

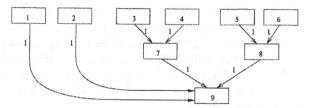

Figure 21.1. A Task Graph Sampled to Illustrate the Execution of Key Message Algorithm

the task number as shown in Figure 21.1. The amount of communication generated by each task in the task graph is one packet. Service rate and arrival rates are assumed as follows[1]:

- $\mu = 10 \times 10^3 \, packets/sec$;

- $\lambda_1 = 0.0001 \times 10^3 \, packets/sec$;

- $\lambda_2 = 9.9 \times 10^3 \, packets/sec$;

Using the formula of the delay in an M/M/1 FCFS queue, we get the delay time as:

$$t_d = (1/(10 - 9.9001)) \times 10^{(-3)} = 10.01001001001 \times 10^{(-3)} sec$$

Using the formula of the delay in an M/M/1 preemptive resume priority queue, we have:

- $t_{d_1} = (1/(10 - 0.0001)) \times 10^{(-3)} = 0.10000100001 \times 10^{(-3)} sec$; and

- $t_{d_2} = (10/((10-0.0001)(10-0.0001-9.9))) \times 10^{(-3)} = 10.010110111\text{-}11 \times 10^{(-3)} sec$

Step 1: *Initialization:*

Initially, the communication costs are all initialized to t_d. Function *All-Path*(TG) returns the paths in the task graph. The path completion time of all paths are calculated using t_d and task weights. Function *CriticalPath*(PathSet) returns path 6-8-9. In this example, the original maximum path completion time is the sum of the task weights and the communication cost. Here, the task weights is 23 *ms* (that is 6+8+9 = 23) and the communication cost is 20.02002002002 *ms* (that is 1*10.01001001001+1*10.01001001001). In the end, the original maximum path completion time is 43.02002002002 *ms*.

Then, a re-initialization operation sets all messages generated from the task graph to low priority. The path completion times of all paths are changed accordingly. After some sets and variables are initialized, the initialization step finishes.

Step 2: *Optimization:*

In this step, the communication between tasks 6 and 8 and between tasks 8 and 9 is optimized first. All path completion times are updated accordingly. After optimization, the path completion time of the critical path 6-8-9 is about 23.2 *ms* (that is 23+2*0.10000100001). The completion time of other paths (i.e., path 5-8-9, 4-7-9, 3-7-9) are more than the optimized critical path completion time. So, they must also be optimized. The procedure of the optimization as illustrated above is thus repeated.

Finally, when optimization terminates, the maximum path completion time is 23.2*ms* and there are six edges optimized. The optimized task graph is shown in Figure 21.2, where optimized edges are highlighted.

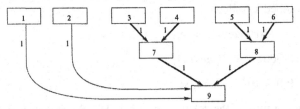

Figure 21.2.   The Optimized Task Graph to Illustrate the Execution of Key Message Algorithm

Step 3: *Result calculation:*

In the last step, the original maximum path completion time, the optimized maximum path completion time and the sets of optimized and unoptimized paths are outputted. Based on this information, the optimization ratio and the improvement ratio can be calculated. They are 75%(6 out of 8 paths are optimized) and 185.4% (43.02/23.2)respectively.

4.   Analysis of Key Message Algorithm

Analytical study is a widely used mechanism to initially evaluate the performance of a particular model or system. The performance of the Key Message algorithm based on the Key Message model in terms of the completion time of a task graph will be analyzed. A queuing model is used to model the network. To focus on the analysis of the communication portion of the completion time, and to reduce the complexity of analysis, the analytical study is limited on some assumptions and parameters.

4.1   Assumptions and Parameters

To simplify the analysis of the Key Message algorithm, the following additional assumptions are used:

- The task weight of a task in a task graph is the total delay a task is experiencing on a node (i.e., including the task queueing time and CPU service time on a node).

- The study focuses on the critical path of a task graph. Obviously, after the communication optimization of the Key Message algorithm, the original critical path in the task graph is still the longest path in the task graph. The completion time of the critical path is the target of the evaluation in the analysis.

- The analysis focuses only on the case in which only one task is mapped to a node. For the case in which multiple tasks are mapped to a node, the analysis can also be applied as explained in the following observation.

Suppose there are T tasks in a task graph of a parallel application, and N nodes in a cluster of nodes. If $N < T$, there are more than one task mapped to a node. If $N = T$, there is one task per node. The difference between these two cases is that the communication cost between tasks that are mapped to the same node is zero. After mapping, the modified task graph is still a DAG. So, for the case $N < T$, it can be analyzed like the case of $N = T$. For $N > T$, the number of nodes is more than the number of tasks. In this situation, there is still one task per node (the unused nodes are idle), the same as the case of $N = T$. As a result, the analytical method in the case of $N = T$ can be applied to the other two cases (i.e., $N < T$ and $N > T$). Based on the above discussion, we can get the following observation:

Observation 1 *In the analysis, we focus on the case of $N = T$. The analytical method in this case is still useful in the other two cases i.e., $N < T$ and $N > T$.*

The following information defines a task graph of a parallel application:

- Tasks in the task graph are numbered from 0 to $T - 1$, where T is the total number of tasks in the graph;

- Task weight, which is the total delay time incurred by a task at a node;

- An edge between task i and task j is represented by an ordered tuple (i, j);

- Edge weight, which represents the number of packets sent between tasks;

- A path in the task graph is represented by a list of edges.

Node and Network Parameters in a cluster are as follows:

- Number of nodes in the system (N);

- Network service rate (μ);

- High priority arrival rate (λ_1): the summation of the arrival rates of high priority messages that are generated by parallel tasks in the cluster;

- Low priority arrival rate (λ_2): the summation of the arrival rates of external background load modeled as a Poisson distribution and low priority messages generated by parallel tasks.

4.2   Path Completion Time

In the analysis, first a DAG task graph is abstracted to a path set

$$\text{PathSet} = \{p_1, p_2, \cdots, p_n\}$$

A path in a task graph is represented by a list of edges. For example, $\{(i_1, i_2), (i_2, i_3), ..., (i_{k-1}, i_k)\}$ is a path p_i that starts from task i_1 and ends at task i_k. To simplify the presentation of the path completion time of a path in the analytical study, a path p_i involving k tasks is re-written as:

$$p_i = \{(t_{i1}, c_{i1}), (t_{i2}, c_{i2}), \cdots, (t_{i(k-1)}, c_{i(k-1)}), t_{ik}\} \qquad (21.1)$$

where, t_{ij} $(j = 1, \cdots, k)$ represents the computation weight of task j in path i; c_{ij} $(j = 1, \cdots, k - 1)$ represents the number of packets task j sends to task $(j + 1)$ in path i.

Then, based on 21.1, a critical path with $k - 1$ edges can be defined as follows:

$$CP_x = \{(t_{x1}, c_{x1}), (t_{x2}, c_{x2}), \cdots, (t_{x(k-1)}, c_{x(k-1)}), t_{xk}\}$$

The path completion time of CP_x (that is, $PathCompTime(CP_x)$ is denoted by pp_x:

$$pp_x = \sum_{j=1}^{k-1} (t_{xj} + C_{xj}) + t_{xk} \qquad (21.2)$$

where C_{xj} $(j = 1, \cdots, k-1)$ represents the total delay time of a message passing from task j to task $(j + 1)$. Using FCFS M/M/1 queueing delay formula, the total delay time of a message passing from task j to task $(j + 1)$ is:

$$C_{xj} = (1/(\mu - \lambda)) \times c_{xj}$$

where μ is the service rate and λ is the arrival rate of packets in a network. Since packets arrive independently, the total delay time of a message is c_{xj} times the average delay time of a packet.

Based on the above analysis, pp_x in Formula 21.2 can be changed to

$$pp_{x-fifo} = \sum_{j=1}^{k-1} (t_{xj} + (1/(\mu - \lambda)) \times c_{xj}) + t_{xk} \qquad (21.3)$$

To calculate the communication cost for different priorities, preemptive priority M/M/1 queueing delay formula is used. Thus, we have:

- For high priority,

$$pp_{x-high} = \sum_{j=1}^{k-1} (t_{xj} + (1/(\mu - \lambda_1)) \times c_{xj}) + t_{xk} \qquad (21.4)$$

- For low priority,

$$pp_{x-low} = \sum_{j=1}^{k-1}(t_{xj} + (\mu/((\mu - \lambda_1)(\mu - \lambda_1 - \lambda_2)))) \times c_{xj}) + t_{xk}(21.5)$$

In priority M/M/1 queueing, λ_1 is the arrival rate of messages with a high priority in the network, and λ_2 is the arrival rate of messages with a low priority in the network. The total arrival rate is $\lambda = \lambda_1 + \lambda_2$.

4.3 Improvement Ratio

symbol	meaning
OptP	the set of optimized paths
OriP	the set of original paths
OriCompTime	the original maximum path completion time
OptCompTime	the optimized maximum path completion time

Table 21.2. Notations Used in the Analysis

The notations used in the analysis are shown in Table 21.2. Then, according to the Key Message algorithm, we have the following equations:

$$OriCompTime = PathCompTime(CriticalPath(OriP))$$
$$OptCompTime = PathCompTime(CriticalPath(OptP))$$
$$ImprRatio = OriCompTime/OptCompTime$$

Since the original critical path is still a critical path in the task graph after the communication optimization using the Key Message algorithm, we get that $CriticalPath(OriP) = CriticalPath(OptP)$. The improvement ratio ($ImprRatio$) is the original critical path completion time ($OriCompTime$) divided by the optimized critical path completion time ($OptCompTime$). The $OriCompTime$ is obtained by using Formula 21.3, while the $OptCompTime$ is obtained by using Formula 21.4.

To analyze the efficiency of the Key Message algorithm, we focus on the $ImprRatio$. Using Formulas 21.3 and 21.4, we have:

$$ImprRatio$$
$$= OriCompTime/OptCompTime$$
$$= (\sum_{j=1}^{k-1}(t_{xj} + (1/(\mu - \lambda)) \times c_{xj}) + t_{xk})/(\sum_{j=1}^{k-1}(t_{xj} + (1/(\mu - \lambda_1)) \times c_{xj}) + t_{xk})$$

Where $\sum_{j=1}^{k-1}(t_{xj}) + t_{xk}$ is determined by a task graph. To simplify the above equation, we define:

$$A = \sum_{j=1}^{k-1}(t_{xj}) + t_{xk} \qquad (21.6)$$

Impr Ratio is then re-written as follows:

$$Impr\,Ratio \;=\; (A + \sum_{j=1}^{k-1}(1/(\mu - \lambda)) \times c_{xj})/(A + \sum_{j=1}^{k-1}(1/(\mu - \lambda_1)) \times c_{xj})$$

In addition, we also define:

$$B \;=\; \sum_{j=1}^{k-1}(1/(\mu - \lambda)) \times c_{xj} \qquad\qquad (21.7)$$

$$C \;=\; \sum_{j=1}^{k-1}(1/(\mu - \lambda_1)) \times c_{xj} \qquad\qquad (21.8)$$

We get:

$$Impr\,Ratio \;=\; (A + B)/(A + C)$$
$$=\; (B - C)/(A + C) + 1 \qquad\qquad (21.9)$$

and,

$$B - C \;=\; \sum_{j=1}^{k-1} c_{xj} \times (1/(\mu - \lambda)) - \sum_{j=1}^{k-1} c_{xj} \times (1/(\mu - \lambda_1))$$

$$=\; \sum_{j=1}^{k-1} c_{xj} \times (1/(\mu - \lambda) - 1/(\mu - \lambda_1))$$

$$=\; \sum_{j=1}^{k-1} c_{xj} \times (1/(\mu - \lambda_1 - \lambda_2) - 1/(\mu - \lambda_1))$$

$$=\; \sum_{j=1}^{k-1} c_{xj} \times \lambda_2/((\mu - \lambda_1 - \lambda_2)(\mu - \lambda_1))$$

$$A + C \;=\; \sum_{j=1}^{k-1} t_{xj} + t_{xk} + \sum_{j=1}^{k-1} c_{xj} \times (1/(\mu - \lambda_1))$$

We assume a cluster system is stable, that is, $\mu > \lambda$. Thus, $(B - C)/(A + C)$ is always more than zero. As a result, ImprRatio is more than 1.

Observation 2 *After the optimization in the Key Message algorithm, the total execution time of a task graph is shorter than that when no Key Message algorithm is used.*

According to Formula 21.9, to increase the *Impr Ratio*, the term $B - C$ must be increased and the term $A + C$ must be decreased.

- For the term $A + C$, its value becomes smaller when $(\sum_{j=1}^{k-1} t_{xj} + t_{xk})$ decreases. As a result, the *Impr Ratio* increases. To achieve this, the average task weight must decrease. So, if the average task weight in a task graph decreases, the *Impr Ratio* increases.

- For the term $B - C$, its value becomes larger when λ_2 and c_{xj} increases. So, if the arrival rate of low priority packets and average edge weight in a task graph increases, the *Impr Ratio* also increases.

Based on the above analysis, we can then conclude that the Key Message algorithm achieves a good performance (a high *Impr Ratio*) under the following conditions:

- For a given task graph, the background traffic load is high; or

- For a certain network traffic load, a task graph is communication intensive (which means the average task weight is small and the average edge weight is large).

4.4   Background Traffic Arrival Rate vs. Improvement Ratio

Assume that t is the average task weight of all the tasks in the critical path and c the average edge weight. That is: $t = (\sum_{j=1}^{k} t_{xj})/k$ and $c = (\sum_{j=1}^{k-1} c_{xj})/(k-1)$. We use t to replace t_{xj} and c to replace c_{xj} in Formulas 21.6, 21.7, 21.8, 21.9. Then we get the following approximation of the *Impr Ratio*:

$$
\begin{aligned}
A &= \sum_{j=1}^{k-1} t_{xj} + t_{xk} \\
&\approx (k-1)t + t \\
&= k \times t \\
B &= \sum_{j=1}^{k-1} [1/(\mu - \lambda)] \times c_{xj} \\
&\approx c \times (k-1)/(\mu - \lambda_1 - \lambda_2) \\
C &= \sum_{j=1}^{k-1} [1/(\mu - \lambda_1)] \times c_{xj} \\
&\approx c \times (k-1)/(\mu - \lambda_1)
\end{aligned}
$$

$$ImprRatio$$
$$= (B - C)/(A + C) + 1$$
$$\approx c \times (k - 1)\lambda_2/((\mu - \lambda_1 - \lambda_2)(\mu - \lambda_1)(kt + c \times (k - 1)/(\mu - \lambda_1))) + 1$$
$$(21.10)$$

Let $t_{xj} = t + \Delta$, $c_{xj} = c + \Delta$. Using L'Hospital rule [17], as $\Delta \to 0$, the convergence of the approximation between using the original ImprRatio in Formula 21.9 and approximation ImprRatio in Formula 21.10 is first order.

c	t	μ	λ_1	k
6	4	100	8.4	6

Table 21.3.   Sample Parameters for Function $ImprRatio = f(\lambda_2)$

Formula 21.10 can be re-written as a function $(ImprRatio = f(\lambda_2))$ with λ_2 as a variable and other parameters as constants. For example, when the constant parameters are set using the values given in Table 21.3, the function $ImprRatio = f(\lambda_2)$ is:

$$f(\lambda_2) = 30 \times \lambda_2/((91.6 - \lambda_2) \times 2228.4) + 1 \qquad (21.11)$$

Its curve (λ_2 vs. $ImprRatio$) is shown in Figure 21.3. As can be seen from the figure, when λ_2 increases, the $ImprRatio$ also increases. It also increases faster when background traffic becomes heavier. Since the Key Message algorithm prioritizes messages in a parallel application, the messages generated from the critical path could jump to the head of queue and are transmitted with little queueing time. As a result, when the background traffic load is higher, the $ImprRatio$ increases.

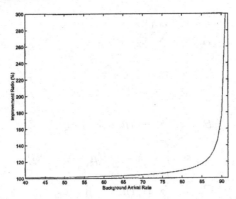

Figure 21.3.   Background Traffic (λ_2) vs. Improvement Ratio

4.5 Computation to Communication Ratio vs. Improvement Ratio

μ	λ_1	λ_2	k
100	8.4	90.45	6

Table 21.4. Sample Parameters for Function $ImprRatio = g(r)$

For computation to communication ratio ($r = t/c$), when average edge weight (c) is a constant, the decrease of the average task weight (t) results in the decrease of the computation to communication ratio of a task graph. To show the relationship between r and $ImprRatio$, similarly, when other parameters are set using the values shown in Table 21.4, formula 21.10 can then be re-written as a function $ImprRatio = g(r)$:

$$g(r) = 4.295/(6 \times r + 0.055) + 1 \qquad (21.12)$$

Its curve (r vs. ImprRatio) is shown in Figure 21.4. As can be seen from the figure, with the hincrement of r, the $ImprRatio$ decreases. A very high improvement ratio is achieved when the computation to communication ratio is very small (< 1). The improvement ratio drops rapidly when the computation to communication ratio changes from 0.5 to 2. The reduction is slowed down with further increase of the computation to communication ratio. This phenomenon can be easily explained. Since the Key Message algorithm only optimizes the communication, the effect of the optimization will become insignificant when the computation is the dominating factor in the application.

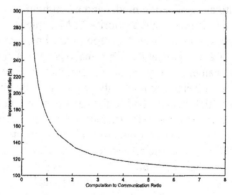

Figure 21.4. Computation to Communication Ratio vs. Improvement Ratio

4.6 Comparison Study

In this subsection, we present a comparison study between our KM approach and Dong et al's double queue hscheme (DQS)[16]. Both exhibit similar features but with totally different purposes. DQS is proposed to reduce the effects of local jobs' communication on the performance of parallel jobs. It divides a single queue of traditional network interfaces into two. One is for the communication of parallel jobs and the other is for the communication of local jobs. Two queues are given different priorities to adjust the allocation of communication bandwidth among them. By giving the parallel jobs' queue a higher priority, through simulation, their study found that scheme improves the performance of parallel jobs considerably with a slight effect on local job communication especially when the size of local jobs' communication is small and moderate. However, they based their study on the *Single Program Multiple Data* (SPMD) programming model, and hence the scheme might not be effective for other programming models. In general, an optimization technique should be applicable for both *Multiple Program Multiple Data* (MPMD) and SPMD programming models. Therefore, it is required that an optimization scheme identify not only the different priorities of communication between parallel applications and local sequential applications, but also the different priorities inside a parallel application. It is common that tasks of a parallel application can be scheduled at different priority levels, but the underlying communication in these tasks is usually not prioritized in DQS scheme. The Key Message (KM) approach presented in this paper addresses this problem.

5.   Conclusions

In this paper, the Key Message approach is evaluated by its modeling analysis. hOur Key Message approach consists of the Key Message model, the Key Message algorithm, as well as its runtime system. The Key Message model is further divided into an application model and a communication model, which are abstracted as a task graph and a priority M/M/1 queue respectively. This model forms the basis for the Key Message algorithm to optimize the communication of a parallel application. Our analysis results show that the Key Message approach can efficiently reduce the completion time of a parallel application running on cluster environments. More specifically, we found that the network with a high background traffic load benefits more from the KM approach than those with lower background traffic loads. On the other hand, when the ratio of computation to communication is very small, a very high improvement ratio is achieved. The essence of this analysis is the simplicity and flexibility of our Key Message model, which leaves the communication issues to be addressed separately by its communication model.

Previous research on priority message assignments do not adequately address or hsolve the communication optimization problem of parallel applications running in distributed environments. Compared to the existing solutions, for example the work reported in [16], the Key Message approach is more flexible and yields better performance[10]. In future research, the Key Message approach will be further investigated in a grid environment.

Notes

1. Note that the assumed number is just for illustrating the algorithm.

References

[1] S.J. Sistare and C.J. Jackson Ultra-High Performance Communication with MPI and the Sun Fire Link Interconnect, *Pro. Supercomputing Conference*, 2002.

[2] C.Dubnicki, A. Bilas, Y.Chen, S. damianakis and K. Li, VMMC-2: Efficient Support for Reliable, Connection-Oriented Communication, *Pro. Hot Interconnects V*, 1997

[3] R. Gillet, MEMORY CHANNEL Network for PCI: An Optimized Cluster Interconnect, *IEEE Micro*, 16(2), 1996, 12-18

[4] Yu-Kwonk Kwok and Ishfaq Ahmad. Dynamic Critical-Path Scheduling: An Effective Technique for Allocating Task Graphs to Multiprocessors. *IEEE Transactions on Parallel and Distributed Systems*,4(2):175-187, Feb. 1993.

[5] J. Hollingsworth Critical Path Profiling of Message Passing and Shared-Memory Programs. *IEEE Transactions on Parallel and Distributed Systems*. Vol. 9, No. 10. Oct. 1998

[6] B.P. Miller, M.Clark, J.Hollingsworth, S. Kierstead, S.-S. Lim and T. Torzewski, IPS-2: The Second Generation of a Parallel Program Measurement System, *IEEE Trans. Parallel and Distributed Systems*, vol. 1, no 2, pp. 206-217, 1990.

[7] C.-Q. Yang and B.P. Miller, Critical Path Analysis for the Execution of Parallel and Distributed Programs, *Proc. Eighth Int'l Conf. Distributed Computing Systems*,pp. 366-375, San Jose, Calif., June 1988.

[8] David R. Surma, Edwin Hsing-Mean Sha: Communication Reduction in Multiple Multicasts Based on Hybrid Static-Dynamic Scheduling. *IEEE Trans. Parallel Distrib. Syst.* 11(9): 865-878 (2000)

[9] L. V. Kale and B. Ramkumar and V. Saletore and A. B. Sinha. Prioritization in parallel symbolic computing 06, 1993

[10] Ming Zhu and Wentong Cai and Bu-Sung Lee. Key Message Approach to Optimize Communication of Parallel Applications on Clusters. *Journal of Cluster Computing*, 6, 253-265, 2003.

[11] A. Gerasoulis and T. Yang. Efficient Algorithms and a Software Tool for Scheduling Parallel Computation, *Scheduling Theory and Applications*. P. Chretienne, E. Coffman, J.K. Lenstra and Z. Liu (Eds.). J. Wiley Publisher. 111-143. 1995

[12] Thorsten von Eicken. Active Messages: an efficient communication architecture for multiprocessors Phd Thesis. U. C. Berkeley. 1993

[13] Steven H. Rodrigues. High performance local area communication with fast sockets Master's Thesis. U. C. Berkeley. 1996.

[14] Scott Pakin and V. Karamcheti and Andrew A. Chien. Fast Messages: efficient, portable communication for workstation clusters and MPPs. V5. No2. 60-73, *IEEE Concurrency*, 1997.

[15] GM, available from http://www.myrinet.com/

[16] Y. F. Dong and X. Du and X. D. Zhang. Characterizing and scheduling communication interactions of parallel and local jobs on networks of workstations V21. No5. 470-484. *Computer Communications*. 1998.

[17] Tuma and Jan J. *Engineering mathematics handbook*. New York: McGraw-Hill. 1998.

[18] A. Barriuso, and A. Knies, SHMEM user's guide, (Cary Research Inc., SN-2516, 1994).

[19] Sven Karlsson, and Mats Brorsson, Priority Based Messaging for Software Distributed Shared Memory. *Cluster Computing* 6, 161-169, 2003.

Index